The Critical Writings of Ingeborg Bachmann

Studies in German Literature, Linguistics, and Culture

The Critical Writings of Ingeborg Bachmann

Edited and Translated by
Karen R. Achberger
and Karl I. Solibakke

Rochester, New York

Translation Copyright © 2021 Karen R. Achberger and Karl I. Solibakke

Translation rights licensed by Piper Verlag GmbH, München, © 1978 / 2005

All Rights Reserved. Except as permitted under current legislation, no part of this work may be photocopied, stored in a retrieval system, published, performed in public, adapted, broadcast, transmitted, recorded, or reproduced in any form or by any means, without the prior permission of the copyright owner.

First published 2021 by Camden House

Camden House is an imprint of Boydell & Brewer Inc.
668 Mt. Hope Avenue, Rochester, NY 14620, USA
and of Boydell & Brewer Limited
PO Box 9, Woodbridge, Suffolk IP12 3DF, UK
www.boydellandbrewer.com

ISBN-13: 978-1-57113-944-3

Library of Congress Cataloging-in-Publication Data

Names: Bachmann, Ingeborg, 1926–1973, author. | Achberger, Karen, editor, translator. | Solibakke, Karl, editor, translator.
Title: The critical writings of Ingeborg Bachmann / edited and translated by Karen R. Achberger and Karl I. Solibakke.
Description: [Rochester] : Camden House, [2021] | Series: Studies in German literature, linguistics, and culture ; 224 | Includes bibliographical references and index.
Identifiers: LCCN 2020057694 | ISBN 9781571139443 (hardback)
Subjects: LCGFT: Essays. | Lectures. | Speeches.
Classification: LCC PT2603.A147 C75 2021 | DDC 838/.91409--dc23
LC record available at https://lccn.loc.gov/2020057694

This publication is printed on acid-free paper.
Printed in the United States of America.

Contents

Acknowledgments

THIS PROJECT HAS ENJOYED the outstanding contributions of colleagues and the generous support of funding agencies over the long period of its genesis. Unable to name them all here, we especially wish to recognize the late Peter K. Jansen, who brought extraordinary skill, wit, and love of language to his translation drafts of Bachmann's essays. It was a pleasure to collaborate with him from 2004 until his sudden death in 2007.

In addition, we wish to thank two St. Olaf College summa cum laude graduates, Amber L. Griffioen and Nancy Simpson-Younger, for their meticulous and tireless research assistance. We also wish to thank Professor Sabine I. Gölz of the University of Iowa for her thoughtful assessment of early drafts of the Frankfurt Lectures.

We also wish to thank the National Endowment for the Humanities (NEH) for the Fellowship for College Teachers. The generous funding provided helped to launch the project that has become this book. In addition, we are grateful to St. Olaf College for its unflagging sponsorship of Karen's effort on this project over the years.

We wish to take this opportunity to recognize the German American Exchange Service (DAAD) for funding Monika Albrecht's short-term St. Olaf lectureship at the time of her work on Bachmann's critical writings in German. And finally, we are indebted to Professor Michael W. Jennings and Princeton University for promoting the work on this volume.

Notes on Translation

BACHMANN IS NOT an easy writer to translate. An acute awareness of the problems inherent in language is manifest throughout her work. Her critical writings, much like her poetic work, demonstrate an approach to language that is deliberate, multifaceted, and deeply subjective. The essays, lectures, and text fragments gathered in this volume reflect the intellectual prowess of a Wittgenstein scholar keenly aware of the power and the limits of words, searching for the utopian moment: "if we had the word."

Bachmann's critical writings bear witness to her incessant and unwavering struggle to give language "a new life, a new chance." Her attempts to allude to what she considered "unsayable" prompted her to create a language rich in neologisms, highly associative, and aurally suggestive. As mediators of her work our goal is to convey something comparable to the polyphonic richness of her finely honed German, respecting the integrity of her intentions, if possible, and transmitting the intellectual substance of her texts into English.

Regarding our translation specifically (in no order of importance):

1. Bachmann made consistent and deliberate use of the male pronoun, and we have respected this in our translations. We made every effort to render her pronouns as well as the gender relevance and complexity of her antecedents accurately.

2. We made no attempt to "normalize" her writing but chose to preserve a sense of her thirst for a new language after 1945. One way that she conveys this aspiration is by placing terms in new and unfamiliar contexts, "alienating" the traditional connotations of words and allowing the reader to experience them in a new light. She also coined neologisms to suggest novel ideas and describe postwar developments; we attempted to render her neologisms with coinages or expressions that capture Bachmann's creativity for an English audience.

3. Where necessary, we altered the renderings of terms in existing English-language translations: for example, we chose to translate the key concept in the Third Lecture, "Concerning the I," as "I without guarantee" in keeping with the singular object in the original: *"Ich ohne Gewähr."*

4. Bachmann occasionally broke with custom in her syntax. At times, her sentences were either incomplete or ran on, perhaps to an extent that is even unusual for German syntax, but clearly excessive in English. We believe that the desired effect is one of unrelenting movement, overflow, or breathlessness, prompting us to preserve the fluidity of her syntactical choices. Though not considered proper in a traditional sense, her fluid syntax is replicated with run-on sentences punctuated by commas instead of semicolons, in order to capture the urgency she strove to evoke. At the same time, we reproduced incomplete sentences and altered the architecture of the clauses as little as possible, sometimes with an apparent disregard for English syntax and rules of punctuation. We found it effective, for instance in the Second Lecture, to preserve the frenzy she incited in an unbroken stream of faultfinding characteristic of a particular type of critic responding to Mannerism: "Or, if you belong to another type, the censorious type, the message is: that has been done before, so it is no longer interesting, has been done better before, it is a weak imitation, plagiarism, the Surrealists could do it too, and better, the *poètes maudits* could do it too, and better, the earlier ones, of course, and better still—think of Marino, of Góngora, think of, think of."

5. Wherever possible, we used published translations of quoted texts by authors other than Bachmann herself. In the instances in which Bachmann cites a German translation of a foreign-language text, we did not translate the German but cited the English original or a published English translation of the work in question. On occasion, however, we were compelled to adjust the English translation to give her position more clarity. Recognized for her literacy, Bachmann did not always quote verbatim or reference her sources; rather, she gave her own accents to originals, appropriating texts to serve her purposes. Occasionally, she altered or deleted individual words, reversed the order of sentences, and placed words in new contexts. In these instances, we either provided new translations of the quotes cited by Bachmann or modified the published translations to match Bachmann's appropriations of the original.

6. Bachmann's style is characterized by a generous application of adverbial fillers, such as *eigentlich*, *da*, *noch*, *aber*, *denn*, etc., and we did not always render the adverbial equivalents into English, since that would have impeded the legibility of highly composite sentences with dense content and intricate syntax.

7. On rare occasions, we felt obliged to change the tenses from those in her texts.

8. The footnotes contain information that we hope will help contextualize the author, the period, or the specific content of Bachmann's critical writings. When we were unable to render the complexity of meanings resonating in the German original, we referenced some of what might be "lost in translation" in the footnotes.

9. As its source text, this translation is based on *Kritische Schriften*, edited by Monika Albrecht and Dirk Göttsche (Piper Verlag, 2005).

Introduction

1. Bachmann as European Intellectual and Critic

Spanning her entire career from the early 1950s to the early 1970s, Ingeborg Bachmann's critical writings demonstrate her talent to speak eloquently from the periphery yet put her finger on the heart of the matter, be it in reference to the cultural, social, or artistic debates raging during her lifetime or in reference to her own poetic objectives. Bachmann's critical writings not only provide a window into the intellectual agendas and discourses prevalent in postwar Europe, but also new perspectives on Bachmann's lasting engagement with European modernism, twentieth-century totalitarianism, and postcolonial oppression. Politically astute, the public intellectual distinguished herself as a talented author and thinker, and at the same time, as a diva whose life was considered sensational, from her early poetic fame during the 1950s to her intimate relationships with well-known men, including the writers Paul Celan and Max Frisch, and concluding in the puzzling circumstances surrounding her accidental death at the age of forty-seven.

Throughout her life, Bachmann wrote both literary and critical works. While Bachmann the poet and novelist is widely read and revered the world over due to the many translations of her works, Bachmann the critic, philosopher, and public intellectual is not read to the same extent. Her essays, lectures, interviews, and speeches, in which she reveals the aesthetic and ethical concerns so central to her life and work, have not received the attention paid to her poems, radio plays, and narrative texts, which have appeared in many languages, often in more than one version of the German original. In contrast to her acclaimed literary works, Bachmann's critical writings have remained largely unknown outside the German-speaking world. Included among these are essays for print and radio, the five Frankfurt Lectures, her acceptance speeches for various literary prizes, autobiographical fragments, and commentaries on individual writers (Giuseppe Ungaretti, Witold Gombrowicz, Franz Kafka, Robert Musil, Marcel Proust, Sylvia Plath, Simone Weil, Thomas Bernhard, Bertolt Brecht), performing artists (Maria Callas), literary milestones (Musil's *The Man without Qualities* [*Der Mann ohne Eigenschaften*] and Proust's *Remembrance of Things Past* [*À la recherche du temps perdu*]), music (both aesthetic deliberations and reflections on her librettos for the German composer Hans Werner Henze), and philosophy (Ludwig Wittgenstein and the Vienna Circle).

The writings presented here—authorized texts published during her lifetime as well as previously unreleased fragments from Bachmann's literary estate—bear witness to an unremitting struggle to give language what the author called "a new life, a new chance," to open our eyes to the truth and, in so doing, to bring about change. In a speech to the Association of the German War Blind, she spoke persuasively about "the task of the writer," stipulating "what art ought to bring about: that our eyes, in this sense, be opened" to "that furtive pain" that sensitizes us "to the experience of truth." Reading Bachmann's critical works, including her many fragmentary reflections on fellow authors, broadens our understanding of her own work and times as well as the personalities and issues she chose to discuss; it shows us what moved her as a reader, what constituted her artistic and moral values and the standards to which she held herself and others. A gifted intellectual conversant in several languages and intimately familiar with Western literary and philosophical traditions, Bachmann engaged in meaningful dialogues with a number of fellow European as well as American intellectuals.[1] She resided in Vienna, Berlin, Zurich, Munich and finally Rome, where she spent the final years of her life.

Bachmann's acute awareness of and sensitivity to contemporary philosophy, psychology, and modern Western aesthetics stemmed from her doctoral thesis on Martin Heidegger as well as her philosophical essays on Ludwig Wittgenstein and the Vienna Circle, and from her familiarity with a broad spectrum of influential thinkers, in particular with exponents of the Frankfurt School, such as Walter Benjamin and Theodor W. Adorno. The political dimensions of her life are evidenced in her opposition to rearming the Federal Republic of Germany in the 1950s and to the Vietnam War in the 1960s. Incensed by the rapid pace with which the "Economic Miracle" came to dominate German and Austrian cultural values, she remained critical of the postwar affluence that paved the way for European unity and the formation of the European Economic Community, precursor to today's European Union, in the late 1950s.

Devoted to a sweeping range of topics, her theoretical writings pursue two common objectives: on the one hand, they consider the critical role that language plays in the postwar era, and on the other, they convey Bachmann's conviction that literature should depict reality in light of the

1 The extent of Bachmann's engagement in European intellectual circles is also evident from her participation on the editorial board of an envisioned, but never realized, international literary journal, the other members of which included such luminaries as Hans Magnus Enzensberger, Günter Grass, Uwe Johnson, Martin Walser, Roland Barthes, Michel Butor, Michel Leiris, Alberto Moravia, Italo Calvino, and Pier Paolo Pasolini.

utopia it has the potential to represent, as she asserts in her final Frankfurt Lecture on Poetics, at the same time adapting itself to encompass all of the arts, whether textual, visual, or aural in nature. With these objectives in mind, this volume follows the author's example and draws the reader's attention to the centrality of Bachmann's critical writings, her utopian approach to language, and her view of language as a "playing field" to stimulate new words and phrases. For Bachmann, the playing field represented a collective sign system grounded in tradition and shackled to established connotations, which a new aesthetic was expected to overcome in order to articulate truths about the postwar order.

2. Growing Up on a Trilingual Border

Ingeborg Bachmann was born in Klagenfurt on June 25, 1926, and died in Rome on October 17, 1973. Since the capital city of the southernmost Austrian state of Carinthia offered few attractions, her family made a regular habit of visiting Ingeborg's grandparents in the Gail River Valley, approximately 60 kilometers west of Klagenfurt.[2] Situated at the geographical and cultural intersection of Austria, Slovenia, and Italy, the so-called "border triangle" (*Dreiländereck*) was pivotal for the trilingual nature of Bachmann's work. The beauty of this largely rural region was subsequently immortalized in the author's early novel *The Cross of Honditsch* (*Das Honditschkreuz*), as well as in her later novel fragment *The Book of Franza* (*Das Buch Franza*). Without a doubt, it was this stretch of Southern Austrian countryside that gave the daughter of an Italian teacher and later high school principal lasting inspiration, stimulating her talent for *Heimatliteratur* or, more specifically, sentimental regional literature. By the time her final works appeared in print, and explicitly in the later volume of short stories, the author had transformed the genre, infusing specific geographies, terrains, and locations with subtle irony. In an early autobiographical gloss, "Biographical Note" ("Biographisches"), Bachmann characterized her deep affinity with her native Carinthia, a border region in which multiple languages are spoken and several cultures intersect:

2 Provincial compared to Vienna, Klagenfurt is surrounded by incomparable Alpine scenery and close to locations that had importance for composers: Brahms wrote his 2nd Symphony while on holiday nearby, Mahler composed many of his works in a chalet in the mountains above the Wörthersee, and Berg wrote his last work, the Violin Concerto, in a summer house near the lake.

> I spent my youth in Carinthia, in the south, near the border, in a valley that has two names, a German and a Slovenian one.[3] And the house in which generations of my ancestors lived—Austrians and Slovenes—bears a foreign-sounding name still to this day. Near the border there is yet another border, the border of language—and I was at home on this side and on the other, with the tales of good and evil spirits hailing from two and three countries; for Italy, which I have never seen, is on the other side of the mountains, only an hour's journey away.

Bachmann began elementary school in 1932, was admitted to secondary school in 1936, and two years later she enrolled in the "High School for Girls," as the National Socialists rechristened the institution. An avid reader, the young girl published her first literary endeavors while still in school, immature yet promising works that she later characterized in her "Biographical Note" as situated between tradition and modernism:

> For a number of years, I read a great deal, most avidly perhaps those poets who were the most alien to me—Gide, Valéry, Éluard, Eliot, and Yeats among the newer ones—and it might be that I learned a thing or two from them. But essentially, what dominates my work to this day is the world of imaginative myths indicative of my childhood home, which remains an example of a genuine and largely unrealized Austria, a world in which many languages are spoken and through which many borders flow.

In March of 1938, the German army marched into Austria, and with the advent of the Nazi regime, this "world of imaginative myths" became seriously tainted for the impressionable and precocious eleven-year-old. Attentive to her surroundings, she came to recognize a brutal seizure of power in the annexation of Austria to the "Third Reich," and for the rest of her life, Bachmann remained burdened by the fact that her father had allied himself with the National Socialist party in Carinthia, presumably as early as 1932. The girl's first substantial works, including the tragedy *Carmen Ruidera* and the historical novel *The Cross of Honditsch*, were penned during the Nazi occupation and subsequent war years. The play,

3 Bachmann is referencing the Gail River Valley here. The name for the Gail in Slovenian is Zilja. Her father's ancestors had long established themselves in the Obervellach (Hermagor) region in a farmhouse with the name "Tobai-Hof," where Bachmann spent many a family vacation during her childhood. From her earliest years, it was not the city Klagenfurt, but these rural areas beyond the city where she felt most at home. We are indebted to Bachmann scholar Andreas Hapkemeyer for his research into the Bachmann family history in the summer of 2019.

largely based on what she was reading in school at the time, but augmented with allusions to Bizet's popular masterpiece, is a drama in verse emulating the classical tragedies of Schiller and Kleist, whereas the novel can be seen as a veiled expression of ideological resistance to the brutal politics of the National Socialist regime. Shortly before the end of the war, Bachmann graduated from high school and enrolled at a local teacher training college. Soon thereafter, the armistice was declared, signaling the end of an extended period of sacrifice and hardship, a caesura the author captured with evocative words in her short story "Youth in an Austrian Town" ("Jugend in einer österreichischen Stadt"), which appeared in 1961: "And one day nobody gives the children report cards any more, and they can go. They are called upon to step into life. Spring descends with clear, raging waters and gives birth to a blade of grass. There is no need to tell the children it is peace. They go away, with their hands in their ragged pockets and a whistle that is meant as a warning to themselves."

Immediately following the end of the military conflict in the Spring of 1945, Bachmann met Jack Hamesh, a Viennese Jew who had escaped to England in 1938 during the Refugee Children's Movement and was later conscripted by the British forces occupying Austrian territories following the end of the war. The eighteen-year-old Bachmann reported, "Jack comes every day, and I have never talked so much in my life." The relationship to Hamesh, with whom she shared a fascination for history, culture, and the literature of Thomas Mann, Stefan Zweig, Arthur Schnitzler, and Hugo von Hofmannsthal, prominent German-language authors with whom Bachmann had managed to become acquainted in spite of her Nazi education, seemed to foreshadow the future poet's intellectual prowess. Full of anticipation, she confided: "This is the most beautiful summer of my life, and if I live to be a hundred years old—this will remain the most beautiful spring and summer. Everyone says you cannot see much of the peace, but for me it is peace, peace!"

Bachmann's sense of the promise that peace would bring found its way into fragmentary journal entries recorded in her *War Diary* (*Kriegstagebuch*), which she penned in the Spring and Summer of 1945, but which were not made available to a broader readership until many years after her death. Comprised of just several pages of entries, her *War Diary* documents the young girl's hunger for intellectual stimulation after the deprivations of war as well as her aspirations for her university studies. Nonetheless, her confessions remain puzzling: "I told Jack that I would like to study philosophy, and he takes me very seriously and thinks it is a good idea. But I did not say a thing about my poems." Already at this nascent stage in her intellectual development, Bachmann's ambivalence about the discrepancy between the language of art and the language of scholarship made itself manifest, a tension in the young girl's mind at the end of the war that would continue to occupy her in years to come. Eager to share her scholarly objectives with Hamesh, she withheld examples of her artistic endeavors, perhaps out of respect for the literary preferences of the soldier or in anticipation of an unenthusiastic response to her poetic experiments. In truth, crafting poetry was never easy for Bachmann, as documented in her "Biographical Note," in which she weighed the semantic and syntactical challenges confronting poets: "Writing poetry appears to be the most difficult task for me, because here the problems of form, of theme, and of vocabulary must be solved all at once, given that poems obey the rhythm of time and yet should order the fullness of the old and new things close to our heart, things in which past, present, and future are resolved."

3. Postwar Encounters with Judaism

Besides contributing to intellectually stimulating conversations on literature and European culture, Hamesh played another significant role in Bachmann's personal development—presumably, the young man represented her first encounter with Judaism. At an early age, Bachmann was compelled to confront the reality that Jews were not tolerated in her homeland, even after Austria's defeat had ended the Nazi regime and its gruesome politics of racial genocide. No doubt, her attraction to Hamesh's "otherness" was heightened by the fact that Bachmann saw herself as exceptional, an emerging artist and intellectual separate from the collective and visibly marked by the exhaustive efforts she invested in her literary output.

Although the young woman was unable to comprehend what it meant for Jews like Hamesh to have survived the Holocaust, deeply anguished by having to confront the collective memory of mass extermination, the close association with him was influential for her early intellectual development. Later, her friendship with the celebrated Austrian author Ilse Aichinger,[4] and perhaps even more unmistakably, her intimate relationship with the Romanian-born German-language poet and translator Paul Celan, celebrated Jewish authors whose lives were permanently scarred by Nazi atrocities, would become testaments to the intellectual and personal insights that Bachmann derived from her early exposure to Judaism. Persecuted by the Nazis, Aichinger made her formative experience central to her literary output, which earned multiple awards, including the Prize

---

4 Ilse Aichinger (1921–2016), Austrian writer and friend of Bachmann from 1952 on. "Ilse und Inge, Inge and Ilse," as friends called them, were often seen together, according to Bachmann's friend and fellow writer Wolfgang Hildesheimer in an interview in December 1986.

of Group 47 (Gruppe 47)[5] in 1952, the year that Bachmann was first invited to attend one of the Group's celebrated meetings. As for Celan and Bachmann's ill-fated relationship, it has been suggested that the Romanian poet was "troubled from the beginning by the initial trauma of the pogrom and the burden of survivor's guilt, while Bachmann's fascination with him was predicated on her subliminal wish to repress the National Socialist involvement of her family."[6]

As soon as Austria's educational institutions reopened in the Fall of 1945, Bachmann left Klagenfurt to study philosophy, psychology, German literature, and art history in Innsbruck. In the following year she chose to continue her studies in Graz, finally transferring to the University of Vienna to pursue a doctorate in philosophy. Her first publication, the socially critical short story "The Ferry" ("Die Fähre"), appeared in the July 31, 1946, issue of the *Carinthian Illustrated* (*Kärntner Illustrierte*) while she was still residing in Graz. Bachmann's path from the Carinthian provinces via Innsbruck and Graz to the Austrian capital was a journey that she would later refer to as her "longest." Heavily damaged in the war and occupied by the four Allied powers, Vienna became a new "homeland on the border: between East and West, between a grand past and a dark future." Above all, the metropolis was a decisive station in her intellectual development, increasingly stimulated as she was by the exposure to pivotal influences and relationships. That same year witnessed the Viennese premiere of a work that would come to have an enduring impact on the young writer, Bertolt Brecht's *The Good Woman of Setzuan* (*Der gute Mensch von Sezuan*). Premiered in Zurich in 1943, the play was the first of Brecht's theatrical works to be performed in postwar Austria and most likely the first masterpiece by one of the vanguards of the twentieth century that Bachmann experienced on the stage. Less than four years later, Carol Reed's noir classic, *The Third Man* (1949), filmed on-site amid the

---

5 Group 47 was an informal association of German writers, as well as some literary critics, founded by German writer Hans Werner Richter (1908–1993) in 1947. Members participated in regular meetings as a platform for the promotion of young, unknown writers and the renewal of postwar German literature. In response to the misuse and corruption of the German language by the Nazis, Group 47 writers advocated a radical "clear-cutting literature" (*Kahlschlagliteratur*), a style of sparse, straightforward language and shortened sentences that described laconically without advancing values.

6 Bernd Witte, "'Ich liebe Dich und will Dich nicht lieben'—Ingeborg Bachmann und Paul Celan im Briefwechsel" ["I love you and don't want to love you"—Ingeborg Bachmann and Paul Celan in correspondence], in *Die Waffen nieder! Lay down your weapons!: Ingeborg Bachmanns Schreiben gegen den Krieg* [Lay down your weapons: Ingeborg Bachmann's writing against war], ed. Karl Solibakke and Karina von Tippelskirch (Würzburg: Könighausen und Neumann, 2012), 87.

rubble and racketeering of the postwar capital, was given its premiere in Vienna's *Apollokino*. In time, the titles, atmosphere, and themes of both masterpieces were to resonate unmistakably in two of Bachmann's most highly acclaimed literary works, the radio play *The Good God of Manhattan* (*Der gute Gott von Manhattan*, 1958) and the novel *Malina* (1971), the central dream chapter of which bears the title "*The Third Man*."

During her initial year in Vienna, Bachmann also established close contacts with the Austrian writer Hans Weigel and the literary circle associated with Café Raimund. The intimate nature of her relationship to Weigel, one of many Jewish intellectuals who had returned to Austria after the war, found its way into Weigel's novel *Unfinished Symphony* (*Unvollendete Symphonie*, 1951), in which Bachmann figures as the model of the promising artist from the provinces with whom the novel's protagonist falls in love. Weigel's novel represents the first of several attempts to transform Bachmann "into the literary object of a male narrative construction."[7]

Bachmann was first introduced to Paul Celan in May 1948 at an event in Edgar Jené's Viennese apartment. An aspiring and gifted poet, Celan was attracted to the young avant-gardists rallying around the surrealist painter and his newspaper, *The Plan* (*Der Plan*). Almost immediately, Bachmann confessed to her parents: "The surrealist poet Paul Celan, whom I had just met two nights ago with Weigel, and who is very fascinating, has, splendidly enough, fallen in love with me, which adds a little spice to my dreary work. . . . My room is a poppy field at the moment, as he inundates me with this flower."[8] Celan lingered in the Austrian metropolis for several weeks before leaving for Paris, his destination of choice, in June 1948. In spite of their sporadic meetings until his suicide in 1970, the poet, whose parents had been victims of the Nazis and who produced an exemplary lyrical oeuvre in the shadow of the Holocaust, wielded a strong influence over Bachmann's artistic output. The publication of their correspondence in 2008 provides ample evidence that the two poets shared intimacies beyond their initial encounter and that they embedded encrypted allusions to their sentiments for one another into their respective verses.

7 Hans Höller, *Ingeborg Bachmann* (Reinbek bei Hamburg: Rowohlt, 1999), 52. Other well-known instances of male writers appropriating Bachmann's person as a model for their literary characters are Max Frisch's novel *A Wilderness of Mirrors* (*Mein Name sei Gantenbein*, 1964) and Thomas Bernhard's novels *Gargoyles* (*Verstörung*, 1967) and *Extinction* (*Auslöschung*, 1986).

8 Quoted from the correspondence between Bachmann and Celan, which was published as *Herzzeit: Briefwechsel* [Heart-time: Correspondence] (Frankfurt am Main: Suhrkamp, 2008) and appeared in Wieland Hoban's English translation as *Correspondence* (London: Seagull, 2010).

Although Bachmann's scholarly work took precedence over her literary production in these early years, she continued to devote time to artistic pursuits while completing her philosophical studies at the university. In fact, the publication of four early poems and a series of prose works in 1949 represented a literary breakthrough. In the same year Bachmann submitted her dissertation, "The Critical Reception of Martin Heidegger's Existential Philosophy," to the University of Vienna and was awarded a doctorate with honors in March of 1950. Evident in the final chapter of her study is the elemental difference she perceived between the language of art and the rational idiom of philosophy, which had absorbed her attention at an early age. She concludes her critical investigation of Heidegger's existentialism by citing Baudelaire's sonnet "The Gulf" ("Le gouffre") "as linguistic evidence of the extreme possibility of expressing the unsayable." With this reference, Bachmann asserted that it was Baudelaire, not Heidegger, who was capable of articulating existential truths. Throughout the work, her historical materialist perspective colored her view that existentialism and fascism emanated from the same social environment and were inextricable from the latent fears of postwar Europeans traumatized by two world wars. After her Neopositivist attack on Heidegger failed to "topple" the author of *Being and Time* (*Sein und Zeit*), as she had naively intended, Bachmann turned to the philosophy of Ludwig Wittgenstein for answers to the existential questions that absorbed her. She even went so far as to single out his work as "the most important" of her "intellectual encounters," since it "traced the problems of philosophy back to the problems of language."[9] Building on her philosophical training, Bachmann's unshakable confidence in the power of language and the transformative nature of art would continually resurface in her literary works as well as in her critical writings, lectures, and speeches.

Once she concluded her formal studies, Bachmann received a stipend to broaden her horizons, traveling first to Paris in October of 1950, where she attempted to rekindle her affair with Celan. Their reunion was ill fated, as one of his communications documents: "Dear Ingeborg, it is past four and I must now go to see my student. It was our first rendezvous in Paris, my heart was beating so loudly, and you did not come."[10] All the same, Bachmann remained in the French capital for two months before journeying to England to spend time with Ilse Aichinger's twin sister Helga. In London, she was invited to read at the Anglo-Austrian Society and was also given the opportunity to meet exiled Austrian writers, among the most prominent of whom were Erich Fried, Elias Canetti,

9 Ingeborg Bachmann, *Wir müssen wahre Sätze finden: Gespräche und Interviews* [We must find true sentences: Conversations and interviews], ed. Christine Koschel and Inge von Weidenbaum (Munich: Piper, 1983), 12.

10 Bachmann and Celan, *Correspondence*, 23.

and Hilde Spiel.[11] Additionally, she contacted Ludwig Wittgenstein to arrange a meeting, but the philosopher was already battling cancer and not willing to meet with her. Succumbing to his illness in 1951, he remained unaware of the decisive role that Bachmann would come to play in his posthumous legacy. Nearly ten years after the philosopher's death, the republication of the *Tractatus logico-philosophicus*, a work instrumental in launching Wittgenstein's exceptional reception in the German-speaking world, can be traced to Bachmann's initiative.

In 1951, Bachmann returned to Vienna, where she found temporary employment as a secretary for the American News Service (AND), a position she found unrewarding. In the fall of 1951, she joined the script department at the Allied radio station Red-White-Red (Sender Rot-Weiß-Rot)[12] in the American sector of Vienna, where she worked first as a script writer and then as an editor until leaving Austria in 1953. Once established in her position, her outstanding dramaturgical talents were discovered, and she was invited to assume partial responsibility for a serialized radio-play production. One of the most successful media projects in the postwar era, *The Radio Family Floriani* (*Die Radiofamilie Floriani*) endured as a popular entertainment feature in Austria until 1960, long after the Allies had withdrawn from Austria following the ratification of the Non-Alignment Treaty in 1955. Bachmann was never particularly proud of her contributions to the popular genre, and in later years, she avoided any mention of this aspect of her career. During this early period in Vienna, however, she also adapted two independent dramas for radio and authored a number of literary reviews. In addition, she would go on to author three independent radio plays, which in varying forms expose the perils of fleeing from reality and illustrate a strong desire to bring about social change through the literary arts.

4. The Task of the Author: Poetry versus Prose

In 1952, the year her first original radio play, "A Deal in Dreams" ("Ein Geschäft mit Träumen"),[13] was given its premiere, Bachmann was invited

11 Erich Fried (1921–1988) was an Austrian-born poet, writer and translator; Elias Canetti (1905–1994), a German-language novelist, playwright, memoirist, and non-fiction writer born in Bulgaria, was awarded the Nobel Prize for Literature in 1981; Hilde Spiel (1911–1990) was an influential Austrian writer and journalist, primarily recognized today for her contributions to Austrian cultural history.

12 The colors of the Austrian flag were used to designate the German-language network, Sender Rot-Weiß-Rot, managed by the American occupation authorities in Vienna.

13 See Ingeborg Bachmann, "A Deal in Dreams," in *Three Radio Plays*, trans. Lilian Friedberg (Riverside, CA: Ariadne Press, 1999), 1–54.

to present her poems at a meeting of Group 47 in Niendorf on the Baltic Coast, which at that time amounted to foreign territory for the young writer from Vienna. Communicating her anxiety at having to read before this illustrious group of authors and intellectuals, she recounted in a short autobiographical study:

> On the second day I wanted to leave; on the third day I read a few poems aloud, suffocating from excitement; a jovial writer read them once more in a loud and distinct voice; a few gentlemen said [something] about them, and afterwards I was approached by a gentleman who said that on the following day I should read the same texts once more in Hamburg for the radio; I was paid 300 marks by the cashier; I thought somebody had made a mistake about the amount and went back to the cashier, but the man said that it was correct, 300 marks was what had been intended, and that was more than [I] earned in a month.

Undoubtedly, the year following was singular for the poet and essayist. On the one hand, she received the Prize of Group 47 in Mainz for her reading of selected poems, including "Great Landscape Near Vienna" ("Große Landschaft bei Wien"), a distinction that stamped her early on as a "writer's writer." On the other hand, her insightful essay, "Ludwig Wittgenstein—A Chapter of the Most Recent History of Philosophy" ("Ludwig Wittgenstein—Zu einem Kapitel der jüngsten Philosophiegeschichte"), appeared in print in July. And lastly, her first volume of poems, *Mortgaged Time (Die gestundete Zeit)*,[14] was chosen for publication by the Frankfurt Publishing House (Frankfurter Verlags-Anstalt).

Firmly rooted in the trauma of post-1945 Germany, the poems in *Mortgaged Time* are expressive of a feeling of urgency: "Keep your eye on the small fishing hut . . . stay calm on deck" (27); by calls to vigilance and action: "Don't look round. Lace up your shoe. . . . Blow out the lupins!"; and by exhortations that "harder days are coming" (43).[15] The strong sense of urgency in Bachmann's poetry, especially following the devastation of World War II, echoes the heightened tone of Brecht's calls to action after World War I in poems like "Cover Your Tracks" ("Verwisch

14 Also translated as "Borrowed Time" and "Time on Loan." For the latter, see Ingeborg Bachmann, "Time on Loan," in *Enigma: Selected Poems*, trans. Mike Lyons and Patrick Drysdale (Riverside, CA: Ariadne Press, 2011), 19.

15 Excerpts from the poems "Leaving Port" ("Ausfahrt"), "Mortgaged Time," "Early Noon" ("Früher Mittag"), and "Every Day" ("Alle Tage") Page numbers in parentheses refer to *In the Storm of Roses: Selected Poems by Ingeborg Bachmann*, trans. Mark Anderson (Princeton, NJ: Princeton University Press, 1986).

die Spuren") in his *Reader for City Dwellers* (*Lesebuch für Städtebewohner*), penned between 1921 and 1928. However, her apprehensions about postwar German society and its latent traces of Nazi ideology fell on deaf ears: "where Germany's sky blackens the earth" (49), where "war is no longer declared, only continued" (53), and where "in a house of death, yesterday's hangmen drink the golden goblet dry" (49), an arresting allusion to Gretchen's introductory song "There was a King of Thule" in Wolfgang Johann von Goethe's *Faust* (part 1, lines 2759–82).

Bachmann's influential Wittgenstein essay, which she revised for broadcast the following year at the American radio station Red-White-Red, attempted to show how Wittgenstein's philosophy of language was born of the philosopher's acclaimed lifestyle of "voluntary austerity." She asserted:

> So it was that the legend superseded reality while he was still alive, a legend of voluntary austerity, of the attempt at a saintly life, the attempt to comply with the proposition that concludes the *Tractatus*: 'What we cannot speak about we must pass over in silence.' And it was—to come straight to the point—the attempt to execute philosophy in silence, an absurd attempt, so it seems, but the only legitimate one for him after he had clearly represented everything sayable (as he demanded of philosophy), everything thinkable, by limiting the unthinkable from within and thus portending the unsayable.

At this time, Bachmann was residing on the Italian island of Ischia in close proximity to the German composer Hans Werner Henze, to whom she had been introduced at a meeting of Group 47. Born within a few days of one another, the composer and the writer remained allies until Bachmann's death, collaborating on a number of projects into the mid-1960s: among these were cycles for orchestra and solo voice, ballets, and three stage works, two of which were premiered successfully.[16] Besides composing the interludes for her second radio play, *The Cicadas*, Henze also set several of Bachmann's poems to music. Subsequently, she produced two essays about her experience as an opera librettist, which can be counted among the most profound articulations of how the writer for the musical stage adapts literary objectives to sustain the dramatic requirements of the genre. Henze's growing renown as a composer assured him an acceptable livelihood in the 1950s, while Bachmann often faced financial hardship, and between July 1954 and September 1955 she scripted editorials for Radio Bremen and the *West German General Newspaper*

16 A third stage work, allegedly conceived as a vehicle for Maria Callas, was never completed.

(Westdeutsche Allgemeine Zeitung, WAZ), adopting the pen name Ruth Keller to protect her integrity as a serious poet.

In August of 1954, Bachmann's significance as an author was affirmed by the publication of a cover story in the German news magazine *Der Spiegel*, designating the poet as an exceptional and promising talent in postwar literary circles. The media coverage focused more on Bachmann's appearance, demeanor, voice, and the formal artistry of her verses than on the socially critical message of her poems, which literary critics had effectively managed to "praise to death," a reception that the poet would come to experience with each new publication. Even though her lyrical achievements enjoyed high esteem in the 1950s, Bachmann remained skeptical about whether her readers were able to acknowledge her deeply serious intentions. Undoubtedly, her misgivings about the modern poetic genre found ample articulation in the "Lectures on Poetics" that she inaugurated at the University of Frankfurt in 1959 as the first among many distinguished authors. Not surprisingly, she concluded her first Frankfurt Lecture with a discussion of "art as a force for change," calling for "a literature that embodies a serious and uncomfortable spirit" and extolling "the writer who wants to bring about change."

The task of the writer, as she defines it, is perhaps best understood against the backdrop of Bachmann's own biography, her emphatic attempts to promote social transformation through art and poetic genius; in desperation she complained that the writer "is seen foaming at the mouth, and he is applauded. Nothing stirs, only that fatal applause." She rejected the writer's knack for facilitating the "enjoyment of a few intricate works" and for stimulating an "appreciation of art, rendering it harmless," and called instead for critical questions to be posed "from now on such that they once again become binding." Bachmann's advocacy for art's obligation to transform society was tempered by her personal unease with her innate capacity for crafting beautiful poetry. In an unfinished preface to an edition of Brecht's poems, she proclaimed: "If there were justice in the world, he would have become the popular poet everybody understands." Beyond her empathy for Brecht's struggles to achieve esteem as a great poet, it was his exceptional approach to language that Bachmann singled out for praise, the kind of language she principally sought to emulate: "He had the big words in the right places, he had a share, as I once tried to say, in utopia, in the millennial struggle against bad language. In our dream of expression."

During the course of 1955, the author took several trips, first to the USA during July and August as a fellow in the International Seminar of the Harvard Summer School of Arts and Sciences. She was part of a group of distinguished international intellectuals invited by Henry Kissinger, then professor of political science, to participate in a colloquium designed to generate enthusiasm for American forms of democracy. The assembly consisted of representatives from nineteen countries in Asia, Europe, and the Middle East, including selected publishers—among them Bachmann's future publisher at Suhrkamp, Siegfried Unseld—literary critics, poets, novelists, journalists, and politicians, an elite cadre singled out to assume leadership roles in their respective countries. After visiting New York City, Bachmann traveled to Paris, then to Rome and Naples.

Her second volume of poems, *Invocation of the Great Bear* (*Anrufung des Großen Bären*), released the following year, reaffirmed her reputation as one of the most gifted poets of the postwar era.[17] Despite the increasing renown of her literary achievements, Bachmann decided to relocate to Munich, where she was offered employment as a dramaturge at the Bavarian Broadcasting Corporation (Bayerischer Rundfunk). In July 1958, on the heels of an awkward encounter with Celan in Paris, Bachmann was introduced to the celebrated author Max Frisch, with whom she entered into an intimate relationship.[18] On October 5, 1958, before relocating to Zurich in order to be in close proximity to Frisch, Bachmann reported to Celan: "In the last few days here, the first since returning to Munich, Max Frisch came to ask me if I could do it, live with him, and now it has been decided," adding that she now felt "safe in warmth, love and understanding."[19] For Bachmann, the relationship with Frisch turned out to be disillusioning, regardless of whether the two resided in Zurich or in Rome, where they leased a joint apartment. Their relationship lasted five years, and apart from the bitter dispute surrounding Frisch's 1964 novel *A Wilderness of Mirrors* (*Mein Name sei Gantenbein*),[20] a number of details about the troubled liaison between the two authors have been leaked, although their personal correspondence has not yet been made available to the general public.

For her third radio play *The Good God of Manhattan*, Bachmann was awarded the prestigious Radio Play Prize of the War Blind in 1959. Her acceptance speech, "Truth is Within Human Reach" ("Die Wahrheit ist dem Menschen zumutbar"), has been widely interpreted as an appeal not only to face the pain of the past, but also to embrace words as

---

17 For this second volume of poems, which was greeted enthusiastically by critics, Bachmann received the Literature Prize of the Free Hanseatic City Bremen.

18 In an interview in December 1986, Wolfgang Hildesheimer recounted how he had introduced his "compatriot" Max Frisch to his dear friend "Inge," both of whom were visiting Paris in July 1958.

19 Bachmann and Celan, *Correspondence*, 143.

20 Frisch's 1964 novel was translated into English in 1965 by Michael Bullock as *A Wilderness of Mirrors* and later reprinted with the title *Gantenbein*. The German title could be translated loosely as "You Could Say My Name Is Gantenbein." Bachmann suspected that she had been negatively portrayed in the novel's glitzy figure Lila.

representations of reality, especially when she asserts that "it cannot be the task of the writer to deny pain, to conceal its traces, to pretend it does not exist." Rather, "that furtive pain sensitizes us to . . . the experience of truth." She also asserts that the writer "must acknowledge its reality and once again, in order to enable us to see it, make it real." Analogous to her utopian perspective on literature, Bachmann acclaimed the fundamental value of truth in literature, especially truth that correlates to physical pain or, perhaps more telling for a Wittgenstein disciple, is solely accessible through modes of silence.

In a similar vein, her Frankfurt Lectures lay claim to a literature that is "sharp with knowledge and bitter with longing." Framed by close readings of prewar and postwar authors, Bachmann made a strong case for the value of human experience in literature. As she contended, an expanding web of superfluous language had rapidly eroded ethical forms of communication in the postwar period. Above all, she insisted that culture's decline in the twentieth century made itself felt in the "flawed language" and "empty phrases" human beings resort to when trying to come to grips with the exigencies of everyday life, while she challenged art and literature to counter this negative development with something unquestionably genuine, what she called "the singular, the irreplaceable."

In the period following the publication of her second volume of poems in 1956 and her final radio play, which was first broadcast in 1958, she directed her creative energies to narrative prose, publishing her first collection of short stories, *The Thirtieth Year* (*Das dreißigste Jahr*), in 1961. The change of genre was received skeptically, especially since the author had long been categorized as a lyric genius. Given the controversy surrounding her prose debut at the time, critics seem to have overlooked that the "fallen lyric poet"—"*gefallene Lyrikerin*," as she was labeled by the celebrated literary critic Marcel Reich-Ranicki—had devoted herself from her earliest years to writing plays, either for the radio or stage, and narrative texts, alongside her lyric output. In addition, she continued to draft essays, while also translating selected verses by the Italian poet Giuseppe Ungaretti. Bachmann's highly personal account of a day spent with the poet on the outskirts of Rome in a literary portrait entitled "On Giuseppe Ungaretti" concludes with the wistful words:

> But great men—what are they really, we rarely encounter them, they are very simple, they laugh delightfully, they are strict without showing it to those who understand nothing about strictness (but I hope I understood his), and they are not fearsome, but rather somewhat more compassionate than others, more generous, more childlike, very much more mature, and in the end there is a correlation between their wisdom and the childlike qualities, according to which

> the gods, who do not exist anymore, once gathered their favorites around them.

Interestingly, she did not turn her back on poetry altogether during the years in which she explored and honed her skills as a prose author. In place of the finely crafted "word operas" of the 1950s, as she designated her lyric output, she produced a small number of masterful verses in the 1960s, haunting lyrics about the inability to write poetry, verses with titles that emphasize the gravity of their message: "Exile" ("Exil"), "After this Deluge" ("Nach dieser Sintflut"), "Truly" ("Wahrlich"), "A Kind of Loss" ("Eine Art Verlust"), "Enigma" ("Enigma"), and "No Delicacies" ("Keine Delikatessen"). Beyond doubt, Bachmann's late poems can be counted among the finest verses written in the German language after 1945. In these, the celebrated lyric icon articulates her refusal to "dress a metaphor with an almond blossom, crucify syntax on a trick of light" in order to "feed eye and ear with first-class word tidbits."[21]

By 1962, the relationship with Frisch had come to a decisive end, and owing to her emotional distress, Bachmann had to be hospitalized on several occasions. Text fragments released by her heirs in 2017 document the author's psychological state and various attempts to undergo treatment.[22] Complementary to these prose fragments, Bachmann also drafted a series of lyrical fragments in the early to mid-1960s, in which she gave ample expression to her physical distress. Not released until 2000, several fragments allude to the author's recurring bouts of anxiety and the therapeutic measures devoted to alleviating her discomfort. Still contending with her lingering illness and fragile mental state, Bachmann was awarded a stipend from the Ford Foundation in 1963, which necessitated her relocation to Berlin, an ideological frontier bearing the mark of Cain in the form of the Berlin Wall. This geopolitical scar of the Cold War was particularly threatening for an author keenly sensitive to emotional loss. In Berlin she befriended the Polish author Witold Gombrowicz, who was also a recipient of financial support from the Ford Foundation. Reflecting on their close association in a short fragment devoted to her colleague, she asserted that "if there was something we understood about one other, without ever admitting it to each other, then it was that we were lost, that this place smelled of sickness and death, for him in one way and for me in another. For a while we lived at the Academy of the Arts, and since I

21 "No Delicacies," in *In the Storm of Roses*, 187–89.

22 The posthumously published volume *Male Oscuro* documents the author's accounts of this period of "dark sickness." See Ingeborg Bachmann, *Male Oscuro: Aufzeichnungen aus der Zeit der Krankheit* [Dark evil: Notes from the time of illness], ed. Isolde Schiffermüller and Gabriella Pelloni, vol. 1 of *Ingeborg Bachmann Werke und Briefe*, Salzburger Bachmann Edition, 30 vols. (Munich and Berlin: R. Piper and Suhrkamp, 2017).

was the only person, at least in the beginning, who could converse with him in French, it was only natural that he asked me some questions, that I answered, that I translated his telegrams into German for him, and that we extended to one another the small courtesies that two foreigners in a foreign city can think of."[23]

5. Finding "Crystalline Words" for the *Todesarten*

During her almost three-year residence in Berlin, Bachmann began to focus more directly on what began as a single novel with the title *Todesarten* and grew to a more ambitious project by the same title,[24] a series of narratives depicting "all possible kinds of death" suffered by women in contemporary Austrian society. Bachmann envisioned this ambitious project as a history of intimate behavior, "a single grand study, a compendium, a handbook, . . . a view of the last twenty years, always with the setting Vienna and Austria." In addition to the three later works completed and published during her lifetime—*A Place for Coincidences* (*Ein Ort für Zufälle*) in 1965, *Malina* in 1971, and the five stories in her second collection *Three Paths to the Lake* (*Drei Wege zum See*) in 1972, Bachmann also drafted three novel fragments and sketched several narrative fragments for the *Todesarten* cycle.[25]

These late examples of Bachmann's literary genius expose the extent to which women are victims of a patriarchal order that strips them of their right to live as independent subjects, denies them agency, voice, and name, and ultimately destroys them. Confronting pain and suffering, her female figures become the preferred vessels of Bachmann's cultural memory work. Accordingly, the unfinished *Todesarten* project serves a dual purpose: on the one hand, it denounces many forms of cultural memory by replacing the real signs of social decay with fictional ones infused with

23 Ina Hartwig's biography of the author offers extensive details concerning Bachmann's lifestyle during her Berlin years, since she met with fellow intellectuals regularly and was generally more sociable than she may have implied in her writings about the city. Ina Hartwig, *Wer war Ingeborg Bachmann? Eine Biographie in Bruchstücken* [Who was Ingeborg Bachmann? A biography in fragments] (Frankfurt am Main: Fischer, 2017).

24 The title of Bachmann's *Todesarten* project has been translated among others as "Ways of Death," "Ways of Dying," "Kinds of Death," "Causes of Death," "Manners of Death," and "Death Styles." For consistency, we have opted to use the German term throughout.

25 In the original German edition, Bachmann's second volume of short stories is entitled *Simultan* (Simultaneous), and *Three Paths to the Lake* is only the title of the final novella in the collection of five prose texts. For the English translation, see Ingeborg Bachmann, *Three Paths to the Lake*, trans. Mary Fran Gilbert (New York: Holmes & Meier, 1989).

a utopian language. For Bachmann, and this confirms her significance for literature today, "beautiful language" lies at the heart of the most meaningful transformations accessible to postwar sociopolitical collectives, if they are resilient enough to confront the truths embedded in pain, loss, and remembrance. On the other hand, Bachmann's prose works endeavor to embed new truths in a comprehensive aesthetic form, a "total work of art" in keeping with Honoré de Balzac's *Human Comedy* (*Comédie humaine*) or Robert Musil's sweeping exploration of early twentieth-century mores in *The Man without Qualities*. The *Todesarten* are as much a literary project as they are a socially motivated anamnesis, mobilizing ghosts and similar manifestations of a violent past to exemplify the transgressions of modern European societies.

In 1964, the author was awarded the prestigious Georg Büchner Prize and on the occasion of the award ceremony delivered a highly controversial speech, "A Place for Coincidences" ("Ein Ort für Zufälle"), in which she likens postwar Berlin to a mental illness. Generally considered to be among the first narratives of her *Todesarten* project, the speech is decidedly literary in quality and has not been attributed to the corpus of the author's critical writings. The long final passage serves as a deeply expressive illustration of the unsettling perspective in Bachmann's virtuosic evocation of a psychosomatic outburst or "incident."

> Berlin room, dimly lit link in the bright suite of rooms, on the high ceiling the consolation of stucco work, a reminder that it was back then in Schöneberg.[26] A cell for reflection between noisy rooms. The silly notions amidst the feathers that everyone has lost, it was long ago, was not long ago. It is a celebration, to which all are invited, there is drinking and dancing, has to be drinking, so something can be forgotten, something, it is—wrong guess!—is today, was yesterday, will be tomorrow, it is something in Berlin. All are dancing silently, the young cheek to cheek. Everybody does drink quite a lot then, a large, black *Kater*[27] rears up to the rose-bordered ceiling. The last guests are screaming their heads off, they no longer know what they are saying: I can, I can, I have, I have, I will, I will! The cars refuse to start, everyone wants to spend the night in this room. The head physician will be late for his game of skat, he has made an exception and looked in one more time, holding his finger to his lips. You do not know if there is hope, but if there is no hope, it is not entirely dreadful, things are dying down, it need not be hope, may be less, need not be anything, it is nothing, it is, is over, is beyond *Scharnhorst*, *Insurance Policies*, *Cigars*, *Chocolates*, *Leiser*,

26 Schöneberg is a city district in the Western part of Berlin, situated until 1990 within the American sector.

27 *Kater* means both tomcat and hangover in German.

> *Fire Insurance*, *Commerzbank*, *Bolle*,[28] beyond, the last airplane has made its approach, the first makes its approach after midnight, everyone flying at the proper altitude, not through the room. It was merely an incident, was nothing more. It will not happen again.[29]

In late 1965 Bachmann returned to Rome, where she was introduced to the Russian poet Anna Akhmatova,[30] to whom she dedicated one of her final poems, "Truly," the closing words of which fuse the legitimacy of art as an agent of truth with the responsibility of the artist: "No one writes this sentence / who does not sign her name."[31] In 1965 Bachmann's growing political commitment led her to sign petitions against the Vietnam War and the statute of limitations for Nazi crimes. In the following year, she launched a literary tour of West Germany, incorporating selected excerpts from the *Todesarten* fragments into her program of readings. At the same time, one of her most flawless poems, "Bohemia Lies by the Sea" ("Böhmen liegt am Meer") originally written in 1964 to commemorate Shakespeare's 400th birthday but not published on that occasion, appeared in print. The poem signaled Bachmann's literary response to the Soviet invasion of Prague in August of 1968, an effort to suppress the liberal reforms initiated a mere eight months earlier. It was also the year that Sylvia Plath's autobiographical novel *The Bell Jar* was published by Suhrkamp in a German translation, prompting Bachmann to draft a short essay on the American author and poet. Esther Greenwood's story resonated with Bachmann as the type of gendered narrative she envisioned for her *Todesarten* project.

In 1971, seven years after her Büchner Prize acceptance speech, Bachmann's *Malina* appeared at Suhrkamp as the long-awaited opening novel of the *Todesarten* project. A poststructuralist tour de force narrated by a nameless female I, *Malina* became an immediate commercial success despite unfavorable reviews. In the following year, Bachmann was honored with yet another literary prize: for her second volume of short stories, *Three Paths to the Lake*, she received the Anton Wildgans Prize, which is granted to an Austrian writer whose early accomplishments

28 Bachmann cites an array of city signs and venues here, some of which are long-standing establishments in Berlin, such as Leiser, a fashionable shoe company, and Bolle, the name of a famous supermarket and dairy chain with branches throughout Berlin.

29 Ingeborg Bachmann, *Ein Ort für Zufälle* [A place for coincidences], with original drawings by Günter Grass (Berlin: Klaus Wagenbach, 1965), 65.

30 Anna Akhmatova (1889–1966) is one of Russia's greatest poets. A literary scholar and translator, she also wrote memoirs and autobiographical pieces.

31 Ingeborg Bachmann, "Truly," in *Songs in Flight: The Complete Poetry of Ingeborg Bachmann*, trans. Peter Filkins (New York: Marsilio Publishers, 1994), 309.

foretell future acclaim. Accepting the award, Bachmann spoke eloquently about her isolation and personal misgivings as the author of literary works preordained to enter into a lasting relationship with a broader readership, while for the writer the creative process remains solitary and desolate, little more than a curse or punishment:

> And as for the issues of the day, I only have to say that the writer must write them away, must subvert the issues of his time, may not allow himself to be corrupted by the empty phrases with which these issues are forced upon him. A writer must destroy the phrases, and if there are recent works that endure, then it will be the few that do without empty phrases. So there is a need not so much for talents, for there are many, but for writers for whom it is possible to keep their character at the height of their talent, and that is what is most difficult. I am aware of the cryptocrystalline nature of these words. We do not know what talent and what character may be, but in speaking I am only able to point, given the impotence of speech, toward something that seems more important to me than the idiotic chatter about the role of the writer yesterday, today, and tomorrow. The crystalline words do not appear in speeches. They are the singular, the irreplaceable. Now and again they appear on a page of prose or in a poem. Since I can only answer for myself, they have become for me the most extreme words: language is punishment.

6. Untimely Death and the Ingeborg Bachmann Prize

In 1973, the final year of her life, Bachmann accepted an invitation from the Austrian Cultural Institute in Warsaw to read excerpts from her work in Poland. During her tour, she paid visits to Auschwitz, Krakow, and Wrocław (formerly Breslau). Once back in Rome, she sustained extensive burns in her apartment on the night of September 25, 1973. Discovering the severity of her injuries, Bachmann's housekeeper and friend Maria Teofili took her to the hospital, where the author succumbed to complications caused by her wounds and substance abuse on October 17, 1973. Bachmann was interred at the cemetery in Annabichl, in close proximity to Klagenfurt. In the mid-1970s, the idea arose to organize a literary festival in the Carinthian capital, and since 1977 "The Days of German Literature" have been hosted annually by the city of Klagenfurt. Currently one of the most prestigious literary honors in the German-speaking territories, the festival's main prize, named after Ingeborg Bachmann, pays tribute to her auspicious role in the history of postwar German poetry and prose.

* * *

The selection of Ingeborg Bachmann's critical works that follows is organized according to topics. Alongside several autobiographical pieces, Bachmann's reflections on her first invitation to speak at a meeting of Group 47, and her personal encounters with fellow authors Giuseppe Ungaretti and Witold Gombrowicz, chapter 1 affords insights into the multifaceted personality of the author. Chapter 2 is devoted to Bachmann's publications and radio essays on philosophy, highly sophisticated texts that examine Ludwig Wittgenstein's legacy, the importance of the Vienna Circle for Austrian intellectual traditions, and the prominence of Neopositivism as a belief system, all of which the young author scripted shortly after having completed her doctorate at the University of Vienna in 1950. Bachmann's subtle assessments of noteworthy literary figures such as Franz Kafka, Robert Musil, Marcel Proust, Sylvia Plath, Thomas Bernhard, and Bertolt Brecht form the core of the third chapter.

Chapter 4 showcases fundamental elements of Bachmann's aesthetics and poetics, calling upon a wide variety of textual sources, among which the essay "What I Saw and Heard in Rome" ("Was ich in Rom sah und hörte") and the radio feature on Simone Weil are perhaps the most prominent. Bachmann's lifelong devotion to the musical arts, her essays on her librettos for two of Hans Werner Henze's operas, her celebrated fragment on the opera star Maria Callas, and her delightfully surreal piece on musical styles and traditions, "Wondrous Music" ("Die wunderliche Musik"), are highlighted in chapter 5. Chapter 6 showcases the five Frankfurt Lectures on Poetics, which Bachmann delivered at the University of Frankfurt in 1959/60. Framing these milestones in her critical works are two of Bachmann's most notable prize acceptance speeches: her highly admired address on the value and accessibility of truth, delivered to the Association of the War Blind in 1959, and the 1972 acceptance speech for the Anton Wildgans Prize, held less than eighteen months before her death, in which she recapitulates many of the issues informing her critical oeuvre. Concluding the speech with the final line of a late poem dedicated to the celebrated German Jewish poet Nelly Sachs, Bachmann addresses language directly: "No dying word, you words!"[32] Given the density of her many observations on embracing a utopian language after 1945, on why adopting an emphatic moral perspective in art and literature is imperative for cultural memory, and on the significance of literature for collective transformation, this final chapter points to the extraordinary legacy of Bachmann's critical writings for a twenty-first-century readership.

---

32 Ingeborg Bachmann, "You Words," in *In the Storm of Roses*, 173.

1: Autobiographical Writings and Intimate Reflections

Biographical Note[1]

I SPENT MY YOUTH in Carinthia,[2] in the south, near the border, in a valley that has two names, a German and a Slovenian one. And the house in which generations of my ancestors lived—Austrians and Slovenes—bears a foreign-sounding name still to this day. Near the border there is yet another border, the border of language—and I was at home on this side and on the other, with the tales of good and evil spirits hailing from two and three countries; for Italy, which I have never seen,[3] is on the other side of the mountains, only an hour's journey away.

I believe that I owe my yearning for travel to the narrowness of that valley and the consciousness of the border. After the war was over, I left, penniless as well as without baggage, and full of impatience and expectation I came to Vienna, a city that had been impossibly distant in my imagination. And once again, it became a homeland on the border: between the East and the West, between a great past and a dark future. And if I subsequently made my way to Paris, London, and Germany, that does not really say much, for in my memory the journey from the valley to Vienna will always remain the longest.

Sometimes people ask me how, as a child growing up in the country, I found my way to literature.—I cannot say exactly how; I only know that I started writing at an age when everybody reads Grimm's fairy tales, that I did not like to work and liked to rest near the railway embankment,

1 Bachmann's reading of this short autobiographical text on Northwest German Radio (NWDR) in November 1952 served to introduce the premiere broadcast of eight new poems and her narrative "A Deal in Dreams." Her first radio play by the same name had been broadcast nine months earlier on February 15, 1952, by the Viennese radio station Rot-Weiß-Rot (Red-White-Red). The title, "Biographical Note," was not used by the author during the reading. Two later drafts of this text were attempted in the mid-1950s, presumably for an event celebrating the publication of her second volume of poems in the Fall of 1956, but this is the only authorized version.

2 Southernmost province of Austria.

3 Although she had traveled to Italy already in September 1952, Bachmann is writing here in this first paragraph from the perspective of her early life in the village before she made the move to Vienna described in the second paragraph.

sending my thoughts on travels to distant cities and countries and to the unknown sea that meets the sky somewhere close to the circle of the world. I always dreamed of seas, sand, and ships, but then the war came, replacing the dream-shrouded world of fantasy with the real one, in which one no longer dreams, but must make decisions.

Later, many things came, as one would scarcely dare to wish for: studies at the university, travel, collaboration on journals and newspapers, and now stable employment with the radio. Those are all daily passages in any life, which are interchangeable and easy to confuse. What remains to be addressed is the question of the influences and models, of the literary climate of which I feel myself to be a part.—For a number of years, I read a great deal, most avidly perhaps those poets who were the most alien to me, Gide, Valéry, Éluard, Eliot, and Yeats among the newer ones, and it might be that I learned a thing or two from them. But essentially, what dominates my work to this day is the world of imaginative myths indicative of my childhood home, which remains an example of an authentic and largely unrealized Austria, a world in which many languages are spoken and through which many borders flow.

Writing poetry appears to be the most difficult task for me, because here the problems of form, theme, and vocabulary must be solved all at once, given that poems obey the rhythm of time and yet should order the fullness of the old and new things close to our heart, things in which past, present, and future are resolved.

Group 47[1]

This is already forgotten, but still true. In 1952, Austrians knew almost nothing about new German writers; now and then someone who had a passport and a visa would travel to Germany, a country that seemed more distant than any other, a small circle of "pioneers," who came back with tales; it would be saying too much that their stories made any sense. Three of them had already been at meetings of a "Group 47" there,[2] probably fallen in with it as accidentally as I did that year; I had never been to Germany, and I do not know what caused the greater anxiety at the time: traveling to that country for the first time, or fear and curiosity, or the mixed feelings about encountering people whose names I had never heard.

I still remember the bus, boarded in Munich to go to the Baltic Sea, the first Coca-Cola drunk in a garden café in Munich, the affable handshakes, the jovial stories told by a gentleman who, as I have since learned, was Walter Kolbenhoff;[3] it seemed rather improbable to me that they could all be writers, because they had neither titles, most of them only first names, nor were they professors, privy councilors; they did not put on airs, and they seemed improbably jolly to me; I had never before seen so many jolly people.

One morning, Milo Dor[4] came into the little office on Seidengasse in Vienna and asked whether he could borrow 50 shillings from me; he needed them, he said, for a German guest, in order to hire a taxi; it was a point of honor—or he probably put it differently—how could we measure up to German literature, if even the fare for a taxi etc. I do not know whether the German writer ever heard that story; he would probably have

1 This unpublished fragment, a preliminary draft written in the early 1960s, is without title. The author begins by recalling her experiences at the tenth meeting of Group 47 in Niendorf, Germany in 1952, at a time when as an Austrian she saw herself particularly remote from "new German writers." What seems to connect these otherwise disparate text fragments is the "already forgotten" but "still true" memory of the distance between Austrian and German writers that she perceived a decade earlier in the early postwar period.

2 Bachmann's Austrian colleagues Ilse Aichinger, Milo Dor, and presumably her early mentor Hans Weigel had attended Group 47 meetings in Germany prior to Bachmann.

3 Walter Kolbenhoff (1908–1993) was a little-known German author and journalist.

4 Milo Dor (1923–2005) was a Budapest-born writer, publicist, and translator of Serbian heritage who lived in Vienna after World War II and studied at the University of Vienna until 1949; one of the early "pioneers," he joined Group 47 in 1951. This memory of a German guest in Vienna is another example of the strange encounter between the penniless Austrians and the jovial Germans at the time.

been the first to laugh about it heartily. We were all in our mid-twenties, notoriously penniless, notoriously hopeless, lacking a future, menial employees, or unskilled workers, some already freelance writers, which is to say adventuresome characters, about whom no one could rightly say how they survived, but, more often than not, at any rate, from forays to the pawnbroker.

It seems that all of us in Vienna had precious little to laugh about; otherwise, my most vivid memory would not be of a transformed Ilse Aichinger,[5] infected by something that entailed youthfulness, mirth, relaxation all at once, an infection redolent with hope, with greater freedom, and with insouciance, so that for all I care this report might sound less like one about a meeting of a literary group, which indeed it was at the very least, but rather about a short span of "youth."

The bus stopped for the night in Frankfurt, and the writers stopped for the night at the house of another writer whose apartment became a hostel, with the guests sleeping on the floor, on mattresses, brewing coffee, greeting other writers, and the newcomer was amazed at everything and at nothing, that was the way it was, and on the next day, the bus continued on its course, stopping in a village up north, where drinks were taken at a pub, those who had money treating the rest and those who did not allowing the others to treat them, and at night the Baltic had been reached and everyone ran to the sea, and everything was strange and surprising, and in the house there were yet other writers, still more, whom I also did not know; one was the artistic director of a theater, from Hamburg, and he too was friendly and not at all like an artistic director of a theater, and [he] too turned out to be a writer; one elderly gentleman was Mr. Rowohlt, certainly no stranger to anyone, and as for the rest, nothing was known about anyone, and conversations were struck up with many of them, and never had a country seemed more exotic than this Germany, and never had there been people more amazing than this Group 47, whose members sat down in rows, though not very orderly ones, on the next day, in a hall, the German writer sitting down on a chair in front, and one started reading, and finally there was quiet. Today, of course, I know who they are.

On the second day, I wanted to leave; on the third day, I read a few poems aloud, suffocating with excitement; a cheerful writer read them

5 Ilse Aichinger (1921–2016), Austrian Jewish writer and medicine student at the University of Vienna who was invited to join Group 47 in 1951, where she met the German poet and radio play author Günter Eich, whom she married in 1953. She was awarded the group's literary prize in 1952 for her short story "Mirror Story" ("Spiegelgeschichte"). Bachmann's memory of Aichinger's transformation after returning from Germany further underscores the differences that Bachmann perceived between Germans and Austrians in that early postwar period.

once more in a loud and distinct voice; a few gentlemen said something about them, and afterwards I was approached by a gentlemen who said that on the following day I should read the same poems once more in Hamburg for the radio; I was paid 300 marks by the cashier; I thought somebody had made a mistake about the amount and went back to the cashier, but the man said that it was correct, 300 marks was what had been intended, and that was more than I earned in a month.

A very friendly Frenchman calmed me down afterwards, saying that it had been good; that was Louis Clappier, who is now dead.

In Hamburg the meeting continued; tapes were played, a radio opera, *The Country Doctor*,[6] so there really were radio operas; a feature broadcast, so there were feature broadcasts, a radio play, *Dreams*,[7] so there were such radio plays, and that "so there were" can no longer be evoked in my memory any more than the novelties incurred by friendship, a haze of friendship, laughter, earnestness, now idealized already, long modified, long displaced.

That meeting never came to an end; two days later some parts of the group reassembled in Frankfurt, then another part in Munich, and the talk never ceased.

6 The story "A Country Doctor" ("Ein Landarzt") by Franz Kafka (1883–1924) was originally published in 1916 and adapted as a radio opera by Hans Werner Henze (1926–2012) in 1951.

7 The radio play *Dreams* (*Träume*) by Günter Eich (1953–1972), German writer and husband to Ilse Aichinger, premiered on Bavarian Radio in 1953.

Attempt at an Autobiography[1]

Born in Klagenfurt on June 25, 1926. Musil says of that place something like this: "Not a place where a person would normally come into the world."[2] But to me, Klagenfurt has always been a credible place. In 1926, my father had already been a teacher in the city for a short while; before that, so the story goes, he had been in Krumpendorf and in Mauthen—and those two places, surprisingly, play a definite role in my thoughts. Mauthen is also the birthplace of the current Federal Chancellor,[3] a pupil of my father's, but also, and that above all else, of Mary, his first fiancée, a woman who was an officer's widow with a child, wrote poetry, and was adored by my father, but evidently with enough astuteness that he realized she would never adapt to that milieu and in all likelihood not to him. For me, Krumpendorf was the most charming lakeside resort; why it was not called Lake Klagenfurt, I cannot really say, and I do not have many memories of the beach at Krumpendorf, only a few snapshots, and the feeling that we often spent the whole day there, eating cold cutlets and hard-boiled eggs, also that we either came from the city on foot or rode on bicycles, each of our parents carrying one of the children on the horizontal bar or in the baby seat.

My father is the youngest of many children of an old family of farmers; our house is called "Tobai," and formerly we owned Ranner farm, which was once situated above the village and burnt down. (Uncle Yuri? A heavy drinker, a most endearing man, although to blame. My grandfather drank too, by the way.) Our parents must have regarded it as a great stroke of luck when they found the apartment on Durchlaßstraße. Before that, in Krumpendorf, they had to live in a one-room apartment. Although I was seven when I left, Durchlaßstraße[4] had already been weighed down with my earliest memories. For instance, the exploding stove: our parents were out one night, and my sister and I were threading pearls (my mother's many-colored necklace pearls), when there was a big

1 Bachmann drafted this text presumably around 1965, during the term of Federal Chancellor Josef Klaus, whom she references in the first paragraph. As a fragment, the text has several gaps, which we have indicated with ellipses.

2 Robert Musil (1880–1942) writes in his diary: "I was born on . . . which is something not everyone can say of themselves. The place, too, was unusual: Klagenfurt in Kärnten; relatively few people are born there. In a sense, both of these are intimations of my future." Robert Musil, *Diaries: 1899–1941*, trans. Philip Payne, ed. Mark Mirsky (New York: Basic Books, 1999), 340.

3 Reference to Josef Klaus (1910–2001), a member of the Austrian Peoples' Party (Österreichische Volkspartei, ÖVP), who served as Austrian Federal Chancellor from 1964–1966 in a coalition of the Social Democratic and People's Parties.

4 The street name appears in "Youth in an Austrian Town," the opening story in Bachmann's first collection, *The Thirtieth Year* (1961).

bang and we called for help. The room and the apartment were already filled with smoke, when Hilde, the girl from downstairs, was coming up the stairs, and then our parents were there too.

I had to go to Bismarck School for the first grade; before long, they let me go by myself, but my father watched over me, to be on the safe side. I must have been overly anxious and overly obedient, waiting at every intersection until not a car was in sight in any direction, so that it took forever to get to Annabichl.[5] At the Glan river, on the bridge, I met two boys that year who were a little older; one of them called to me, "Hey you, come over here, I'll give you something"; I remember how happy I was; I went up to the boy beaming, because he wanted to give me something, and when I reached him he slapped me in the face.[6]

. . . invented. My father confirms that; one year before I started school, I put that together for myself. Had presumably eavesdropped now and then when my father was tutoring my cousin Ernst. At that time, he had been living with us for a year, and we very much enjoyed playing with him. (Wish for a big brother.) At Christmas, between the panes of the double-glazed window—for refrigeration—a guineafowl or some other animal for the holiday roast, of interest especially to my sister, because it was dead, and because of the colorful and jet-black feathers.

At Bismarck School a less than pleasant deskmate, a girl with lice. Very good grades, but no real memory, do not know whether I liked going or not; my memories remain concentrated on home.

The big turning point is the move to a house of our own. The first night spent among the boxes, no electric light, but all of us full of confidence, because my father must have been beside himself with joy. He had bought a savings certificate, had stopped smoking and drinking for the sake of the house; he hardly ever drank anything before, only beer, but he was a passionate smoker. The frugality of my parents, which had nothing oppressive about it, nothing avaricious, but also had no influence on me, rather on my brother. Only later to be admired, the consistency; in some respects, the way we were raised could be called exemplary, the lack of luxury but not of joy, never a vulgar word, almost no toys, no pampering, no help in school matters, no emphasis on grades. We learned early how to swim; in Vellach[7] we had liberties that we did not have in the city where we were at home. No problems at school, only later rebellion and inklings of turmoil, when my little brother arrived, my idol, to which my mother reacted with annoyance. Strange reaction: that I shall never have a

---

5 Annabichl, a northern suburb of Klagenfurt, where Bachmann's grave is located today.

6 Bachmann's fragmentary text omits the "he" and "me" in the last clause.

7 Vellach, a small Carinthian spa town southeast of Klagenfurt, is the southernmost municipality of Austria, close to the border with Slovenia.

child, could not imagine one of my own, because I loved my brother too much, found him more beautiful than all other children.

The pardonable lies: when I was asked—for the first time, by the way—which poets had left an impression on me, I felt that I owed it to the others or myself or some authority to say something about Éluard, Apollinaire, and Eliot, and Yeats; those were still very exclusive names in Vienna back then, after the *tabula rasa* of collective ignorance, and I knew those writers by name, still more, I even knew a poem by Breton, which I did not understand but of which I was in awe, in addition I "silently surrendered" to a poem by Éluard for personal reasons. Eliot meant nothing to me; Yeats is someone I do not know to this day. Why such childish lies? I might just as well have said that Swedish furniture fascinated me; some people found it fascinating; I had never seen any, but then I saw some samples, and I preferred my rustic wardrobe. But I felt "obligated." Ah, wilderness, stupidity.

What really did leave an impression on me? Let anyone laugh who wants to. I read the novels of Lernet-Holenia closely, especially selected pages, and the reason was that I realized I could learn German, nuances that went beyond German, punctuation, subjunctives; I studied those pages like a medical intern who observes surgical procedures for the first time. *The Two Sicilies*[8] for instance, that was a book that I learned from. Now I am reminded of that, since I am reading an inconsequential novel by Lernet, but once again with a magnifying glass: how does he form a sentence, etc. And yet it would be wrong to say that he "influenced" me; I was kept in detention after school, because we did not learn anything in class, and here there was something to be learned. And how could I even have learned German from an Éluard or a Yeats, and I was in dire need of schooling. That more than anything. Influence was something I did not need, even back then: I was a self-sufficient writer without knowing it, and today, after much experience, it falls off like dead skin. I did not need one, any standard; in all of contemporary literature and also among the classics there is no one who could seduce me. I call all of those children who borrow from Brecht and Joyce and others *beati loro,* or lucky the one who does not forget.

My questionable freedom: I am unimpressionable. My adventures take place in different ways, for instance the baffled amazement now and then at an opening in Balzac (but that has nothing to do with influence)—How does the man do it? I have never figured it out, and I admire where I am unable to figure anything out . . .

8 *Beide Sizilien* (1942, one year after *Mars in Aries*) is considered Alexander Lernet-Holenia's second-most important novel. Neither has appeared in English translation.

On Giuseppe Ungaretti[1]

His face was friendly, the face of an old man, of a man who forgives, who has had many worries, many experiences and prefers not to get in anyone's way with them. That day at noon, he was not the great man; he did not say anything significant, and it would be just as possible to associate him with his oeuvre as it would be to remember him without his oeuvre, as may, in fact, be the case with all proper human beings. *Ungaretti, uomo di pena.*[2]

I think it is wrong to tempt speech across so many different experiences, across such sweeping differences of age.

At Fiumicino,[3] on a horrible day on which he wanted to take me to a flight that for an entire day did not want to or could not be, or simply was not, available, we drank together and waited for hours, and finally recognized by . . .ists of the sort that can only be found at Fiumicino, who wanted to know what the "Professore" was up to or to what country the trip was destined for . . ., spent one of the strangest days that I can remember. Since I discovered that Giuseppe Ungaretti had never been sick, that he knows neither what headaches nor what ailments are, like those that all normal people are subject to, it has seemed even more peculiar to me that only he realized I was fraught with pain and that he stayed with me until the damned plane finally departed.

Ever since, I have traveled and lived with four lucky charms, the *portafortuna* that he gave me that day, and if I now no longer use all of them, but give them merely a friendly glance and even leave them at home, I will always remember that he wanted to protect me from something, and because I no longer die of agony at Fiumicino and because my house is protected, each room by one lucky charm, the fact that I met the man no longer seems quite as arbitrary and strange to me.

Even if respect and reverence forbid it—if the beauty of a venerable face forbids it, I nevertheless believe, as we sometimes allow ourselves to gaze at a star and think that its light shines on us, that something shone on me and now protects me, and even if it is becoming more and more fragile, like the light about which he writes in his final poems, it is still

---

1 This text is without title and was presumably drafted in the late 1960s. Giuseppe Ungaretti (1888–1970), an Italian Symbolist poet, critic, and translator, was the founder of the Hermeticist movement in literature. Bachmann "made the acquaintance of the great old man himself" in 1961 after translating his first collection of poems into German.

2 Ungaretti, man of sorrow. A reference to Ungaretti's poem "Pilgrimage" ("Pellegrinaggio"), in which the poet describes himself with this phrase. Bachmann translated this poem into German as "The Patient Sufferer" ("Dulder").

3 Resort town on the Tiber; home of the Leonardo da Vinci Airport.

strong enough that I shall sense it on me even in its utmost fragility and remoteness.

He said to me, do not write that you regard me as a great poet, and I promised him that I would not; rather, write that I am a *ragazzino*,[4] a simple favor that anyone can easily fulfill for someone.

But the great men—what are they really, we rarely encounter them, they are very simple, they laugh delightfully, they are strict without showing it to those who understand nothing about strictness (but I hope I understood his), and they are not fearsome, but rather somewhat more compassionate than others, more generous, more childlike, very much more mature, and in the end there is a correlation between their wisdom and the childlike qualities, according to which the gods, who do not exist anymore, once gathered their favorites around them.

I do not know Ungaretti's gods; I do not believe that he was ever told that existence was duty, for duty is called *dovere*[5] here, and "must" is a tragic gift, the serenity of which is never questioned; we must live, we must do our job, then the helpful are given helping hands.

I do not believe that Giuseppe Ungaretti ever thought he had to help me, or anyone else for that matter; rather, I hope that he considered it more important to write a sentence or to describe Blake's hell,[6] to live his life and nothing but his life. That is more helpful than the gifts of many others.

Like the lucky charms, the sentences surround one, and that is the gift.

If an old man is capable of creating joy, then he has never been unfaithful to himself when he first penned *allegria*.[7]

But it is the joy of shipwrecks.[8]

To learn this joy, to return to the voyage like an old sea lion who simply cannot do otherwise,[9] that is neither existence nor duty, but the splendid vice of life, and to live and to live once again.

---

4 Italian for little boy.

5 "Dovere" is both an intransitive verb meaning "must" or "should" and a noun meaning "duty."

6 An unclear reference to William Blake (1757–1827), an English Romantic poet and artist known for complexly imagined theologies.

7 A play on Ungaretti's poetry collection *Allegria*. The title means "joy."

8 A play on Ungaretti's poem "Allegria di naufragi," which Bachmann translated as "Freude der Schiffbrüche" ("Joy of the Shipwrecks"), in Ingeborg Bachmann, *Werke in vier Bänden*, ed. Christine Koschel, Inge von Weidenbaum, and Clemens Münster, 4 vols., new edition (Munich and Zurich: Piper, 1993), vol.1, 556.

9 Another phrase from the same Bachmann-translated poem: "Und plötzlich nimmst du / die Fahrt wieder auf / wie / nach dem Schiffbruch / ein überlebender / Seebär." In Bachmann, *Werke in vier Bänden*, vol. 1, 557.

And those who cannot will never be able to write, since existence is not a duty but a vice, but those who understand a great deal will also understand a little . . .

The tribute of which a great poet is assured is less than the admiration for a life subjected to losses, humiliations, insults, travails, and the incessant infamy to which a writer is exposed who escapes his four walls like everyone else; it is a triumph that consists in something immense, in the *illumino*,[10] and that is how things come together in my view: the man I left in a taxi today on a random street in Rome and who made me a present of his plume or his laughter, meaning that I have understood everything, even though that too passes by.

It is the enigma of great men that they take leave of us laughing.

10 A play on the Ungaretti poem "Mattinata" ("Morning"), also translated into German by Bachmann, which reads "M'illumino / d'immenso" (I illuminate myself / by means of the immense).

Admittedly[1]

Admittedly, I no longer know why I live here,[2] for I write about Vienna, or, rather, when I write, I am in Vienna. And admittedly, I do not drink a "one-horse carriage," or a "tall brown one," or a "capuchin" here, but a "cappuccino";[3] the apartments are expensive, but the food is cheaper, suddenly all my friends are named Giulio or Giorgio or Luciano, Ginevra, Marina, Alda. Admittedly, you already dream in another language, but supposedly that means absolutely nothing; that is to say, you have to be able to count in another language, but that is precisely what I cannot do, I cannot multiply or divide or add, basically the smallest operations, in Italian, and these I will never learn. Admittedly, life is like it is everywhere here: on any given day someone will get married, someone will be appointed to a professorship, someone will hang himself, be committed to a mental hospital; all will be as it is everywhere else, and no Colosseum, no Capitol can help you through it, and so what can help you escape, surely not only to get away from everything, but rather to live? Admittedly, the people here are not any better than anywhere else, but only spend five minutes on the street and a slight flash of craziness, a temptation to give it all up are suddenly abandoned. Admittedly, the people are a little more attractive here and very friendly, but you know, of course, what is behind that. But do you really? You really know nothing whatsoever. For me, it is enough that the people here are not unfriendly, but rather friendlier. Admittedly, you cease taking things all too seriously here; for in 2,500 years a lot of water has flowed down the Tiber, and really everybody here is aware of that. Written in advance of life is the word Pazienza, that is patience, patience. Here crises, crises of state, private crises that resemble childhood diseases. People know that getting along with each other is paramount. Admittedly, I have learned here how to get along with everyone else. I have learned it repeatedly, but I also admit that when the door to the room in which I work falls shut, then there is no doubt: Thinking is a solitary pursuit, being alone is a good thing.

---

1 Translated by Nancy Simpson-Younger while a St. Olaf undergrad in 2006, with grateful acknowledgment to the late Peter K. Jansen for his input.

2 Bachmann is writing this piece in Rome.

3 The "one-horse-carriage" (*Einspänner*), "tall brown one" (*großen Braunen*), and "capuchin" (*Kapuziner*) are traditional coffee beverages served in Viennese coffeehouses. "Cappuccino" is Italian.

Witold Gombrowicz[1]

I first met Mr. Gombrowicz[2] in Berlin in the spring of 1963, the two of us were the first guests of the Ford Foundation and, in similar ways, probably both grateful and ungrateful. What I was able to guess, although I cannot prove it, is that Gombrowicz was ill at ease, despite that small windfall, which allowed him, for the first time after so many years, to live without daily worries and in halfway comfortable circumstances, ill at ease perhaps less because of any scruples, which neither he nor I felt, because they would have been highly misplaced at a time when a person no longer has a roof over his head—so I believe to have guessed correctly that the money did not affect his integrity and his way of living; it pleased him, but as so often happens, comforts for which a person ought to be grateful are encumbered by immense changes.

Gombrowicz came from Argentina, subsequent to a hundred detours; I too came from many countries, and if there was something we understood about one other, without ever admitting it to each other, then it was that we were lost, that this place smelled of sickness and death, for him in one way and for me in another. For a while we lived at the Academy of the Arts, and since I was the only person, at least in the beginning, who could converse with him in French, it was only natural that he asked me some questions, that I answered, that I translated his telegrams into German for him, and that we extended to each other the small courtesies that occur to two foreigners in a foreign city.

Gombrowicz was one of the few discreet people I have met in my life, and that is another reason I have little to say; when one discreet person encounters another, who is similar, there is much silence and only now and then an exchange. The things that concerned him, besides the proximity to Poland,[3] were several books, among them Sartre's book on

---

1 Written in 1963, when Bachmann and Gombrowicz were both recipients of a Ford Foundation scholarship in (West) Berlin, this manuscript is without title and was not published during the author's lifetime.

2 Witold Gombrowicz (1904–1969) was a Polish diarist, satirist, and playwright who wrote on themes of youth, identity formation, and anti-nationalism. While his first novel (*Ferdydurke*, 1937) was well received in Poland, his work was not well known in Buenos Aires, where he lived from 1938–1962 in relative poverty, especially during the war. Fame came only in the last years of his life. In the 1960s, several of his works were translated and his dramas staged in theaters in France, Germany, and Sweden; the Ford Foundation scholarship allowed him to return to Europe, where he was awarded the Prix International in 1967, two years before his death near Nice, France.

3 In 1963, while Bachmann was writing this piece, the Polish authorities had begun a campaign against Gombrowicz's work, reaffirming their earlier ban of his *Dziennik* (Diaries), published in serial form from 1953–1969 in *Kultura* and generally considered his most outstanding work. More than a mere record of

Genet, about which he talked more than once, but I am unable to reconstruct his sometimes brilliant and arrogant remarks; I remember him, but I do not jot down sentences.

I remember walking together through the streets of Berlin, so alien to both of us, often laughing and calling out, "Voyez, il y a quelqu'un,"[4] for the streets were so infinitely empty, to us at any rate.[5]

One day we went into a small restaurant in Berlin to eat; the waiter thought that we did not understand German; in the end I spoke German to him; it was one of the many shocks that very often repeated themselves for me in Berlin. But it was not the waiter who said to me, this is not a Polish hangout, you know. He said something else, he was cautious, not knowing where to place us and whether we were Westerners or Easterners or something altogether different, but he did say something appalling, both of us stood up immediately and paid and left.

One day G. was taken to a hotel on Kurfürstendamm, I sent him a cable, and I suspect that it was my only display of affection and understanding. The hotel was horrible, staleness in every object, and we examined a letter from his translator and a contract; in the end he said: we, you and I and the others, we will commit collective suicide here, and the poor Ford Foundation will have to pay for that on top of everything else.

That was something we talked and laughed about for a while, even though it was no laughing matter, for deep down both of us knew that we might in fact do it. Even though it would no longer be at the Ford Foundation's expense.

But who was that man really? I think he was one of the loneliest people I have ever met, he was completely forsaken by everything, by Poland, by Argentina, by Berlin, and all Berliners were put off by his manner of speaking and arguing. If I may use a French expression, it was an *incompatibilité*, not ill will on either side.

Because I too come from a country with a reputation for characterlessness and "difficulty," in the sense of the truly "difficult,"[6] it was possible for me to understand both sides. I could understand that to my Berlin friends, this man, who was in search of a dialogue they were neither able nor willing to conduct, was totally absurd. To me, he was anything but that, for the absurdity of any man and any class and any race is something always on my mind, and G.'s intelligence was unquestionably of a

---

the author's life, his Diaries are a philosophical essay rich in literary devices and incorporating his views on politics, national culture, and religion.

4 French for "Look, a man is coming!"

5 This story is also related in Gombrowicz's *Berliner Notizen* [Berlin notes] (Pfullingen: Neske, 1965), 72.

6 In German, *Schwierigen*: a pun on the title character in Hugo von Hofmannsthal's 1921 comedy *Der Schwierige* (The Difficult Gentleman).

kind that could not even be remotely understood and certainly not with the best of goodwill in Berlin.

Yet, it was not that difficult to understand him. His essence was one of great goodness, a gentleness that masqueraded as arrogance. He was the most unassuming person imaginable. I went to see him one more time, before I myself fell ill, in his first, abominable apartment in Berlin, among a cacophony of noise, and he was listening to the Beethoven quartets, which I myself later bought because of him, but he was listening to them through a set of headphones, because he did not want to disturb anyone, while his surroundings, the entire Kurfürstendamm, assaulted him with an infernal racket; I left sooner than I had intended, because I could not stand the street noise any longer.

At that time he could already speak German fairly well, which amazed me, because it must be enormously difficult for a sixty-year-old man to learn yet another language, he must also have met a few people who thought highly of him, but I do not know anything about that. I believe he told me about a few young people who came to see him.

It may indeed sound foolish if I limit myself to such vague statements when speaking of a person whom I really did know, with whom I went on many walks, shared many meals, but memory is a merciless authority, it does not condone lies.

Something that I know better than the facts or the phrases, of course, is my impression of him. My affection for him was sincere, and he knew it too. He cannot ever have doubted it, either. He did doubt the sincerity of all the others, and he may have been right about that. They had no language in common, and the two of us, as the result of our many and complicated detours, did share a common language after all. It was not only the advantage of conversing in French, but the advantage of sadness, the disadvantage of all of its consequences, even though we had to discontinue our one single literary debate as soon as it had begun, because he was torturing me; yes, I remember it vividly; while we were already strolling on the street, he asked me, what do you think of Goethe, what of Schiller, what of Kleist, etc. I muttered this and that and wanted to know which of Goethe's or Kleist's works, while he proceeded to accuse me repeatedly that I was bent on "complicating everything"; in the end, we were standing in the hallway of the Academy building, which was certainly the right setting, the only setting suitable for those unreal conversations, and I suddenly turned to walk towards my room. And then he took a few steps after me and said, I hope you are not crying, I simply wanted to torture you, and if I succeeded in that, then everything is all right.

At the time, I really did have to cry and to laugh as well.

Perhaps that was one of his most essential qualities. He wanted to torture people, and he could not. As I have already related, he was a human being with a big heart, *au fond*[7] and against everything he wanted to be. Although I am not in the habit of pigeonholing people according to their views, their eccentricities and manners, those being irrelevant to me—when I must think and am allowed to think of someone, then in connection with G., it would always occur to me first that he had a heart. And probably for that reason he was also a great writer.

It would be wrong to blame so many others for not noticing that quality in him, because he was obviously intimidating in his strange demeanor, his pride, his eccentricity, etc., but never so to me, for I should not want to see pride and eccentricity disappear from the world.

Well, what then was his problem? He was ill, and so was I. I could no longer go to see him, he did not come to see me. But that is entirely irrelevant.

---

7 French for fundamentally, essentially.

2: Philosophy

Commentary

INGEBORG BACHMANN COMPLETED her studies in philosophy at the University of Vienna in 1949, only two years after Martin Heidegger published his "Letter on Humanism" ("Brief über den Humanismus"). Originally written in response to a series of questions posed by Heidegger's French colleague Jean Beaufret, the letter was a response to a lecture that the French existentialist philosopher Jean-Paul Sartre held at the Club Maintenant in Paris in late October 1945. The text of Heidegger's missive was drafted in December 1946, but did not appear in print until it had been expanded into an essay. At the time, the Heidegger-Sartre exchange represented a singular occurrence in twentieth-century philosophy, since it was among the first of many productive dialogues between German and French intellectuals after the defeat of the Nazi regime in May 1945.

Of great interest to Bachmann, the "Letter on Humanism" unveils a theory of language that is perceived as the constituting element of Being. Centered on how thinking defines speech, Heidegger argues that speech manifests language and that, in turn, language should be recognized as the "house of Being." Largely ontological, but also spatial in nature, his argument is justified in a famous passage at the outset of the text:

> Language is the house of Being. In its home man dwells. Those who think and those who create with words are the guardians of this home. Their guardianship accomplishes the manifestation of Being insofar as they bring the manifestation to language and maintain it in language through their speech. Thinking does not become action only because some effect issues from it or because it is applied. Thinking acts insofar as it thinks. Such action is presumably the simplest and at the same time the highest, because it concerns the relation of Being to man. But all working or effecting lies in Being and is directed toward beings. Thinking, in contrast, lets itself be claimed by Being so that it can say the truth of Being. Thinking accomplishes this letting. Thinking is *l'engagement par l'Être pour l'Être* (engagement by Being for Being).[1]

---

1 Martin Heidegger, "Letter on Humanism," trans. Frank Capuzzi and J. Glenn Gray, in *Basic Writings*, ed. David Farrell Krell (New York: Harper and Row, 1977), 193–94.

Bachmann, whose literary career was devoted to how language molds culture, was fascinated by Heidegger's approach to language as an existential form and yet highly critical of his controversial affiliation with the Nazi Party in the early 1930s. Written in the late 1940s, when the noted philosopher was still banned from the classroom, her dissertation, entitled "The Critical Reception of Martin Heidegger's Existentialist Philosophy," was an attempt to contest Heidegger's ideas, focusing on what Bachmann considered the irrational side of his philosophy. Though she never overcame her ambivalence toward Heidegger's political legacy, she was willing to adopt his ontology of language, thought, and truth in one of her best poems, "Exile." Included in her second volume of poetry, *Invocation of the Great Bear*, released in 1956 to critical acclaim, "Exile" enlists the notion of language as a living space or dwelling:

> I with the German language
> This cloud around me
> Which I keep as a house
> Press through all languages[2]

One of the underlying impulses in Bachmann's lyrics in the 1950s and a cornerstone of her prose works in the 1960s, Heidegger's thinking calls attention to language's agency when recognizing the truth of Being as a corrective for human history. Expressive of human experience, language becomes a testimonial to the violence that culture has incited in the course of many centuries. Attempting to distance himself from the numerous fallacies that litter the past, the philosopher advocated for silence as the most telling mode to recognize forms of truth. For him, silence or, more specifically, the absence of meaningless speech, defines the space of intelligibility. Heidegger even went so far in *Being and Time* as to insist that a reticence sensitive to existential truths unravels the mystery of Being from a fundamental perspective: "As a mode of discoursing, reticence articulates the intelligibility of *Dasein* [being, existence; literally, "being there"] in so primordial a manner that it gives rise to a potentiality-for-hearing that is genuine, and to a Being-with-one-another that is transparent."[3] Referenced here and in other key texts by Heidegger, silence becomes an important faculty for confirming the significance that our conscience places on the truth of Being. By the same token, in *Being and Time*, the philosopher's most celebrated work, one can read: "*Conscience discourses solely and constantly in the mode of keeping silent.*"[4]

2 Ingeborg Bachmann, "Exile," in *Songs in Flight*, 313.

3 Martin Heidegger, *Being and Time*, trans. John Macquarrie and Edward Robinson (Oxford: Blackwell, 1962), 208.

4 Heidegger, *Being and Time*, 318; italics in original.

Dovetailing history, speech, and what the philosopher considered to be the conscience of Being, Heidegger's "Letter on Humanism" came almost twenty years after *Being and Time* and its ontological approach to language parallels a number of the central notions postulated by both the Vienna Circle and one of its primary precursors, the Austrian philosopher Ludwig Wittgenstein. By dint of the fact that Bachmann's philosophical training took place at the University of Vienna, the focal point for the Vienna Circle, it is not surprising that she was influenced by logical positivism and, in the early 1950s, by Wittgenstein's critical analysis of language. Uniting experts from the natural and social sciences, logic and mathematics, the Vienna Circle gathered regularly from 1924 until shortly before Austria was annexed by Nazi Germany in 1938. To a large extent, the movement was inspired by Wittgenstein's attention to symbolic logic, especially his verifiability principle or criterion of meaningfulness. In his early treatise on logic, which bears the Latin title *Tractatus Logico-Philosophicus*, the philosopher argues that what is articulated about aesthetics, ethics, and human existence should be consigned to silence. Spelling out Wittgenstein's significance for the "Vienna Circle," Bachmann explains:

> One consistently encounters the name Wittgenstein in philosophical literature in connection with the "Vienna Circle," the only original movement in empirical philosophy in contemporary times: the once disdained and dreaded "Vienna Dynasty" of logical positivists who, at least in part, founded a new school inspired by this singular thinker. Yet it would be incorrect to identify Wittgenstein with the school, which frequently happens, and to overlook what ensures his work the highest pedigree, over and above his fundamental contribution to symbolic logic and a "mathesis universalis" (newly formulated as a "uniform system of scientific knowledge"). It is not the clarifying, negative propositions, which limit philosophy to a logical analysis of scientific language and surrender investigating reality to scientific fields of study, but rather it is his desperate efforts to probe the unspeakable, thus infusing the *Tractatus* with a tension in which it renounces itself.

Now viewed as one of the most significant contributions to intellectual discourse in the twentieth century, Wittgenstein's treatise is devoted to identifying the relationship between language and reality and to circumscribing the limits of what can be reasonably expressed: "What we cannot speak about we must pass over in silence."[5] Casting Wittgenstein's iconic

5 Ludwig Wittgenstein, *Tractatus Logico-Philosophicus*, trans. D. F. Pears and B. F. McGuinness (New York: Routledge, [1961] 1974), §7. Hereafter abbreviated as *TLP*.

pronouncement about what is representable or what can be articulated in the context of an ethical critique of language, Bachmann ends her essay on the philosopher with the following thoughts:

> Whether he renounced his silence and took the step to a confession of faith is uncertain and highly improbable. "God does not reveal himself in the world"[6] (6.4320) is one of the bitterest sentences in the *Tractatus*. But does Wittgenstein not let us know that the ethical form, which, like the logical one, is not representable, manifests itself and is reality? "What we cannot speak about, we must pass over in silence," he says at the close of the *Tractatus*, and he means precisely the reality that we are not able or permitted to imagine. Or did he conclude that we have lost the game with our language, because it does not contain a word that has any substance?

Admired as a seminal thinker of the twentieth century, Wittgenstein's objectives were predicated on the notion that absolute values cannot be expressed in the language of the empirical world. That is why Wittgenstein's subject has limited access to what lies beyond the realm of the experiential. In a succession of rational assumptions, the philosopher reveals how the world might be "represented" in correct and logical statements, how one might "speak" about that world meaningfully, and what insights could be gained from a critique of the language in which discrete elements of that world are illustrated "from within." As Bachmann interprets Wittgenstein, his was "the attempt to execute philosophy in silence, an absurd attempt, so it seems, but the only legitimate one for him after he had clearly represented everything sayable (as he demanded of philosophy), everything thinkable, which limits the unthinkable from within and so presages the unsayable."

Curiously, Bachmann's approach to language and truth in her literature combines both philosophical perspectives: Wittgenstein's constraints on the I as revealed in factual sentences about the real world, on the one hand, and Heidegger's hermeneutics of being seen through the lens that language affords, on the other. The result is the literary perspective of an aesthetic I, a subject with a fervent moral bent who is at once committed to the reality of today's experiences and yet open to truths in a world

---

6 The *Tractatus* employs an austere and succinct literary style. The work contains almost no arguments as such, but rather consists of declarative statements, or passages, that are meant to be self-evident. The statements are hierarchically numbered, with seven basic propositions at the primary level (numbered 1–7), with each sub-level being a comment on or elaboration of the statement at the next higher level (e.g., 1, 1.1, 1.11, 1.12, 1.13). In all, the *Tractatus* comprises 526 numbered statements.

still to come. Even when these truths are consigned to silence, because we lack the vocabulary to articulate absolute values beyond the merely empirical, it remains the prerogative of the writer to craft the "beautiful word" and give it significance when proclaiming it. In essence, and this aspect seems to find strong affirmation in Bachmann's works, modes of silence reveal much more about the inner nature of the human condition than could any proliferation of purely logical terms.

Submitted to the philosophy department at the University of Vienna in 1949, Bachmann's dissertation argues that modern poetry is eminently suitable to express subject matter not accessible to philosophical discourse, mostly because she believed postwar German literature had an obligation to repudiate the violent and sinister facets of the human psyche. Her starting point was the analytical structure of "logical positivism," which aimed to transform philosophy into a scientific discipline, aligning it with the instruments and methods of empirical logic. Bachmann describes the rationale behind the Vienna Circle and insisted that the movement "harkens back to the classical positivism of Auguste Comte and John Stuart Mill and beyond that to nineteenth-century English positivism." She adds: "yet it carries less historical baggage and is more original than existentialism, which is felt to be so very modern—or, if you will, more modern even than vitalism and phenomenology or various types of metaphysics."

She also asserts that the Austrian capital exhibited a remarkable kinship to Neopositivist thought. In her radio script on the Vienna Circle, she points to "a long-standing tradition of empiricist philosophy in Austria, a philosophy that was specifically concerned with the sciences." While Neopositivism may have given credence to the laws of modern logic, its philosophical statements remain empty and, certainly at face value, devoid of meaning. Yet, in spite of their lack of meaning, the statements mirror essential laws, constituted as rules of grammar, with which the inexpressible can be processed and, in due time, perhaps even articulated. Reminding her readers of the origins of the movement, Bachmann writes:

> Around the year 1930, when the currents of modern philosophy that are at work today had already entered the consciousness of the era, a study group in Vienna addressed the public with a manifesto entitled "Scientific World View: The Vienna Circle" ["Wissenschaftliche Weltauffassung. Der Wiener Kreis"]. The slim pamphlet presented a concise introduction to the genesis, orientation, and goals of that study group. Its philosophical program was formulated in the soberest and most objective terms—yet it triggered a palace revolution in German philosophy, and the hostilities increased over the years in which the school achieved international recognition. As "logical positivism" or "Neopositivism," it dominates the field today, especially

> in the Anglo-Saxon and Scandinavian countries, while it was never able to gain a real foothold in Germany, France, and Italy.

Rallying foundational debates in the natural and social sciences, the Neopositivist movement strove to develop a logical derivation of meaning, as well as an empirical approach to classical metaphysics and the integration of exact instruments of epistemology into rational thought. Cognizant that philosophy should amount to a "logical analysis of language," which precludes forming irrational statements about the mystical side of the world, Neopositivists claim that philosophical propositions shed light on what comprises reality. The intention is to perceive language as a control function, since any bona fide representation of reality must be relinquished to scientific methods and their respective nomenclatures.

In contrast to the central thinkers of the Vienna Circle, whose analytical precision was affirmed by Rudolf Carnap and Otto Neurath,[7] Bachmann exhibited greater license in her approach to categories of communication extending beyond the parameters established in Neopositivist theories. Ultimately, she believed she was able to overcome the restrictions imposed on any logical derivation of language, giving literature the prerogative to negotiate the boundaries of purely cognitive processes and convey the wide range of ambient experiences that individuals are subject to, whether explicitly or subliminally.

At the end of her dissertation, Bachmann liberates art from modes of thought constrained by scientific proofs. At the same time, she eschews assumptions that art is devoid of logic. While art might not be called upon to confirm or refute statements about reality in a scientific way, it can nonetheless claim to articulate the irrational pervading reality. In Bachmann's eyes, the irrational is symbolized in the mythological violence that the Titans Uranus and Chronos exhibited toward their children. Citing Western creational myths, she reconsidered the prevailing factors that both constitute and subvert symbolic orders. Illustrating the impulses leading to the formation of cultures, myths also trace the irrational side of the human psyche back to a single inspiration: the imposition of culture on a singularly destructive and malevolent nature, human and otherwise. Correspondingly, if Chronos personifies time in mythological contexts, then the suggestion is that time or, more specifically, its elapse from the moment of inception to the present, is also intimately linked to the violence inherent in most cultural contexts. Dwelling on

7 Rudolf Carnap (1891–1970), leading member of the Vienna Circle and advocate for logical positivism, is considered one of the giants among twentieth-century philosophers; Otto Karl Wilhelm Neurath (1882–1945), also one of the leading figures of the Vienna Circle, was a philosopher, philosopher of science, sociologist, and political economist, before he fled his native country in 1934.

the boundaries between philosophy, art, and myth in her highly regarded essay on Wittgenstein, Bachmann explains:

> The impetus behind this kind of philosophizing is the same one about which Baudelaire speaks in his poem "The Gulf" ["Le gouffre"]. All it has to offer, in its particular passion for the whole truth, is the arid, formulaic, "eternal" truth of logic—sentences we must overcome to see the world properly. This philosophizing cannot contribute to the solution of the problems of our lives. Reminiscent of Pascal, Wittgenstein moves in and with his abyss; what he is not allowed to name inundates him from all peripheries and he is abandoned to the "drame cardinal" [cardinal drama]. "Ah, jamais sortir des nombres et des êtres!" [Ah! never from beings, numbers to be free!][8]

Here, Bachmann points out that formulaic logic cannot provide insights into the most enigmatic problems of our existence, and she associates Wittgenstein with the nineteenth-century poet Baudelaire as well as with the seventeenth-century French mathematician Pascal, insisting that all three thinkers transcended the formulaic to fathom the world in its complexity. Hence, Bachmann's allusion to the cardinal drama of mankind, the "passion for the whole truth," which engages more than mere logic and is bound up with overcoming the mysteries underlying number systems as well as the riddles of human existence.

Analogous to Wittgenstein's approach to what is unsayable about truth and beauty, Bachmann's passion for art and literature hinged on an aptitude for extremes, for giving voice to the horror that subtends our daily lives and for which we often lack adequate terms. The principle of mythical violence—consistent with the violence perpetrated by Uranus and Chronos—and the abyss posed by the unsayable prompt Bachmann to advocate for an aesthetic of the grotesque. Indeed, it seems plausible that the frequent allusions to atrocities and destruction in her works were predicated on the author's childhood experience of war and a strong desire to grasp the inexpressible facets of human misery. In her later texts—the prose fragments associated with the *Todesarten* project, and more specifically the novel *Malina*—there are innumerable examples of collective terror, all of which can be associated with the abyss referenced in her early Wittgenstein essay. Following the philosopher's lead, Bachmann claimed that truth is most readily revealed through what cannot be articulated, given that the space of the unsayable "points beyond reality insofar as something reveals itself in the logical form that is unthinkable to us, and because it is unthinkable, it is impossible to speak about it."

8 Translation of Baudelaire: Charles Baudelaire, "The Gulf," in *The Flowers of Evil*, trans. James N. McGowan (Oxford: Oxford University Press, 1998), 345.

Bachmann's devotion to Wittgenstein's philosophy of the sayable and the unsayable was documented not only in her radio scripts—among these "The Vienna Circle: Logical Positivism—Philosophy as Science" ("Der Wiener Kreis: Logischer Positivismus—Philosophie als Wissenschaft") and "The Sayable and the Unsayable—The Philosophy of Ludwig Wittgenstein" ("Sagbares und Unsagbares—Die Philosophie Ludwig Wittgensteins")—but also in her essay on the philosopher, all of which were penned in the early 1950s. Examples of her philosophical prowess, these carefully crafted texts have been included in this volume. They set out to locate the modern individual and the limits of his world and language by referencing Wittgenstein's philosophy of language as a central criterion. Also included in the volume is the fragment of a radio script on logical mysticism—posthumously titled "Logic as Mysticism" ("Logik als Mystik")—that was believed lost but has since resurfaced. These pieces exhibit the cerebral nature and analytical style of rigorous scholarship, as they delve into the disparity between inner-worldly experience, which is paradigmatic for a rational language, and metaphysical perceptions that extend beyond the empirical realm. Bachmann's distinction between an empirical and a metaphysical subject mirrors Wittgenstein's approach, when she asserts that

> we stand, think, and speak on this side of the border. Feeling the world as a limited whole arises when we ourselves, as a metaphysical subject, are no longer part of the world, but rather a "border." However, the path across that border is concealed. It is not possible for us to place ourselves outside the world and to express sentences about the sentences of the world. For that reason, there can also be no value—"and if it did exist, it would have no value" (§6.41). There can be no sentences of ethics, since a sentence can express nothing of a higher nature. The will can also not be the bearer of the ethical, for the world is separate from our will. Nothing that language is capable of expressing—the facts of the world—is alterable by an act of will. Only the peripheries of the world are alterable, and about these we are obliged to remain silent.

If the philosophical I finds itself within the limited sphere of a sensory world in which space, intellectual freedom, and communicative possibilities are regulated by logic, every attempt to permeate the boundaries of the empirical realm to experience the mystical or the transcendental must end in failure. In any case, calling upon cognitions beyond the empirical to comprehend the constitution of the world seems no longer feasible, at least not from a Neopositivist perspective.

Despite the apparent inability to surpass the boundaries of the empirical, a transcendental crevice can still be determined in which utopian aspirations and desires manifest themselves. For Bachmann, the probability of transcending reality correlates to the quest for truth in art. In turn, artistic or literary truth is related to the classical notion of *eros* or the love of genuine beauty. From a Platonic perspective, *eros* evokes the objective of comprehending what is good, beautiful, and true. In Plato's *Symposium*, Socrates argues that *eros* is initially felt for a person, but as contemplation deepens, love becomes an appreciation for the beauty within that person and eventually an appreciation for beauty itself in an ideal sense. As Plato expresses it, *eros* can help the soul to "remember" beauty in its pure form. When the notion of ascending to the loftiness of an absolute love of beauty is linked to the idea of movement, the quest for truth that culminates in a love for the beautiful can also be aligned with the Aristotelian quest for pure human knowledge. For Aristotle, knowledge and truth are predicated on constant change, a never-ending progression from potentiality to actuality. Entrenched in this process is the idea that knowledge entails striving for the continual perfection of the soul, and in keeping with Bachmann's approach to art, a soul that continuously progresses toward aesthetic truth and artistic fulfillment.

Pinpointing the need to strive for truth, Bachmann's acceptance speech for the prestigious Radio Play Prize of the War Blind in 1959, which opens the chapter on Bachmann's lectures in this volume, examines cases in which boundaries that obstruct perfection in an everyday world are overcome. "A borderline example is embedded in each and every case, also in the most commonplace one of love, one that we can detect upon closer scrutiny and one that we should possibly always endeavor to detect." True to every manifestation of life, the idea of "imperfect perfection" is measured against constantly expanding horizons. These new horizons embrace ever higher echelons of beauty until one achieves what has to be the most beautiful and perfect of all, absolute freedom. Bachmann's assertions about perfection, which are based on classical models, have become canonic for modern cultural theory:

> I am certain that we must remain within the given order, that there is no escape from society, and that we must test ourselves against one another. Yet, from within those limits, our eye is fixed on the absolute, the impossible, the unattainable, be it of love, of freedom, or of any pure entity. In the interplay of the impossible and the possible we expand our possibilities. That we create it, this state of tension that allows us to grow, that, I believe, is what matters; that we orient ourselves toward a particular goal that admittedly recedes again into the distance whenever we approach it.

For Bachmann, doubts lingered about the extent to which our sensory perception can be measured against an aesthetic truth moving beyond the empirical or tangible to embrace the visionary. A faculty of clairvoyance, truth as Bachmann interprets it, insists on a dialectical tension between the impossible and the possible. This dichotomy took on significance when she suggested that truth could redeem a postwar world shackled in dark imprisonment (*Dunkelhaft*). Similar to the visionary mysticism in Ludwig Wittgenstein's treatise, the clairvoyance that Bachmann ascribed to the artist is reminiscent of an even earlier philosophical approach to the singularity of the artistic experience, an approach that was also seminal for the development of Wittgenstein's mysticism. The allusion is to Arthur Schopenhauer and the Romantic philosopher's concept of the "world-eye," which he attributes to the pure subject of knowing. In chapter 30 of the second volume of his monumental study *The World as Will and Representation* (*Die Welt als Wille und Vorstellung*), Schopenhauer explains:

> I have therefore described the pure subject of knowing, which then remains ever as the eternal world-eye. This eye looks out from all living beings, though with very different degrees of clearness, and is untouched by their arising and passing away. It is thus identical with itself, constantly one and the same, and the supporter of the world of permanent Ideas, i.e., of the adequate objectivity of the will. On the other hand, the individual subject, clouded in his knowledge by the individuality that springs from the will, has as object only particular things, and is transient and fleeting, as these things themselves are.[9]

Rising above the visual and literary arts in Schopenhauer's philosophy, music becomes the preeminent metaphysical art form and, as such, it is on a level with the Platonic ideas themselves. Consequently, auditory signals are the direct manifestations of human will, or the vital essence central to Schopenhauer's deliberations.

What is more striking for Bachmann's purposes is that Schopenhauer's pure manifestations of will coincide with the objects in Wittgenstein's theories. In fact, Wittgenstein's objects form the substance of the world, from which an adequate representation of the world's structure can be derived. Once the objects have been named, they form basic facts. As Bachmann discovered, these facts help to construct sentences that formulate logical premises and, by association only, point to metaphysical or mystical truths extending beyond the empirical. In essence, Wittgenstein places language in a position similar to the one Schopenhauer reserved for music. Likewise, Wittgenstein's I can be interpreted as a direct correlate to the pure subject in Schopenhauer's system. For the pure subject, the I, assumes a position outside the system, and it is only from this exterior position that the world's ethical and aesthetic dimensions can

9 Arthur Schopenhauer, *The World as Will and Representation*, trans. E. F. J. Payne, 2 vols. (Mineola, NY: Dover Publications, 1966), vol. 2, 371.

be comprehended. Sensitive to the limitations of individual experience, Schopenhauer and Wittgenstein, as well as Bachmann in her aesthetics, share a deep moral compassion for the innate suffering of humankind.

Bachmann's discontent with the postwar order, sublimated in her assessment of society as a "murder scene" (*Mordschauplatz*), requires literature to acknowledge ethical claims about the world. Were we to substitute the pure subject with the artist who unfolds a sovereign vision of the world, we would arrive at a similar realization with respect to the kind of truth that can only be achieved in literature. Bachmann alleges: "it cannot be the task of the writer to deny pain, to conceal its traces, to pretend it does not exist." Expanding on her beliefs in her address to the War Blind, she contends:

> On the contrary, he must acknowledge its reality and once again, in order to enable us to see it, make it real. For all of us would like to be able to see. And that furtive pain sensitizes us for the experience, and in particular for the experience of the truth. When we reach that state, the lucid, afflictive moment in which our pain bears fruit, we say quite simply and fittingly: my eyes have been opened. We do not say that because we have perceived the external reality of an object or event, but because we have grasped something, although we may not be able to see it. And that is what art ought to bring about: that our eyes, in this sense, be opened.

Bachmann's advocacy for the dialectics of the impossible and the possible, for what evolves from the potential to the actual, becomes an opportunity to progress to a utopian level of truth in art. Art's capacity for opening our eyes must have been particularly poignant for the blind war veterans listening to Bachmann speak in October 1959. Their visual faculties had been sacrificed in the war and the perceptive powers she extolled in her speech could only be recuperated on an ideal level through aural exposure to the literary arts. Specifically referencing how art can transcend affliction, Bachmann argues:

> Who, if not those among you who have met with a grave misfortune, could better testify that our power reaches farther than our affliction, that a person deprived of many things is capable of pulling himself up again, that it is possible to exist in disillusionment, that is to say, without illusion. I believe that human beings are permitted one sort of pride—the pride of one who does not give up in the dark imprisonment of the world and never ceases to keep an eye on what is just.

In order to convey that the subject, generally subservient to a mundane world of objects, struggles to cross the frontier between the possible and the impossible, Bachmann calls for a new language and a utopian form of literature. Her standpoint vacillates between a condemnation of superficial communication (what she called "idle talk") and an appeal for a higher form of communication deeply imbued with hope (what she called "a new spirit"). Her eye is set on realizing the beautiful word, buoyed by the utopian aspiration of liberating modern societies from epistemological blindness. The hope she harbors for the beautiful word is voiced in the following stanza of "Word and Afterword," incorporated into her second volume of poems:

> Word, be one of us,
> enlightened, distinct, beautiful.
> Certainly an end must come
> to its cautious living.

Ultimately, and this is the point at which Bachmann blends philosophy with literature, the beautiful word proves to be the most pliant instrument for redeeming the world from the evil that humankind has wrought since time immemorial.

> Come and do not fail,
> for we stand in strife with so much evil.
> Ere dragon blood protects our adversary,
> this hand will fall into the fire.
> You, my word, deliver me![10]

---

10 Ingeborg Bachmann, "Word and Afterword," in *In the Storm of Roses*, 113.

The Vienna Circle: Logical Positivism— Philosophy as Science[1]

NARRATOR: Around the year 1930, when the currents of modern philosophy at work today had already entered the consciousness of the era, a study group in Vienna addressed the public with a manifesto entitled "Scientific World View: The Vienna Circle." The slim pamphlet presented a concise introduction to the genesis, orientation, and goals of that study group. Its philosophical program was formulated in the soberest and most objective terms—yet it triggered a palace revolution in German philosophy, and the hostilities increased over the years, in which the school achieved international recognition. As "logical positivism" or "Neopositivism" it dominates the field today, especially in the Anglo-Saxon and Scandinavian countries,[2] although it was never able to gain a real foothold in Germany, France, and Italy. And in Vienna itself . . .

1ST SPEAKER: In Vienna itself, the Vienna Circle is dead. Between 1933 and 1939 its most prominent representatives were offered appointments at foreign universities; several members went into exile, others fell victim to National Socialism. What is still alive today are proceedings, stenographic records, transcribed discussions, essays in the collected volumes of *Knowledge* (*Erkenntnis*), the official publication of the Circle, which was edited by Rudolf Carnap and Hans Reichenbach. In 1939, *Knowledge* was banned and then superseded by the *Journal of Unified Science*, which appeared in England.

NARRATOR: But first let me recount the prehistory of this new achievement, the only real one in the empiricist movement of the modern era. —As its name suggests, it harks back to the classical positivism of Auguste Comte and John Stuart Mill[3] and beyond that to nineteenth-century English positivism. And yet it carries less historical baggage and is more original than existentialism, which is felt to be so very modern—or, if you

1 It has been conjectured that Bachmann's radio essay on the Vienna Circle was aired in April 1953, although no documents exist to validate that date.

2 Bachmann gleaned this information, and much of her knowledge about the Vienna Circle, from Victor Kraft's 1950 book *Der Wiener Kreis: Der Ursprung des Neopositivismus; Ein Kapitel der jüngsten Philosophiegeschichte* [The Vienna Circle: The origin of Neopositivism; a chapter of the most recent history of philosophy] (Vienna: Springer, 1950).

3 This school of thought stressed scientific empiricism and rules for inductive logic.

will, more modern even than vitalism[4] and phenomenology[5] or various types of metaphysics.[6]

Undoubtedly, Vienna represented fertile soil for its genesis. A professorship for "Philosophy of the Inductive Sciences" had existed at the University of Vienna since the end of the nineteenth century, having been inaugurated for Ernst Mach.[7] Hence, there was a long-standing tradition of empiricist philosophy in Austria, a philosophy that was specifically devoted to the sciences.

In 1922, Moritz Schlick was appointed to that professorship. Like his predecessors Boltzmann and Stöhr, he came to philosophy from physics—a student of Max Planck's who maintained close personal connections to Einstein and Hilbert. But what distinguished him from all the others was his thorough knowledge of philosophy. And Schlick became the nucleus of a circle of students and philosophically interested scientists, among them Rudolf Carnap and the celebrated mathematicians Menger and Hahn.

1ST SPEAKER: But it was by no means accurate that Schlick alone set the tone and the others concurred with his theses, given that intellectual endeavors were carried out by the entire group. An array of results was harvested in lively discussions, in a steady exchange of pros and cons, as well as through successful and unsuccessful experiments, much like researching in a laboratory.

2ND SPEAKER: The most influential impulses, however, came from Ludwig Wittgenstein,[8] certainly one of the most unusual and legendary figures in philosophy. Never present in person, Wittgenstein conducted occasional conversations with Moritz Schlick and in subsequent years conducted a tutorial in his Vienna apartment, an exclusive seminar, which he also maintained at Cambridge, where he died a year ago, admired and feared—a solitary man whose greatness is acknowledged even by his enemies.

---

4 Vitalism proposes that an innate determining force, not scientific principles, governs biological processes.

5 Phenomenology emphasizes revelation through immediate sensory perception and intuition, as opposed to logical analysis.

6 Metaphysics examines the nature of being.

7 Mach (1838–1916) sought to rid philosophy of metaphysical assumptions, replacing them instead with empirical analysis.

8 For Bachmann's analysis of Wittgenstein's writings, see "The Sayable and the Unsayable" and "Ludwig Wittgenstein—A Chapter of the Most Recent History of Philosophy" in this volume.

1ST SPEAKER: Wittgenstein's *Tractatus Logico-Philosophicus*, the only work personally authorized by the author,[9] already implies the main theses of Neopositivism. That difficult work is a curiosity in terms of its structure. It is comprised of brilliantly formulated aphorisms and begins with the succinct sentence: "The world is everything that is the case."[10] And it closes with one that is all but mystical: "What we cannot speak about we must pass over in silence"[11]—that is to say a declaration that even his own statements contained no meaning at all.

2ND SPEAKER: That enigmatic pronouncement, however, which has generated much interpretation, is not quite as enigmatic as it appears at first sight.

Wittgenstein's point of departure is the basic thesis of the English philosopher Bertrand Russell,[12] which asserts that the world is composed of facts completely independent from one another. "The world is everything that is the case" means that the world is the totality of facts or that it can be dissolved into facts. Beyond that, it is nothing.

1ST SPEAKER: Accordingly, knowledge, as a reflection of the facts that are independent from one another, must always be particular. All general propositions are only logical inductions from particular statements.

PROFESSOR: Thus the sentence, "Every person is mortal" has the same meaning as the statement "Peter is mortal and Hans is mortal." The "and" connecting these two particular statements serves to demonstrate the truth of the general proposition that "every person is mortal." Its truth is merely determined by the truth of the two particular statements "Peter is mortal and Hans is mortal." But a new, general truth that is more than the truth of the particular statements does not ensue.

1ST SPEAKER: Derived from logic, this harmless example reveals less harmless consequences. It demonstrates that logic, taken quite literally and banally, signifies absolutely nothing. To use Wittgenstein's words, its character is purely tautological. All of its statements are empty; they cannot give us any clarity about reality.

---

9 Eventually, Wittgenstein's other writings would come to light—among them the *Blue Book* and the *Brown Book* (published 1958) and the *Philosophical Investigations* (published 1953).

10 *TLP*, §1.

11 *TLP*, §7.

12 Russell was Wittgenstein's early teacher and mentor.

2ND SPEAKER: Let me anticipate the ultimate consequence of that insight: since the Neopositivists defined philosophy as a "logical analysis of language" that does not examine reality, it cannot teach us anything about that reality, as it has presumed to do until now. It cannot shed any light on anything, it is merely an activity—an "analysis," exerting a form of control and nothing more. And processing reality must be left entirely to the natural sciences.

1ST SPEAKER: Surrendering the examination of reality to the special fields of the natural sciences, something that had *de facto* occurred a long time ago, was finally confirmed for the first time in German philosophy.

CRITIC: I have a question: if philosophy is to be restricted to the analysis of the language of natural sciences and its analytical tool, logic, is regarded with such skepticism, if logic is perceived as completely incapable of understanding reality—how, then, could that same logic become a decisive weapon in the hands of the Neopositivists?

1ST SPEAKER: Before logic could become a "weapon," as you put it, in the hands of philosophers, traditional logic underwent a fundamental transformation toward the end of the last century, primarily due to the application of symbols in analogy to mathematics.

In their "Principia Mathematica,"[13] Russell and Whitehead demonstrated that the basic concepts of mathematics—the natural and extended numbers, the concepts of analysis and set theory—could be constituted according the basic concepts of logic, on the basis of logical principles, if two new axioms were included: the axiom of infinity and that of selection.

2ND SPEAKER: Simply put, they discovered that mathematics is only a branch of logic and that we are also dealing with a set of purely formal operations in logic, that it is possible to calculate with concepts and statements without considering their content.

1ST SPEAKER: After all, in mathematics numbers do not signify objects from the world of our experience, and geometry does not designate real space.

13 Wittgenstein partially responds to this work in his *Tractatus* and *Philosophical Investigations.*

PROFESSOR: An equation like Kant's celebrated "7 + 5 = 12,"[14] for instance, does not refer to any real set of facts. What happens is that two groups of units are transformed into a single group in accordance with an arithmetic rule. In the realm of a purely cognitive order the same units are grouped differently.

1ST SPEAKER: In a similar manner, the logical signifiers, which we call symbols, do not designate the objects and the relations between them, but we attribute the former to the latter when we think.

2ND SPEAKER: A decisive correction has been undertaken with respect to the old empiricism that insisted on basing logic and mathematics upon experience. But what has also been corrected is Kant's thesis that there are laws a priori—that is to say laws independent from experience—that are nevertheless synthetic.

1ST SPEAKER: Neopositivism assumes an intermediate position. It views the laws of logic as a priori, to be sure, but its statements are at the same time empty and devoid of meaning. The laws constitute rules of grammar with which the substance of sensory experience can be more easily processed.

CRITIC: Let us admit that it is impossible to go back to a point before that reformed logic today. Notwithstanding, what can be the consequence of the reform of an individual philosophical discipline for philosophy as a whole?

2ND SPEAKER: A series of embarrassing consequences.—Resulting from the new logic, the first was a doctrine that made the Neopositivist school famous: the doctrine of verifiability.

---

14 See Immanuel Kant, "The Critique of Pure Reason," in *The Critique of Pure Reason, The Critique of Practical Reason and other Ethical Treatises, and The Critique of Judgment*, trans J. M. D. Meiklejohn (Chicago: Encyclopaedia Brittannica, 1952), 18: "We might, indeed, at first suppose that the proposition 7 + 5 = 12 is a merely analytical proposition, following . . . from the conception of a sum of seven and five. But if we regard it more narrowly, we find that our conception of the sum of seven and five contains nothing more than the uniting of both sums into one. . . ." In the one instance the sum is analytical or after the fact; in the other, the sum is synthetic and can be extrapolated into a general rule.

NARRATOR: Based on preliminary results, a preliminary conference was held in Prague in 1934, where Carnap, together with the physicist Philipp Frank, had already formed an "outlier" of the Vienna Circle. In September 1935, the First International Congress of Scientific Philosophy followed in Paris, which was held on the premises of the Sorbonne under the aegis of the French government. Russell gave the opening speech. Approximately 170 members from more than twenty countries participated. At Carnap's behest, a committee for the standardization of logical symbols was constituted, and the Congress finally affirmed its readiness to collaborate on the *International Encyclopedia of Unified Sciences*, as proposed by the Vienna Circle, a work that has meanwhile been published, at least in part, in America. In 1936, the Second Congress took place; it was devoted to the problem of causality with regard to quantum physics and biology. Niels Bohr gave the first lecture. In 1937, Paris once again hosted the Congress; in 1938 it was held at Cambridge. After that, the war put a stop to all activities.

2ND SPEAKER: Reduced to its simplest denominator, the doctrine of verifiability, developed with great success by the Vienna Circle, states that a sentence only has meaning if it can be verified, that is to say, if it can be determined whether it is true or false.

1ST SPEAKER: That touches on the Achilles' heel of classical philosophy, as well as of modern metaphysics and existentialism. For in order to determine whether a sentence is true or false, at least two observers are absolutely required. As a matter of principle, if two observers cannot perform the verification, then the truth of the sentence cannot be tested and the sentence cannot be a scientific one.

CRITIC: That would mean that only those sentences can be "verified" that refer to the world of objects, to bodies and their movements?

1ST SPEAKER: Precisely.

CRITIC: And the propositions of introspective psychology? The sentences of classical philosophy . . .?

1ST SPEAKER: If you mean the expression of the entire realm of an existential, metaphysical, and religious being, the expression conveyed about the entire range of emotions, then the Neopositivist will answer that sentences articulating those things are unverifiable and therefore meaningless.[15] Problems that have been debated for centuries, such as the problem of realism and idealism, the problem of the existence of God, the problem of the intellect, to name only a few of them, have been characterized as pseudo-problems by the Neopositivist. There is no room in philosophy for questions to which no answer can be expected.[16]

2ND SPEAKER: There have been enemies of metaphysics from time immemorial. But their objections suffered from the lack of an adequate method to guarantee a radical triumph over metaphysics. While metaphysics was believed to be impossible because it contradicted the knowledge of experience—

PROFESSOR: —like English empiricism, for instance—

2ND SPEAKER: —and while Kant thought that metaphysics was impossible, because its questions transcended the limits of human cognition—

1ST SPEAKER: —logical positivism finds itself in a position to give a more incisive answer. And what makes that more incisive answer possible is the logical analysis of language.

2ND SPEAKER: The new logic, which had become a highly specialized tool for the work on a theory of science in the Vienna Circle, also paved the way for basic investigations into the philosophy of language.

PROFESSOR: Let us remember that there are numerous languages: ordinary languages and foreign languages, scientific languages in the most diverse fields, a signal language for flags, sign language for deaf-mutes . . .

2ND SPEAKER: But what we have in mind is not one of the languages actually used, but a language with a simplified and perfected form—a pure system of representation. That language will now be scrutinized with respect to what it might represent—

15 From here through the Critic's speech starting with "The unmasking of such . . .", Bachmann relies heavily on her doctoral dissertation on "The Critical Reception of the Existential Philosophy of Martin Heidegger," often quoting from it verbatim. See Ingeborg Bachmann, *Die kritische Aufnahme der Existentialphilosophie Martin Heideggers*, ed. Robert Pichl (Munich: R. Piper, 1985), 16–23.

16 See "The Sayable and the Unsayable": "For what cannot even be the subject of a meaningful question cannot, inherently, ever be the subject of a meaningful answer."

PROFESSOR: —that is to say its semantic function—

2ND SPEAKER: —and how it represents—

PROFESSOR: —that is to say its syntactical rules.

CRITIC: But did Wittgenstein not deny that such an examination was possible? Did he not say that it was impossible to undertake the logico-grammatical analysis of language and to engage in philosophy?

2ND SPEAKER: Indeed. His proposition, "What we cannot speak about we must pass over in silence," refers to that problem. With the help of new logic, however, Rudolf Carnap found a solution: It is possible to speak of language, if another language, a metalanguage, is applied. And consequently, philosophy consists in metalogical analysis. To that end, it is necessary to establish a system of signs that, in turn, constitute words of the scientific language, such that philosophy is equipped to analyze the statements of natural science.

CRITIC: I think it would be better to leave those abstract trains of thought and show how logical analysis works, using a concrete example. You suggested a while ago that metaphysical propositions, when regarded in that fashion, lead to a negative result.

1ST SPEAKER: They do. That is easy to prove. Let us take—with your permission—Martin Heidegger's text "What Is Metaphysics?" Rudolf Carnap extracted a few sentences from that work to demonstrate that the violation of logical syntax can result in a meaningless sequence of words.

CRITIC: What do you mean by meaningless?

1ST SPEAKER: To rule out any misunderstanding: I do not mean "nonsensical" by any means. "Meaningless" designates a pseudo-sentence, in which the grammatical syntax is acceptable, though the logical may not be.

PROFESSOR: If I were to say, "Caesar is a prime number," then the demands of syntax are met. But since "prime" is a property of numbers and not of people, the logical syntax is violated.

CRITIC: Let us move on to Heidegger.

PROFESSOR: In the text, "What Is Metaphysics?," one can read: "What is to be examined is only that which is, and nothing else; alone what is, and further—nothing; solely what is, and beyond that—nothing. What is it about that nothing? . . . Does the nothing exist only because the 'not,' that is to say negation, exists? Or is it the other way around? Does negation only exist because the nothing exists? We assert: The nothing is closer to the source than the not and the negation. Where do we search for the nothing? How do we find the nothing?—We know the nothing.—Fear reveals the nothing. What we feared and why we feared it, was actually—nothing. Indeed, the nothing itself—as such—was there. What is it about that nothing? The nothing itself nots."[17]

1ST SPEAKER: Now I propose that you write down a few of the quotations. But please write them in a vertical column to leave room for the corresponding translations that I intend to give you.

1. What is outside?
2. Nothing is outside.
3. What is it about that nothing?
4. We know the nothing.
5. The nothing nots.

That selection has been made to shorten the game of questions and answers and also to be able to translate questions and answers into a language that is familiar to us.

2ND SPEAKER: Then the Heideggerian sentence, "What is outside?," would find its equivalent in the same sentence in our customary language, viz.: "What is outside?" But in the logically correct language it would be: "There is not, or there does not exist, or there is not present, anything that is outside." That scientific sentence may also be expressed in symbols, which for the sake of simplicity, we shall ignore for the time being. Something like "There is rain outside" would correspond to the second sentence, "There is nothing outside." In a logically correct language, the sentence must still signify: "There is not anything that is outside." Com-

17 This is a selection of sentences from Heidegger's "What is Metaphysics?." Bachmann lists them in the proper order, but occasionally omits as much as a page and a half of argument between them. See Heidegger, "What is Metaphysics?," trans. David Farrell Krell, in *Basic Writings*, 97–99.

patible to the third sentence, "What is it about that nothing?," would be "What is it about that rain?" or "Can we say anything more about that rain?"—The fourth sentence, "We know the nothing," would be consistent with the sentence "We know the rain" in everyday language; with respect to the fifth sentence, "The nothing nots," the sentence "The rain rains." But in the logically correct language, the three latter forms are beyond being likely.

1ST SPEAKER: The difficulty begins as soon as the word "nothing" appears as though an object of that nature existed. And, in the end, the meaningless word "to not" is brought in to top things off. Even if we made up our minds to introduce the word "nothing" as an object, the sentence would contain a contradiction, because that sentence ascribes to that object an existence for which its definition as "nothing" has been rescinded. If the sentence were not already meaningless, it would have to be characterized as contradictory and thus nonsensical.

CRITIC: Within the boundaries of this analysis you may be right. But you are forgetting that Heidegger himself is aware that he violates the laws of logic. "In the turmoil of a more pristine questioning," he sees the idea of logic dissolving and therefore no longer feels beholden to it. He says: "Question and answer with respect to the nothing are both inherently absurd."[18] How do you respond to that?

1ST SPEAKER: The response is that science cannot afford to become involved in a "turmoil of counterlogical questioning," as Heidegger demands of it. Obviously, he perceives the separateness of the two realms: science and metaphysics, since he regards the practice of philosophy, as he conducted it, as incompatible with the thought processes of science.

CRITIC: The conviction that the two realms are incompatible is something, at any rate, that these two extreme positions of modern thought share.

2ND SPEAKER: Our intention here, incidentally, is not to single out Heidegger for criticism. Logical criticism aims to eradicate meaningless words and pseudo-sentences devoid of sense. Without exception, that pertains to all forms of metaphysics.

---

18 Heidegger, "What is Metaphysics?," §11. The text is his inaugural lecture at the University of Freiburg in 1929.

CRITIC: But could sentences be found within metaphysics that have meaning and stand up to that criticism?

1ST SPEAKER: Meaningful sentences can only be based on experience, and experiential sentences only occur in the individual disciplines of empirical science. A truly metaphysical proposition is inaccessible to empirical science and its methods. Nevertheless, it aspires to be more than an analytical judgment—to use Kant's words—that is to say more than a "tautology," as Wittgenstein more accurately characterized analytical judgments.

CRITIC: Presumably, unmasking these and similar pseudo-propositions of the metaphysicians goes hand in hand with uncovering the philosophical pseudo-problems that you mentioned earlier. Among them you included the problem of God and the problem of the intellect, but also the problem of the reality—or ideality—of the world. Classical empiricists and positivists were also aware of that problem, suggesting that it must exist for the Neopositivists as well? For applying a philosophy devoid of epistemological questions is simply unthinkable!

2ND SPEAKER: It is true that the epistemological questions—that is to say the question of the nature of our knowledge and the cognition of the world—are of central importance for Western philosophy. Nevertheless, the Vienna Circle rejected that form of questioning, albeit only insofar as the question involved an absolute reality of the world, one that transcended what could be experienced.

1ST SPEAKER: The question as to what is "real," on the other hand, can readily be answered: Real is anything that is verifiable—anything intersubjectively verifiable.

2ND SPEAKER: Anything that in principle can be verified by at least two observers!

1ST SPEAKER: Being real means being integrated into the spatiotemporal system of the intersubjectively verifiable. And in that sense logical positivism and realism are not opposites. Only reality as a concept, transcendental reality, must be rejected, since that would introduce a metaphysical perspective into philosophy.

2ND SPEAKER: What reality is—or existence as such, as the more recent terminology puts it—cannot be defined at all, because no criterion can be determined for it.

1ST SPEAKER: A second reality, a greater one that we do not experience and that lies behind our empirical perspective, is something that we can only think, assume, assert. We can posit a hypothesis, but we know for certain from the start that it will never be verifiable.

1ST SPEAKER: So why posit such a hypothesis?

2ND SPEAKER: If it is a question of empirical reality, for instance whether a mountain range in an unknown region is real or only the stuff of legend, then ocular scrutiny can provide an unambiguous answer. But if we go on to introduce yet a second reality outside of our consciousness and contrapose it as the truer one to empirical reality—how could it be proven? To presume to measure our reality against that absolute, indefinable reality is a meaningless aspiration.

1ST SPEAKER: That is the reason why the question of the ideality or reality of the world was categorized as a spurious or pseudo-problem by the Vienna Circle. All of the historical theses about "true" reality: metaphysical idealism and metaphysical realism, phenomenalism, solipsism, and older forms of positivism—fall out of the realm of scientific knowledge, because they aspire to answer an impossible question.

CRITIC: After everything you have reported here, it is possible to come away with the impression that the Vienna Circle did not consist of philosophers but of enemies of philosophy, that the Vienna school did not want to make a contribution to the development of philosophy but to its abolition. In fact, it is even possible to come away with the impression that it constitutes the reactionary movement in the philosophy of our time.

If this pre-Socratic stance is sustained epistemologically, if the question of existence, which after all is posed with great earnestness not only by existentialism but by all metaphysicians today, is dismissed with a wave of the hand and the discussion disintegrates . . . on the basis of dogmatic premises . . .

1ST SPEAKER: You are going on the offensive now . . .?

CRITIC: Essentially, I want to reserve that for later. You might perhaps explain what, by and large, the task of such a philosophy can be . . ., for surely it cannot exhaust itself in criticism and in sorting and clarifying material that has already been considered by the individual sciences from biology to physics? Or can it? Based upon your definition, must it not aim at a unified . . .

1ST SPEAKER: I know what you want to say: According to its definition, philosophy must have its eye on a unified world view. In a certain sense, all philosophy, even logical positivism, remains true to its—if you will—age-old purpose. For logical positivism knows better than any other the problem of a unified system.

PROFESSOR: That is not an earth-shattering innovation. Descartes tried to develop a *mathesis universalis* [universal mathematics][19] and, as he himself says, Leibniz regarded it from his early years on as his task "to devise a sort of alphabet of human thought, in order that a combination of the letters of that alphabet and an analysis of the words thus formed"[20] might enable us to find everything and to judge it.

2ND SPEAKER: The Vienna Circle formulated the problem of the unified system as the "unified system of scientific knowledge." Let us remember that Kant had already narrowed philosophy, in so far as it was *cognition*, to epistemology, and, even previously, classical positivism had already surrendered all knowledge of objects to the various scientific disciplines. The Vienna Circle perceives an advantage over those initial advances in that it combines all of the sciences to create one unified science. And philosophy assumes the task of representing scientific insights, of elucidating all of the concepts and statements that have been made. All of its questions concern *language*—and hence we have returned to our point of departure, at which we defined philosophy as a logical analysis of *language*.

1ST SPEAKER: Or, to express it another way: Instead of the individual disciplines of philosophy that have existed up until now, such as the philosophy of nature, the philosophies of the organic, of the soul, and of history—philosophy now takes on the task of analyzing the natural sciences, such as biology, psychology, and the historiography of scientific achievements.

---

19 Bachmann refers to Descartes's efforts to develop a set of universal mathematical symbols.

20 Gottfried Wilhelm Leibniz (1646–1716), *Dissertatio de arte combinatoria* [Dissertation on the art of combination] (Leipzig: John Simon, Fickium, and John Polycarp, Seuboldum, 1666) 62.

PROFESSOR: Let me give an example: Kant had attempted to solve one of the basic problems of physics philosophically, the problem of space and time. The Vienna Circle considers the question of the structure of space and time as a question of the *syntax* of the coordinates of space and time.

1ST SPEAKER: Thus it has become a linguistic problem.

2ND SPEAKER: Or one of the most interesting basic problems of psychology, one that haunted the centuries in the guise of the body/soul problem, is confronted by simply relating the language of psychology to the language of physics. Philosophy must bring these two partial languages of science into harmony with the universal language of science.

PROFESSOR: For instance, if you see the color red, the scientist observes three things: a physical stimulus, a brain-physiological process, and an entirely subjective quality of experience.

2ND SPEAKER: That simple example already involves three individual sciences. Physics describes the physical circumstances that must be in play for a person to see red; the physiologist describes the brain-physiological process that occurs, and the psychologist . . .

1ST SPEAKER: Well, this is where things become difficult. For the psychological state of affairs is treated differently by psychologists using different methods. But an entirely radical theory was developed, since the Vienna Circle had to insist that the sentences of psychology be translated into equivalent sentences of physics, in order to be able to apply the unified language to all of the individual scientific disciplines.

2ND SPEAKER: We recall that, as a matter of principle, a scientific sentence is considered meaningful only if it can be verified by at least two observers—correctly formulated: if it is intersubjectively verifiable.

1ST SPEAKER: The real problem of a unified language lies in the question as to whether it can also be used to represent the psychic realm. For events occurring in another person's psyche cannot be verified directly for the most part. In the case of our example of seeing the color red we have indications stemming from the physical world. But beyond that we are dealing with a psychic experience of a qualitative kind that cannot be communicated.

2ND SPEAKER: At first the Vienna school believed that all psychological sentences of that sort had to be liquidated as pseudo-sentences. But that radical view incurred vehement opposition, not only on the part of philosophers, but also on the part of psychological experts.

CRITIC: This is also the stance that I find more disturbing than any of the other theses that have been proffered so far. For if statements about psychic events are declared impossible, as is happening here, then science would have to renounce a large part of its previous statements, indeed the largest part of the humanities would have to be jettisoned. And I am prepared to subscribe to what I said a while ago: that we are dealing not with philosophers but with the enemies of philosophy in the Vienna Circle.

1ST SPEAKER: To be sure, relinquishing the humanities would have been the ultimate consequence of such a stance. But that radical physicalist theory, incidentally developed by Rudolf Carnap in his early writings, was subjected to revision by himself and critics in his own camp. It was discovered that any psychic experience in another person—however particular and subjective it may be—such as the experience of color or of pain—can be communicated or understood, because it is determined by a frame of reference and characterized by an entirely unambiguous structure that manifests itself permanently and everywhere.

PROFESSOR: If you receive the message from another person, "I am seeing red," then you know what is intended, because the structure is the same as though you yourself are seeing red. You know: the other person is seeing something of the same sort as the color that you yourself have experienced on occasion—even though probably not with the same particularity.

1ST SPEAKER: But to return once more to the unified language: it is true that not everything can be translated into universal language, because psychic states and processes are not fully translatable. There is a conceptual system of psychic elements and another pertaining to physical ones, systems that stand side by side, but independently from each other. Science cannot do without either of them.

CRITIC: For the first time, you have made a kind of concession and relinquished your dogmatic viewpoint. And so perhaps I may call attention to a few things, since you have pointed to a deficiency in this unquestionably persuasive system. I do not doubt that the Vienna Circle, with its passion for exactitude and accuracy, has performed feats in the fields of logic and mathematics; I also do not doubt that its collaboration with modern physics has closed a gap in the philosophical thought of our time—but I believe that its excessive scientism has blinded logical positivism to *other* possibilities. The impression is that all questions that concern human beings are evaded. I ask myself what the reason for that might be.

Confronted with an indifferent, overpowering universe, human beings must stand their ground on their own strength. And their own strength signifies science here. That is the only way to account for the cult of science and technology and the insistence on a purely intellectual cognition of the world. It is also remarkable that this philosophy is not the creative achievement of an individual, but resulted from a kind of teamwork and is predicated on an anonymous consciousness.

1ST SPEAKER: If, by teamwork, you mean a fruitful exchange of ideas and mutual inspiration, then I cannot stop you. I did not want to overwhelm you with a surfeit of names. But among the Neopositivists of the Vienna Circle there were a number of notable personalities, such as Schlick, Carnap, Reichenbach. . . . It is true, however, that they never claimed to be prophets and always deferred to their work. Their view of the world, their personal convictions were something that they never carried to market.

CRITIC: I am not interested in personal confessions. And no one will doubt that the results of the natural sciences are a genuine store of knowledge today. But a total picture, a philosophical system that has no consideration for the human being, including the whole wealth of his existence and the abundance of his problems, one in which there is no philosophy of the person, cannot sustain the demands of our time—a time that still carries heavy baggage due to the calamitous consequences of a way of thinking that is foreign to metaphysics.

1ST SPEAKER: If you take the unfortunate history of the Circle into account, some things become self-evident.

NARRATOR: Schlick was murdered by a former student in 1936. His writings were left unfinished, and the loss of his prominence was irremediable. Carnap went to the University of Chicago that same year. The meetings of the Circle ceased at that time, and after Germany's annexation of Austria in 1938 it disbanded altogether. Its participants were scattered to the four corners of the earth. The sale of its publications was prohibited for political reasons, because some of the collaborators were Jews; the activity of those who could not be charged with any actionable offense was regarded as "subversive."

What would have resulted from a continuation of the work under more auspicious circumstances is hard to say. Today, the direction taken by the Vienna school is pursued in other countries, which could be a source of pride for the school, were it still in existence. Together with like-minded thinkers in the United States and England, Reichenbach and von Mises, Carnap and Popper are carrying on the work. But these former members of the study group and foreign academics like Kaila in Finland, Jörgensen in Copenhagen, and Maurice Boll in France have not contented themselves with preliminary insights; they have continued to develop these while partially moving beyond them. The distinction that all of them together continue to share is the way in which their work opposes the threat to Western culture posed by inauspicious irrationalism and subjectivism and the fact that they subject the material and the tools of philosophy to a thorough scrutiny devoid of preconceived notions.

Where should a fresh start be made today? Perhaps with Ludwig Wittgenstein, who has yet to be discovered, the greatest and at the same time least-known philosopher of our epoch. The closing pages of his *Tractatus Logico-Philosophicus* contain sentences that might bring a sea change, the end of positivism without abandoning its insights. Before suspending his words in silence, Wittgenstein says:

PROFESSOR (reading): "The facts all contribute only to setting the problem, not to its solution."[21]

"We feel that even when all possible scientific questions have been answered, the problems of life remain completely untouched. Of course there are then no questions left, and this itself is the answer."[22]

"There are, indeed, things that cannot be put into words. They *make themselves manifest.* They are what is mystical."[23]

"My propositions serve as elucidations in the following way: anyone who understands me eventually recognizes them as nonsensical, when he has used them—as steps—to climb up beyond them. (He must, so to speak, throw away the ladder after he has climbed up it.) He must transcend these propositions, and then he will see the world aright."[24]

---

21 *TLP*, §6.4321.

22 *TLP*, §6.52. Bachmann omits Wittgenstein's underscoring of "all possible."

23 *TLP*, §6.522.

24 *TLP*, §6.54.

Ludwig Wittgenstein—A Chapter of the Most Recent History of Philosophy[1]

When Ludwig Wittgenstein died two years ago in Cambridge, a cursory notice appeared in several papers: "At the age of . . . the renowned philosopher . . ." Well, he was anything but known; he was actually the most unknown philosopher of our time, a man for whom a word of his countryman Karl Kraus holds true, who once said of himself: "I am famous, but word has not gotten out yet."[2] Wittgenstein made sure that word did not get out, for reasons that we are not free to disclose.[3] Furthermore, the only book that he published during his lifetime bears a title with so little "appeal" that no one, with the exception of a small circle of experts, ever wanted to own it. If he was accessible to only a few in his work, then his biography was accessible to none; after finishing the *Tractatus Logico-Philosophicus*, he eschewed the world and fame, erased his tracks, relocated to the rural provinces for a number of years to work as a village teacher; and with respect to his final years in Cambridge, where he held the G. E. Moore Chair in Philosophy, it was reported that he lived in a cottage and only tolerated one simple chair as furniture. The legend superseded reality while he was still alive, a legend of voluntary austerity, of the attempt to live a saintly life, the attempt to comply with the proposition that concludes the *Tractatus*: "What we cannot speak about we must pass over in silence."[4] And it was—to come straight to the point—the attempt to execute philosophy in silence, an absurd attempt, so it seems, but the only legitimate one for him after he had clearly represented everything sayable (as he demanded of philosophy), everything thinkable, by limiting the unthinkable from within and thus anticipating the unsayable.

One consistently encounters the name Wittgenstein in philosophical literature in connection with the "Vienna Circle," the only original movement in empirical philosophy in contemporary times: the once disdained and dreaded "Vienna Dynasty" of logical positivists who, at least in part, founded a new school inspired by this singular thinker. Yet it would be incorrect to identify Wittgenstein with the school, which frequently happens, and to overlook what ensures his work the highest pedigree, over and above his fundamental contribution to symbolic logic and a "mathesis

1 Essay, first published in July 1953 in *Frankfurter Hefte* (now *Journal of Social Democracy*). Republished in 1960, 1964, and 1978.

2 Karl Kraus, "Ich bin berühmt" [I am famous], *Die Fackel* [The torch] 847 (March 1931), in *Die Fackel*, 12 vols. (Frankfurt am Main: Zweitausendeins, 1968–1976), vol. 11, 48–54.

3 As an Austrian of Jewish origin, Wittgenstein's relationship with his native country was strained by the annexation (*Anschluss*) in 1938, and it was Bachmann who initiated a Wittgenstein renaissance during the early to mid-1950s.

4 *TLP*, §7.

universalis" (newly formulated as a "uniform system of scientific knowledge"). It is not the clarifying, negating propositions, which limit philosophy to a logical analysis of scientific language and surrender the investigation of reality to scientific fields of study, but rather it is his desperate efforts to probe the unspeakable that infuses the *Tractatus* with an inner tension in which the speakable is revoked. Its failure to satisfy a positive definition of philosophy, which in the case of the other Neopositivists becomes fruitful ignorance, is worthy of continued discussion.

When in the year 1929 the Vienna working group led by Moritz Schlick[5] came out with the brochure *The Scientific Conception of the World—The Vienna Circle*, inciting a wave of protest in German philosophy with its cool, objective program, Wittgenstein's *Tractatus* had already been available for eight years. In the same year, the second edition of Heidegger's *Being and Time* appeared, which seemed to corroborate the circle's struggle against the pervasive irrationalism from Germany, the land of depression. In Vienna, the fierce antagonism of the group to Austrian clericalism, exemplified in the doctrines promulgated by the state philosopher Othmar Spann, was another aspect that was called for. It should not go without saying that the aggression, the shrill polemics against all forms of metaphysics, above all Neurath's,[6] were sometimes too narrow-minded or became ends in themselves. However, the insights garnered from a genuine passion for integrity and accuracy on the part of most of the collaborators justified the claim that the circle made for itself as an international school of exceptional repute.

Vienna was favorable terrain for the emergence of Neopositivism. Ever since a chair for the "Philosophy of Inductive Sciences" had been established at the University of Vienna for Ernst Mach at the end of the nineteenth century, there had been a longstanding tradition in Austria of empirical sciences dedicated almost exclusively to the fundamental problems of the natural sciences. In 1922, Moritz Schlick was appointed to this chair; he had studied with Planck and maintained close personal contacts with Einstein and Hilbert. Like his predecessors Boltzmann and Mach,[7] he came to the discipline from physics, but was ahead of them due to his thorough training in philosophy. A circle of students and

5 German philosopher Moritz Schlick (1882–1936) was the founding father of Logical Positivism and the Vienna Circle.

6 Philosopher, sociologist, and economist Otto Neurath (1882–1945) was one of the leading figures of the Vienna Circle.

7 Leonard Boltzmann (1844–1906) was an Austrian physicist and philosopher whose greatest achievement was in the development of statistical mechanics. Ernst Mach was an Austrian physicist and philosopher, noted for his contributions to physics, such as the study of shock waves, and a proponent of empirio-criticism, a philosophy asserting that all we can know is based on sensations and that knowledge should be confined to pure experience.

scholars interested in philosophy soon formed around him: Rudolf Carnap, the formal logician, as well as the eminent mathematicians Menger and Hahn were among them. Schlick was the only scholar in the group who occasionally spent time with Wittgenstein at his home and the one he influenced most decisively. However, the opinions of the circle with respect to Wittgenstein were not unanimous. It should not be overlooked that the leading positivist logician, the one who denied ordinary thinking entitlement to every "riddle" that is stimulated by a mystical experience of the unsayable, maintained his skepticism with respect to the weight of that mystical experience. The "unio mystica" of the philosopher who perceives the unsayable presence of the real in a few moments of grace was also the tenor of the final words uttered by Schlick, whose murder in 1934 represented an irreplaceable loss for the circle. After his death, an increasingly rigorous, "physical" course was pursued, and Carnap and Neurath joined together to reject Schlick's and Wittgenstein's "primeval experiences."

We find the main theses of Neopositivism prefigured in the *Tractatus Logico-Philosophicus*, which, viewed from the perspective of its form, is a curiosity. It consists of discrete, brilliantly written, numbered aphorisms, and begins with the succinct sentence: "The world is all that is the case" (1). Wittgenstein adopts Bertrand Russell's basic thesis that the world is composed of facts totally independent from one another. Beyond the totality of the facts, there is nothing that the world can be reduced to. As a reflection of these independent facts, our perception is forever discrete. Having revealed that, we also form general propositions that seem to refute this premise, such as: "All humans are mortal." Yet the truth of an assertion, general enough to be reliable for all of us, is determined by the truth of the individual assertions: "Peter is mortal" and "Hans is mortal." In this case, the copula "and" assumes the function of guaranteeing the truth of the general proposition. A new meaning, a new universal truth beyond the truth of the individual assertions, cannot be derived from a general proposition.

This innocuous example has less harmless consequences. It demonstrates that logic—understood both literally and plainly—does not signify anything. It has, to cite Wittgenstein, a purely tautological character. Consequently, logic is not able to explore reality or teach anything about it. Although philosophy is characterized as the logical analysis of language, it remains incapable of expressing anything about reality; it is simply an activity that exerts a form of control.

Its analytical tool, logic, experienced a profound transformation at the end of the previous century by using symbols, a transformation analogous to that of mathematics. In their *Principia Mathematica*, Russell and Whitehead had already shown that the basic mathematical concepts (the natural and augmented numbers, the elements of analysis and of set theory) can be constituted with logical terms on the basis of plausible precepts, if one includes two new axioms: the axiom of infinity and the axiom of choice. Mathematics was discovered as a branch of logic. "The logic of the world, which is shown in tautologies by the propositions of logic, is shown in equations by mathematics" (6.22), as Wittgenstein purports. Let us understand this properly. Since the numbers in mathematics do not signify objects of our empirical world and geometry does not describe real space, the symbols of logic are incapable of denoting real objects and their relationships to one another. Only when we think do we attribute relationships to the objects.

Neopositivism, therefore, undertakes a delicate correction, on the one hand of empiricism, on the other of Kant: it may be true that the laws of logic are a priori, but their statements are simultaneously empty and meaningless. That also suggests that Kant's thesis about their being synthetic is untenable. The only propositions that are meaningful and signify something are empirical propositions—in essence, propositions that relate to the facts associated with reality. These propositions occur in the individual empirical sciences. However, specifically philosophical propositions, as metaphysics postulates them, have to be signified as tautologies, as pseudo-propositions, despite their claiming to being more, since they are inaccessible to empirical science and its methods.

How pseudo-propositions were "unmasked" in the Vienna Circle will now be shown in Rudolf Carnap's criticism of Heidegger.

In his essay "The Elimination of Metaphysics through Logical Analysis of Language,"[8] Carnap provides a few examples from Martin Heidegger's "What is Metaphysics?" to show that constructions of this sort are based on a transgression of logical syntax. "What is to be investigated is being only and—*nothing* else; being alone and further—*nothing*; solely being, and beyond being—*nothing*. *What about this Nothing?* . . . *Does the Nothing exist only because the Not, i.e., the Negation, exists?* Or is it the other way around. *Does Negation and the Not exist only because the Nothing exists?* . . . We assert: *the Nothing is prior to the Not and the Negation*. . . . Where do we seek the Nothing? How do we find the Nothing. . . . We know the Nothing. . . . *Anxiety reveals the Nothing.*— That for which and because of which we were anxious, was 'really'—nothing. Indeed: the Nothing itself—as such—was present. . . . *What about this Nothing?—The Nothing itself nothings.*"[9]

---

8 Rudolf Carnap, "The Elimination of Metaphysics Through Logical Analysis of Language," in *Logical Empiricism at Its Peak: Schlick, Carnap, and Neurath*, ed. Sahotra Sarkar (New York: Garland, 1996), 10–31.

9 The translation cited is the one provided in the published English translation of Carnap's essay: Carnap, "The Elimination of Metaphysics," 19. Emphasis in the original.

Carnap attempts to emphasize the meaningless individual constructions by developing a scheme in which he compares the propositions to their grammatical analogy under "I" and the notation of symbolic logic under "III":

I. *Meaningful Sentences of Ordinary Language*	*II.* *Transition from Sense to Nonsense in Ordinary Language*	*III.* *Logically Correct Language*
A. What is outside? Ou(?) Rain is outside Ou(r)	A. "What is outside?" Ou(?) Nothing is outside Ou(no)	A. There is nothing (does not exist anything) which is outside. ~(∃x).Ou(x)
B. What about this rain? (i.e. what does the rain do? or: what else can be said about this rain?) ?(r)	B. "What about this Nothing?" ? (no)	B. None of these forms can even be constructed.
1. We know the rain K(r)	1. "We seek the Nothing" "We find the Nothing" "We know the Nothing" K(no)	
2. The rain rains R(r)	2. "The Nothing nothings" No(no)	
	3. "The Nothing exists only because . . . " Ex(no)	

Carnap argues in the following fashion: as question and answer, the construction of the sentence in II A does not correspond to the demands that must be placed on logically correct language, although it is still meaningful because it is translatable into logically correct language (III A). Its inappropriateness is revealed, however, if we proceed to the sentences under II B, which can no longer be formed using a logically correct language. For in II B 1, the word "nothing," with which a negative existential statement was constructed in ordinary language, is used as a noun.

In sentence II B 2, the meaningless word "to nothing" is introduced, rendering this sentence senseless for two reasons. First, sentence II B 3, the only sentence that is not equivalent to the grammatical analogy in I B, shares the fallacy of the previous statements by using the word "nothing" as a noun; second, even if it were admissible to introduce "nothing" as a designation of an object, it would contain a contradiction, because in the same statement the existence that was denied to the entity by definition is attributed to it once again.

Admittedly, Heidegger eludes this argumentation—Carnap is fully aware of that. "In a whirl of a more basic questioning" he believes to see the idea of logic dissolved and for that reason no longer feels himself beholden to it. But the Neopositivist must hold fast to the notion that a secondary, larger, "true" reality can only be posited, a reality in which the "nothing" is said to exist; yet it is certain from the onset that this reality will never allow itself to be verified.

Thus, Wittgenstein starts with the investigation of logic, which means the investigation of everything that is subject to the principles of logic: "And outside of logic, everything is accidental" (6.3). Matters that are subject to the laws governing logic as well as those that are under investigation do not provide explanations for the law. "The whole modern conception of the world is founded on the illusion that the so-called laws of nature are the explanation of natural phenomena" (6.371). Everything that happens in the world, happens as it does, and all that is, is as it is: "It is not how things are in the world that is mystical, but that it exists" (6.44). "Meaning," which by definition would have to be derived from an explanation, is not in the world.

We imagine the world as the totality of all facts, and our images are, by the same token, attributable to these facts. Between the image and the reality it depicts there is something shared that allows for depiction: the form (spatial form in the case of the depiction of what is spatial, colored form in the case of what is colored, and so forth). Moreover, under all circumstances every form is logical form and, accordingly, every image is also a logical image. "Logical pictures can depict the world" (2.19). In other words: since logical images are thoughts, everything that is thinkable is also possible, and since language is the totality of all sentences, philosophy must, of necessity, be the criticism of language—the logical analysis of language. For: "The totality of true propositions is the whole of natural science" (4.11). "The result of philosophy is not a number of 'philosophical propositions,' but to make propositions clear" (4.112).

Beginning with the clear representation of what is sayable, Wittgenstein points unexpectedly to the fact that philosophy would signify what is unsayable. What is this unsayable, then? First, we encounter it as the impossibility of depicting the logical form itself. Rather, the logical form manifests itself. It is mirrored in the proposition. The proposition points to it. What is manifested cannot be said; it is mystical. Here, logic experiences its limit, and since logic pervades the world, since the world enters into the structure of the logical form, its limit is the limit of our world. Thus, we understand the sentence: "The limits of my language mean the limits of my world" (5.6).

We stand, think, and speak on this side of these limits. Feeling the world as a limited whole arises when we ourselves, as a metaphysical subject, are no longer part of the world, but rather a "border." However, the path across that border is concealed. It is not possible for us to place ourselves outside the world and to express sentences about the sentences of the world. For that reason, there can also be no value: "and if it did exist, it would have no value" (6.41). There can be no sentences of ethics, since a sentence can express nothing of a higher nature. The will can also not be the bearer of the ethical, for the world is separate from our will. Nothing that language is capable of expressing—the facts of the world—is alterable by an act of will. Only the limits of the world are alterable, and about these we are obliged to remain silent. None of the questions that we are accustomed to directing at philosophy can be answered by it. With the question about the "meaning of being," we are left to our own resources.

The impetus behind this philosophizing, which cannot contribute to the solution of the problems of our lives, especially one which, in its passion for the whole truth, only has the arid, formulaic, "eternal" truth of logic to offer—sentences that we must overcome in order to see the world properly—is the same impetus about which Baudelaire speaks in his poem "The Gulf." Reminiscent of Pascal, Wittgenstein moves in and with his abyss; what he is not allowed to name flows to him from all borders and he is abandoned to the "drame cardinal." "Ah! never from beings, numbers to be free!"[10]

In the Vienna Circle, one certainly limited oneself to following the conspicuous motto of the *Tractatus*: ". . . and everything that one knows, has not mere rumbling and roaring, can be said in three words." The logical analysis of language was perfected, facilitated by preparatory work on a "unified system of scientific knowledge," on a universal language as Leibniz had already aspired to, a language into which all scientific partial languages can be translated. A close collaboration with mathematics and physics closed a gap in the philosophical thinking of our time. At illustrious international conferences, the Vienna School was able to extend its influence to the English-speaking and Scandinavian countries. Germany, France, and Italy, however, were consistently hostile toward Neopositivism. Even in Vienna, things have become quiet as far as the Vienna Circle is concerned. Between 1933 and 1939, its most outstanding

10 Baudelaire, "The Gulf," 345.

representatives were offered positions at foreign universities; some emigrated, and others became victims of National Socialism. The publication organ of the Circle, *Knowledge* was banned as "subversive" and had to be superseded by the *Journal of Unified Science* in England. What these ideas would have developed into under more favorable circumstances is difficult to say. The logically oriented texts that reach us today from the former members of the consortium—Rudolf Carnap, v. Mises, Popper, and Reichenbach, who continue to work with kindred thinkers in the United States and England—indicate the passing of Neopositivism's heyday; it has exhausted itself in the treatment of details.

But the time for Wittgenstein's discovery has surely come. From England, we learn that a second, as yet unknown work, *Philosophical Investigations*, has appeared in print; there are also reports of the existence of a *Blue Book*, which Wittgenstein did not want to have published until after his death.

Whether he renounced his silence and took the step to a confession of faith is uncertain and highly improbable. "God does not reveal himself in the world" (6.4320) is one of the bitterest sentences in the *Tractatus*. But does Wittgenstein not also let us know that ethical form, which, akin to logical form, might not be representable, still manifests itself and is reality? "What we cannot speak about, we must pass over in silence," he says at the close of the *Tractatus* and he means precisely the reality that we are not able or permitted to imagine. Or did he conclude that we have lost the game with our language, because it does not contain a word that has any substance?

Logic as Mysticism[1]

1ST SPEAKER: Two years ago, when Ludwig Wittgenstein died in Cambridge, a few Viennese newspapers carried a brief notice: "At the age of . . . the well-known philosopher . . . has died in . . ." But he was by no means well known; he was actually the least-known philosopher of our era, a man to whom the words of his countryman Karl Kraus apply, who once said of himself: "I am famous; it's just that the word hasn't gotten around yet."[2] However, Wittgenstein took care that the word did not get around. The only work that he published during his lifetime bears the less than alluring title, *Tractatus Logico-Philosophicus*, and to this day is known only to a small circle of specialists.

If he was accessible only to a few readers in his work, in his life he was accessible to no one. After finishing the *Tractatus*, he avoided the world and fame, he carefully covered his tracks, moved to Lower Austria for a long time to work as a village school teacher; in regards to his final years at Cambridge, where he had succeeded the English philosopher Moore as professor of philosophy during the war, it is reported that he lived in a cottage in which he only tolerated a simple chair as furniture.

Hence, legend superseded his life even while he was alive, a legend of voluntary poverty, of the attempt at a saintly life, the attempt to live in compliance with the sentence that closes the *Tractatus* . . .[3]

2ND SPEAKER: . . . on the other hand thought that metaphysics was impossible because its questions transcended the limits of human cognition.

PROFESSOR: —like Kant, for instance—

1ST SPEAKER: —logical positivism finds itself in a position to provide a more trenchant answer. And this more trenchant answer is aided by the logical analysis of language.

2ND SPEAKER: The new logic, which in the Vienna Circle developed into a highly specialized tool for working on a theory of science, also paved the way for basic investigations into the philosophy of language.

1 Bachmann's radio essay "Logic as Mysticism" was long considered lost until this fragment was discovered among the author's papers. Presumably, it is a preliminary draft of the missing radio essay, written in 1953 after Bachmann finished her Wittgenstein essay and prior to her radio essay "The Sayable and the Unsayable," both of which appear in this volume.

2 Kraus, "Ich bin berühmt," *Die Fackel* 847, 48–54.

3 There is a break in the manuscript at this point.

PROFESSOR: Let us bear in mind that there is a large number of languages, one's own language as well as foreign languages, scientific languages for the most diverse fields, a signal language for flags, the sign language of deaf-mutes . . .

2ND SPEAKER: It was not one of the languages in actual use that the Neopositivists had in mind in their investigation, but a language of a simplified and even more perfected nature—a pure system of representation. That language should then be examined with regard to what it represents—

PROFESSOR: —that is to say its semantic function—

2ND SPEAKER: —and to the manner in which it represents—

PROFESSOR: —that is to say its syntactical rules.

CRITIC: Does Wittgenstein not deny that such an examination of language is possible? Does he not say in his *Tractatus* that since language itself resists representation, it is impossible to speak about language?

1ST SPEAKER: Indeed. The sentence with which he closes the book,

PROFESSOR: "What we cannot speak about we must pass over in silence,"[4]

1ST SPEAKER: also refers to that problem, and we will continue to pursue it.

2ND SPEAKER: Wittgenstein begins by closely examining sayable sentences. He notes with respect to any correct sentence that it represents the facts in the realm of logic, but also the existence and nonexistence of facts. It is a model of reality. And the conformity between the facts and the model constitutes the truth that it contains.

1ST SPEAKER: Let us once again recall Wittgenstein's thesis that the logical form that serves us for those models does not belong to the facts of the world, that there is a limit of the sayable, one that coincides with the limit of my world—

---

4 *TLP*, §7.

2ND SPEAKER: but not with the limit of reality as such.

1ST SPEAKER: And "limit of my world" implies "limit of my language."[5] Our reach extends only as far as our language reaches, according to which we accurately represent and picture how the world is.

2ND SPEAKER: But what, then, have we accomplished with the representation and the picture of the world? Nothing whatsoever, is Wittgenstein's surprising answer.

PROFESSOR: "*How* things are in the world is a matter of complete indifference for what is higher. . . . It is not *how* things are in the world that is mystical, but *that* it exists."[6]

2ND SPEAKER: Anyone who has reached that passage when reading the *Tractatus*, after its terse equations, examples from symbolic logic, and after the sobering clash with the arid truths of logic, will suddenly understand the adventure that has been launched by this book.

PROFESSOR: "The world is everything that is the case."
"The world is the totality of facts . . ."[7]

2ND SPEAKER: That is how the *Tractatus* begins, rigorous, brittle, pithy. Not one word could be omitted, not one word presumes to mean more than it happens to express. And then the "mystical," a word with a limitless field of meaning, laden with doubtless and doubtful experiences of an unnamed faith.

CRITIC: What is the impact of the mystical in Wittgenstein, we have to ask. Is that sentence not disturbingly reminiscent of Heidegger's question—certainly a senseless question in Wittgensteinian terms: "Why are there essents, why is there anything at all, rather than nothing?"[8] Is Hei-

---

5 Reference to *TLP*, §5.6: "The limits of my language mean the limits of my world."

6 *TLP*, §6.432 and 6.44. While Wittgenstein's originals have underlining to emphasize certain terms, we have followed Bachmann's practice of not underlining Wittgenstein's quotations.

7 *TLP*, §1–1.1. Bachmann omits the word "alles" (everything) in quoting the opening sentence.

8 Martin Heidegger, *An Introduction to Metaphysics*, trans. Ralph Manheim (New Haven, CT: Yale University Press, [1959] 1968), 1. The word "essent" is a

degger's speechlessness in the face of being not reminiscent of Wittgenstein's speechlessness? Do the positivist and the philosopher of being not find themselves enmeshed in the same aporia?

1ST SPEAKER: The experience at the core of Heidegger's mysticism of being may be similar to the one that prompts Wittgenstein to speak of the mystical. But it would be impossible for Wittgenstein to ask the Heideggerian question, since he denies what Heidegger presupposes: that in the process of thinking being is articulated. Where Heidegger's philosophy begins, Wittgenstein's ends.

PROFESSOR: Because: "What we cannot speak about we must pass over in silence."[9]

1ST SPEAKER: It is also impossible to speak in the "sense" of being, for there is no meaning in a world that can only be represented but not explained.[10] We stand and speak on this side of the boundary across which our path is blocked.[11] It is not possible for us to position ourselves outside of the world and to form sentences about the sentences of the world, as generally occurs in metaphysics. Sentences about the sentences of the world are pseudo-sentences. Since we cannot propose sentences about the sentences of the world, there cannot be any sentences about ethics either. For a sentence cannot express anything higher; there is no second order of propositions besides those that articulate facts. Nor can the will be a bearer of ethics, for the world is independent from our will. Nothing that language can do—that is, represent the facts of the world—can be changed by the will. What can be changed are the limits of the world, but we must be silent about them. And not one of the questions that we have been accustomed to directing to philosophy is philosophy able to answer. With the question of the "sense" of being, we are left to our own devices.

2ND SPEAKER: The movement behind a philosophy that cannot contribute anything to the solution of our existential problems and, as a result of its passion for the whole truth, has little more to offer than a formulaic "eternal" truth of logic is the same in which Baudelaire speaks of Pascal, culminating in the bitter wish:

---

translation of the German *Seiendes* or *das Seiende*, meaning "existents," or "things that are."

9 *TLP*, §7.

10 See *TLP*, §6.41: "The sense of the world must lie outside the world."

11 Bachmann refers here to the boundary created by the limit of our language, described by Wittgenstein in *TLP*, §5.61.

PROFESSOR: "—Ah! never from beings, numbers to be free!"[12]

2ND SPEAKER: Numbers and beings, those are the entities that are quantifiable and measurable, that do not know the experience of the metaphysical subject as a limit, that need not fall silent in the face of the unsayable, because they are exclusive of language.

1ST SPEAKER: But we must not lose track of Wittgenstein's other steps: as we already know, he made a distinction between representation and what was to be represented, between form and world. Logic, the examination of which is equivalent to the examination of all inevitabilities for Wittgenstein, has yet to be defined.

PROFESSOR: "Logic is not a body of doctrine but a mirror-image of the world."[13]

1ST SPEAKER: That means that there is only logical necessity in the world, because the world conforms to the logical form.

PROFESSOR: "And outside logic everything is accidental."[14]

2ND SPEAKER: For example, the law of causality—and that is of immense significance—reveals itself to be not a law but the *form* of a law. It says nothing about the world, and neither does it say anything about the world that can be described in terms of Newton's mechanics—or, more accurately today, in terms of Einstein's theory of gravity. The law of causality, Newton's mechanics, and Einstein's theory of gravity are nothing but descriptions of the world with the help of a logical form, a network of circumscribed freedom. The descriptions may be accurate, as any calculation is, and the scientific descriptions may be optimal—but nothing has been said about reality. Above all, reality will never be "understood" in all eternity on the basis of descriptions. What is described is only how the world is, and that is irrelevant, or at least relevant only to the practice of life. And Wittgenstein adds:

PROFESSOR: "The whole modern conception of the world is founded on the illusion that the so-called laws of nature are the explanations of

12 Baudelaire, "The Gulf," 345.
13 *TLP*, §6.13.
14 *TLP*, §6.3.

natural phenomena. Thus people today stop at the laws of nature, treating them as something inviolable, just as God and Fate were treated in past ages."[15]

1ST SPEAKER: We have learned that theories, whatever their subject may be, do not explain and indeed cannot explain anything, since there is only one form of necessity, that of logic, and hence meaning—once again we recognize the circular argument in the question of meaning—must lie outside the world and not in its states of affairs.[16] And all worldviews are due to premature interpretations that are being submitted to us today and in the conflicts in which we are entangled; to these we owe the value systems to which we either acquiesce or against which we rebel, because we are unable to appreciate that there is no value in the world—or more precisely in the world that is bounded by us.

PROFESSOR: "And if there were one, it would have no value. For all that happens and is the case is accidental. What makes it non-accidental cannot lie *within* the world, for otherwise it would again be accidental. It must lie outside the world."[17]

2ND SPEAKER: Outside the world—meaning: outside language. As Wittgenstein does, we too quickly reach his first conclusion and the conclusion that he unexpectedly gave to the *Tractatus* and to which so many riddles have become attached, and yet we still have to allow for several more questions and criticisms.

The conclusions are: even if our language were perfect and were able to describe the world perfectly, not a single problem that concerns us would be solved—nevertheless, our questions will also not be overcome by revealing them to be pseudo-questions.

1ST SPEAKER: As we know, the most radical representatives of Neopositivism believed that the unmasking of pseudo-problems alone was enough to overcome them!

2ND SPEAKER: But Wittgenstein yields a more genuine radicalism, which does not even stop at his own work: since the entirety of scientific knowl-

15 *TLP*, §6.371 and 6.372. Bachmann combines the two sentences (§6.371 and 6.372) into one paragraph.

16 Bachmann explains this concept in more detail above.

17 Bachmann is paraphrasing *TLP*, §6.41 here.

edge is without value—precisely because there is no value in the world—we must be rid of it.

PROFESSOR: "We feel that even when all *possible* scientific questions have been answered, the problems of life remain completely untouched.

"Of course there are then no questions left, and this itself is the answer."[18]

"There are, indeed, things that cannot be put into words. They *make themselves manifest*. They are what is mystical."[19]

My propositions serve as elucidations in the following way: "anyone who understands me eventually recognizes them as nonsensical, when he has used them—as steps—to climb up beyond them. (He must, so to speak, throw away the ladder after he has climbed up it.) He must transcend these propositions, and then he will see the world aright."[20] The appropriate philosophical method would actually entail: saying nothing other than what can be said, in other words sentences of natural science—something that has nothing to do with philosophy—and then every time someone attempts to say something metaphysical to prove that he has failed to give meaning to certain signs in his sentences. That method would be dissatisfying—he would not feel that we were teaching him philosophy—but it would be the only strictly correct one to adopt.

CRITIC: Perhaps I might interrupt to add something: philosophy, if I understand correctly, has ceased to be an independent source of higher knowledge to Wittgenstein. It has become a subservient form of questioning. Whatever the result of such questioning may be—for the most part, it would seem to be one of extreme empiricism—Wittgenstein's altered conception of philosophy might be the beginning of an era in which it no longer seems paradoxical that the actual object of the philosopher's quest is not the nature of human cognition, experience, and transcendence and so forth, but language. If we accept that premise, we would be quite astonished that Wittgenstein's own work, the *Tractatus*, does not pass the test by the standards of his own claims. He asserts that his own propositions may be recognized as meaningless and extols, in a sense, his philosophy as the end of philosophy. That contains an inconsistency that cannot be overlooked.

18 *TLP*, §6.52.
19 *TLP*, §6.522.
20 *TLP*, §6.54.

1ST SPEAKER: But of course that "inconsistency," as you call it, results from the logical investigations and from language theory as a whole, as it appears in the *Tractatus.* Sextus Empiricus, incidentally, articulated an idea echoed in Wittgenstein's *Tractatus* when he designated his philosophy as a kind of purgatory, not only for the ideas of other philosophers but also for his own.[21] If you want to understand Wittgenstein, you must first remember that thinking consists of a sort of silent use of language. Wittgenstein, who wanted to determine the limits of possible cognition, also wanted to describe the limits of what could be said. Thus, with respect to that intention, he is tasked to examine the nature of language.

CRITIC: Then the results can only be of a scientific and not of a philosophical nature. Or else he would have to penetrate into the essential nature of language using words. But how? In order to write anything intelligible, writing would have to make use of words, and instantly his thinking would lose its sublime *détachement* and be subject to what he aims to avoid. He himself says that no point exists outside language, from which one could write about language. Banished from its traditional position, philosophy would then be without one altogether, because by devoting itself to the study of language it would have to become grammar—something entirely different from what Wittgenstein has in mind. For him philosophy would have to reach a height, a height so exceptional, that it would ultimately cancel itself out. There is an assumption here that Wittgenstein passed up an opportunity that he might have seized, other than this *salto mortale.*

2ND SPEAKER: Let me draw on something you said about philosophy as grammar. Wittgenstein's theory of language is not an ordinary one. If it were, it would not assert that so many things remain unrepresented.

---

21 Writing in Greek around 200 CE, Sextus Empiricus would not have used the term *purgatorio*, nor would he have had any notion of its allusions to Dante, although one of his sixteenth-century Latin translators may have used the term in the literal sense of "cleansing" to translate the Greek word *katharsis*, a common philosophical term. He likens the formulae of the Skeptics to "cathartic medicines" that "purge the body of humors" and "carry off themselves with the humors": "Pyrrhonic Sketches," I. 206, trans. Mary Mills Patrick. In *Sextus Empiricus and Greek Skepticism.* Cambridge and London: Deighton Bell and Company and George Bell and Company, 1899, accessed via Project Gutenberg, https://www.gutenberg.org/files/17556/17556-h/17556-h.htm#PYRRHONIC_SKETCHES. He also writes, that "Just as cathartic drugs flush themselves out along with the various materials in the body, so these arguments apply to themselves along with the other arguments that are said to be probative": "Pyrrhonic Sketches," 2.188, cited in Benson Mates, *The Skeptic Way: Sextus Empiricus's "Outlines of Pyrrhonism"* (New York: Oxford University Press, 1996), 135.

A grammarian writes about the ordering of words and the particularities of speech that do not stand for objects. Nor is his approach a descriptive theory. In his introduction to the *Tractatus*, [Bertrand] Russell says that the work contains a theory about an ideal language, the grammar of which is so exact that we can express our thoughts without the possibility of confusion. In reality, however, it is a theory about the essential nature of all languages that is deeply enshrouded in the kinds of symbolic elements that languages contain. That becomes clear when we consider what one of the most essential parts of the theory looks like.

1ST SPEAKER: Wittgenstein says that ordinary words signify things that are complex. However, it is possible to develop an understanding of the meaning of a word by explaining it using words that describe the details of things. He proposes that the process of logical analysis ultimately leads to a word that can no longer be explained by using other words, but only by pointing to the thing for which it stands. Those things, however, would have to be simple elements and the meanings would have to correspond to the simple words for which they stand.

CRITIC: That would mean that if those simple elements, those simple things, did not exist, language would necessarily be meaningless. And Wittgenstein reached that conclusion not by examining a common word but by applying abstract argumentation. This aspect of Wittgenstein's theory comes very close to being metaphysics, one that is sometimes called "pluralism" or "logical atomism" and that initially emerged in Plato's "Theaetetus."[22] It is an identity of word sense and object that must appear impossible to anyone who does not concede that the objective of a philosopher's endeavors is an analysis of language.

2ND SPEAKER: By way of a criticism of language, we come to Wittgenstein's posthumous work, *Philosophical Investigations*,[23] which casts a completely new light on that very problem . . .

---

22 "Theaetetus," one of Plato's later dialogues, deals with the relationship between the one and the many.

23 The *Philosophical Investigations* were first published in 1953, two years after Wittgenstein's death. Ludwig Wittgenstein, *Philosophical Investigations*, trans. G. E. M. Anscombe, P. M. S. Hacker, and Joachim Schulte, revised, bilingual edition (Chichester: Wiley-Blackwell, 2009). Abbreviated as *PI*, giving section and page numbers. The "e" following the page number denotes reference to the English-language page in this parallel text edition.

CRITIC: Permit me to add here that the identification about which I was speaking is not the only piece of metaphysics in Wittgenstein's *Tractatus*—the entire theory of language is slightly dubious in the sense that it attempts to force the diversity and the wealth of language into a simple, rigid net, one that is executed with geometric precision. When studying the *Tractatus*, the reader feels: this is how things must be. But the moment the book is cast aside we remember that this is not how things are. To express myself in a less subjective manner: a metaphysical system need not be presented in the traditional guise as a theory about the world. It may also be offered to us as a theory about the language in which we describe the world! Yet it was one of Wittgenstein's intentions, after all, to reveal to the metaphysicians that their words are empty. This is where the deeper motive for the strange message of the *Tractatus* can be found. Truly, it is a metaphysics to end all metaphysics. I would also like to correct myself and assert that it may not be the inconsistency of the work—rather, the error could be located in the method.

1ST SPEAKER: Well, it is in fact true that Wittgenstein subjects part of the *Tractatus* to a revision in the *Philosophical Investigations*, and the most trenchant as well as most convincing criticism concerns his older theory of simple elements. We do not know what prompted him to conduct that revision—almost thirty years separate the two books, thirty years of virtually unknown life and intellectual activity. In the preface to this book, which was edited by his students and collaborators, Wittgenstein states:

PROFESSOR: "Until recently I had really given up the idea of publishing my work in my lifetime. All the same, it was revived from time to time: mainly because I could not help noticing that the results of my work (which I had conveyed in lectures, typescripts and discussions), were in circulation, frequently misunderstood and more or less watered down or mangled. This stung my vanity, and I had difficulty in quieting it.

"Four years ago, however, I had occasion to reread my first book (the *Tractatus Logico-Philosophicus*) and to explain its ideas. Then it suddenly seemed to me that I should publish those old ideas and the new ones together: that the latter could be seen in the right light only by contrast with and against the background of my older way of thinking.

"For since I began to occupy myself with philosophy again, sixteen years ago, I could not but recognize grave mistakes in what I set out in that first book."[24]

---

24 *PI*, 4e.

1ST SPEAKER: Although the *Tractatus* rarely serves as a direct point of reference in the *Philosophical Investigations*, it is nevertheless indispensable to an understanding of what they impart to us. A close perusal also demonstrates that the comprehensive concept of the *Tractatus* is present without being articulated. For Wittgenstein, philosophy remains a special, all-embracing entity, and because of its extraordinary position, it continues to be barred from ever producing anything itself. If it were productive, it would only cause new problems, rather than finding solutions for the existing ones.

2ND SPEAKER: The revision, however, takes the case of the simple elements mentioned above and the words that are no longer reducible as its point of departure, which our critic unmasked as metaphysics—something that it, in fact, did not want to be. Wittgenstein no longer offers a theory now but draws us into a dialogue about the simplest of commonplace things.

CRITIC: And what does that "Socratic" dialogue look like?

2ND SPEAKER: He starts by demonstrating a primitive language to us. A bricklayer calls out the names of the things that he wants, and a helper gives them to him. Wittgenstein calls what the two people do a "language game." In that "game," the two people act as they speak. When the bricklayer calls out: "Five bricks," then the number "five" no longer stands for something that corresponds to the other individual things that he had asked for.

1ST SPEAKER: At this point, it turns out that words that are used like the things corresponding to them need not be explained using other words until the simplest elements have been reached. If we explain a word, reduce it, then the other person to whom it is to be explained plays an important role. Some people understand quickly; some will never understand.

2ND SPEAKER: An additional insight is that when the simple elements have been reached, those that can no longer be explained but only "pointed out," i.e., those that can be shown or produced, then those elements are not—as Wittgenstein had thought earlier—the meanings of the simple words that they signify. For the bearer of a name, for instance, that name is not his meaning after all. If the bricklayer, for example, asks his helper for bricks and there are not any left, then the helper, if he has understood his foreman, may also shake his head in reply. Or let us assume that the correct use of a word for a color, sky blue for instance, is judged by reference to a color scale. Nonetheless, the existence of the scale is not required for the word "sky blue" to preserve its meaning.

1ST SPEAKER: No one wanting to study Wittgenstein's work can be spared the perusal of the examples, the language games in the *Philosophical Investigations.* These examples must be followed sentence by sentence to ensure the success of the remedy for which Wittgenstein devised them. We can only attempt to represent the basic concepts, which are present by implication.

2ND SPEAKER: Wittgenstein no longer works with impressive generalizations, as he did in the *Tractatus.* He has become convinced that the great errors of philosophy, his own included, come from the desire to bring everything into clear, simple patterns. His language games are methodological devices designed to show how language works, and the comprehensive idea of that method is the thesis that the meaning of a word comes more from its customary context than from its connection with objects or an inner experience. The loss of meaning occurs when we excise a word from the environment that gives it life, when, for example, we repeat it in isolation until it runs empty. Therefore, we must not interfere with the practice of language:

PROFESSOR: "For philosophical problems arise when language *goes on holiday.*"[25]

1ST SPEAKER: Yes, in fact, Wittgenstein thinks that the use of words in everyday language speaks for itself with sufficient clarity, that this clarity is already a perfect one.

PROFESSOR: "But this simply means that the philosophical problems should completely disappear."[26]

1ST SPEAKER: Paradoxically: the task of philosophy in Wittgenstein's terms is the abolition of philosophy in terms of traditional teachings. So there is one idea that is identical with a basic idea of the *Tractatus*—the idea of the one language that we cannot touch and whose traits we only need to look at in order to understand. It is the idea that turns against the doctrine of essence in philosophy, essentialism—the doctrine of meta-

25 *PI*, §38, 23e

26 *PI*, §133, 56e. Bachmann removes Wittgenstein's emphasis. The original reads: "should *completely* disappear."

physics that has generated metaphysical systems for thousands of years. A second thought found in the *Tractatus* has been retained; we are already familiar with it: in speaking a language we speak about things, that is to say we practice natural science. Philosophy is not a natural science: it does not speak about things but attempts to speak about language. Yet it cannot, for it is impossible to speak about language without once again entering into language. How language is constituted is something that "shows itself." "Showing oneself" and "being self-evident" are one and the same.

2ND SPEAKER: That concept contains a striking affinity with existential philosophy, which also says, after all, that we can only speak about factual things, whereas everything else is unmediated, but existentialism still clings to the doctrine of essence and allows philosophy to represent a form of life. By contrast, according to Wittgenstein's language theory philosophy cannot even endure as a form of life—form of life is language itself, and there are as many forms of life as there are languages. Philosophy must disappear completely. Only practical experience is what is given.

CRITIC: Having listened to your account of the basic thoughts in Wittgenstein's *Philosophical Investigations*, I should once again like to interject something to ask a related question, as well as to raise some doubts.—At one point in this discussion, mention was made of the ideal of philosophy, of the extraordinary position that Wittgenstein ascribed to philosophy in the *Tractatus* and that even at that early point drove him to a negative definition of philosophy. You have forgotten to mention that that high ideal is retained in the *Investigations* as well—the thought that philosophy is all-embracing and therefore not allowed to produce anything itself. On the basis of that ideal, which is simply taken for granted and is not derived from "practice," an attack is launched against the existing philosophical systems and movements. So Wittgenstein's work does contain a philosophical doctrine. That doctrine amounts to the introduction of an opposition, an arbitrary one it seems to me, between "natural" language and the language of philosophers. Hence, we have to regard this work as another "castle in the air," one that has to disappear on the basis of the assertions it contains. I am not sure that that is very satisfying.

1ST SPEAKER: You are right—the net result of the *Philosophical Investigations*, which inadvertently repeat the *salto mortale* of the *Tractatus*, is not an easy one to assess. A number of problems remain unsolved. We have to choose between alternatives; either we must give up the universal claim of philosophy, which Wittgenstein paradoxically wants to keep, and regard it as no longer anything but a historically cleaved group of problems. The insights of the *Philosophical Investigations*, the new theory of language, the refutation of the doctrine of essence, and the discovery of the wealth of linguistic forms would then still constitute a noteworthy result, even though it would have to be positioned in different contexts. Or we retain the ideal of philosophy and return to essentialism.

2ND SPEAKER: That, however, seems hardly possible any more, after the fruitful analyses of the work provided above.

1ST SPEAKER: Or we make use of what that work has taught us; we learn to see the problems of philosophy in entirely new frames of reference and once again embark on the quest, realizing the "infinite" task of thinking with which we have been charged, a task from which even the "end of philosophy" cannot absolve us. And that is what Wittgenstein gives us to understand, in the words with which he closes his preface:

PROFESSOR: "I should not like my writing to spare other people the trouble of thinking. But if possible, to stimulate someone to thoughts of his own."[27]

---

27 *PI*, 4e.

The Sayable and the Unsayable[1]

WITTGENSTEIN: "The world is all that is the case."

"The world is the totality of facts."

"The world is determined by the facts, and by their being *all* the facts."[2]

1ST SPEAKER: Thus begins the *Tractatus Logico-Philosophicus* by Ludwig Wittgenstein, a not particularly ample philosophical work that appeared in Vienna in the year 1919.[3] Its concise, austere language is the first thing to strike anyone who devotes himself to it. And the reader will also be struck by the fact that it is not a philosophical text based on a systematic structure, but one consisting of loosely sequential, numbered aphorisms. Not every train of thought is resolved, not always is there an effective transition from one thought to the next. That is why the *Tractatus*, despite its clear, precise formulations, has often been called an opaque book, an esoteric book, accessible only to initiated readers, that is, to specialists. But we believe that it is a very necessary and important book for anyone interested in philosophy and modern scholarship and that it can help us perceive the world accurately.

2ND SPEAKER: The very first sentences of the *Tractatus* present Wittgenstein's starting point. He speaks of the world as the totality of facts. In philosophical terms, that is a completely uncritical, simple premise, one he took from his English friend and mentor, the philosopher Bertrand Russell. Russell starts with the thesis that the world is composed of facts that are totally independent of one another. And the world, beyond the totality of facts, is—nothing. That is why our understanding of the world, as a reflection of facts that are totally independent of one another, can always only comprehend parts.

1ST SPEAKER: But very often, we articulate our understanding in generalities. We can say, for instance, "All humans are mortal."

1 Radio Essay, aired by Sender Red-White-Red in Vienna on September 16, 1954.

2 *TLP*, §1–1.11. Although Bachmann does not capitalize all parts of the Latin title, Wittgenstein does. Unabridged, the second sentence reads: "The world is the totality of facts, not of things."

3 Bachmann's date is incorrect. Wittgenstein sent the *Tractatus* to his mentor Bertrand Russell in 1919; it first appeared in Vienna, not in 1919, but in 1921 and inspired the "logical positivism" of the Vienna Circle philosophers.

2ND SPEAKER: If we examine that "generality" closely, we discover that it has the same meaning as "Peter is mortal" and "Hans is mortal." The "and" that connects those two individual propositions usually serves to ensure the truth of the generality, "All humans are mortal." The universal truth that we believe to have derived is solely defined by the truth of the two individual propositions, "Peter is mortal" and "Hans is mortal." By no means, however, does a new general truth emerge. This modest and trivial example of the logical discipline demonstrates that logic—understood quite literally and banally—proves nothing. It has—to use Wittgenstein's words—a purely tautological character.[4] All of its sentences are empty; they cannot provide us any indication of reality.

1ST SPEAKER: It is the natural sciences that are concerned with reality, with the totality of facts. They describe the facts and convey insights. Not being a science, however, philosophy, like logic—which is its tool—cannot teach us anything about reality. For all sentences referring to reality are scientific sentences, and the generalizing propositions that we encounter in traditional philosophy, such as the one mentioned a moment ago, "all humans are mortal," are only meaningful because they are based on empirical sentences and provide no new knowledge that is specifically philosophical.

CRITIC: If philosophy cannot convey any knowledge to us, if only the natural sciences can do that, then what does philosophy actually accomplish?

1ST SPEAKER: As a "logical analysis" of the sentences expressing scientific experience, philosophy can exert a method of control; it can discover the sources of errors and eliminate inaccuracies. Yet it must entrust the processing of reality entirely to the natural sciences.[5] The forfeiture of any exploration of reality to the specific fields of the natural sciences, one that de facto had taken place a long time ago, has thus received confirmation for the first time in German philosophy.

2ND SPEAKER: Wittgenstein's approach to philosophy, "logical analysis," is not as new as it appears. For we rediscover in it the analytical method promoted by rationalism and empiricism, a method that is almost as old as

4 If a sentence is tautological, it is true by virtue of its logical form. Logical sentences of the form "If P, then P" are tautological sentences.

5 See *TLP*, §4.113: "Philosophy sets limits to the much-disputed sphere of natural science."

philosophy itself.[6] That it fell into oblivion in German philosophy—that oversight can be blamed on the nineteenth century. Fichte's, Schelling's, and Hegel's[7] systems had completely superseded it, until it reawakened in a new form in the twentieth century and appeared in the most recent history of philosophy as Neopositivism, at least in part inspired by Wittgenstein. The real reason for its comeback, however, was a revolution in mathematics and logic—when suddenly at the end of the nineteenth century the richness of the analytical method once again asserted itself in those fields. It was discovered that in mathematics as well as in logic, so-called paradoxes arise, which challenge the foundations of both of these disciplines. Some logical paradoxes, to be sure, had been known since classical antiquity. Most of us are acquainted with the story of the liar: Epimenides the Cretan says that "all Cretans are liars."[8]

Now paradoxes were encountered in mathematics as well, and they were far more alarming, since they threatened to eliminate entire fields of mathematics. Since both logic and mathematics were threatened, it meant that our entire order of representation—our *language* in the widest sense—was affected, not only the one sentence or the other within that language. What was to be done now? How could those problems—the basic problems—be solved?

1ST SPEAKER: The philosophers who recognized how extraordinarily important it was to employ logic—Bertrand Russell in England and the Neopositivists in Vienna—hit upon a concept which, albeit obvious, was in truth entirely new: that the reason for those paradoxes necessarily lies in the fact that throughout the centuries we have used sentences in philosophy, as well as in our language, that appeared as if they were expressive of meaning, but in reality did not convey any meaning at all; that we have fallen prey to a mystification of our language without realizing it, because we trusted language blindly. Indeed, Plato and other philosophers after him tried to examine the truth of propositions by subjecting them to a strictly analytical method. Descartes, as we know, even decided to regard all propositions as false, for which their truth was not absolutely self-evi-

6 Despite this statement, rationalism and empiricism have traditionally been at odds. Rationalism holds that reason alone, without experience, can arrive at fundamental truths about the world; empiricism holds that the mind is a blank slate, and experience is necessary for any sort of knowledge. Philosophers like Immanuel Kant tried to synthesize rationalism and empiricism, which is perhaps what Bachmann is suggesting that Wittgenstein has accomplished.

7 These three "German idealist" philosophers expanded on Kant's work, but aimed not at analysis, rather at a grand synthetic picture of the world integrating all aspects of reality.

8 This sentence is known as Epimenides's paradox.

dent. But no one had ever asked whether some questions were intrinsically meaningless.

2ND SPEAKER: For Wittgenstein and his Neopositivist colleagues, the examination of the meaning of sentences and forms of inquiry moves into the foreground of philosophical analysis and becomes more important than the question of truth. For a change, the covert nonsense—the nonsense hidden in language—had to be investigated thoroughly. And the distrust suddenly assumed such large proportions that Moritz Schlick, one of the preeminent thinkers of the Vienna School, once exclaimed that what philosophers were afraid of today was not that they could not solve the problems of philosophy but that philosophy would never come up with a genuine problem. Today, most of its problems have already become recognizable as pseudo-problems.

1ST SPEAKER: Since philosophical difficulties were discovered to be rooted in language, we understand why Wittgenstein's work encompasses a theory of language. It will show us how the world may be "represented" in correct and meaningful sentences, how we can "speak" about the world, and what philosophy can achieve as a critique of our speaking about the world.

Furthermore, Wittgenstein is said to have called his first book *Tractatus* because he wanted to conduct a sort of "trial," in the legal sense, of philosophy and our philosophical speech.[9] In his preface, he writes:

WITTGENSTEIN: "The book deals with the problems of philosophy, and shows, I believe, that the reason why these problems are posed is that the logic of our language is misunderstood."[10]

1ST SPEAKER: Hence, for Wittgenstein the natural starting point of his philosophical inquiry became the exploration of logic. As an aphorism in the *Tractatus* states:

---

9 Although the word "Tractatus" (Latin "treatise") does not carry any legal implications, a treatise is a systematic analysis of evidence and arguments to support a case. *Tractatus* was the title given to the English translation (published in 1922) and was suggested by G. E. Moore as an allusion to Spinoza. Wittgenstein generally referred to the book as *Logisch-Philosophische Abhandlung*, the title of the 1921 publication.

10 *TLP*, preface, 3.

WITTGENSTEIN: "Outside logic everything is accidental."[11]

1ST SPEAKER: And everything outside logic must be accidental, since logic fills the world.

WITTGENSTEIN: "The limits of the world are also its limits."[12]

2ND SPEAKER: Let us try to follow that train of thought: Wittgenstein is speaking about the world that confronts us with objects and facts. That one world and its states of affairs are represented in sentences that are verifiable—

1ST SPEAKER: —that is to say, scientific sentences—

2ND SPEAKER: —and in another passage he adds that we are also able to represent *all* of reality with our sentences.

1ST SPEAKER: What is meant is that the sciences explore reality and bring it into an order of representation.

CRITIC: But what causes Wittgenstein to speak of the "limits of the world"?

1ST SPEAKER: He takes a step back and says that there is one thing we are *not* able to represent, and that is *what* our sentences, which represent reality, have in common with reality.

2ND SPEAKER: His assertion touches on a peculiar phenomenon, to which we never give a thought in everyday or scientific practice. For instance, we represent a certain natural occurrence using the sentence, "it is raining"—or, in the natural sciences, express a so-called natural law, such as the laws of gravity, in a formula. The sentence expressed in everyday language as well as the mathematical formula represent reality, even though it is apparent that they do not have the slightest connection to that reality. They are merely signs signifying something without having anything in common with the signified. Nevertheless, the question remains as to how

11 *TLP*, §6.3.
12 *TLP*, §5.61.

we are able to function using those signs, our language in the most extensive sense of the term!

1ST SPEAKER: And this is Wittgenstein's answer: of necessity, it is the logical form which the two have in common, because otherwise sentences would not be able to represent reality at all. And the logical form is the "boundary" that was the subject of our critic's query a moment ago, for while it makes representation possible, it can no longer be represented itself. Something pointing beyond reality becomes evident here. It points beyond reality insofar as something reveals itself in the logical form that is unthinkable to us, and because it is unthinkable, it is impossible to speak about it.

WITTGENSTEIN: "We cannot think what we cannot think; so what we cannot think we cannot say either."[13]

1ST SPEAKER: That is how Wittgenstein formulates the "borderline situation" that results in the representation of reality for science. And in the treatise or "proceeding"—his "Tractatus Logico-Philosophicus"—he then examines the *sayable* sentences and specifies the conditions under which sentences are sayable, which also signifies: "meaningful." He calls those sentences "models" of reality.[14]

2ND SPEAKER: The term "model," incidentally, is one that we also encounter in modern physics in which, for instance, the model of the atom is an object of discussion. In physics that term has also been chosen, in order to make it evident that the description of the atom has nothing to do with the atom itself, that the logical form is the only correspondence between representation and the reality that representation is unable to grasp, as Wittgenstein would say.

1ST SPEAKER: Once again, let us remember Wittgenstein's thesis that the logical form, with which we can describe the facts of the world, does not belong to the facts of the world, that with its help something can be said meaningfully, but that it is the limit of the sayable and coincides with the limit of the world—

---

13 *TLP*, §5.61.

14 Bachmann is making reference here to Wittgenstein's "picture theory of language." According to the *TLP*, "We picture facts to ourselves" (§2.01), and "a picture is a model of reality" (§2.12). A linguistic proposition, then, "is a picture of reality" and therefore "a model of reality as we imagine it" (§4.01).

2ND SPEAKER: —but not with the limit of reality as such.

1ST SPEAKER: And "limit of my world" means "limit of my language."[15] For our reach extends only to the point that is attained by our language, according to which we accurately represent and depict *how* the world is.

CRITIC: Allow me to summarize the arguments that have been put forward so far: I believe that we are dealing here with a strictly empiricist, positivist, rationalistic philosophy, which employs an analytical method developed on the basis of modern logic. Above all, its theses illuminate the relationship between philosophy and natural science. In the history of philosophy from antiquity to the present, we encounter similar trends time and again, but whereas in earlier centuries a neat separation had not yet been realized between philosophy and natural science, in our own century, it has come about almost on its own as a result of the progressive specialization of the individual sciences. A number of questions, the answers to which were once sought by using philosophical, speculative methods, have long since been overcome. Psychology, physics, biology have provided the answers to these. For philosophy, this was a progressive loss of terrain, but one that by no means became cognizant to all philosophers. However, that it occurred is beyond doubt. And at that moment, a Neopositivist school entered the fray, accepting the consequences both deliberately and radically, declaring that what we had been accustomed to calling philosophy was, on the one hand, natural science in disguise and, on the other, could either be unmasked by psychology as anthropomorphic or by the new forms of logic as grammatically or syntactically meaningless empty talk.

With respect to the term "meaningless empty talk," the "Vienna Circle," the think tank of the Viennese Neopositivists, applied "pseudo-sentences" to the metaphysics of the historical systems as well as to more modern ones. But what seems to be the question is whether it is possible to shelve Western metaphysics in all of its forms from one day to the next, manifold and contradictory as they might appear, for the sole reason that some regard it as impossible to answer the questions it raises.

1ST SPEAKER: The Neopositivists did not allege that metaphysics was impossible because its questions could not be answered. That would have been the viewpoint of the older empiricists and positivists, who erred in turning empiricism into an ideology, one that contained its own metaphysics, roughly that the world as it is presented to us experientially be-

15 See *TLP*, §5.6: "*The limits of my language* mean the limits of my world."

comes absolute as reality. In Neopositivism or logical positivism, on the other hand, an attempt was made to formulate the questions that have arisen in philosophy since its inception in a meaningful way, or if that was not possible, to eliminate the questions altogether. For what cannot be the subject of a meaningful question cannot fundamentally be the subject of a meaningful answer.

In the process, "pseudo-propositions," "pseudo-problems" were encountered in metaphysics, such as the problem of the ideality or reality of the world, the problem of the intellect and the problem of God, which cannot inherently be solved. And those problems were eliminated from philosophy. A sentence, for example, that asserts the reality or ideality of the world, does not, after all, represent a fact; like all statements of the same sort, it serves a very different purpose. It expresses an awareness of being alive. It is shaped by our emotional and intentional attitudes towards our environment, towards the universe, towards our fellow human beings, towards the tasks in our lives. That is why metaphysics holds such great value for many people. But the awareness of life can also find expression through artistic creativity. In that sense, metaphysics is related to the work of art. However, in metaphysics the sense of life finds expression in a structured set of propositions that seem to be linked to one another in logical relationships, logical derivations; and thus a theoretical content is assumed. A work of art does not tender arguments. Metaphysics, however, proposes arguments and insists that it imparts insights. But what is capable of imparting insights will never be anything but a scientific sentence, even when it makes its appearance in the guise of a metaphysical one.

2ND SPEAKER: Wittgenstein's stance is marked by a hostility toward metaphysics. From one sentence to the next, the *Tractatus* insists on a sharp, tidy separation of genuine propositions and pseudo-propositions: representation and depiction of the world must be left to the natural sciences, and wherever ambiguities and vagueness exist, logical analysis steps in to establish clarity. That is now philosophy's task. And it is no longer traditional forms of empiricism and positivism, with their faith in science and in the world as an ideology and a method, but little more than method. No longer is there an attempt to interpret the world in one way or another; reality is deliberately left untouched and "undetermined," because it is no longer in our power to define its character. If we can represent objects accurately and in a practical way, then questions about "essence" and "appearance" become irrelevant, since they do not help us advance by even a single step and indeed they have often been a hindrance, leading to useless or erroneous results in the empirical sciences. And yet for Wittgenstein, who shares that neutral attitude—one might also contend, unphilosophical attitude—towards the world with other Neopositivists, one question still remains: what have we accomplished with an accurate and usable representation and depiction of the world? And he gives us his answer on one of the closing pages of the *Tractatus*, an answer that allows us to comprehend the adventure upon which this book has embarked: "Nothing at all."

WITTGENSTEIN: "*How* things are in the world is a matter of complete indifference for what is higher. . . . It is not *how* things are in the world that is mystical, but *that* it exists."[16]

2ND SPEAKER: Wittgenstein strikes a new chord with that aphorism, one that he sustains to the end of the book and that reveals the problematic nature of his mode of thinking, hostile as it is to conundrums. The assertion of the worthlessness of our knowledge of "*how* the world is" is directed in equal measure against positivism, that is to say against Wittgenstein's own philosophical inquiry, and against metaphysics, which strives to explore the essence of things, searching for the absolute, true character of the world and of objects beyond their modes of appearance. That assertion refers to the incomprehensibility of the fact *that* the world exists at all, calling it quite unabashedly by the name: "the mystical"—a word with a limitless field of meaning, laden with doubtful and undoubtful experiences.

CRITIC: Will you permit me to ask what significance the mystical has to Wittgenstein? Is that assertion not disturbingly reminiscent of Heidegger's question, surely a meaningless one in the Wittgensteinian sense: "Why are there essents, why is there anything at all, rather than nothing?"[17] Is Heidegger's speechlessness in the face of being not also Wittgenstein's speechlessness? Do the positivist and the philosopher of being not end up in the same aporia?

2ND SPEAKER: The experience underlying Heidegger's mysticism of being may be similar to the one that prompts Wittgenstein to speak of the mystical. But it would be impossible for Wittgenstein to pose the Heideggerian question, since he denies what Heidegger presupposes, i.e., that in the process of thinking, being enters language. Where Heidegger's philosophical inquiry begins, Wittgenstein's ends. For, as the final sentence of the *Tractatus Logico-Philosophicus* reveals:

16 *TLP*, §6.432 and §6.44.

17 Heidegger, *Introduction to Metaphysics*, 1. As noted above, the word "essents" is a translation of the German *Seiendes*, meaning "existents" or "things that are."

WITTGENSTEIN: "What we cannot speak about we must pass over in silence."[18]

2ND SPEAKER: To speak of the "meaning" of being is impossible, according to Wittgenstein's theses, for there is no meaning in a world that can only be represented, described—but not explained. In order to be able to explain the world, we would have to be able to position ourselves outside the world, we would have to be able, in his words, "to make propositions about the propositions of the world," as the metaphysicians fondly think they are able to do. Besides propositions that speak about facts, they also have propositions of a second order that speak *about* the propositions pertaining to facts. They accomplish a conferral of meaning. Wittgenstein rejects those attempts rigorously. If there were meaning in the world, then that meaning would be without meaning, because in that case it would belong to the facts, to what is representable among other representable things, equal in rank to the latter, an object of knowledge like other objects and thus worthless. For:

WITTGENSTEIN: "How things are in the world is a matter of complete indifference for what is higher. The sense of the world must lie outside the world. In the world everything is as it is, and everything happens as it does happen:. . . ."[19]

CRITIC: If we do not elicit an answer to the question, which we are accustomed to ask of philosophy, the question about the "meaning of being," if we are left to our own devices with respect to that question, because thinking and language fall short for us, how will the questions of ethics, which are so closely related to it, be answered? For ethical norms, the "thou-shalt" propositions and the values we apply to give us direction, are also propositions of the second order and anchored in metaphysics. But if a reality of the second order, one in which the designation of meaning and the moral law governing our lives are rooted, is denied, then ethics in its entirety would be jettisoned by Neopositivist philosophy, and the zero point would have been attained in Western thought, the realization of an absolute nihilism, one that not even Nietzsche, the eradicator of traditional Western value systems, was able to conceive.

18 *TLP*, §7.

19 *TLP*, §6.432 and §6.41. The quote ends: "*in* [the world] no value exists—and if it did exist, it would have no value."

1ST SPEAKER: Wittgenstein's philosophy is of course a negative philosophy, and he could have called his *Tractatus*, in the spirit of Nicholas of Cusa, *De docta ignorantia* [On Learned Ignorance]. For what we are able to articulate is without value, and we are unable to speak about the realm where that value is rooted. Thus—he infers—we cannot articulate any true and verifiable sentence of ethics either:

WITTGENSTEIN: "Ethics is transcendental."[20]

2ND SPEAKER: With that, Wittgenstein implies that the moral form, which does not belong to the facts of the world, is analogous to the logical form. It can no longer be represented, but it manifests itself. Like the logical form, with the help of which we depict the world, it is the limit of the world, one that we cannot cross. And he continues:

WITTGENSTEIN: "The solution to the riddle of life in space and time can only lie outside space and time."[21]

2ND SPEAKER: And, once again, we arrive at the decisive sentence:

WITTGENSTEIN: "For how things are in the world is a matter of complete indifference for what is higher. *God does not reveal himself in the world.*"[22]

1ST SPEAKER: It is the most bitter sentence in the *Tractatus*, echoing Hölderlin's verse, "The gods, ah, how little they heed us!"[23] But much more precisely, it suggests that God remains the hidden, the *deus abscon-*

---

20 *TLP*, §6.421. See also Wittgenstein's *Lecture on Ethics*: "Ethics . . . is a document of a tendency in the human mind which I personally cannot help respecting deeply and I would not for my life ridicule it." Ludwig Wittgenstein, "A Lecture on Ethics," *The Philosophical Review* 74, no. 1 (1965): 12.

21 *TLP*, §6.4312. Bachmann modifies the quote slightly. The original is as follows: "The solution of the riddle of life in space and time lies outside space and time."

22 *TLP*, §6.432. Bachmann's emphasis. The original is as follows: "*How* things are in the world is a matter of complete indifference for what is higher. God does not reveal himself in the world."

23 The actual quote, from "Brot und Wein" (Bread and Wine), runs: "Endlessly there they [the gods] act and, such is their kind wish to spare us, / Little they seem to care whether we live or do not." Friedrich Hölderlin, "Bread and Wine," in *Poems and Fragments*, trans. Michael Hamburger (Ann Arbor: University of Michigan Press, 1967), 248–49.

ditus, who does not reveal himself in a world that we can depict in a formal schema. That the world can be articulated—thus depicted—that the sayable is possible is only due to the unsayable, the mystical, the limit, or whatever we choose to call it.

2ND SPEAKER: When discussing Wittgenstein's theory of language, which concerns the representation of the world, we called attention to its connection to the analytical method in effect since the beginning of Western thought and to the empiricist and rationalistic attributes of his philosophy. And today we witness the significant influence of the "positive" part of the *Tractatus* on the development of modern thought in the last few decades, especially in the Anglo-Saxon countries, in which it has become the "Bible," as it were, of the scientific methodological thinking of our time.

But what is the context in which we are to place the other component of Wittgensteinian thought, his desperate wrestling with the inexpressible, the unsayable?

1ST SPEAKER: Because of his efforts in that area, Wittgenstein should perhaps be identified as *the* great representative thinker of our age, since he found modes of expression for the two extreme tendencies in Western intellectual currents. He stands at the pinnacle of contemporary scientific thought, the thought that accompanies the development of technology and the natural sciences and leads the way for it; and yet it is he who tells us, citing a passage from Nestroy: "Progress has in general the feature that it looks much greater than it really is."[24] That is why the other component of his philosophy, the mystical one, which aims to overcome the scientific mode of thought, touches us so deeply.

2ND SPEAKER: We do not think that we are too far afield in referencing Pascal as a precursor for a thinker who combined both components. Wittgenstein, following a precise ideal for twentieth-century science, is the philosopher to whom Pascal would be more likely to attribute the "esprit de la géométrie" than to any other thinker after himself. But can we also attribute to him the "esprit de finesse"?[25] For Pascal, it is the combination of those two intellectual forms that constitutes the great thinker; without the "mysticism of the heart," which stands before or behind thought as a

24 Johann Nestroy, *Der Schützling* [The Protégé], in *Gesammelte Werke*, ed. Otto Rommel, 6 vols. (Vienna: Schroll, 1962), vol. 4, 10. This quote served as the motto for Wittgenstein's *Philosophical Investigations*.

25 Blaise Pascal distinguished the rigid, geometric mind (*l'esprit de la géométrie*) from the acute, subtle mind (*l'esprit de finesse*).

mystical experience of reality involving the complete person, a philosophy was "not worth one hour of pain" according to him.[26]

1ST SPEAKER: A harsh verdict, jotted down by Pascal while reading Descartes.

2ND SPEAKER: In order to fathom Wittgenstein's mystical attributes and make them understandable, one must perhaps take a step in a direction that moves beyond his own sparse terms.

WITTGENSTEIN: "God does not reveal himself in the world."[27]

2ND SPEAKER: That is expressed toward the end of the *Tractatus*. What does it mean? It means that the world as the totality of facts, which permits only scientific representation, does not reveal God; that as limited beings in a limited world we cannot establish any proof of the existence of God, because God, after all, is not a fact in the world. And to infer from the lower to the higher order is impossible, since every inference is a logical inference—which is to say a tautology, devoid of content. But:

WITTGENSTEIN: "There are, indeed, things that cannot be put into words. They *make themselves manifest*. They are what is mystical."[28]

1ST SPEAKER: And that is also how we must understand Wittgenstein's treatment of ethics. Values are something "higher," thus they do not belong to the world. Let us listen to his formulation:

WITTGENSTEIN: "There is no value in the world, and if there were, it would have no value."[29]

---

26 See Aphorism #79 in the Brunschvicg Édition, which Pascal himself originally erased: "[Descartes.—We must say, summarily: 'This is made by figure and motion,' for it is true. But to say what these are, and to compose the machine, is ridiculous. For it is useless, uncertain, and painful. And were it true, we do not think all philosophy is worth one hour of pain.]" Blaise Pascal, *Pensées*, in *The Provincial Letters, Pensées, and Scientific Treatises*, trans. W. F. Trotter (Chicago: Encyclopaedia Brittannica, 1952), 186.

27 *TLP*, §6.432. "In" is italicized in the original text.

28 *TLP*, §6.522.

29 *TLP*, §6.41. Bachmann modifies the quote slightly. The original is as follows: "*in* [the world] no value exists—and if it did exist, it would have no value."

2ND SPEAKER: That means: the world is value-neutral; it consists of facts of equal rank, which are as they are, impervious to our will, which we call the agent of the ethical. Yet, the ethical values belong to our existential problems, because they lend the characteristics of good and evil, of the valuable and the valueless to our actions. That cannot be denied, and Wittgenstein never even comes close to denying it. But what he does make clear once and for all is that *science* cannot contribute anything to a resolution of existential problems. We are left to our own devices with respect to these. Indeed, he does not imply that there are no values, that ethics is impossible or that it is impossible to believe in God—he only implies that, strictly speaking, it is impossible to *speak* about all those things. Language can only speak about facts and it constitutes the limit of our world, yours and mine. The transcendence of the world occurs in a realm that language does not attain and that thought does not grasp. It occurs where something "*makes* itself manifest," and what makes itself manifest is the mystical, the inexpressible experience—

1ST SPEAKER: the experience not of the empiricist but of the mystic.

2ND SPEAKER: Wittgenstein's creed is thus a negative one, given that he cannot express it. However, the closing sentences of the *Tractatus* suffice to let us deduce it.

WITTGENSTEIN: "We feel that even when all *possible* scientific questions have been answered, the problems of life remain completely untouched. Of course there are then no questions left, and this itself is the answer.

"The solution to the problem of life is seen in the vanishing of the problem.

"(Is not this the reason why those who have found after a long period of doubt that the sense of life became clear to them have been unable to say what constituted that sense?)"[30]

1ST SPEAKER: And so the book arrives at conclusions that the other positivist scientists greeted with a lack of understanding.

WITTGENSTEIN: "The correct method in philosophy would really be the following: to say nothing except what can be said, i.e., propositions of natural science—i.e., something that has nothing to do with philosophy—and then, whenever someone else wanted to say something metaphysical, to demonstrate to him that he had failed to give a meaning to certain

30 *TLP*, §6.52–§6.521.

signs in his propositions. Although it would not be satisfying to the other person—he would not have the feeling that we were teaching him philosophy—this method would be the only strictly correct one.

"My propositions serve as elucidations in the following way: anyone who understands me eventually recognizes them as nonsensical, when he has used them—as steps—to climb up beyond them. (He must, so to speak, throw away the ladder after he has climbed up it.)

"He must transcend these propositions, and then he will see the world aright."[31]

1ST SPEAKER: Does Wittgenstein not reach the same conclusion as Pascal? Let us listen to what the author of the *Pensées* says 300 years earlier: "The last proceeding of reason is to recognize that there is an infinity of things which are beyond it."[32]

2ND SPEAKER: Wittgenstein took that last step of reason. He who asserts, "God does not reveal Himself in the world," also asserts implicitly, "Vere tu es deus absconditus."[33] For what else would there be to be silent about, if not about that which transcends the boundaries—about the hidden God, about the realms of ethics and aesthetics as mystical experiences of the heart, which ensue in the dimension of the unsayable? These are encompassed by the pronouncement: "What we cannot speak about we must pass over in silence." Being silent about something does not simply mean being silent. Negative silence would be agnosticism—positive silence mysticism.

1ST SPEAKER: That interpretation of Wittgensteinian silence admittedly goes beyond what he himself said; but we regard the conclusion as legitimate in order to make the *Tractatus* understandable, also because Wittgenstein's life gives us an indication about all those things that he thought could only be accomplished in silence.

Ludwig Wittgenstein enveloped himself in silence all his life; it would be difficult to put it in any other way, puzzling as it might be that a man in the public eye, certain of fame and prominence, could so successfully withdraw from his generation that he eluded it. In 1919 he published the *Tractatus Logico-Philosophicus* in Vienna,[34] where a few years later,

---

31 *TLP*, §6.53–§6.54.

32 Pascal, *Pensées*, 221–22, Aphorism 267.

33 "Truly you are a God who hides himself": Pascal, *Pensées*, 221–22, Aphorism 242. Pascal quotes Isaiah 45:15.

34 Bachmann's publication date is inaccurate; see note 3.

inspired by his thinking, Moritz Schlick initiated the "Vienna Circle." While the Vienna Neopositivist school, which was almost exclusively based upon Wittgenstein's sublime intellectual endeavors on the subjects of modern logic and philosophy of science, even though his mystical "caprices" were regarded with suspicion, gained increasingly more international acclaim, Wittgenstein never surfaced; he avoided the debates, refused opportunities to lecture at universities, and finally moved to Lower Austria, where he lived for years as a village schoolteacher, years for which no one can give an account. He "quit" philosophy. For "racial" reasons he had to leave Austria in 1938, and he turned to England, where he succeeded G. E. Moore as a professor of philosophy at Cambridge. With respect to his remaining years, we know that he gathered a small circle of students around himself; they report that he lived in a shack and tolerated only a simple chair in it as the single piece of furnishing. Hence, legend had superseded his life even while he was still living—a legend of voluntary poverty, of an attempt at a saintly life,[35] the attempt to live in obedience to the sentence which concludes the *Tractatus*:

WITTGENSTEIN: "What we cannot speak about we must pass over in silence."[36]

2ND SPEAKER: Not until after Wittgenstein's death in 1951 did a genuine interest in his work and person begin. In Germany, it was Ewald Wasmuth who called attention to him and in an essay expressed hope, as a Christian philosopher, that in his final writings, news with respect to the existence of which was reported from England, Wittgenstein might have taken the step beyond silence towards affirmation. It was the time during which mention was made of the philosopher's *Blue Book* and of *Philosophical Investigations*—of an extensive legacy of works that would give us a more comprehensive impression of his thinking.[37] Last year a posthumous work did in fact appear in England under the title *Philosophical Investigations*, edited in large part by the philosopher. In a preface, he explains this "re-entry" into the philosophical discipline:

---

35 Bachmann gives the impression that Wittgenstein only came to England and took an academic appointment in 1938 after the Nazis took control of Austria; however, his stint as an elementary school teacher ended in 1927 and he taught in Cambridge from 1929 onwards. After the *Anschluss*, he was unable to return to Vienna, and he became a British citizen at that point.

36 *TLP*, §7.

37 The *Philosophical Investigations* were first published in 1953, two years after Wittgenstein's death. The *Blue and Brown Books*, also called *Preliminary Studies for the Philosophical Investigations*, were not published until 1958.

WITTGENSTEIN: "Until recently I had really given up the idea of publishing my work in my lifetime. All the same, it was revived from time to time: mainly because I could not help noticing that the results of my work (which I had conveyed in lectures, typescripts and discussions), were in circulation, frequently misunderstood and more or less watered down or mangled. This stung my vanity, and I had difficulty in quieting it."[38]

1ST SPEAKER: And speaking about the *Philosophical Investigations* themselves, he continues in another passage:

WITTGENSTEIN: "I make them public with misgivings. It is not impossible that it should fall to the lot of this work, in its poverty and in the darkness of this time, to bring light into one brain or another—but, of course, it is not likely.

"I should not like my writing to spare other people the trouble of thinking. But if possible, to stimulate someone to thoughts of his own.

"I should have liked to produce a good book. It has not turned out that way, but the time is past in which I could improve it."[39]

2ND SPEAKER: Whether this book could have turned out better is a question we shall have to leave unanswered. In the form in which it is available, as a conglomerate of thought paradigms, it presents a number of difficulties. Again, systematic coherence is lacking. Rather, we are drawn into a Socratic dialogue that touches on many things; hence, Wittgenstein's intention is not immediately apparent to us. It seems to progress without a set purpose—and he asserts, for instance:

WITTGENSTEIN: "I can know what someone else is thinking, not what I am thinking. It is correct to say 'I know what you are thinking', and wrong to say 'I know what I am thinking.'"[40]

2ND SPEAKER: We chose this example, because it is accompanied by a decisive commentary, an exclamation that could follow every one of the examples:

WITTGENSTEIN: "(A whole cloud of philosophy condenses into a drop of grammar!)"[41]

---

38 *PI*, 4e.

39 *PI*, 4e.

40 *PI*, "Philosophy of Psychology—A Fragment," xi, §315, 233e.

41 *PI*, "Philosophy of Psychology—A Fragment," xi, §315, 233e.

1ST SPEAKER: And with that we have found his purpose, the same that figures openly in the *Tractatus*: to show that the problems of philosophy are problems of language, that it is the failures of language that create philosophical problems. That is why in *Philosophical Investigations*—expanding on the *Tractatus*—he sets about giving examples of the proper or improper functioning of language in order to show us the difference between proper and improper thinking. For:

WITTGENSTEIN: "language itself is the vehicle of thought."[42]

2ND SPEAKER: Previously, in the *Tractatus* we can read:

WITTGENSTEIN: "Philosophy does not result in 'philosophical propositions', but rather in the clarification of propositions."[43]

2ND SPEAKER: In *Philosophical Investigations* that clearer understanding of propositions is to be achieved on a large scale. The control begins with the sentences of everyday language, with a perception of his sole philosophical ideal: total clarity. Here is how he himself understands it:

WITTGENSTEIN: "But this simply means that the philosophical problems should completely disappear."[44]

1ST SPEAKER: It is Wittgenstein's conviction that philosophy must be brought to rest, so that it ceases to be "lashed" by questions that call *its own essence* into question, and he believes that we can silence the problems if our language functions well and meaningfully, if, in its *application*, it lives and breathes. Only when language, which is a form of life, is taken out of use, when it becomes idle—and that is what it does, in his opinion, when it is used in philosophizing in the traditional sense—only then do problems arise.[45] These problems are not to be solved, but eliminated.

Thus, the investigations actually move in the sphere of the *Tractatus*, but they expand on it with detailed analyses for every facet. They quit the realm of abstraction and provide images. Language is now no longer

42 *PI*, §329, 113e.

43 *TLP*, §4.112.

44 *PI*, §133, 56e. As before, Bachmann omits Wittgenstetin's emphasis on the word "completely."

45 Wittgenstein writes: "For philosophical problems arise when language *goes on holiday*." *PI*, §38, 23e.

termed a system of signs—which of course it remains—but compared instead to an old city in its manifold nature. It can also be viewed—as:

WITTGENSTEIN: "A maze of little streets and squares, of old and new houses, of houses with extensions from various periods, and all this surrounded by a multitude of new suburbs with straight and regular streets and uniform houses."[46]

1ST SPEAKER: And since language is a maze of paths—as he calls it in another passage—philosophy must join in the fray against the blighting of our intellect by means of language. Philosophy must destroy castles in the air and uncover the foundation of language; it must be comparable to a therapy, for philosophical problems are diseases that must be cured. Not a solution, but a cure is what is called for.

Thus philosophy has to accomplish a paradoxical task: the elimination of philosophy.

CRITIC: Like the *Tractatus*, the *Philosophical Investigations* also yield a particularly peculiar outcome. They intend to abolish what we have practiced as philosophy for millennia in the most diverse forms. And they intend to achieve that by investing positivism with the authority to render a conclusive description of the world, but also by throwing it on the scrap heap as a worldview and a philosophy that explains the world, together with all other philosophies that ask questions about being and existence. But to me, a crucial point seems to lie in the fact that after the elimination or dismissal of the kind of problems that are designated as "existential concerns," those same problems persist nevertheless, because it is human nature to question and to see in reality more than the positive and the rational, which in Wittgenstein's opinion does not constitute all of reality. And many among us will remain unsatisfied with this definition, however indisputable, of the knowable and the unknowable, of positive science and the boundaries that take place in the metaphysical subject as logical and ethical forms, but which can no longer be articulated. Though Wittgenstein may have pursued silence in a positive way, perhaps even making positive acts apparent by displaying the great virtues of the thinker in his works—intellectual integrity and reverence for a reality inaccessible to human understanding: what he bequeaths to us is a vacuum, a metaphysical realm devoid of all content.

1ST SPEAKER: That is certainly true. But what you call a vacuum is open to genuine beliefs. To be sure, there is no longer any room for the bat-

46 *PI*, §18, 11e.

tle of Western metaphysical schools, for a philosophical faith armed with logical arguments against another philosophical faith. But Wittgenstein's failure to profess Christianity, as was expected of him, must not, on the other hand, shake our understanding of the "boundaries," which are not mere boundaries but also fissures through which the epiphanies can enter, the mystically or religiously felt experiences that affect our agencies and exclusions. It is simply that there is no room in his work for a profession of faith, since it cannot be articulated, rather it would already renounce that work, once articulated. And besides, Wittgenstein, as passionate as Spinoza before him, probably wanted to *liberate God from the stigma of addressability.*[47]

2ND SPEAKER: We must look to the historical situation in which Wittgenstein found himself in order to understand the reason for his stance. His silence may very well be regarded as a protest against the distinctive anti-rationalism of the age, against the metaphysically diseased mode of Western thinking, particularly the German variety, which revels in laments over the loss of meaning and appeals for metanoia, in prognoses of decline, transition, and rise of the West, pitting trends of anti-rationalist thought against the "perilous" positive sciences and a technology "running amok," in order to consign humanity to a persistent primitive state of mind.

And silence can also be regarded as a protest against the tendencies of our age that place implicit faith in science and progress, against the know-nothing attitude toward "total reality," frequently prevailing in the Neopositivist school, which took its cue from Wittgenstein's work, and among the scientist thinkers who were the school's intellectual partners.

Wittgenstein was once deemed Janus-faced by a Viennese philosopher, and it is true that he understood better than anyone else the dangers of the heightening antagonisms in the thinking of his century: irrationalism and rationalism, which he withstood and overcame in his work. Of course, he arrived without a petty prescription for a much sought-after synthesis, but with the one for a cure—as a therapist.

WITTGENSTEIN: "We feel that when all possible scientific questions have been answered, the problems of life remain completely untouched. Of course there are then no questions left, and this itself is the answer."[48]

---

47 See Spinoza's, *Ethics* (1677), § I, Proposition 17, where he writes: "So there can be nothing outside [God] by which he is determined or compelled to act. Therefore, God acts from the laws of his nature alone, and is compelled by no one, q.e.d." Benedict de Spinoza, *Ethics*, ed. and trans. Edwin Curley (London: Penguin, 1996), 13.

48 *TLP*, §6.52. In the original, "all possible" is underscored.

3: Modern Literature

Commentary

FROM THE TIME OF her earliest attempts to compose literature in the early and mid-1940s, Bachmann was passionately focused on whether society could successfully transform itself after the defeat of the Nazi regime. Her personal vision of art was linked to a peaceful Europe, one that would aspire to political maturity and social justice and one in which literature would play a more decisive role for the collective than in the past. Although the collapse of European fascism in 1945 seemed to inaugurate a period of sustained prosperity, the author's personal experience of the war years motivated her literary reflections on a legacy of violence, which Bachmann saw as an unremitting threat to the new order. Her distinctive reading of fascism, not as an aberration in the ideological disposition of a political collective, but as the nucleus of the relationship between the sexes, informs her literary works and clearly pervades her critical thinking.[1] Bachmann's concept of private fascism has significance for an Austrian, who did not live long enough to experience any redress for the corrosive legacy of collective fascism in her native country. Since admissions of culpability for Nazi crimes did not take place in Austria until the late 1980s, many years after her death, Bachmann claimed that fascism endured in the private domain long after denazification in West German public life had taken place.

The author's focus on latent and explicit injustices also led her to correlate pre-war persecution and postwar devastation with numerous instances of human cruelty in the long history of Western culture. Steeped in historical and cultural allusions, Bachmann's texts can be compared to the layers in an archaeological dig, in which multiple examples of human malevolence appear stratified over time—from the atrocities of Greek mythology cited in her poems and the funerary cult of Egyptian antiquity in the *Franza* fragment to the Siberian tortures featured in the second chapter of *Malina*. When reading her texts, we quickly sense an overwhelming longing for peace. According to Bachmann, peace lays the groundwork for a utopian language, much as a utopian language, once realized, lays the groundwork for a civilization sustained in peace.

---

1 See Bachmann, *Gespräche und Interviews*, 144.

Intrinsically just and pure, Bachmann's concept of utopian language propels literature beyond a random "conglomeration of things past and things inherited." On the contrary, great literary works call upon an inventory of signs from "a realm of unknown boundaries, both open-ended and forward-looking." Prophetically, Bachmann insists that the blank page is a promise of what is to come, arguing that, given the right intention, every page harbors the potential to become great literature or, at the very least, a splendid text. The task of the writer, whose merit can only be measured against the constellation of signs on the page, is to connect what was with what is and what will be. "Without admitting it, the writer constantly campaigns for admission to the fellowship of 'literature,' and even if he is never informed as to whether permanent membership has been granted to him—he hopes for it and never abandons that hope." The manifestation of that hope is a "great book" resounding with the beauty of words grounded in infinite truth. "Great books do not put the less great ones or the worthless ones to shame, since they come into being on another planet. But without those books, literature would only be a conglomeration of written texts, for they are so necessary that it is self-evident that they have to come about."

While Bachmann's most haunting texts are routinely steeped in historical, religious, or philosophical traditions, her sensitivity to the legacy of great books was closely aligned with a literary crisis in the postwar era. Fueled by Theodor W. Adorno's indictment of the poetic medium after the tragedy of Auschwitz, many European writers were challenged to find a language that would allow the literary arts to flourish after 1945. Closely paralleling her aspirations for a utopian literature, Bachmann also affirmed a deep appreciation for the purity of the word, insisting that cultural "misconceptions" need to be overcome before the word can ring true and be "beautiful." Forced to confront prevailing attitudes about the potency of fascist ideals in the post-war era, the dubious morals fueling the "economic miracle" in Europe, and the treacherous relationship between the sexes and the generations in the postwar era, Bachmann cited existential threats as the greatest deterrent to social advancement. In an interview conducted shortly before her tragic death in October 1973, she alluded to the dangers undermining an apparently well-ordered existence, asserting that "for many thousands of years (existence) has been consistently destroyed." Absent the hope for a nonviolent collective, the impetus for a new literature is lost: "I truly believe in something, and I call that 'a day will come'. . . if I can no longer believe in it, then I can no longer write."[2] Astute and visionary, Bachmann defined the fundamentals of modern literature as a radicalism extending well beyond the arrangement of signs on the page. She offered an example of what she was looking for

2 Bachmann, *Gespräche und Interviews*, 145.

in a short essay praising the role of silence in the works of her Austrian colleague Thomas Bernhard: "when the questions about what constitutes modernity, what is new, fall silent, then, without a doubt, that means that it cannot be read on the surface, is not an experiment in arranging letters on the page, not a calligraphic test of courage, but a radicalism embedded in a way of thinking and extending to the limits."

Bachmann's notion of "extending to the limits" or advancing to the periphery of what language can articulate accentuated how the stigmata of the human condition redefine collective visions. Not only with respect to language as form, but also to reality as content, she demanded that literature combat the underlying weaknesses of Western societies. Bachmann's fixation on physical and moral transgressions was intended to raise the level of awareness for cultural decay and to instill moral values into postwar art. In a similar vein, she extolled the works of Bertolt Brecht. Bachmann suggests that Brecht, surely one of the most influential authors of the twentieth century, "never ceased to think grandly, from the lowliest to the most resplendent of words," and since he "had the resplendent words in the right places, he had a share, as I once tried to say, in utopia, in the millennial struggle against flawed language."

Although Bachmann substantiates how modern texts, owing to their radicalism, propel language to its limits, they are, by the same token, artifacts or missives from previous centuries. Analogous to phantasmagorias and ghosts, great literature is embedded in a memorial space in which new words arise out of the confluence of timeworn texts and non-literary factors, as something more than simply aesthetically pleasing arrangements of signifiers on the page. Drawing attention to representations of reality, Bachmann's insistence on the unity of sign, image, and sound foreshadows a desire to capture numerous gradations of meaning. To that end, reality can only be experienced in a visionary language grounded in experience, "as if language itself could drive knowledge home and reveal an experience the writer has never had. Where it is only toyed with to produce a novel feeling, it soon takes revenge and unmasks the intention."

Consequently, Bachmann blurs traditional distinctions between literature and more formal genres of memory, specifically chronicle and historical narrative, making her works a study of what a new cultural order should aspire to be and, perhaps even more persuasively, what it should avoid becoming at all costs. From her early years on, she seemed disquieted by the fact that collective aspirations were bound up with commercial success and, in spite of the proliferation of new knowledge in modernity, with an unfortunate disposition to eschew intellectual depth and compromise moral standards. To substantiate her point, in the last of her five Frankfurt Lectures she juxtaposes the nineteenth century against the twentieth, describing how the proliferation of superficial communication and arbitrary meanings had negatively impacted the social order. "In the twentieth century, a previously inconceivable, frenzied fever curve of criteria has superseded the succession of changing views and standards, which had progressed so slowly until the end of the nineteenth century that there was still time to view them individually. Each of them left its mark, whereas now the only constant, as if in mockery, seems to be commercial success." Conceding that the new century had been enriched by its forerunner, she warns that this enrichment also led to a loss of stability:

> The state of affairs, which was bound to appear and which comes to us from the nineteenth century, has made us richer, to be sure, than any generation before us, but also less stable and more endangered, more vulnerable to arbitrary meanings. For today we are familiar with not only the literature of all peoples, even including that of Africa; we are also aware of the existence of all grammars, treatises on poetics and rhetoric, aesthetics, and all of the prospects for law and form in literature.

At the same time, and perhaps as the result of her call for a cathartic spirit after 1945, Bachmann counted on postwar authors to articulate an uneasy legacy of perpetrators and victims. For, having survived the war years herself, she never doubted that enduring antagonisms would bleed into the new order. This is the sociocultural fabric in which the *Todesarten* project is embedded, a framework affirming assumptions about how postwar societies gave preference to old forms of brutality over new models of lasting peace. Specifically, the texts of the unfinished cycle of novels depict circumstances in which women are destroyed by the men closest to them, circumstances that fed on fascist values, most notably Leo Jordan's exploitation of his wife in the *Franza* fragment and the father figure's systematic abuse of his daughter as recounted in the dream chapter of *Malina*, which opens with the ominous image of "the cemetery of the murdered daughters." Emphasizing the historical plight of women, these tragedies are best understood in the context of the author's statements near the end of her life in which she argued that the origins of fascism lie "in the relationship between a man and a woman."[3] Above all, Bachmann's nuanced notions of the cultural violence that women have sustained in the course of civilization lend her works political relevance.

In a political sense, Bachmann pointed to the origins of language, constantly accentuating her distrust of any vernacular that reiterates deceptive ideals and transmits cultural misconceptions from one generation to the next. Arguing that authors must stake a strong moral claim, she derided literature that obscures facts and affirmed that a new spirit can only be found in an emphatic desire to represent reality. Accordingly, she

3 Bachmann, *Gespräche und Interviews*, 144.

was adamant that the author fix language "within the framework of the limits drawn" and "make it alive again with ritual, give it a gait that it does not receive anywhere else except in the literary work of art." Bachmann's ritual prompts her readers to experience "beauty, to feel beauty," rather than "aesthetic satisfaction." Her devotion to ritual, to a celebration of beauty in literature, fuses the task of the writer with collective hopes for humankind in general and individual dreams in particular.

> Literature, which is itself unable to say what it is and only reveals itself as a thousand-fold and multi-millennial infraction against flawed language—for life only has a flawed language—and which therefore confronts it with a utopia of language; this literature, then, however closely it might cling to the age and its flawed language, must be praised for desperately and incessantly striving toward this utopia. Only for that reason is it a source of splendor and hope for humankind. Its most vulgar languages and its most pretentious ones still share in a dream of language; every word, every syntax, every period, punctuation, metaphor, and symbol redeem something of our dream of expression, a dream that is never entirely to be realized.

The mechanics of seeking what might have been lost or what remains deeply hidden within the continuum of cultural memory is only one of the many challenges addressed in this chapter, featuring a selection of Bachmann's critical writings on Franz Kafka, Robert Musil, Marcel Proust, Sylvia Plath, Thomas Bernhard, and Bertolt Brecht. Validating how their literary achievements write traces of the past into the present and reflect diverse facets of collective memory, the author points out that great literature transcends all periods—past, present, and future. The technique of blending periods is perhaps most pronounced in Proust's and Musil's mammoth novels, signature achievements stemming from the politically unstable two decades between the two world wars. These writers were masterful in conveying how the old world of the nineteenth century had lost its bearings and the new world of the twentieth had entered a void, a space in which all that was once functional has fallen into disarray. Kafka undoubtedly belongs in this gallery of early-twentieth-century authors, and Bachmann's radio essay on his novel *Amerika* closes with an appreciation of the author's innate gift for using language to represent a "nonfunctional" modernity: "it is precisely the pure, clear language, which almost pedantically does justice to even the paltriest things, that makes the 'nonfunctioning' evident, and indeed the magic of Kafka's work would be inexplicable without the peculiar phenomenon of his language and its method of representation."

Also programmatic for Bachmann's statements about utopian literature is the desolation weighing heavily on individuals in modernity, aptly illustrated in her affinity for the precarious existences of modern literary figures. Like the narrator of her celebrated short story "The Thirtieth Year," many of these figures "survive by taking up arms against the stock language that transmits hollow stereotypes and disjointed realities," clearly making them vehicles of Bachmann's social criticism: "In your four walls you can cultivate a domestic happiness of the patriarchal style or a libertinage or whatever you want—outside you twirl in a functional world of utility that has its own ideas about your existence." Attributing disjointed realities to her own protagonists, Bachmann also draws attention to the scarred and traumatized characters in the works of other authors. Not only do these figures embody a lack of continuity in the narratives they inhabit, but they also fall prey to the stories in which they ostensibly exercise a pivotal function. Their tendency to derail, to cite Bachmann's term, is what also drew her to Esther Greenwood, the protagonist of Sylvia Plath's novel *The Bell Jar*. In a short essay on the novel Bachmann explains:

> Perhaps *The Bell Jar* has an unfortunate title; its striking trait in the beginning is the almost incredible streak of humor, the comic, infantile, clownish element in this nineteen-year-old Esther Greenwood, a girl with straight A's in school, winning every prize and every scholarship, a girl who slowly derails in New York in a flurry of dinners, parties, pointless kisses, and she derails in such an imperceptible way that even after a third reading you are still asking yourself where that hidden catastrophe started, and how. And I am inclined to consider that factor, like everything that is not verifiable in a book, the best and strangest element.

For Bachmann, literature is almost never read as it should be, for its moral commitment to the plight of its protagonists, but instead as a testing ground for critics and historians who want to prove something significant about existential affairs or metaphysics.

> All of us want to put literature to the test or to demonstrate something with it. Moreover, philosophy, psychiatry, and all manner of disciplines jump on it, and it is forced into legalities or conditions or disclosures with which—and that is astonishing—it complies today, only to contradict them tomorrow. Literary historians—we have become gradually inured to this—break it up into time periods, shading it to match notions of ancient, medieval, and modern. Literary criticism and literary scholarship of a philosophical bent analyze it with respect to metaphysical and ethical problems—but literary scholarship has also resorted to other tools: sociology, psychoanalysis, and art history, not just philosophy—the span is that

> broad. Scholars examine literature with regard to stylistic periods, risking an eidetic assessment or hoping for existential gain.

Plath's genius triumphs over the "eidetic" aspirations of her critics to tell a story with such urgency that it leaves no doubt about its status as art. The question of Plath's genius as a writer "is the only question that never forces itself on the readers, for if someone has a story to tell and has so little time to think about it, everything seems to fall into place all by itself, and all of the simple questions of art are subordinated to that sense of urgency, without resulting in anything other than art, and not the template of artistic adventure, of exhibitionism, of betrayal and self-deception that 'distinguish' almost all new novels and drive the critics, who are becoming more and more timid, into a corner."

Carefully weighing the flaws afflicting Western civilization, Bachmann's utopian approach to postwar literature is particularly ambitious. Not only does her thinking capture the anxieties of European intellectuals in the first decades following the Second World War, but it also recognizes the shattered memories following two world conflagrations and the specter of nuclear destruction in the 1950s. Conflagrations materialize in Bachmann's fictional realm as written, spoken, and even sung traumas. Examples of these traumas can be found in *Malina*, as well as in her earlier prose works, specifically in "A Wildermuth" and "The Thirtieth Year." To this end, she adapts motifs from the archive of Western civilization and matches them to the fragile realities of the postwar era. Inviting her readers to cull traces of traumatic memory, Bachmann requires from them a deep appreciation for symbolic and thematic layering as well as a sympathy for how expertly form and meaning, or subject and object for that matter, lend themselves to deconstruction.

Configuring literary spaces in which the individual succumbs to the violence of the collective, Bachmann asserted that a new language should counteract the past and articulate hope for the future. Only when literature promises to unearth collective memories can a new, appropriate, or even beautiful language attain the legitimacy to confront hard realities. Undeniably, the traumatic content of Bachmann's texts—portrayals of loss, existential *angst*, cruelty, tainted relationships, and "ways of death"—mirrors what Bachmann sought from great literature. She was convinced that a return to the source of all utopian communications, a proper or beautiful language—what she called *"die schöne Sprache"* in place of flawed language or *"die schlechte Sprache"*—would ensure literature's prominence as the harbinger of a peaceful collective. Seen from a broader perspective, Bachmann's approach to literature affirmed that cultural memory after 1945 was as fragile as the new political order confronting postwar European societies.

Franz Kafka: *Amerika*[1]

2ND SPEAKER: "As Karl Rossman, a poor boy of sixteen who had been packed off to America by his parents because a servant girl had seduced him and gotten herself a child by him, was standing on the ship slowly entering the harbor of New York, a sudden burst of sunshine seemed to illuminate the Statue of Liberty, so that he saw it in a new light, although he had already been watching it for a long time. The arm with the sword rose up as if newly stretched aloft, and round the figure blew the free winds of heaven."[2]

1ST SPEAKER: Is that really the opening of a book by Franz Kafka?

2ND SPEAKER: ". . . and round the figure blew the free winds of heaven . . ."

1ST SPEAKER" "Free winds of heaven" are something we never again find in his work, neither before nor after. The novel *Amerika*, recently reissued by S. Fischer in Max Brod's edition, remained an exception. This is what Max Brod has to say:

2ND SPEAKER: "He worked at it with unending delight, mostly in the evenings and late into the night. Kafka knew quite well that this novel was more optimistic and 'lighter' in mood than any of his other writings."[3]

1ST SPEAKER: *Amerika* is indeed a book full of light, even though its young protagonist, who is banished from his home, is also haunted by a "trial"; he is no more successful than Josef K. and K. in the novels *The Trial* and *The Castle*; he is beset with misfortunes and subjected to serious tests. To be sure, on occasion the impression arises that the appearance of humorous, at times almost harmless elements is the result of an optical illusion. The confused world in which Karl Rossmann finds himself is no less terrifying, no less hostile than all of the other worlds conceived by Kafka's magical imagination. For the reader, what appears as total futility and darkness in *The Trial* or in *The Castle* is attributed to Karl's childlike

1 Bachmann's text is a radio script that was aired by Radio Hessen on December 9, 1953. This is also the year in which Kafka's novel was reissued by Max Brod (1884–1968) as an installment of his postwar Kafka edition for S. Fischer Verlag.

2 Franz Kafka (1883–1924), *Amerika*, trans. Willa and Edwin Muir (New York: New Directions, 1946), 1. Translation slightly altered.

3 Max Brod, "Afterword," in Kafka, *Amerika*, 276–77.

innocence. It is almost as if every page makes the reader want to persuade himself: of course, things are not at all as Karl Rossman encounters them. Were he older, more reasonable, more experienced and less gullible, then everything would become clear to him and would return to the most perfect order. In other words: we think that the confusion is not the product of reality, but is owed to his puerile perspective. It is true that Kafka, out of a joy for storytelling, often allows young Karl Rossman to react innocently, even downright foolishly, and some contexts would actually take on a different quality if a "reasonable" person were to encounter them. But it must not be forgotten that it is Rossman's proclivity to blind trust that causes him to slide from one misfortune into the next and determines his approach to the world time and again. When all is said and done, he fares better than the clever people, the shrewd operators. That allows us to surmise that the naiveté of this American world cannot be all that genuine, for as Günther Anders once observed, only chance and women are able to effect change in Kafka's works, never the protagonists' own actions.[4] But that peculiar . . . does not become an urgent theme until he writes the great novels *The Castle* and *The Trial*. There, it is not children but intelligent adult males who confront a world they would be able to come to grips with, but at that point there is no longer a redeeming authority, the hope for an escape, the excuse of a childlike nature. As has already been said, Karl Rossman's struggle for a place in society and for his basic needs is more modest and more impetuous, but not a bit less desperate. And his first insight is articulated in the desperate verdict:

2ND SPEAKER: "It is impossible to defend oneself, where there is no good will."[5]

1ST SPEAKER: Because he does not understand his rights in his inexperience and youth, and would not even know how to use them if he did, he is the only one of the three protagonists in Kafka's three novels who reaches his goal. To be sure, he is not spared anything. He happens to meet his American uncle on the steamer that brings him to New York. Everything seems to come together in a wondrous manner. He is introduced to a new life and to a job in the shipping company that has made his uncle respectable and wealthy—until one day he accepts an invitation to a country estate near New York, an invitation that takes a peculiar turn; instinctively he realizes that his conduct toward his uncle is being tested, he wants to

4 Günther Anders, *Franz Kafka* (London: Bowes and Bowes, 1960), 31–35.

5 Kafka, *Amerika*, 174.

back off before it is too late and is prevented from doing so. He is handed a letter from his uncle.

2ND SPEAKER: "Against my wishes you decided this evening to leave me; stick, then, to that decision all your life."[6]

1ST SPEAKER: Thus begins the boy's life of suffering, the stations of which, while searching for a job, are the road, a hotel, and the dreadful asylum granted by the singer Brunelda, whose tyrannical regime is willingly tolerated by her lover Delamarche and by Robinson, the little Irishman. But everything vile and low repels Karl, and his hope to secure a decent job never diminishes. In Kafka's approach to the world, the hopelessness of which is mostly irredeemable, redemption is sanctioned: in the heavenly and mundane project of the nature theater of Oklahoma, Karl's bitter experiences and disappointments lose their gravity; there, he will be able to forget everything that has previously transpired. The announcement on a recruiting poster for the theater amounts to a promise:

2ND SPEAKER: "The great Theater of Oklahoma calls you! Today only and never again! If you miss your chance now you miss it forever! If you think of your future, you are one of us! Everyone is welcome! If you want to be an artist, join our company! Our Theater can find employment for everyone, a place for everyone! If you decide on an engagement we congratulate you here and now! But hurry, so that you get in before midnight! At twelve o'clock the doors will be shut and never opened again! Down with all those who do not believe in us!"[7]

1ST SPEAKER: The notion that he could be welcome anywhere prompts Karl to sign up; his trust in the possibility of life in a community has never been greater, and armed with that trust he passes the simplest and most difficult test: he is accepted. To be sure, the world persists in its chaotic state as a system of obstacles, but those who have made that choice, like Karl Rossmann, are granted refuge and peace. Evocative of a religious ritual, a banquet unites the new members. They find *the* entrance, in contrast to the man who is told by the gatekeeper in one of Kafka's parables:

6 Kafka, *Amerika*, 85.
7 Kafka, *Amerika*, 252.

2ND SPEAKER: "This gate was made only for you. I am now going to shut it."[8]

1ST SPEAKER: The book closes with the departure for Oklahoma and the view of a pristine landscape.

2ND SPEAKER: "For two days and two nights they journeyed on. Only now did Karl understand how huge America was. Unweariedly he gazed out of the window, and Giacomo persisted in struggling for a place beside him until the other occupants of the compartment, who wanted to play cards, got tired of him and voluntarily surrendered the other window-seat. Karl thanked them—Giacomo's English was not easy for anyone to follow—and in the course of time, as is inevitable among fellow-travelers, they grew much more friendly, although their friendliness was sometimes a nuisance, as for example whenever they ducked down to rescue a card fallen on the floor, they could not resist giving hearty tweaks to Karl's legs or Giacomo's. Whenever that happened, Giacomo always shrieked in renewed surprise and drew his legs up; Karl attempted once to give a kick in return, but suffered the rest of the time in silence. Everything that went on in the little compartment, which was thick with cigarette smoke in spite of the open window, faded into comparative insignificance before the grandeur of the scene outside.

"The first day they traveled through a high range of mountains. Masses of blue-black rock extended in sheer wedges all the way to the tracks; even craning one's neck out of the window, one could not see their summits; narrow, gloomy, jagged valleys opened out and one tried to follow with a pointing finger the direction in which they lost themselves; broad mountain streams appeared, rolling in great waves in their boulder-strewn beds and drawing with them a thousand foaming wavelets, plunging underneath the bridges over which the train rushed; and they were so near that the breath of coldness rising from them chilled the skin of one's face."[9]

1ST SPEAKER: In 1913 Kafka published the first chapter, "The Stoker"; in the following year he wrote the other chapters—then he suddenly interrupted his work on the novel, never to take it up again. It remained unfinished, but we know that Kafka intended to give it a heart-warming resolution, that "within the Nature Theater of Oklahoma, his young hero

8 Franz Kafka, "Before the Law," in *The Complete Stories*, trans. Willa and Edwin Muir (New York: Schocken, 1976), 4.

9 Kafka, *Amerika*, 275–76, translation slightly altered.

Karl Rossmann" was to find "a profession, his freedom, a stand-by, even his old home and his parents" again.[10]

Kafka never traveled to America, and the America he presented may not correspond to the real one in a number of respects. Accordingly, Karl is once interrogated by a policeman in a manner that seems less than credible for New York around 1900. But that is beside the point. In *Amerika*, Kafka created a world ever so convincingly and discovered it for his protagonist, one that is full of open space and colors, full of delight in every observation and rich description of details. Yet it is no longer the natural world; its causality appears ruptured, and no longer do the characters' actions adhere to the motives that psychology suggests, even though everything that happens can be "rationally" accounted for and its elements are connected to one another by a network all of its own, of a quasi-logical character that is woven in great detail. The separation of reality and unreality, which is abolished in the other two novels, is still perceptible, although even in this Kafka novel, reality no longer functions either.

It is precisely the pure, clear language, which almost pedantically does justice to even the paltriest things, that makes the "nonfunctioning" evident, and indeed the magic of Kafka's work would be inexplicable without the peculiar phenomenon of his language and its method of representation.

But let us resist the temptation to add yet another judgment and another interpretation to the countless judgments on Kafka's literary quality and the countless interpretations of his oeuvre. This first period of calm, after the noisy debates of the initial years following the war, affords us an opportunity to read him once again. Great literary figures are accorded their due in periods of calm, for when all interpretations have become outdated and all exegeses are worn out, their work reveals itself by way of the inexhaustible truth to which it is beholden.

---

10 Brod, "Afterword [to *Amerika*]," 277. Bachmann's version of the quote as rendered here reverses the order of "his freedom" and "a stand-by" in Brod's original.

Into the Millennium[1]

In order to anticipate potential misunderstandings, Musil attempted to describe his book in the draft of a "Voluntary Declaration."[2]

"It is not the long-awaited great Austrian novel, although . . .

"It is not an account of an era in which Mr. . . . comes to realize his true nature . . .

"It is not a confession, but a satire . . .

"It is not a satire, but a positive paradigm."

When an author promises that his work provides a positive paradigm, he exposes himself to scrutiny not only of his poetics, but also of his intellectual capacity. Musil once proposed to inscribe "deportment unusual, ability slight, albeit inclined to excesses," into the diploma with which he wanted to take leave of German literature. But then the day came when the critics perceived his work to be, among other things, the greatest approach to the history of philosophy and the most relentless novel of ideological criticism since Voltaire's "Candide." So Musil did experience a bit of justice; for he wanted to write so much more than a novel, to do more than tell the story of the fall of Kakania[3] and level criticism against the desolate ideas of his era.

Yet, he did not want to exceed his realm of expertise—something that he was accused of from time to time. He was always aware that "a creative writer should not go so far as to produce a philosophic system (nor is he able to do so)."[4]

He did not "go all out"; rather he offered examples and directions, partial solutions, not *the* solution. He not only wanted to come to an understanding of reality, but also to include contingency or, as his hero

1 This is the heading for "Part III" of Robert Musil's (1880–1942) unfinished novel in four parts, *The Man Without Qualities* (1930–43). Bachmann's short essay on Musil appeared in the February 1954 volume of *Akzente*, which at the time of publication was a new journal edited by Walter Höllerer and Hans Bender.

2 Robert Musil, "Selbstanzeige" in *Der Mann ohne Eigenschaften I*, ed. Adolf Frisé, Sonderausgabe, 13. Edition (Reinbek bei Hamburg: Rowohlt, 2006 [based on the 1978 edition]), 1939. Musil's title "Selbstanzeige" has a double meaning in German: either "voluntary declaration," as in the case of unpaid taxes, or "self-advertisement," as in the case of writing a blurb for one's own book. The draft has not been translated into English.

3 Kakania refers to the pre-war Austro-Hungarian dual-monarchy, which was informally known as *kaiserlich-koniglich* (Imperial and Royal) or KK. The term was intended to characterize the Habsburg Monarchy as a state of mind, bureaucratic and with a highly stratified formal society in Musil's novel.

4 Musil, *Diaries*, 451.

Ulrich once put it, to "take in the open horizon, from which life itself aligns with the spirit."[5]

The hero of his fragment, Ulrich, a young mathematician with rigorous, scientific training in logic, was already conceived as a "Man Without Qualities," a hero lacking the prerequisites for action and the aptitude for carrying out the usual conflicts that transpire in a novel.

A conflict is always a moral conflict, and Ulrich, about whom we learn that he ranges among the decadent "moral imbeciles," would not be able to engage us if the author had not intended an adventure for him that is totally unheard of as the adventures of a hero go. The author awakens in him the wish to activate his thinking and behavior anew, instead of conforming to the collective or "howling with the wolves." This somewhat theoretical undertaking is prefaced by the idea that reactivation can only come from a new moral impetus, and given that the root of all morality is belief, that it can only come from a new belief. The man without qualities does not set out in painful search for a lost credo and a lost morality, but rather experiments courageously with the unleashing of intellectual nuclear power, and, if need be, exercising suitable caution, opens up forces that he and his era are not yet able to make use of.

Ulrich's conflict precedes all conflicts. For him, it is a matter of the "moral" of the moral, because our moral is situated in a mode of thought that is centuries out of date. Ulrich recognizes that the moral values directing our society are functional concepts: the same action can either be good or evil, and in the end, the fact that its commandments are helplessly contradictory proves to be the sole characteristic of the European moral code. (In the case of the serial murderer of prostitutes, Moosbrugger, we witness the dissonant interplay of forensic medicine, justice, and pastoral ministry.)

The path Ulrich's thinking pursues coincides with the pathway of love. What is related of Ulrich and his sister Agathe, in whom he believes to have found his double, the shadow of himself, is not a love story but "the ultimate love story," less an attempt at anarchism in love than one to see passion united with the basis of all passion, once referred to as the passion of God. Without being religious, Ulrich and Agathe venture onto a path that has a great deal in common with that of the "born again." They devote themselves to the testimonials of great mystics in order to

---

5 The quotation as given by Bachmann appears to be a partially inaccurate version of the passage "Ulrich zeigte die lächerliche gegenteilige Gesinnung, das Leben müsse sich dem Geist anpassen," which is found on page 540 of volume 1 of the 2006 version: *Der Mann ohne Eigenschaften I*, ed. Frisé, 540. Bachmann appears to have substituted "den offenen Horizont hereinnehmen" (take in the open horizon) for the first, independent clause in that passage, which translates as "Ulrich showed the ridiculously contrary conviction. . . ."

discover how to dissolve the boundaries of consciousness and world, and they attain the "other state"[6] for a brief period, in which they are dissolved morally into a "primeval atomic state."[7]

All of Ulrich's thoughts revolve around the question: What can be believed after all? Mysticism as a constant state of being moved by God seems "wanton" to him; he creates the concept of a "clear-sighted mysticism"[8]—the possibility for a temporary deviation from the accepted system of undergoing experience. He is at odds with converting this deviation to a direct proclivity for God. As a scientist, he knows that it cannot foster knowledge. Every turn, if it is to be fruitful, must occur for the sake of "sensing to the best of one's knowledge." Everything else, "would only be like Icarus's wax wings, which melted with the altitude, he exclaimed. If one wishes to fly other than in dreams, one must master it on metal wings."[9]

The recourse of the man without qualities to the idea of the millennium, his laying claim to the "other state," the *unio mystica*, is less disconcerting if one conceives of Musil as a possible utopia and keeps the utopia in mind, not as telos but as direction. Musil's thinking is teleophobic, agile, it runs up against the prevailing regulations in which every entity is "an ossified unicum of its possibilities."[10] Indeed, every order seems absurd to him and analogous to wax figures if one takes it seriously and holds fast to it beyond its time. He privileges the thought that the "world—as an order—is only one of x attempts and God probably provides partial solutions, from which the world continuously forms a relative totality that does not conform to any one solution. Candidly, God is suspect. We have to surrender ourselves to that suspicion."[11]

This notion, in which the driving force of the spirit is kept alive and prepared, is all that remains for Ulrich after the trip into the millennium with Agathe has failed. Love as denial, as a state of emergency, cannot endure. The exuberance, the ecstasy, endures—as does belief—for only an hour. It may be true that the "other state" showed the way from society to absolute freedom, but Ulrich knows now that the utopia of this other life bestows no instructions for the practical experience of life and has to be superseded by a life in society, by the utopia of the given social condition.

6 Musil's term "der andere Zustand" refers to the *unio mystica* of the sibling love between Ulrich and Agathe in *The Man Without Qualities.*

7 Robert Musil, *The Man Without Qualities*, trans. Sophie Wilkins, 2 vols. (New York: Alfred A. Knopf, 1995), vol. 2, 1020.

8 Musil's "taghelle Mystik,": Musil, *The Man Without Qualities*, 2:1184.

9 Musil, *The Man Without Qualities*, 2:831.

10 Our translation. Neither of the two published English translations of Musil's "Posthumous Papers" includes this passage and others that follow.

11 Our translation.

Musil calls the latter the utopia of "inductive stance."[12] Nonetheless, both utopias bring about ideologies that progress from closed to open.

Not only has Kakania's case demonstrated that thinking in closed ideologies leads directly to war; but also the permanent war of opinions continues to prevail.

Musil's directions do not want to tempt us to anything, only to lead us out of thinking in conventional stereotypes. They force us to contemplate, to think precisely and courageously.

Aside from that, what meaning does the question have as to whether this monstrous "novel" is to be seen as a failure or not? And how do we really do justice to it?

Steeped in melancholy, Musil once said of Ulrich that he is an "important statement, gone lost."[13]

An important statement—one could designate the book as such. The statement should not be lost.

---

12 Musil, *The Man Without Qualities*, 2:948. This term, "induktive Gesinnung" in German, is a metaphor for Ulrich's intimacy with his sister and alludes to the moral weakness inherent in such an overtly immoral relationship.

13 Our translation.

The Man Without Qualities[1]

1ST SPEAKER: Before we turn to the subject that we have chosen, we will have to ask, who was Robert Musil? We ask, because for some time his name has been on the lips of some—because a few literary histories have devoted a paragraph to him, be it ever so short, and because, what seems even more important to us, a large German publishing house has recently issued a new edition of his work, which had been out of print.

2ND SPEAKER: (reading without emotion) Robert Musil, born in 1880 in Klagenfurt, Austria, into a family of the lower nobility, died in Geneva in 1942. An early novel, *The Confusions of Young Törless* [*Die Verwirrungen des Zöglings Törless*, 1906], attracted the attention of German critics by virtue of its innovative psychology and caused a stir by dint of its choice of subject, since the attempt was made to depict the troubles of a young boy during puberty. Although Musil was later to distance himself expressly from German Expressionism, Expressionist prose took its cue from that work. Moreover, German literary critics were impressed by the stupendous psychological knowledge of an author who succeeded in bringing even the most inexpressible emotional experiences to the surface and finding suitable images for them.

Separated by long intervals, two volumes of novellas appeared: *Unions* [*Vereinigungen*, 1911] and *Three Women* [*Drei Frauen*, 1924].

1ST SPEAKER: In these prose pieces, Musil's descriptive power had already advanced far beyond his first novel. And yet, after the considerable success of his first work, hardly anyone took notice of them. What good did it do for Musil that Hofmannsthal expressed high praise for one of the novellas?[2] Musil had ventured to take a path that the public did not expect of him.

2ND SPEAKER: In 1920, he began work on a novel, one that he was to leave unfinished twenty-two years later. The first and second volumes appeared in 1930 and 1932; the publication of the third volume had to be

1 Bachmann's radio essay is the result of her lasting interest in the vast and unfinished novel of her fellow Carinthian author, Robert Musil. Based on a letter to Bachmann dated April 14, 1954, referencing the essay's transmission, we can assume that the text was completed and produced in the early months of 1954.

2 "I remember that Hofmannsthal praised 'Grigia' highly." Musil, *Diaries*, 458.

put up for subscription by his widow to help defray the printing costs.[3] That was in 1943.

1ST SPEAKER: And at that time it seemed as though Musil's access to his German readers had been lost forever. *The Man Without Qualities* [*Der Mann ohne Eigenschaften*]—the work we are speaking of—the labor of Musil's entire lifetime, no longer found an echo. It had never found much favor. That said, the first two volumes were at least recognized by a few critics as a singular masterpiece, one without parallel in German literature and one having merits that could not be assessed adequately, because the benchmarks were lacking. That is what prompted the somewhat reserved and hardly appropriate comparisons with Joyce's *Ulysses* and Proust's *Remembrance of Things Past* [*À la recherche du temps perdu*], Balzac's *The Human Comedy* [*La Comédie humaine*] and Voltaire's *Candide*. Reckoned among the most exalted company from a literary perspective, Musil was rarely read, and the result was a curious sort of fame, one that puzzled him no end:

MUSIL: "This curious reputation! It is strong, but not loud. I have often had occasion to wonder about it: it is the most paradoxical example of the presence and absence of a phenomenon. It is not the great reputation enjoyed by authors in whom the mainstream recognizes its mirror image (albeit in refined form); it is not a reputation of the caliber enjoyed by the favorites of literary conventicles. I dare assert of my reputation (not of myself) that it is the reputation of a great writer with small printings. It lacks social weight. I lack the tens of thousands of readers who just manage to keep up, and have to keep up, with other writers."[4]

1ST SPEAKER: This can be read on a page headed by the words, "I can't go on." "I can't go on . . ."—these words are expressive of a heart-rending truth: the tragic endeavor to complete this *one* work, which spanned several decades and was ultimately doomed to failure. Critically important to him, Musil complained bitterly about his desperate struggle for subsistence as an author in a nation that did not allow him to serve it as a writer.

2ND SPEAKER: Musil came from a well-situated and traditional Austrian family of civil servants, scholars, engineers and military men. For many years, his father had held a professorship at the Brünn Institute of Tech-

3 Although the first volume was published in 1930, as Bachmann claims, the second was published in 1933.

4 This passage has been edited out of the English translation of Musil's *Diaries*.

nology and was later ennobled while serving as Counselor to the Patent Court. His mother was the daughter of one of the builders of the first continental railway, which extended from Linz to Budweis. Like many sons born into an upper-middle-class milieu, he was sent to a military academy—

1ST SPEAKER: —the world of the confused young Törless—

2ND SPEAKER: —and prepared to launch a career as an officer in the Austro-Hungarian army. Before his first promotion, he defected. While studying ballistics, he had discovered his aptitude for technology. He resolved to study mechanical engineering, passed the state examination for engineers, and became an assistant professor at the Stuttgart Institute of Technology.

1ST SPEAKER: Our interest in the writer's biography is not attributable to a questionable attempt to be thorough but rather to a definite purpose. Before we enter into Ulrich's life, the man without qualities, whose message will be of particular concern for us, he [has] already passed through the stations of Musil's own existence, with hardly any effort to conceal the parallels. Reflecting upon that time in his life, Ulrich calls it one of his attempts to become a man of consequence—one among others that are doomed to failure, but one to which he owes the early stirrings of his morality.

MUSIL: "From the moment Ulrich set foot in engineering school, he was feverishly partisan. Who still needed the Apollo Belvedere when he had the new forms of turbodynamo or the rhythmic movements of a steam engine's piston before his eyes! Who could still be captivated by the thousand years of chatter about the meaning of good and evil when it turns out that they are not constants at all but functional values, so that the goodness of works depends on historical circumstances, while human goodness depends on the psychotechnical skills with which people's qualities are exploited?"[5]

1ST SPEAKER: In a word: like the author himself at an earlier stage, Ulrich had developed a strong vision of the engineer's persona. The men of technology whom he met had several advantages over military men: they possessed admirable competence and daring and with every hour they moved the world ahead another step, and yet. . . . Something disturbing

5 Musil, *The Man Without Qualities*, 1:33.

struck him about them. In no way did their emotions and way of thinking keep step with the daring of the specialist. Thus they stuck "tiepins topped with stags' teeth"[6] or tiny horseshoes in their neckties, they wore suits reminiscent of the early days of motoring, and they would no sooner have thought of applying the adventurousness of their thinking to their own very existence than they would have agreed—

MUSIL: ". . . to use a hammer for the unnatural purpose of killing a man."[7]

2ND SPEAKER: Once again, Musil revised his professional plans: from Stuttgart he went to Berlin to study logic and experimental psychology with Carl Stumpf, the prominent experimental psychologist, with the result that only a few years later he was a candidate for academic positions at the universities of Munich and Graz.

1ST SPEAKER: Viewing that period in relation to the man without qualities makes it emerge as the most significant experiment in Musil's life. Ulrich undergoes a similar intellectual experience when training to become a mathematician. He did it because he was "in love"[8] with the method of thinking as sharply and coolly as the blade of a knife. He loved mathematics because of the kind of people who "could not endure it,"[9] those types—

MUSIL: ". . . who were prophesying the collapse of European civilization on the grounds that . . . mathematics, the mother of the exact natural sciences, the grandmother of engineering, was also the arch-mother of that spirit from which, in the end, poison gases and fighter aircraft have been born. . . . He conceived it as the wellspring of an awesome spiritual sea change for a science before which God opens one fold of his mantle after another.

"'People simply don't realize it,' Ulrich felt. 'They have no idea how much thinking can be done already; if they could be taught to think in a new way, they would change their lives.'"[10]

---

6 Musil, *The Man Without Qualities*, 1:34.

7 Musil, *The Man Without Qualities*, 1:35.

8 Musil, *The Man Without Qualities*, 1:37. Bachmann alters the quote slightly: in Musil's original, it reads "He was in love with science not so much on scientific as on human grounds. He saw that in all the problems that come within its orbit, science thinks differently from the laity."

9 Musil, *The Man Without Qualities*, 1:37.

10 Musil, *The Man Without Qualities*, 1:37.

2ND SPEAKER: Even though the offer was gratifying, Musil declined an academic appointment. By then, he had written *The Confusions of Young Törless* and felt that there was now only one path left open to him.

1ST SPEAKER: That path offered no guarantees—neither economic security, nor steady advancement—it offered him nothing but inextinguishable doubts and clandestine assurance, disappointment, loneliness, and that happiness in unhappiness which dissociation from their era grants to those who exemplify it. What transpires after that is random at best:

2ND SPEAKER: He lived in Vienna as a librarian until the outbreak of the First World War, in which he served on the Italian front. After the war he became a special advisor in the Federal Ministry of the Armed Services and ultimately moved to Berlin, where in those years—it was the time of the Weimar Republic—the tensions and conflicts of German intellectual life were the most noticeable. Despondent after Hitler's takeover and without a compelling external reason, Musil returned to Vienna and resumed his work on *The Man Without Qualities*, the first and second volumes of which had by then been published. He was now a freelance writer, in the grimmest sense of the word. His inheritance had been lost in the Great Inflation. 1938 came. He was one of the few who left Austria voluntarily, sharing the fate of most political or Jewish émigrés. Unknown, without means, without friends, he lived in Zurich, a man without a name, one of too many uninvited guests. After that, in Geneva until his death on April 15, 1942. At Saint Georges Cemetery only eight people bid farewell to him. Not until his widow put the posthumous volume up for subscription did talk about Musil resume. It was to take almost ten more years for the talk to reach Germany.

1ST SPEAKER: And that same man, while in exile, had once written:

MUSIL: "I dedicate this novel to German youth . . . the youth who will come after a time and that will have to begin exactly where we stopped. . . . This novel takes place before 1914, a time that young people will no longer know at all. And the novel does not describe this time the way it really was, so that one could learn about it from this book. But it describes the time as it is mirrored in a person outside the mainstream."[11]

11 Musil, "From the Posthumous Papers," in *The Man Without Qualities*, 2:1131–801, 2:1723 and 2:1722.

1ST SPEAKER: So what does this novel have to say to today's readers? Let us first look at that person of no consequence, whose name we know to be Ulrich, and in whom the world of his era is mirrored. Let us redeem the man reflected by immersing ourselves in the mirror, viewing and accepting the world as an example, not as reality.

2ND SPEAKER: A young man, about whom we know that he—just like us—is a person of no consequence and that he has grappled with a variety of professional opportunities, returns to Vienna one day in the year 1913, at a moment when his life seems to be veering into a void. He recalls that one's native soil is credited with the mysterious ability to allow roots to grow—

MUSIL: ". . . and he settled there with the feeling of a hiker who sits down on a bench for eternity, but with the thought that he will be getting up again immediately."[12]

2ND SPEAKER: Since he has sufficient means, he takes up residence in a small palace and resolves to take a year's furlough from life.

1ST SPEAKER: Taking a furlough from one's life means: doing nothing. And for a healthy young man capable of doing many useful things, that is almost forbidden. For Ulrich, it seemed worth the "effort" not to do anything for a whole year.

2ND SPEAKER: What might be the disposition of a young man who deems it an "effort" to do nothing at all?

1ST SPEAKER: Well—let us say that he is a rather impractical man, who will appear unpredictable in his dealings with people and pursues completely eccentric activities. He is—let us say—a man without qualities.

2ND SPEAKER: The time has come for us to attempt to define what "a man without qualities" is. The term invites the most diverse associations—from a person bred in a test tube to a person without character.

1ST SPEAKER: In a word, Ulrich is neither one nor the other, rather he possesses a greater sense of possibilities than he does of reality, and this

12 Musil, *The Man Without Qualities*, 1:14.

quality—no, not quality, otherwise he would have one after all—makes him a man without qualities. As a man without qualities, he is subject to a twofold control: that of his disciplined thinking and that of his sensitivity to matters of feeling. Of course, he has a sense of reality too, for he is neither a dreamer nor an idealist with a penchant for escapism. But his sense of a reality that has not come about yet, of possibility, propels him into an intellectual battle, one fought out on the frontline of a reality that is yet to be created. At the risk of exposing him to a misunderstanding it must be said that he is a utopian. Early on, Ulrich realized that his epoch, despite the knowledge that gives it an advantage over any other, even with all of its overwhelming knowledge, seems incapable of intervening in the course of history. And the reason that that is so, as Ulrich perceives it, lies in the fact that today's reality is shaped only to a small extent by humanity itself; humanity is no longer creative because people have been transformed into a mere heap of qualities and habits and they *experience* life using conventional schematics. Indeed, they are no longer capable of experiencing anything genuine *themselves.* And this is how Musil describes that modern disease:

MUSIL: "Experiences . . . have gone on the stage, into the reports of research institutes and explorers, into ideological or religious communities, which foster certain kinds of experience at the expense of others as if they are conducting a kind of social experiment, and insofar as experiences are not actually being developed, they are simply left dangling in the air. Who can say nowadays that his anger is really his own anger when so many people talk about it and claim to know more about it than he does? A world of qualities without a man has arisen, of experiences without the person who experienced them. . . ."[13]

1ST SPEAKER: Ulrich discovers for himself that he is "equally near as far" from having all of the qualities that others have, that he is utterly indifferent to all of them. He is capable of separating the value of an action or the value of a quality from the purposes they serve and of extricating them from the connections in which they are entangled. He takes a very close look at them and examines them like an anatomist.

MUSIL: "A character, a profession, a fixed mode of being, are for him concepts that already shadow forth the outlines of the skeleton, which is all that will be left of him in the end."[14]

13 Musil, *The Man Without Qualities*, 1:158.
14 Musil, *The Man Without Qualities*, 1:269.

1ST SPEAKER: That makes him shudder. It is safe to assume, of course, that Ulrich, Musil's hero, comes from a family with which we are already acquainted. To a certain extent, he is a descendant of Hofmannsthal's *The Difficult Gentleman* [*Der Schwierige*, 1918] and a descendant as well of all the lovable and unlovable malcontents who have breathed the air of Nestroy. He has that keenness of vision that has at times flourished in Vienna, a penchant for mordant criticism and self-criticism, and like other worthy spirits before him, he strides above the disquieting undercurrent that is never mentioned and to which he knows he will fall prey as soon as his consciousness and his skepticism desert him. From that ancestry and from that climate he has inherited the unacknowledged disposition of the suicide victim or the mystic, the disposition for irony and for "not wanting to be original" and—last but not least—for an antipathy to metaphysics.

2ND SPEAKER: That family of "difficult characters" to which Ulrich, among others, belongs, was at home in the nation that is preserved in our history books because it has ceased to exist, in a state that even when it existed "somehow only went through the motions"—in the Austro-Hungarian Empire. But it is idle to say anything about that nation, since Musil himself summed it up most succinctly:

MUSIL: "There, in Kakania, that state since vanished that no one understood, in many ways an exemplary state, though unappreciated, there was a tempo too, but not too much tempo. . . . Of course cars rolled on these roads too, but not too many! The conquest of the air was being prepared here too, but not too intensively. A ship would now and then be sent off to South America or East Asia, but not too often."[15]

1ST SPEAKER: There, in Kakania . . .

MUSIL: "On paper it was called the Austro-Hungarian Monarchy, but in conversation it was called Austria, a name solemnly abjured officially while stubbornly retained emotionally, just to show that feelings are quite as important as constitutional law and that regulations are one thing but real life is something else entirely. Liberal in its constitution, it was administered clerically. The government was clerical, but everyday life was liberal."[16]

1ST SPEAKER: About the struggles between its many nationalities:

15 Musil, *The Man Without Qualities*, 1:28.

16 Musil, *The Man Without Qualities*, 1:29.

MUSIL: "They were so violent they jammed the machinery of government and brought it to a dead stop several times a year, but in the intervals and during the deadlocks people got along perfectly well and acted as if nothing had happened."[17]

1ST SPEAKER: There in Kakania is where Musil set the "Parallel Action"—the central plot of the novel, insofar as it is possible to speak of a "plot." The tale of that highly organized, cultural and political venture, that rescue action for the spiritual "values of the West," is the fabric into which the hero's individual destiny is woven. The fact that this macabre patriotic venture was set in the Danube Monarchy, which Musil portrayed with so much knowledge, so much furtive love and devastating criticism, would suggest that we are dealing with a historical novel, the swan song of a dying Kakania. But Musil himself once tried to define his work in order to obviate possible misunderstandings.

MUSIL: "It is not the great Austrian novel people have been awaiting for ages . . .

"It is not a depiction of the time, in which Herr . . . recognizes his spitting image.

"It is not a confession, but a satire . . .

"It is not a satire, but a positive construction . . ."[18]

2ND SPEAKER: To be sure, the first part of the novel is to a large extent satire and contemporary criticism. It takes us through the maze of prevailing superannuated ideas, and we are introduced to the representatives of those ideas, people who make the collapse of their culture plausible.

1ST SPEAKER: All of the novel's figures, with the exception of Ulrich, could be called incarnations of ideological types. Let us venture an appraisal:

2ND SPEAKER: The "great writer" Arnheim: his favorite idea is to only do business in the context of intellectual issues, to apply the philosophies of Maeterlinck or Bergson, for instance, to the questions of the price of coal or of cartel regulations. He thinks of his own era as one without gods and therefore likes to talk about the need for organizing internal sensitivity to save humanity from a soulless existence. He travels a great deal, is received [by] politicians, gives speeches, sits on all juries to award prizes,

17 Musil, *The Man Without Qualities*, 1:30.

18 Musil, "From the Posthumous Papers," 2:1763.

signs all manifestoes, writes all prefaces, proposes all birthday toasts, expresses his opinion on all important events, makes a profession of combating the demonization of the times by exercising his intelligence. His inherent problem: his behavior is mercantile and addresses idealistic points of view—an administrator of the large-scale industry of the spirit of our time.

1ST SPEAKER: General Stumm von Bordwehr, in charge of the Department of Military Training and Education in the War Ministry:

2ND SPEAKER: entrusted with the task of "keeping a smidgen of an eye on the goings-on" in the "Parallel Action" and interested in familiarizing himself with the most important "civilian issues" of the world. A lover of art and music, who envisions a broad popular participation in the issues of the armed forces and their weaponry as a worthy goal for mankind. His ultimate advice to the Parallel Action: short of convening a conference on world peace, one might as well furnish munitions to the army and the fleet.

1ST SPEAKER: Count Leinsdorf:

2ND SPEAKER: The real inventor of the Parallel Action, a typical Austrian aristocrat, bent on pursuing *Realpolitik*. In his opinion this is:

MUSIL: ". . . not doing the very thing you would love to do; however, you can win people over by letting them have their way in little things!"[19]

2ND SPEAKER: His wish is not to realize noble ideas but—

MUSIL: ". . . to mobilize the people!"

2ND SPEAKER: Which means, in his estimation: answering all proposals with the proposal to form an association, for

MUSIL: ". . . when a good many people are for something, the chances are that something will come of it."[20]

19 Musil, *The Man Without Qualities*, 1:376.
20 Musil, *The Man Without Qualities*, 1:380.

2ND SPEAKER: In sum, he was endowed with unwavering, healthy political views, believed in the mandatory unselfish subordination of every individual to the entity of the state, believed in the "goodness" of the folk and ascribed all of their less good-natured vociferations to "subversive elements."

1ST SPEAKER: The Jewish banker Fischel, on the other hand:

2ND SPEAKER: A representative of the business community, who harbors doubts about the patriotic action, has to wage a tragic war in his own home against the circle of his daughter's Christian-Germanic friends and their explicit anti-Semitism. Once a respected free-thinker, he suddenly finds himself cast in the role of a "Jewish capitalist." Aside from that, he believes in a form of progress that somehow has to resemble the image of his bank's thriving profitability, and—

MUSIL: "As a capable man in his field he knew, of course, that only where one has a thorough knowledge of the facts can one have a conviction. . . . The immense expansion of activities does not allow for such competence outside one's own field."[21]

1ST SPEAKER: Lindner, a university professor, a.k.a. "the do-gooder"—

2ND SPEAKER: transforms everything with which he comes into contact into an ethical challenge. His character training and physical exercise for the fortification of his personality do not prevent him from falling in love—how embarrassing!—with Ulrich's "morally impaired," beautiful sister and from failing in raising his son, who, subjected to his father's virtuous regimen, will soon come to represent one prototype of the coming generation, a consequence of the rebellion against pharisaical fathers: Lindner himself would call his son, to borrow a word from his vocabulary, a ne'er-do-well.

1ST SPEAKER: The list goes on, from the socialist Schmeißer and the homosexual Meingast, modeled after the philosopher Klages, to the ambitious young poet Friedel Feuermaul with his bombastic outbursts on the theme "humanity is good." Musil is supposed to have been inspired by Franz Werfel for that portrayal. Without a doubt, two of the most important figures are Moosbrugger, a serial murderer of prostitutes, and

---

21 Musil, *The Man Without Qualities*, 1:141–42.

the dubious figure of Clarisse, a friend of Ulrich's from his youth. Two pathological figures, two radical incarnations of the disease of the times.

Moosbrugger's significance for the novel is reflected in a note penned by Musil:

MUSIL: "Nations have a mind that is not legally accountable. . . . Comparison with the insane. They don't want to. But they have at each other."[22]

2ND SPEAKER: Moosbrugger exemplifies the dark side of life. His world is a mystical one. He is a derailed emblem of the order, a cipher that is no more exotic than the other images of the world. And because he suffers vicariously for humanity, as Clarisse believes, he carries his weight in the novel's religious ambiguity—

1ST SPEAKER: an ambiguity confirmed by Musil's remark that this is a religious book, subject to the premises of unbelievers.

2ND SPEAKER: Finally, Clarisse, obsessed with the ideology of Nietzsche and Klages, driven by a longing for redemption, she surrenders to madness. In her the most incongruous religious tendencies are mingled—she feels superhuman and sees herself as the great hermaphrodite, as a twofold being of woman and man; she does not want to be "one," like Ulrich and Agathe, but "two"; however, she is also Christ and wants to replicate the stations of the cross and she believes that she can take the sins of the world upon herself with continually escalating acts of sacrifice, until she succumbs to her insanity.

1ST SPEAKER: Musil has unveiled a giant shadow of decay over the entire novel. A shadow over the nation cast by the characters and a shadow over the characters cast by the nation. Explicitly, Musil designates the monarchy as a particularly striking example of the modern world, because it was the first state to which God had denied confidence in its mission. Given its internal and external collapse, it stands for the fate of the modern world in its entirety. Ulrich's counterpart, the Prussian Arnheim, modeled after Rathenau and afflicted with the same human and political misperceptions as the figures frequenting the aesthetic salon of the Viennese Diotima, merely represents the fate of Germany in this little theater of the world, which serves to illustrate the fate of Europe.

Accordingly, we will have to forgo consideration of the complex external plot, which must be one of the primary attractions of the whole

22 Musil, "From the Posthumous Papers," 2:1756.

work for every reader, with its captivating portrayal of milieus and characters, its morbid sense of humor and bitter comedy. It is only a starting point for the author—the starting point for a bold historical-philosophical experiment that loses its way and ends up as *belles lettres.*

2ND SPEAKER: In truth, the book has little to do with narrative prose. It is practically crushed by an excess of reflection, by the mediated nature of its presentation. It is a conglomerate of essays, aphorisms, the interior monologues of Ulrich and two dozen secondary characters.

1ST READER: And yet it is composed and structured from beginning to end like no other book in this century. Musil is an intellectual strategist who works on the execution of his design with the most riveting intelligence, making use of all linguistic resources, every possible style, every shift of consciousness, every adventure that might be probable. And he is driven by the coldest and most peculiar kind of passion.

MUSIL: "This book has a passion that in the area of *belles lettres* today is somewhat out of place, the passion for rightness/precision."[23]

2ND SPEAKER: Several years before he went to work on his vast novel, Robert Musil had published a culturally critical essay entitled "Helpless Europe." There, for the first time, he took an adamant stance with respect to the idea, still widespread today, that the "crisis" of Europe stemmed from the increasing mechanization of existence, that the use of our intellect, the mounting insights of scientific thought and, consequently, modern technology led to spiritual corrosion and was responsible "for everything." In contrast, he maintained the position that what was no longer intact could no longer be preserved and that the intellect could not corrode anything that was not already corroded.

MUSIL: "The difficulty, then, cannot be anything other than a skewed relationship, an abiding miscommunication between the intellect and the soul. We do not have too much intellect and too little soul, but too little intellect in matters of the soul."[24]

23 Musil, "From the Posthumous Papers," 2:1760.

24 Robert Musil, "Helpless Europe," in *Precision and Soul: Essays and Addresses*, ed. Burton Pike and David S. Luft, trans. Philip H. Beard (Chicago and London: University of Chicago Press, 1990), 131.

1ST SPEAKER: This insight is the root of Ulrich's conflict. Indeed, Ulrich's thoughts take that very thought as their starting point. And although his character is conceived as a "man without qualities," as a protagonist who lacks the prerequisites for action, and nonetheless motivated by that thought, he embarks on an adventure that is entirely novel for the hero of a narrative. He resolves to reactivate his thought and action instead of "running with the pack."

2ND SPEAKER: If that undertaking strikes us as somewhat academic, it is prefaced by the thought that the reactivation can only arise from a new morality—

1ST SPEAKER: and since faith is the root of morality, only from a new faith.

2ND SPEAKER: The man without qualities does not go in search of lost faith and lost morality, but experiments boldly, and cautiously if necessary, to unchain a spiritual atomic energy. And he releases forces that he and his era are not able to utilize.

But lest we misunderstand: a conflict is always a moral conflict, and in contrast to the other characters of the book, Ulrich, whom Musil ironically counts among the "morally impaired decadents," deals with a conflict that antedates all conflicts. His concern is the "morality of morality," because our morality finds itself in a state of thought that is centuries behind the times. Ulrich recognizes that the moral values to which everyone around him orients themselves are "functional concepts." That suggests: the same action can be good as well as evil, and ultimately the sole characteristic of European morality turns out to be that its commandments hopelessly contradict one another.

In one of the first encounters with his sister Agathe, Ulrich is sufficiently carried away to vent these ideas freely for the first time:

ULRICH: "You asked me what I believe . . . I believe that all our moral injunctions are concessions to a society of savages.

"I believe none of them are right.

"There is a different meaning glimmering behind them. An alchemist's fire.

"I believe that nothing is ever done with.

"I believe that nothing is in balance but that everything is trying to raise itself on the fulcrum of everything else.

"That's what I believe. It was born with me, or I with it.

"I seem, without having had a say in the matter, to have been born with another kind of morality.

"You asked me what I believe. I believe there are valid reasons you can use to prove to me a thousand times that something is good or beautiful, and it will leave me indifferent; the only mark I shall go by is whether its presence makes me rise or sink.

"Whether it rouses me to life or not.

"Whether it's only my tongue and my brain that speak of it, or the radiant shiver in my fingertips.

"But I can't prove anything, either.

"And I'm even convinced that a person who yields to this is lost. He stumbles into twilight. Into fog and nonsense. Into unarticulated boredom.

"If you take the unequivocal out of our life, what's left is a sheepfold without a wolf.

"I believe that the bottomless vulgarity can even be the good angel that protects us.

"And so, I don't believe.

"And above all, I don't believe in the domestication of evil by good as the characteristic of our hodgepodge civilization. I find that repugnant. . . .

"But maybe I believe that the time is coming when people will on the one hand be very intelligent, and on the other hand be mystics. Maybe our morality is already splitting into these two components. I might also say into mathematics and mysticism. Into practical improvements and unknown adventure!"[25]

1ST SPEAKER: Adventuring into the unknown is what Ulrich undertakes with his sister.

2ND SPEAKER: He has not seen her again since his childhood and becomes reacquainted with her at the funeral of his father, at a moment when her life also begins to drift into a void. A wondrous, shy affection arises between the two of them. Ulrich withdraws more and more from the cultural hustle and bustle and discovers the Siamese twin in Agathe, the shadowy duplicate of himself.

1ST SPEAKER: His path of thought coincides with that of love, and what happens now is not just the development of any love story but that of the "final love story." Brother and sister find themselves on a path that has

25 Musil, *The Man Without Qualities*, 2:835–37.

much in common with the path of "those possessed by God." They study the testimonies of great mystics in order to understand how consciousness and world might be surpassed, and for a short time they attain the "other state" in which they are morally dissolved into a primeval atomic state—the "other state."

2ND SPEAKER: In an unpublished poem, "Isis and Osiris" ["Isis und Osiris"], Musil offers perhaps the most stunning variation on the theme of sibling incest, allowing the dreamlike recurrence of the central theme to achieve the exquisite solution that is Ulrich's and Agathe's fervent wish.

MUSIL: On the leaves of the stars there lay the youth
moon in silvery rest,
and the hub of the sun's wheel
spun and watched him.
The red wind blew from the desert,
and the coasts were empty of sails.

And gently the sister severed
the sleeper's sex and ate it,
and in exchange she gave her soft
red heart and placed it on him.
And in the dream the wound closed.
And she ate the lovely sex.

Lo, the sun burst out in thunder,
when the sleeper started from his sleep,
stars were reeling, just as boats
rear up on their moorings,
when the great storm breaks.
Lo, his brothers now ran after
the fair robber in hot pursuit,
And he shouldered his bow,
And the blue space came crashing down,
forests cracked under their steps,
And the stars ran along in fear.
But no one, however far he ran,
Overtook the elfin creature with her bird-like shoulders.

Only the youth whom she called every night,
finds her, when moon and sun trade places,
this one of all the hundred brothers,
and he eats her heart and she eats his.

1ST SPEAKER: All of Ulrich's thoughts now revolve around the question: what, if anything, can be believed? As a constant acquiescence to God, mysticism seems "immoral" to him: he forms the idea of a "day-bright mysticism"—as the possibility of a temporary deviation from the accustomed order of experience. Translating that deviation into a direct appeal to God goes against his grain. As a scientist he knows that it cannot foster cognition. In order to be fruitful, any appeal must follow "intuition informed by the best of one's knowledge." As he one day cries out to his sister, everything else:

ULRICH: ". . . would only be like Icarus's wax wings, which melted with the altitude, he exclaimed. If one wished to fly other than in dreams, one must master it on metal wings."[26]

1ST SPEAKER: The man without qualities' recourse to the idea of the millennium, his desire for the "other state," for the *unio mystica*, is less disconcerting if it is understood as a utopian concept. And if that utopia is envisioned not as a goal, but as a direction. For Musil's thought is opposed to goals, it is mobile. It defies the ruling systems in which each thing is nothing more than an individual concretization of its possibilities. Indeed, any system seems absurd to him, comparable to a waxwork figure, when it is taken seriously and held on to beyond its time. He prefers the idea that the world—as a system—is only one of x number of experiments and that God might offer partial solutions—a partial solution from which the world derives a relative totality time and again, but one to which no solution corresponds. To be sure, God is dubious. We have to surrender to intuition.

2ND SPEAKER: So what significance can be attributed to the utopia of that "other state"? Superficially, it manifests itself in the siblings' tendency to withdraw from the world; they travel to Italy. Ulrich experiences that "journey to Eden" as something that is deeply connected to his rejection of the world and as an experiment, the failure of which will cause him to sacrifice his own life, or so he has decided.

1ST SPEAKER: Let us say in advance: the experiment fails and with it the utopia of the other state, and suddenly Ulrich can no longer find the reason why he has to kill himself. Brother and sister separate. In order to avoid having to love Ulrich again, Agathe will have affairs with other men. And Ulrich will go to war, though he could find safe haven in Switzerland,

26 Musil, *The Man Without Qualities*, 2:831.

and though he despises the war, in which he perceives a sort of "other state" all over again—

MUSIL: ". . . but one mingled with evil."

1ST SPEAKER: And Musil resumes his interpretation of this love story:

MUSIL: "Ulrich-Agathe is really an attempt at anarchy in love. Which ends negatively even there. That's the deeper link between the love story and the war."[27]

2ND SPEAKER: If mention is made of its connection to war in this love story, then it has to be made clear from the outset that war is the all-embracing problem of the novel. Every one of the lines drawn by Musil leads to war, most obviously the Parallel Action of course, and everybody welcomes it in his own way, because something has been found at last that is called "conviction" and "faith"—something that Ulrich disdains and against which he posits as utopia, the "other state," pure contemplation. That utopia has a tragic ending.

Musil knows that the utopia is doomed to failure because:

MUSIL: "Withdrawal from the world is pointless. That is evident from the fact alone that it has always made God its goal, an unreal and unattainable entity."[28]

1ST SPEAKER: Yet, that utopia, as a guiding concept, is also the prerequisite for another guiding concept, which can free the human being from his ideological shackles. For is Ulrich, after his journey to the millennium has failed, not left with the intuition in which the driving force of the spirit remains forever awake and in readiness? Love as denial, as an exceptional state, cannot endure. Rapture, ecstasy—like faith—last only an hour. To be sure, the "other state" showed the way from society to absolute freedom, but Ulrich knows now that the utopia of that other life does not offer any prescriptions for everyday existence. For a life in society, that utopia must be superseded by a utopia of the pre-existing social conditions. "Utopia of inductive reason":[29] that is another term Musil sometimes uses for it.

---

27 Musil, "From the Posthumous Papers," 2:1752.

28 This passage has been edited out of the English edition of the "Posthumous Papers."

29 Musil's principle of "inductive reason" is an inductive attitude that does not depend on first and last principles, but approaches the world as an "open

But both ideologies would succeed in supplanting closed ideologies with open ones.

2ND SPEAKER: In the end, Musil was unable to complete the closing chapters. The intellectual summation was to be the "end result of the utopia of inductive reason." For Ulrich, that meant:

MUSIL: ". . . knowing, working, being effective without illusions [as well as the end results of the utopia of inductive reason]."[30]

1ST SPEAKER: And the awareness comes to him at a moment when madness erupts, in the summer of 1914, the moment that precipitates the collapse of culture and the concept of culture. And what now places . . .

system," as inherently without closure, without end and decision or judgement. "In its orientation towards the radical openness of the world, this attitude of inductive thinking is one that in the context of the unending connectedness of the world is able to reach only 'partial solutions,' a provisional fixing or definition. Simultaneously, inductive thinking always constitutes an element of doubt with regard to its goal, which Musil calls its 'utopia.'" Fred Ulfers, "The Utopia and Essayism of Robert Musil 1/4," European Graduate School video lectures, 2007, accessed January 30, 2021, https://egs.edu/lecture/the-utopia-and-essayism-of-robert-musil-2007-1-4/.

30 Musil, "From the Posthumous Papers," 2:1756. Words in brackets have been translated from Bachmann's version of the quote, but are not present in Musil's original text as translated.

The World of Marcel Proust: Views of a Pandemonium[1]

AUTHOR: As I was beginning to take notes for this essay on Marcel Proust, I received a letter from the editors of a journal, who were likewise interested in the subject. It contained some remarks with which I would like to preface my text, because it gave me cause to doubt something that had seemed self-evident, namely that Proust's novelistic oeuvre was bound to elicit a passionate response today.

This is what they wrote:

SPEAKER: "We cannot take it as a given, and far be it from me to regret that, that this subject will elicit a literary, snobbish interest in our readers. On the contrary, what we have to assume on the part of those interested in literature is the unquestionable prejudice against Proust as an elitist, decadent, difficult, and in any case outdated writer, who basically only poses stylistic problems."

AUTHOR: Thus I was warned against taking the impact of this oeuvre for granted and adding yet another interpretation to the many that already exist, yet one more dealing with stylistic analysis, structural analyses, and questions of composition.

The research on Proust in Germany began with a celebrated book by Ernst Robert Curtius, who as early as 1925 surmised that the author of *À la recherche du temps perdu* would soon be mentioned together with the names of Balzac, Stendhal, and Flaubert.[2] Later, Walter Benjamin and most recently Günther Blöcker called attention to the new realities in Proust, and I would have nothing to add to those excellent studies if it were not for my wish, even at the risk of excessive one-sidedness, to liberate Proust's book from the blemish of snobbery, aestheticism, and classicism that in the eyes of many seems to cling to it. To anyone who knows how to read it properly, it is a forbidding, tragic, and revolutionary book, one that can continue a tradition only by breaking with it. Because it is as sweeping as *The Thousand And One Nights*, full of allusions and rich in reality, there are many ways of reading it, and one of them might be to examine it with regard to brilliance and coloristic effects, nuances and reverberations—but surely another might be to enter the new inferno that this book contains, the circles of hell in which Proust's characters,

---

1 Bachmann's radio essay on Marcel Proust's masterpiece was first aired by Radio Bavaria on May 13, 1958.

2 Ernst Robert Curtius, *Marcel Proust* (Frankfurt am Main: Suhrkamp, 1952), 10.

here and now, are condemned to live.[3] Today we know that Proust did not originally intend to name his book *À la recherche du temps perdu* but *Sodome et Gomorrhe* [Sodom and Gomorrah, trans. *Cities of the Plain*]—a title he was to retain for only one of its many volumes. Prior to Proust, a similar case was Baudelaire, whose *Flowers of Evil* was to have appeared under the title *The Lesbians.*[4] There is a passage in Proust's journals that addresses this strange proposition:[5]

SPEAKER: "How could Baudelaire be so interested in Lesbians as to plan to put them in the title of his main work? If an author like Vigny is prejudiced against women and explains that with the mystery of their peculiar physiology and psychology, then it is understandable that in his disappointed and jealous love he wrote: 'Woman will be in Gomorrah, and man in Sodom.' At least they are irreconcilable enemies, whom he sets far apart from each other. 'And casting confused glances at each other from afar, the two sexes will die, each on its own side . . .' Baudelaire's case is altogether different."[6]

AUTHOR: Proust's case is also different. But first we must ask ourselves how one is to approach the scandalous truths, the traces of which this book seeks to investigate. Proust is the first writer to enter the two accursed cities Sodom and Gomorrah, almost inevitably given his explorations of the individual and society. To be sure, the subject had been fermenting for

---

3 A reference to Dante's *Inferno.*

4 *Les fleurs du mal,* Baudelaire's celebrated collection of poetry, appeared as *Les Lesbiennes* c. 1845–1847, as *Les limbes* (Limbo) c. 1848–1851, and finally as *Les fleurs du mal* in 1857.

5 The passage is actually not in Proust's journals, but in an essay entitled "A propos de Baudelaire," *La Nouvelle Revue Française* 16, no. 93 (1921): 641–63. This and all subsequent footnotes reference the published English translations from the French.

6 The published translation of this passage reads: "How did he come to be so interested in Lesbians that he actually proposed to use the word as the title of that whole superb work? When Vigny, raging against women, thought to find the secret of their sex in the fact that the female gives suck: / *Il rêvera toujours à la chaleur du sein;* / in the peculiar nature of their physiology: / *La femme, enfant malade et douze fois impur;* / in their psychology: *Toujour ce compagnon dont le couer n'est pas sûr* / it is easy to see why, in his frustrated and jealous passion, he could write: / *'La femme aura Gomorrah et l'homme aura Sodome.'* / But he does, at least, see the two sexes at odds, facing one another as enemies across a great gulf: / *Et, se jetant de loin un regard irrité / Les deux sexes mourront chacun de son côté.* / But this did not hold true of Baudelaire. . . ." Proust, cited in André Maurois, "Remembrance of Things Past (II): Love and its Passions," in *Proust: A Biography,* trans. Gerard Hopkins (New York: Meridian Books, 1958), 223.

quite a while, from Saint-Simon to Balzac and Zola, who admitted that it held the highest psychological and social interest, although he had hopelessly searched for a way of presenting it that would not give rise to "an uproar." While Proust is not afraid of the uproar, he is wary of applause from the wrong audience, from those who are unable to recognize his artistic intentions. But he succeeded in preventing both by virtue of the compelling purity of his portrayal. The critics scarcely protested, but to this day that aspect of his work is met with passive resistance, or it is simply passed over. One of the earliest French critics wrote:

SPEAKER: "It is dreadful. I cannot speak about it!"[7]

AUTHOR: Whenever a new writer enters into a realm that is yet unexplored and indistinct, it seems a sacrilege. When Dumas fils made prostitution and Flaubert made adultery the premise of the most precise depictions—both of which are phenomena that have always existed—these subjects had never before been literary subjects. Then, as now, the taste of readers was characterized by a horror of any confrontation with reality. But since it usually takes a generation to acquire the ability to acknowledge new realities, the time ought to have come to view Proust's audacities with detachment.

In keeping with his method of composition, he not only resurrects the two biblical cities in one or two chapters, but he also picks up the motif time and again; it pervades his entire book and culminates in a vision of human misery and doom, a sinister, horrifying wartime scene that is part of the final volume and to which we shall return.

In the beginning we hardly understand the allusions when we make the acquaintance of the Baron de Charlus, around whom, as around the grand master of Sodom, all other figures are positioned, and we are told that he is in mourning for his late wife—"but like a cousin, like a grandmother, like a sister."

We ask ourselves the same question that Proust himself posed on Baudelaire's account. How could he, and why could he, be so deeply absorbed by sexual inversion?[8] Why is one half of his world populated by people like Charlus and Morel, Jupien and Saint-Loup, and on the other side with Mademoiselle Vinteuil and her female friend, with Albertine and Esther? And how can he give us a compelling picture of human nature and a picture of human sufferings and human passions by referring to these figures?

---

7 The source for this quotation has not been located.

8 Sexual inversion is a term for homosexuality found primarily in older scientific literature.

It might be assumed that, like André Gide in the same period, he might have been searching for a new awareness of life, that his goal was vindication and transfiguration and the resurrection of a Greek ideal. But Proust was not after romanticism, but rather after truth and nothing but the truth. His premise is that homosexuality is an incurable disease, thus pathological, and he reasons:

SPEAKER: "An idealization of Sodom is not possible. The homosexuality of Plato's young people and of Virgil's shepherds has been completely gone for nineteen hundred years. To glorify it as a passion freely chosen by a human being, from a taste for beauty, friendship, and male intelligence, is an absurdity. Only geniuses who are great enough and independent enough to live above their time in a young and pristine world are able to rise to a sublime friendship. The others experience only confusion; they mistake their mania for a friendship that bears no resemblance at all to it. Thus this passion is an expression neither of an ideal of beauty nor of satanic libertinism, for that would mean that it was willed. But it is a disease, one with social consequences."[9]

AUTHOR: Proust's purpose is to examine the phenomenon anew; besides the mysterious vagary of nature that he observes at the beginning of *Sodom and Gomorrah* and that Baron de Charlus and Chamberlain Jupien submit to, Proust is concerned with the confrontation between the individual and society. The latent revolt of the individual against society, of nature against morality, led him to develop the concept of the *homme traqué*, the hounded person, the person at bay, for which the inverted individual[10] is only a particularly apt example.

That is why we are able to identify with the human constitution of Proust's characters. That is also why Dostoevsky's characters, who are almost without exception epileptics like the writer himself, strike us not as particularly diseased or demented individuals, but as sufferers and lovers with whom we can identify.

The history of the inverted contributes the most deplorable features to the image of the *homme traqué*, for it is a history of lies, concealment, and hypocrisy, of lifelong anxiety and fear. The constant repression of passion is the key to Baron de Charlus's personality. His goodness and his baseness, his anger and his sense of humor, his tyrannical as well as his obsequious manner would otherwise be incomprehensible to us. There is a passage in Nietzsche where the philosopher asks the stranger:

---

9 The source for this quotation has not been located.

10 See footnote 8.

SPEAKER: "What do you desire, what do you need for your comfort?—For my comfort . . . what are you saying! Give me, I beg you—What? What! Go on . . .

"One more mask. Another mask!"[11]

AUTHOR: Charlus's entire life is played out from behind a mask. Only for the space of a few seconds does he risk a gesture that discloses his true nature, exposing himself to those who resemble him. In the very next moment, trembling with dread at being detected, he puts on a mask—yet another mask. In a salon he can be always found at the side of the most elegant woman. He displays indifference toward young men, insouciance and arrogance. Gentle and solicitous as he might appear, he does not allow people to be introduced to him. And yet he never feels safe. Does anybody harbor doubts? Does anyone suspect him? In the end it is not he who is a riddle to the others, but rather all those who surround him become riddles for him. For the masked, the whole world wears a mask whose perspective is torture to him. He can no longer distinguish his friends from his enemies; he thinks that he is hearing disparaging insinuations everywhere; he perceives everyone as a judge and stands before a ceaseless tribunal.

He behaves like a criminal and, among equals, as though he belonged to a gang of thieves. At last he goes so far as to accuse everyone of debauchery, in order to be able better to defend himself.

The demonized sphere around Charlus has its analogy in the ordinary one, for a dominant idea in Proust's work and world is the idea of the futile search of humankind for enjoyment, for *plaisir*. That search is its secret mainspring and it determines human actions and behavior without being acknowledged openly. The sacrifices that are made are disproportionate to its fulfillment, since fulfillment never occurs when we need it, but at a time when we have long since begun the pursuit of a different goal.

The inverted simply allow us to comprehend, with heightened intensity, the impossibility of our desire, since in their search for happiness they conduct themselves in a more delusional manner than the rest of us do as a rule.

SPEAKER: ". . . their happiness is far greater than that of any normal lover could ever be. Knowing so well the hazards that beset their search for a

11 "And whoever you may be: what would you like now? What do you find relaxing? Just name it: I'll give you whatever I have!—'Relaxing? Relaxing? How inquisitive you are! What are you saying! But please, give me— —.' What? What? Just say it!—'Another mask! A second mask!'" Friedrich Nietzsche, "What is Noble?," in *Beyond Good and Evil*, trans. Judith Norman (Cambridge: Cambridge University Press, 2002), 169.

partner, they feel that their form of love is not, like that of heterosexuals, born of the moment, is not a mere instant's fancy, but must be far more deeply in rooted in . . . life . . . the answer to their call has come from somewhere far beyond the passing minute, that the 'beloved' thus miraculously given has been his affianced love from days before his birth, has found his way to this moment of meeting from the depths of limbo, from those stars where all our souls inhabit before they are incarnate. Such love, they will be more than ever tempted to believe, is the only true love."[12]

AUTHOR: This notion of love differs from that of Classicism and Romanticism, which had been dominant in literature until that time. Proust's portrayals of love are wholly novel and are based on a more precise exploration of its genesis, its crystallization, its waning, and, ultimately, its indifference.

He arrives at a tragic conception of love, one that had previously been masked for us. Decisive for the depth of our feeling or the persistence of our passion is not the value of the woman or the man we love but our own condition. We bestow the other person with music, passion, and perfume, and nurture that person's being. That is why we find it so hard to understand the love affairs of others. All of Proust's lovers are devoted to individuals who are not worthy of them, who are positioned far below them. Odette, a demimondaine, spoils years of Swann's life as well as his social position, a superior, sophisticated man; Albertine, vulgar and mediocre, becomes the narrator's great love and corrupts and enchants him even beyond her own death; Charlus, one of France's greatest celebrities, is obsessed with the plebeian violinist Morel; the young, radiant Saint-Loup loses his fortune to Rahel, a woman whom anyone else could have had only a short time earlier for just a few francs.

All love is hapless, and its cruel law forces the lovers into a cycle of fear, jealousy and deception as well as an agony that not even death and absence are able to cure. Only the vacuum stemming from oblivion allows them to adapt to reality—at least for a while, until another person steps into that scene. Every time, the narrator, the "I" of the novel, assumes that a single person signifies the entire world: his grandmother, his mother, Gilberte, the Duchess of Guermantes, and Albertine, and every time he traverses the full measure of the trail of tears that represents love, until time does its part and oblivion sets in.

Proust's tragic concept of love—love as something catastrophic and fateful—is shaped by his personal experiences and occasionally suffers from "translations" carried out by him, from Albert to Albertine—but

12 Maurois, *Proust*, 220–21.

only in the sense that durable relationships or marriages are omitted from his analysis.

And the moments of happiness, of joy and fulfillment, expire when subjected to analysis and meticulous dissection. Among the exceptions are moments of contemplation and mystical immersion. The famous passage that constitutes the beginning of the volume *La prisonnière* [*The Captive*], when the narrator is absorbed in the vision of Albertine sleeping, coincides with a standstill of plot, action, and movement; immediately thereafter the awakening revives the pain as hell returns, and the web of lies with which both characters weave their artful embroideries continues. The mysteries surrounding Albertine will work their spell again, Gomorrah will cast its shadows over them, and there will be conversations that are a long agony:

SPEAKER: "'Albertine, can you swear that you have never lied to me?' She gazed fixedly into space before replying: 'Yes . . . that's to say no. I was wrong to tell you that Andrée was greatly taken with Bloch. We never met him.' 'Then why did you say so?' 'Because I was afraid that you believed other stories about her.' 'That's all?' She stared once again into space and then said: 'I ought not to have kept from you a three weeks' trip I went on with Lea. But I knew you so slightly in those days!' 'It was before Balbec?' 'Before the second time, yes.' And that very morning, she had told me that she did not know Lea! I watched a tongue of flame seize and devour in an instant a novel which I had spent millions of minutes in writing. To what end? To what end? Of course I realized that Albertine had revealed these two facts to me because she thought that I had learned them indirectly from Lea; and that there was no reason why a hundred similar facts should not exist. I realized too that Albertine's words, when one interrogated her, never contained an atom of truth, that the truth was something she let slip only in spite of herself, as a result of a sudden mixing together in her mind of the facts which she had previously been determined to conceal with the belief that one had got wind of them. 'But two things are nothing,' I said to Albertine, 'let's have as many as four, so that you may leave me with some memories. What other revelations have you got for me?' Once again she stared into space. To what belief in a future life was she adapting her falsehood, with what gods less accommodating than she had supposed was she seeking to make a deal? It cannot have been an easy matter, for her silence and the fixity of her gaze continued for some time. 'No, nothing else,' she said at length. And, notwithstanding my persistence, she adhered, easily now, to 'nothing else.' And what a lie! For, from the moment she had acquired those tastes until the day when she had been shut up in my house, how many times, in how many places, on how many excursions must she have gratified them! The daughters of Gomorrah are at once rare enough and numerous enough for one not to pass unnoticed by another in any given crowd. Thenceforward, a rendezvous is an easy matter."[13]

AUTHOR: Besides Albertine, Mademoiselle Vinteuil, the daughter of the composer whose sonata and septet play such an important role in the book, is located at the center of Gomorrah. Her father died of grief over her; his image only serves to elicit a habitual and degrading mockery from her and her female friend. But a few years later, something remarkable happens. In a Paris salon the work is performed posthumously, under conditions no one anticipates, but which incite the belief in the narrator that public fame and the immortal work of art only come together through an interplay of the most sordid elements. In the present case, the immediate cause could be traced to the relationship—

SPEAKER: "—that existed between M. de Charlus and Morel, relations which made the Baron anxious to give as wide a celebrity as possible to the artistic triumphs of his young idol, and to obtain for him the cross of the Legion of Honour; the remoter cause which had made this assembly possible was that a girl who enjoyed a relationship with Mlle Vinteuil analogous to that of Charlie and the Baron had brought to light a whole series of works of genius which had been such a revelation that before long a subscription was to be opened under the patronage of the Minister of Education, with the object of erecting a statue to Vinteuil."[14]

AUTHOR: According to Proust, the alliance between demeaning passion and art is one of the most enigmatic events in life, and once again it harkens back to his idea of love as pure illusion and self-deception, once again, but one that is at the same time capable of releasing the most sublime powers. Without our sufferings, even of the most debasing sort, we would be inhuman in our self-righteousness, and we would be vacuous, for only our pain enables us to understand and recognize others, to discriminate and to create art.

The tense relationship between the individual and society, between the former's personal sphere and his public manifestation, undergoes a further intensification as a result of the struggles for power and position relentlessly imposed upon the individual in society. The war of all against all expresses itself in snobbery, or rather in a great variety of snobberies. There is no one in Proust's world, neither duchess nor cook, neither

13 Marcel Proust, *The Captive*, in *In Search of Lost Time*, trans. C. K. Scott Moncrieff and Terence Kilmartin, rev. by D. J. Enright (New York: Random House, 2012). Kindle version, 2693–95.

14 Proust, *The Captive*, 2601–2.

physician nor person of letters, who is not caught in the act of employing weapons against those below and above him. And we are witness to the unmasking of everyone. The excluded would like to become the chosen; the chosen defend their privileges and punish those who are excluded with contempt. It makes little difference what social groups Proust bases his observations on, since his conclusions are universal. Although he never prided himself on expressly playing the role of a social critic, he exposed the inescapable mechanisms with stupendous force and, at the same time, gave them expression. The reproach that he viewed the public life of his era, its social and political evolution, with indifference must be the most foolish that has ever been leveled against him. Rather, it requires an extra step to see more than social criticism in *À la recherche du temps perdu* and to read it as a panorama of the human condition.

Now I should like to turn to another aspect of Proust's oeuvre, but one that in the end will coincide with the one I have just indicated; based on the perspective of the last volume, *Le temps retrouvé* [*Time Regained*], the truths that have been discovered coalesce into one and the same balance sheet. In that book, Proust the author as well as Marcel Proust, the "I" of the novel, takes us into the Paris of the First World War, which is now no longer the city in which he played as a child on the Champs Elysées with Gilberte, his first love, and no longer the city in which he experienced his first social conquests and gained access to the exalted world of the aristocracy, or the city of his years with Albertine, the imprisoned and fugitive lover, but a Paris that has changed as much as its people have—in the cruel grip of passions that transcend the individual.

SPEAKER: "The town from being a black shapeless mass seemed suddenly to rise out of the abyss and the night into the luminous sky, where one after another the pilots soared upwards in answer to the heart-rending appeal of the sirens, while with a movement slower but more insidious, more alarming—for their gaze made one think of the object, still invisible but perhaps already very near, which it sought—the searchlights strayed ceaselessly to and fro, scenting the enemy, encircling him with their beams until the moment when the aeroplanes should be unleashed to bound after him in pursuit and seize him. And squadron after squadron, each pilot, as he soared thus above the town, itself now transported into the sky, resembled indeed a Valkyrie."[15]

AUTHOR: It is a time when everything, except the war, has been put on hold. But it is not the war that happens where the shots are fired or a war that could be depicted in a painted battle scene, but its reflection, which is more real: its invasion of everyone's language, its reverberation in the life

15 Marcel Proust, *Time Regained*, in *In Search of Lost Time*, 3162.

of the salons and in fashion and its ability to turn places into other places. The narrow hawthorn path of Méséglise has become Hill 307. The bridge over the Vivonne and the idyll it represents have been blown up. The Parisian ladies have discarded their pearls, and in order to demonstrate their patriotic spirit, they are wearing tight dark military tunics over short skirts and gaiters resembling those of the *poilus*. Those once ostracized as Dreyfus partisans have long ceased to be so; in the eyes of the trendsetters, the new enemies are the enemies of three-year conscription. All varieties of views are there, from blind Germanophilia to blind Germanophobia, and between their representatives we recognize the conciliator Saint-Loup, the once so radiant friend, who will soon find his death.

SPEAKER: "I do not wish to imply that the 'calamity' had raised Saint-Loup's intelligence to a new level. But just as soldier heroes with commonplace and trivial minds, if they happened to write poems during their convalescence, placed themselves, in order to describe the war, at the level not of events, which in themselves are nothing, but of the commonplace aesthetic whose rules they had obeyed in the past, and talked, as they would have ten years earlier, of the 'blood-stained dawn,' 'Victory's tremulous wings,' and so on, so Saint-Loup, by nature much more intelligent and much more of an artist, remained intelligent and an artist, and it was with the greatest good taste that he now recorded for my benefit the observations of landscape which he made if he had to halt at the edge of a marshy forest, very much as he would have done if he had been out duck-shooting. To help me to understand certain contrasts of light and shade which had been 'the enchantment of his morning,' he alluded in his letter to certain paintings which we both loved and was not afraid to cite a passage of Romain Rolland, or even of Nietzsche, with the independent spirit of the man at the front, who had not the civilian's terror of pronouncing a German name, and also—in thus quoting an enemy—with a touch of coquetry . . ."[16]

AUTHOR: Time and again, by means of such snapshots Proust succeeds in reminding us of the horror as well as the heinous occurrences of those years. Just as the lyrical letters of the friend contrast with the trench in which he is lying, the conduct of the queen of Parisian salons, Madame Verdurin, in whose residence military men and politicians come and go, contrasts with the sinking of the Lusitania.

SPEAKER: "So it was that the Verdurins gave dinner parties (then, after a time, Mme Verdurin gave them alone, for M. Verdurin died) and M. de

16 Proust, *Time Regained*, 3157–58.

Charlus went about his pleasures and hardly ever stopped to reflect that the Germans—immobilized, it is true, by a bloody barrier perpetually renewed—were only an hour by car from Paris. The Verdurins, one would imagine, did think about this fact, since they had a political salon in which every evening they and their friends discussed the situation not only of the armies but of the fleets. They thought certainly of these hecatombs of regiments annihilated and passengers swallowed by the waves; but there is a law of inverse proportion which multiplies to such an extent anything that concerns our own welfare and divides by such a formidable figure anything that does not concern it, that the death of unknown millions is felt by us as the most insignificant of sensations, hardly even as disagreeable as a draught. Mme. Verdurin, who suffered even more from her headaches now that she could no longer get croissants to dip in her breakfast coffee, had eventually obtained a prescription from Cottard permitting her to have them specially made in a certain restaurant of which we have spoken. This had been almost as difficult to wangle with the authorities as the appointment of a general. The first of these special croissants arrived on the morning on which the newspapers reported the sinking of the *Lusitania*.

As she dipped it in her coffee and gave a series of little flicks to her newspaper with one hand so as to make it stay open without her having to remove her other hand from the cup, 'How horrible!' she said. 'This is something more horrible than the most terrible stage tragedy.' But the death of all these drowned people must have been reduced a thousand million times before it impinged upon her, for even as, with her mouth full, she made these distressful observations, the expression which spread over her face, brought there (one must suppose) by the savor of that so precious remedy against headaches, the croissant, was in fact one of satisfaction and pleasure."[17]

AUTHOR: Because the war exercised a profound and striking effect on Proust's novel, nearly undermining its original outline, it seems important to present a few samples and new points of view according to which his characters are allowed to develop continually, pathologically, even as they succumb to the shock of war. More and more he turns to a ruthless observation of collective sentiments, which resemble individual feelings, and in this hectic, even morbid atmosphere he records the derailments of people, of classes, and of nations. Even more than in the case of the Dreyfus affair, in which Proust for the first time observed the problematic nature of convictions and how they change, opinions and how they too are transformed, the war wrenched him out of the world of fine taste, convention, and of an aristocratic and artistic outlook on life. Only by recognizing what changed abruptly and what remained unvarying during the

17 Proust, *Time Regained*, 3178–79.

war did he preserve his distance from any milieu that might have rendered him suspect, so that, viewed from the end of the book all of the episodes take on their appropriate accents. Correspondingly, his characters turn into the "monsters" that assume such dreadful cogency for us. Saint-Loup becomes the hero he has unconsciously always been; Madame Verdurin ascends, with exaggerated displays of chauvinism, to the highest circles; a formerly anti-militaristic historian switches his attention to military events; Charlus, already shunned now by many and forsaken and moving towards a dreadful decline, remembers his Bavarian ancestors and cannot aspire to destroy Germany.

SPEAKER: "And for this attitude of his the reason was, again, that the great collections of individuals called nations themselves behave to some extent like individuals. The logic that governs them is an inner logic, wrought and perpetually re-wrought by passions, like that of men and women at grips with one another in an amorous or domestic quarrel, the quarrel of a son with his father, or of a cook with her mistress, or a wife with her husband. The party who is in the wrong believes nevertheless that he is in the right—this was so in the case of Germany—and the party who is in the right sometimes supports his excellent cause with arguments which appear to him to be irrefutable only because they answer to his own passionate feelings. In these quarrels of individuals, the surest way of being convinced of the excellence of the cause of one party or the other is actually to be that party: a spectator will never to the same extent give his unqualified approval. Now within a nation the individual, if he is truly part of the nation, is simply a cell of the nation-individual. It is ridiculous to talk about the power of propaganda. Had the French been told that they were going to be beaten, no single Frenchman would have given way to despair any more than he would if he had been told that he was going to be killed by the Berthas. The real propaganda is what—if we are genuinely a living member of a nation—we tell ourselves because we have hope, hope being a symbol of a nation's instinct of self-preservation. To remain blind to the unjustness of the cause of the individual 'Germany,' to recognize at every moment the justness of the cause of the individual 'France,' the surest way was not for a German to be without judgment, or for a Frenchman to possess it, it was, both for the one and for the other, to be possessed of patriotism."[18]

AUTHOR: Proust's irony confirms his sovereign, incorruptible view of the course of events, even though he took sides both in the war and in the Dreyfus affair—for France, for Dreyfus. But that never prevented him from examining the realm of murderous compulsions that only those last

18 Proust, *Time Regained*, 3179–80.

few years allowed him to recognize with the eye of a scientist. Maturity makes a misanthrope of him, and out of a novel that commences with enchantment and figures seen with tenderness ensues an increasingly somber work. The characters change color and become darker: the Duchess of Guermantes is completely corrupted; Madame de Marsantes betrays the incurable pride of the aristocracy as a result of hypocritical humility; Saint-Loup ends up as an inhabitant of Sodom and a customer of the totally depraved Jupien. Without the war, which delayed the publication of the novel and prompted Proust to continue his work on it, *À la recherche du temps perdu* would have turned out much shorter and come closer to the classic ideal of the French novel, but it would not have taken on the disturbing, oceanic quality to which it owes its uniqueness.

After Proust presents us the main characters once again, with all of the stigmata that the war has imposed on them, night falls. A night in which the narrator all of a sudden finds himself in a Parisian bordello. He recognizes Jupien, his former factotum, in the owner, who has been transformed into the custodian of the Baron's vices. The events of that night constitute the core of the final phase; they are set in the innermost circle of hell, a horror show of human misery and human damnation in which the scum from below—the common folk—encounters the scum from above—high society.

The universal absurdity is mirrored by this specific instance of insanity. The great pandemonium is represented by a small one—and Proust the writer, the aesthete of yesteryear, has reached the point at which the horror surrounding him renders any visions of horror superfluous. This is also the night in which Jupien relates:

SPEAKER: "A slap in the face or a box on the ear helps to educate not only children but poets."[19]

AUTHOR: Still under the spell of the events he has witnessed in this house, Proust replies:

SPEAKER: "Meanwhile, this house is anything but what you say it might become. It is worse than a madhouse, since the mad fancies of the lunatics who inhabit it are played out as actual, visible drama—it is a veritable pandemonium. I thought that I had arrived, like the Caliph in the Arabian Nights, in the nick of time to rescue a man who was being beaten, and in fact it was a different tale from the Arabian Nights which I saw enacted

19 Proust, *Time Regained*, 3244.

before me, the one in which a woman who has been turned into a dog willingly submits to being beaten in order to recover her former shape."[20]

AUTHOR: But nobody will regain his former stature. This is the hour in which all have become "Pompeians," upon whom the fiery rain might fall at any moment.

SPEAKER: "In an instant the streets became totally black. At moments only, an enemy aeroplane flying very low lit up the spot upon which it wished to drop a bomb. I set off, but very soon I was lost. I thought of that day when, on my way to La Raspelière, I had met an aeroplane and my horse had reared as at the apparition of a god. Now, I thought, it would be a different meeting—with the god of evil, who would kill me. I started to walk faster in order to escape, like a traveler pursued by a tidal wave; I groped my way round dark squares from which I could find no way out. At last the flames of a blazing building showed me where I was and I got back on to the right road, while all the time the shells burst noisily above my head. But my thoughts had turned to another subject. I was thinking of Jupien's house, perhaps by now reduced to ashes, for a bomb had fallen very near me just after I had left it—that house upon which M. de Charlus might prophetically have written Sodoma, as the unknown inhabitant of Pompeii had done, with no less prescience or perhaps when the volcano had already started to erupt and the catastrophe had begun."[21]

AUTHOR: After that macabre nocturnal excursion, the end of the war is captured in a few short reflections, in utterances, obituaries, and meditations that to the younger readers among us sound as if they had been written not after the First World War, but after the Second, in a frame of mind that persuades us that the scrutiny of facts has the edge over prophecy.

The meticulous stocktaking of this positivist, who did not allow himself any glimpse beyond what was given, into whose world no light shone from above, and whose ecstasies served only the search for truth, has brought more of the mystery of humans and objects to light than have undertakings with loftier aspirations. The work arose from the struggle of the spirit against time, from the inability to find in fleeting real life a fixed point, an idea that could have given it direction.

SPEAKER: "How many for this reason turn aside from writing! What tasks do men not take upon themselves in order to evade this task! Every

20 Proust, *Time Regained*, 3245.
21 Proust, *Time Regained*, 3246.

public event, be it the Dreyfus case, be it the war, furnishes the writer with a fresh excuse for not attempting to decipher this book: he wants to ensure the triumph of justice, he wants to restore the moral unity of the nation, he has no time to think of literature. But these are mere excuses, the truth being that he has not or no longer has genius, that is to say instinct. For instinct dictates our duty and the intellect supplies us with pretexts for evading it. But excuses have no place in art and intentions count for nothing: at every moment the artist has to listen to his instinct, and it is this that makes art the most real of all things, the most austere school of life, the true last judgment."[22]

AUTHOR: That is how Proust becomes the translator, the interpreter of the reality that has revealed itself to him in his time and that existed within him, and his book was bound to result in the abandonment of all people and objects that had touched him, because truth could not be made to speak in any other way. Years after the war he once again returns to Paris, to the "world," as someone who had left the city. Once again, he enters the salon of the Princess of Guermantes and, once again, he is surprised. For after the passing of so many years, he finds himself facing people upon whom ashes have fallen, whom he no longer recognizes, old men and old women, and young people, whom he has never seen before. What has time wrought? Old friends have fallen out with one another and new friendships have been made; political passions have cooled; families have been disbanded; the social classes have undergone a new displacement; beautiful and precious things have vanished, and those who were loved are loved no longer. An unforgiving torrent has swept away victors and vanquished alike toward death. But he himself is no longer recognized either. He has to acknowledge that he too has grown old—and a notion of time comes to him that calls into question any notion of an afterlife, even one that affects art. Yet, that realization is also the only one to afford him the creative impulse and will to execute his work of art. He now begins to fear death and to count the days, not because he fears his own destruction, but because he senses that he has already passed through all the circles and died many times. The "I" that loved Albertine died when it ceased to love her, and the "I" that loved the Duchess of Guermantes died when it ceased to love her. No longer was he someone capable of such passions and sufferings but one who saw a task before him that had to be completed at any cost. That anxiety superseded every other.

SPEAKER: "To me it seems more correct to say that the cruel law of art is that people die and we ourselves die after exhausting every form of suf-

22 Proust, *Time Regained*, 3299–300.

fering, so that over our heads may grow the grass not of oblivion but of eternal life, the vigorous and luxuriant growth of a true work of art, and so that thither, gaily and without a thought for those who are sleeping beneath them, future generations may come to enjoy their déjeuner sur l'herbe."[23]

AUTHOR: He imagines that he is perched on a mountain peak and peering down into the depth of the years, endangered by the attempt to hold on with all his might to avoid sliding down, and he closes his work with a sentence that sets up its beginning. The end has become a beginning. The last word comes before the first.

SPEAKER: "So, if I were given long enough to accomplish my work, I should not fail, even if the effect were to make them resemble monsters, to describe men as occupying so considerable a place, compared with the restricted place which is reserved for them in space, a place on the contrary prolonged past measure, for simultaneously, like giants plunged into the years, they touch the distant epochs through which they have lived, between which so many days have come to range themselves—in TIME."[24]

AUTHOR: But what happens to ourselves as we look back upon this novel, upon its venues, which are not ours, upon the lives and deaths of these monsters that he has preserved for us? They are there, I think, in order for us to take possession of them—of a new, frightening openness so that we may enter every succession of love, jealousy and deception, ambition and disenchantment, ultimately truth and destruction. It is not a book that deals with one character or another, but one in which the one or the other generic figure might be imbued with life—a book of pure associations in which every sentence and every passage is an "open sesame" and unlocks a door within us.

SPEAKER: "In reality every reader is, while he is reading, the reader of his own self. The writer's work is merely a kind of optical instrument which he offers to the reader to enable him to discern what, without this book, he would perhaps never have perceived in himself. And the recognition by the reader in his own self of what the book says is the proof of its veracity, the contrary also being true, at least to a certain extent, for the difference

23 Proust, *Time Regained*, 3487. "Luncheon on the grass" is a reference to Manet's large oil painting of 1862–63 of the same name, depicting a female nude and a scantily dressed female bather on a picnic with two fully dressed men in a rural setting.

24 Proust, *Time Regained*, 3499.

between the two texts may sometimes be imputed less to the author than to the reader. Besides, the book may be too learned, too obscure for a simple reader, and may therefore present to him a clouded glass through which he cannot read. And other peculiarities can have the same effect as inversion. In order to read with understanding many readers require to read in their own particular fashion, and the author must not be indignant at this; on the contrary, he must leave the reader all possible liberty, saying to him: 'Look for yourself, and try whether you see best with this lens or that one or this other one.'"[25]

AUTHOR: The freedom that Proust grants to his readers has also been employed here, since there are many different ways of reading him: as a social critic, as a theoretician of art, as a philosopher—and several readings have been assayed in this essay, readings that certainly cannot render a picture of the whole, but which were intended to show him as he wanted to be seen—as the creator of characters who from this moment on live among us with their sufferings and fallacies, for the purpose of our solace, and as the creator of places that will now be remembered because, although we shall not find them on any map, they are inhabited and loved by those characters and are witness to as much misery as those miraculous settings that generated great myths and were populated by heroes, demigods, and gods. For Proust, who at the end of his life freely renounced everything to liberate the imprisoned images of the world, fasting and working in pain alone in his four bare walls, and finally attained a greater degree of truth than any writer before him, may be characterized by the words with which he eulogized Ruskin:

SPEAKER: "Though dead, he still shines for us, like long extinct stars whose light is still traveling towards us. Generations after us will still see nature with those eyes, closed forever now and resting in the depth of the grave."[26]

AUTHOR: It was this positivist and mystic, for whom the world of art alone was absolute, staunchly denying himself any prospect and hope beyond the imprisonment in the here and now, who wrote of one of his literary figures, the poet Bergotte: "They buried him, but all through that night of mourning, in the lighted shop-windows, his books, arranged three by three, kept vigil like angels with outspread wings and seemed, for him who was no more, the symbol of his resurrection."

---

25 Proust, *Time Regained*, 3336.

26 The passage is cited from Proust, "A Propos de Baudelaire."

Unpublished draft

Recently I received a letter from the editors of a journal for whom I am supposed to pen an essay on Proust and who wrote to me with great candor: . . . Having read that passage with some consternation, consternation because I know that book very well and, to make no bones about it, admire. . . . But now I knew that I had to start from a different set of premises, i.e., that Proust's work is still almost unknown in Germany and, where it is not, that prejudices are possibly fed by erroneous judgments. Scholarship on Proust does indeed present a very strange and curious picture, and the more panegyric it is, the more desolate it leaves the reader. Even the famous essay by Ernst Robert Curtius, to name but one example, though a particularly brilliant one that discovered that manuscript for Germany, cannot change the situation in any way. Qualities of style and refinement are described with admiration in that essay, and though I should be the first to admit that all those things are indeed remarkable, they suggest a sensitive, talented writer, a *decadent*, a splendid portraitist of a vanished era.

But since new readers come of age every day for an author, later generations with a new perspective, the work changes, if there is enough strength in it, such that readers resurrect it with every new reading, unmistakable, to be sure, but revealing itself in new ways, so that a reader might say what he has gleaned from it today.

But of course it is totally impossible to talk about it and at the same time to initiate a listener into those lives, those six volumes—fourteen is the number in the French Gallimard edition—to familiarize him with Combray and Méséglise and Guermantes, those oracular sites situated in France as Delos is in Greece, to introduce him to Swann and Baron Charlus, to Gilberte and Albertine, people about whom Proust claims in the end: and should they emerge as veritable monsters in time.

I should like to take him at his word with respect to the veritable monsters that he hoped and feared he would create. That is not the vocabulary of a nervous man who was wary of the light.

À la recherche du temps perdu is a fearsome book, a book of truth, it is one of those books about which we would hope that we never understand them completely, never read them completely; it is a book of radical disenchantment, an adventure of the wretched and violated heart, a book without a trace of palliation and one of towering beauty.

Playing Watten and Other Writings (On Thomas Bernhard) An Attempt[1]

Since nothing remains undiscovered, nothing unprinted, nothing without praise; furthermore, the misfortune besetting books of literary criticism must be found in a place other than where it is usually sought; finally, the infelicity of criticism that toils on many fronts: indeed all of these factors might be due to criticism's complete lack of admiration for matters of quality.

For several years now, books by Thomas Bernhard have appeared, not as a consequence of the writer's being overly prolific, but obviously from a wellspring of the highest and most intense productivity, and of the most recent of those books, *Prose* [*Prosa*], *Playing Watten* [*Watten: Ein Nachlaß*], and even *Gargoyles* [*Verstörung*], with its colossal monologue of Prince Saurau . . . pages so painful for the reader that I would hesitate to swear I had read them all, indeed am unable to read them all.

That someone writes at a distance [from] contemporary literature and even increases that distance by adopting solitude, not allowing [it] to diminish between the two covers of a book, is in itself reason enough not [to] know what to make of him. Where does he belong, what does he want, where are the references (to what?), what conversation is interrupted by this monologue (that is to say none at all), what does he have to say and to whom? And society, the readers, the public, the confrontations, the demands, the benefit?

When the questions about what constitutes modernity, what is new, fall silent, then, without a doubt, that means that it cannot be read on the surface, is not an experiment in arranging letters on the page, not a calligraphic test of courage, but a radicalism that is embedded in a way of thinking and extends to the outer limits. How extensively these books reflect the times, something they do not even propose doing, will be grasped by a later era, just as a later period came to understand Kafka. Everything in these books is precise, assuredly of the most searing precision; yet we do not fathom the thing that is so precisely portrayed here, which is ourselves.

The question of style, which even the most brilliant minds of the ages have never been able to answer, whether it is the collective traits, the personal idiosyncrasies, the complete disappearance of any idiosyncrasy, a style of inconspicuousness, as it were—in keeping with the old adage that

1 Bachmann's gloss on Bernhard has not been dated, but was presumably penned after *Watten* appeared in 1969. Comprised of discrete fragments, the text provided here is an attempt to collate several pieces into a coherent commentary on the younger author and fellow Austrian.

the best-dressed person is dressed [inconspicuously]—[is] no more easily answered today than it has ever been. Style is without doubt inconspicuous, if what is meant by that is that it is both overlooked and perceived; idiosyncrasy comes out of compulsion, and in Bernhard's works everything is compulsive, the use of dreadful, stupid, dear Sir civilities, distances, a vocabulary of fright, a stigmatization; adjectives bestow dignity once again, the verbs are [among the] most extensive variety permitted by the German language, talking downward, not merely talking against, talking out of, talking into, talking up, in Bernhard everything becomes talking downward, talking from above.

Great books do not put the less great ones or the worthless ones to shame, since they come into being on another planet. But without those books, literature would be a conglomeration of written texts, for they are so necessary that it is obvious that they have to come about.

All of Bernhard's books bear the stamp of necessity, inevitability, of the inexorable, beginning perhaps with *Amras*, in which the anxiety is even stronger than the mastery over that anxiety, the vitreous calm when confronting a crumbling world. Processes become simpler, their meaning more obvious in the totality of their meaninglessness. Here a few lines from *Playing Watten* on the objects manufactured today: "Industry makes everything too small nowadays, I say to the truck driver, they make everything too short and too tight, and of the very poorest quality. Basically, people go around in clothes that are a swindle, because they are too short, too tight, and of poor quality. But people have long ago lost the feeling for quality. For durability. For first-class workmanship. Everything you touch falls apart after only a short while."[2]

The no-longer-going-to-the-card-game, the no-longer-going-to-the-theater, which, significantly, is the real event and not, as many believe, that there is a crisis of the theater, of drama, of comedy, rather going to the theater is the issue here and why it is not possible to do so. Playing cards is the issue, and why that is not possible. At issue are many things that can no longer be remedied, the uneducable, the incorrigible; as long as we do not know what is incurable, we shall also be unable to catch hold of the very least at the place where it . . .[3]

In the end, a great predicament presents itself that is greater than anything that we expected, and we can expect very little these days, to be sure. Is there cause for praise here? Is fame on the rise, the fame of German literature, which has had to wait, like everything else, for its moment of glory?

---

2 Thomas Bernhard, *Playing Watten*, in *Three Novellas*, trans. Kenneth J. Northcott (Chicago: University of Chicago Press, 2003), 76–77.

3 Bachmann's text is an anacoluthon.

Bertolt Brecht: Preface to an Anthology of His Poetry[1]

Brecht is a very peculiar poet. He already has a reprimand on his report card, and that is the reason that he has not been allowed to join the conversation.

He is still standing in the corner and has not been permitted to take his seat.

In Rome, there is a small theater that he would have liked, it has benches like those in old schoolhouses, with grooves for pens and a hole for the inkwell; there, Brecht is not performed, but someone else is played, recklessly, passionately, which Brecht might have liked.

Brecht wrote many poems, some of which I read very early, others I have not yet read, there are so many of them, some say that they have the typical Brecht tone, while other poems do not; they slipped through his fingers without prior ado; and some lines read as if they had been penned by the best German poets, verses under which we usually note: "poet unknown."[2]

Brecht is best when he is "unknown." "And the sky with its stars holds the cross high aloft," but what did he mean by that?[3] Fortunately, that is something no one will know, for no swarm of literary scholars will ever figure out what someone meant by being held aloft.

A radical intelligence, a lead weight, the lightness of air, those are prerequisites; what is doable is done. The best is not doable, although it has demonstrably been done.

La grazia sola[4] is a concept he would not have admired, except for the literal meaning of the words, and what is there besides the literal meaning?

---

1 Bachmann's draft of a preface to an anthology of Brecht's poetry was written presumably in 1969, but remained unpublished during her lifetime.

2 During the Nazi period, Heinrich Heine's poem "Loreley" was published in German textbooks followed by the attribution "poet unknown." Bachmann is also referring to Brecht's own adaptation of *Sechs chinesische Gedichte* (Six Chinese Poems), which uses the phrase "unknown poet, 100 BC" to refer to one of the original Chinese authors.

3 Presumably, Bachmann is alluding to two lines from the third stanza of Brecht's poem "Concerning a Drowned Girl" ("Vom ertrunkenen Mädchen"): "Evenings the sky grew dark as smoke, / At night the stars held light high aloft." In *Selected Poems*, trans. H. R. Hays (New York: Reynal & Hitchcock, 1947), 49. Translation slightly altered.

4 *La grazia sola* (Latin: *Sola gratia*), Italian for "by grace alone," is one of the five Protestant doctrines (*solas*) according to which salvation is possible *only* through a sovereign act of grace from God—an undeserved and essential divine gift. Brecht would certainly not have accepted the concept of divine salvation, yet

Brecht is so simple that posterity cannot do him much harm either, although he smells of sweat; if someone wants to smell sweat, then let him, but if he cannot tolerate smells, then there are many other things that remain besides that. That Brecht might be more than intelligent, that he might have wit and that the intellectual pace in any poem cannot be replicated, that is something that does not occur to them; they stride along, so they think, and they cannot hear that he has left them far behind.

When half an era has gone by, greater affinities are felt and more of that "I feel the air of another planet";[5] it is the mortal enemies that feel it.

Undeniably, everybody knows that Brecht wrote for the class struggle, that he wrote first as an anarchist, then in the spirit of class conflict, finally as someone firmly anchored in the system. There is nothing that anyone can do to counter that, because quibbling is of no use: he did it, and who are we to judge him? Some choose to judge for specific reasons, while others choose alternative motives, but no one really knows anything about the past. Who knows why Dante consigned some to hell, others to paradise; a regiment of classicists, truly remarkable, eminently serviceable; there were battles then, now there are others, and it is possible to examine the refuse, except that we merely look at the lines of others in yet another light. What seems to be left over?

If there were justice in the world, Brecht would have become the popular poet everyone understands, for his inflection, his contradictions, his macabre sense of humor would have afforded him that distinction, but no one loves the people less than those who presume that they have

---

Bachmann seems to suggest that he would have embraced a more literal, secular meaning of grace.

5 First line of Stefan George's poem "Transport" ("Entrückung") in Arnold Schoenberg's preferred translation by Carl Engel, Dr. Peter Hesterman's pages on Eastern Illinois University website, accessed January 27, 2021, http://www.ux1.eiu.edu/~pdhesterman/pdfs/modernism/Entrueckung%5BTransport%5D.pdf. Schoenberg set the poem to atonal music for soprano in the fourth and last movement of his String Quartet No. 2 (1908). In quoting from George's poem here, Bachmann connects Brecht to the composer Schoenberg, whose atonal compositions she references throughout her work as a metaphor of the new poetic language to which she herself aspires. Schoenberg's breakthrough to a radically new musical language, inspired by George's poems, including "Entrückung," is for Bachmann a further instance of the kind of "beautiful language" that Brecht manages to create in his writing. Associating the poet with the composer and his words with music, for a public that "cannot hear (!) that he has left them far behind," Bachmann pays tribute by weaving into this preface a montage of Brecht quotes in which she lets the poet's words, "the typical Brecht tone," resound with the clarity and wisdom, "the grand gestures," she so deeply reveres.

devoted too much time to the people; the people do not appreciate their own sense of humor.

Brecht acquired those traits by observing people, but people never looked back at him; they gaze at him in bleary-eyed wonder, failing to appreciate the natural turns, yes, the sea is blue, so blue,[6] and certainly not directly in the face,[7] they fail to recognize their own humorous traits.

I believe he does not have a public. He is as foreign as Hölderlin, and his pathos, a pathos I admire, the lofty tone, also remains unappreciated. See there two cranes,[8] and there, to sweep it away, the wind.[9]

Brecht has such grand gestures, ones that are so folk-like, that, while some are not sufficiently folk-like, the others are much too magnificent to move our gut feelings or whatever it might be.

The attempt to rescue him is ironic, catastrophic, contradictory, glorious.

Exemplary:

He had the big words in the right places, he had a share, as I once tried to assert, in utopia, in the millennial struggle against bad language. In our dream of expression.[10]

Do it in an exemplary way.

---

6 "Yes, the sea is blue, so blue," a quote from Bertolt Brecht, Kurt Weill, and Dorothy Lane, "What the Sailormen Say (The Sailors' Tango)," trans. Chris Hazell in the CD liner notes to Ute Lemper, with RIAS Sinfonietta Berlin, conducted by John Mauceri, *Ute Lemper Sings Kurt Weill*, vol. 2 Decca Compact Disc 436 417-2, 1993, 11–14.

7 "Not directly in the face," a quote from Wilhelm Michel's untitled review of Brecht's play *St. Joan of the Stockyards* (*Die heilige Johanna der Schlachthöfe*), *Kölnische Zeitung*, February 1933.

8 "See there two cranes": "Sieh jene Kraniche," also rendered as "look at those cranes" and as "see how those cranes," the title of the "Duet of the Cranes," in Act II, scene 14 of Bertolt Brecht, *The Rise and Fall of the City of Mahagonny*, trans. W. H. Auden and Chester Kallman (Boston: David R. Godine, 1976), 71. Brecht's poem "Terzinen über die Liebe" (Tercets on Love) also begins with these same words: "Sieh jene Kraniche in großem Bogen" (rendered as: "See how those cranes fly arcing through the sky"). Bertolt Brecht, "Tercets on Love," in *Love Poems*, trans. David Constantine and Tom Kuhn (New York: Liveright Publishing Corporation, 2015), 56–57. The Willet/Manheim edition of the collected plays also uses the Auden/Kallman translation.

9 Probable play on the line "There shall remain of these cities but the wind that blew through them!" Bertolt Brecht, "Concerning Poor B.B.," in *Selected Poems*, 15–17.

10 In her fifth Frankfurt Lecture, Bachmann articulates her belief in the power of poetic language to redeem something of "our dream of expression, a dream that is never entirely to be realized."

Will you still do something for yourself? Full of hope and resolve, with strong motions, in an exemplary way.[11]

"Anything else would be too bitter."[12]

The folk are not loristic.[13]

We do not live forever.[14]

No, certainly not.

With his poems, in any case, and with his songs he fell between all stools, and when that happens, there is room to be discovered. The clever people love the songs, which are not in the very least about them, and all of the rest understand neither the one nor the other, the hymns, the darkness, the incantation, the forests, the . . . unknown god.

In a good sense, Brecht is a . . ., he ingested literature as well as the gutter, or rather the literature of the gutter and of the gallow-birds, the

---

11 Citation from the last three lines of Brecht's 1937 poem for film star Carola Neher, where the poet asks: "Will you do something for yourself? / Hopeful and responsible / With good movements, exemplary?" Bertolt Brecht, "Washing (C.N.)," trans. Michael Hamburger in *Bertolt Brecht: Poems 1913–1956*, ed. John Willett and Ralph Manheim, second edition (New York: Methuen, 1979), 290. Translation slightly altered. Bachmann omits Brecht's question mark.

12 The last three lines of Brecht's poem "The Leavetaking" ("Der Abschied") read: "We speak of the weather and of our / Enduring friendship. Anything else / Would be too bitter." Bertolt Brecht, "The Leavetaking," trans. Naomi Replansky, in *Poems 1913–1956*, 275.

13 Citation from the final two lines of Brecht's poem "Da das Instrument verstimmt ist" (Since the instrument is out of tune), which ends: "If we want to remain a force for those below, we cannot write in a folkloristic vein, for the folk are not loristic." Brecht's coinage *tümlich*, rendered here as "loristic," suggests both "popular" or "folksy" (*volkstümlich*) and "simple-minded" or "inane" ("*dümmlich*"). Bertolt Brecht, "Da das Instrument verstimmt ist," in *Werke: Große kommentierte Berliner und Frankfurter Ausgabe*, ed. Werner Hecht, Jan Knopf, Werner Mittenzwei, and Klaus-Detlef Müller, 30 vols. (Berlin and Weimar/Frankfurt am Main: Aufbau/Suhrkamp, 1988–1998), vol. 14, *Gedichte 4*, 418. The poem has only recently been translated into English by Tom Kuhn: "Now the instrument is out of tune," in *The Collected Poems of Bertolt Brecht*, edited and translated by Tom Kuhn and David Constantine (London: Liveright, 2019), 643–44.

14 "We do not live forever" is the last line of Brecht's untranslated poem "Nimm Platz am Tisch" [Take a Seat at the Table], in *Werke: Große kommentierte Berliner und Frankfurter Ausgabe*, ed. Werner Hecht, Jan Knopf, Werner Mittenzwei, and Klaus-Detlef Müller, 30 vols. (Berlin and Weimar/Frankfurt am Main: Aufbau/Suhrkamp, 1988–1998), vol. 15, *Gedichte 5*, 215–16. This has also only recently been translated into English by David Constantine: "Sit down to eat," in *The Collected Poems of Bertolt Brecht*, 961.

lofty tone, the unending skies, in other words, we may as well say it, he is an unknown poet who sometimes becomes the poet unknown.[15]

It is easy to sit in the theater and take in the show, after all, something is taking place, but what happens in poems? And who determines that, and who dares to talk about it?

In a melange of Chinese, of Southern German, of pathos of the very best pedigree, of the malicious, of the Roman, of an unsurpassed Shakespeare, everything is there, it is the great manual, the keyboard, the omniscience, the omnipotence to do everything that transcends ability. Because he is able to do everything, he can indeed do more, he is not always able to be a master, rather he says: at last her hair,[16] or: It was a day,[17] or: the terse contraction, the proverbial wisdom: *non operare.*[18]

It is necessary to be a great operator to always be able to sit down modestly in the end and utter: Well, I do not know, or I do indeed know.

That Brecht might also be buried in his secret, that was my first notion of Brecht, and it will also be my last.

But the secret is nothing special, on the contrary, it is the natural thing, it is the only coffin lid that always opens.

In its best hours, reading touches that secret and brings it to life. Words that initiate the creaturely and the creative.

In the second year of my flight,[19] albeit not the first.

Between Ovid with his desperate song of exile, "*Et tu* . . .,[20] and Brecht, the epochs do not converge, nor the adventures, not even the adventures of writing, yet the space of a continent does converge, though the great progeny who meets up with a great forebear is not a leveling

---

15 "Poet unknown": See footnote 2 above.

16 Brecht, "Concerning a Drowned Girl," 49. The poem ends: "First her face, her hands, at last her hair. / Then she was carrion with the carrion in the water."

17 Opening words of Brecht's poem, "Remembering Marie A." ("Erinnerung an Marie A."): "It was a day in that blue month September / Silent beneath a plum tree's slender shade / I held her there, my love so pale and silent / As if she were a dream that must not fade." Bertolt Brecht, "Remembering Marie A.," trans. John Willett, in *Poems 1913–1956*, 35. Here, as throughout the preface, Bachmann chooses to let Brecht speak for himself by offering us a compilation of the poet's own inimitable words and phrases.

18 Italian for "do not operate," suggesting that we should leave Brecht's language just as it is since there is no need to rework or improve on his constructions—the noun "operatore" refers to a construction worker.

19 Bertolt Brecht, "In the Second Year of my Flight," trans. Michael Hamburger, in *Poems 1913–1956,* 251. The poem begins: "In the second year of my flight, / I read in a paper, in a foreign language / that I had lost my citizenship."

20 Possibly a reference to "Solomon Song," originally from the *Threepenny Opera* (*Dreigroschenoper*), where Brecht's Caesar cries "You, too, my son!" Bertolt Brecht, "Solomon Song," in *Selected Poems,* 73–75

element, rather its opposite, even if it only (only!) involves a letter to the tax office.[21]

For Brecht, any and every occasion was truly great, and he was not equal to every one of them, but no tone was lofty enough for him, even for the lowliest subject, and so the lesson is not Yea yea, Nay nay, but Come as a great man.

He is the last German within a grand tradition; his grassland was very rocky; it caused him much bewilderment, more than we might think; he never ceased to think grandly, to think what was grand, to think from the lowliest to the most grand, for thinking is nothing if not that: so he was right, the old man.

21 Presumably, Bachmann is comparing the great Roman poet Ovid (43 BCE–17 CE) with Brecht, bringing both authors into the spatial and temporal sphere of a European continent that was once under Roman rule. She also references the petition Brecht filed with the German tax office in 1927 in which he claims tax exemption for being little more than a professional playwright.

The Bell Jar / The Quintessential Horror (On Sylvia Plath)[1]

Sylvia Plath[2] killed herself in London at the age of thirty. Respect for those close to her, the right to privacy, to secrecy, forbid us to say more about it.

Nevertheless, *The Bell Jar* may justifiably be called an autobiographical novel, but by no means because in it someone offers her private affairs to a public addicted to sensational revelations; rather, autobiographical in the sense in which the intellectual figure[3] of a thoughtful, disintegrating, beaten and ruined creature can be singularly interesting and captivating for another person.

Perhaps *The Bell Jar* has an unfortunate title; its striking trait in the beginning is the almost incredible streak of humor, the comic, infantile, clownish element in this nineteen-year-old Esther Greenwood, who is a girl with straight As in school, winning every prize and every scholarship, and who slowly derails in New York in a flurry of dinners, parties, pointless kisses. She derails in such an imperceptible way that even after a third reading you are still asking yourself where that hidden catastrophe started, and how. And I am inclined to consider that factor, like everything that is not verifiable in a book, the best and strangest element.

The night scene in New York, after Esther has cast her clothes and her underwear from a high-rise to the wind, and in the next scene we find her on a bus going home to her mother, in a borrowed dirndl dress, with two bloodstains on her face.[4]

After that, scene after scene, the race into suicide, into an insanity that, while never identified, even though the conversation with the physicians is recorded, is described in a cluster of symptoms with uncanny

1 Bachmann's essay on Sylvia Plath (1932–1963) was drafted in 1968, the year in which *The Bell Jar* was released by Suhrkamp Verlag in translation. The assumption is that Bachmann was introduced to Plath's widower Ted Hughes (1930–1998) in 1966 and that she was already acquainted with examples of Plath's works at the time she met him.

2 Plath is an American novelist and poet known for an intensely personal style and an ever-growing fascination with death.

3 Bachmann would later characterize her own novel *Malina* with the phrase "intellectual, imaginary autobiography," which she borrowed in part from Hans Magnus Enzensberger's afterword to the German translation of Carlo Emilio Gadda's *La cognizione del dolore* (The Recollection of Pain, 1963), first published in 1966.

4 Bachmann is referring to the scenes in chapters 9–10. Sylvia Plath, *The Bell Jar* (Cutchogue, NY: Buccaneer Books, 1971), 91–92.

precision, where other authors (such as Marguerite Duras[5]) fail completely, because they obviously do not understand that the clinical depiction of mental illness, of psychosis, also entails an exact description, and that it is not sufficient to string together random delusions because they have something "poetic" about them. There is nothing poetic about illness, and the great invalids, from Dostoevsky to Sylvia Plath, know that; illness is the quintessential horror, it is something with a lethal outcome.

Now the critic also ought to ask how Sylvia Plath writes, questions of style, of point of view, how does she do it?

It is the only question that never forces itself on the readers, for if someone has a story to tell and has so little time to think about it, everything seems to fall into place all by itself, and all of the simple questions of art are subordinated to that sense of urgency, without resulting in anything other than art, and not the template of artistic adventure, of exhibitionism, of betrayal and self-deception that "distinguish" almost all new novels and drive the critics, who are becoming more and more timid, into a corner.

There are very few new things happening on the literary scene; I do not believe that Sylvia Plath is something new, she has neither shattered the English language, nor has she resurrected it, and she has not accomplished anything that might inspire her critics to particularly extravagant notions.

But like the writers who have been to hell, she will be among the first, because she was among the last,[6] and since the publication of Malcolm Lowry's[7] posthumous papers, I have not known anything in English literature capable of such derailment and in which there are passages that are as frightening as they are moving.

. . . is, in which the figs from the fig tree of which she dreams have strangely ripened nonetheless, not all of them but the one—for Esther it means becoming "a famous poet."[8]

And in the end, the title is also forgotten, for there is no book that can less easily be imagined under a bell jar than this one about Esther, . . .

---

5 Author of *Le ravissement de Lol V. Stein* (The Rapture of Lol V. Stein), which describes the events of the night in which the title character parts with her fiancé.

6 An ironic reference to the Biblical story of Judgment Day, in which "many who are first will be last [in heaven], and many who are last shall be first" (Matthew 19:30).

7 Malcolm Lowry (1909–1957) was an English novelist concerned with the loneliness of the modern age.

8 In chapter 5 Esther reads a story about a Jewish man and a beautiful dark nun who meet under a fig tree. Later, the figs become a symbol of the life choices that face Esther. See Plath, *The Bell Jar*, 45.

4: Visual Rhetoric and Poetics

Commentary

> I saw, where Rome's streets come to an end, the triumphant sky moving into the city, the sky that did not stoop under any gate and that spread itself across the seven hills, blue after raids along Sicily's coasts and full of the island fruits of the Tyrrhenian Sea, unscathed after inroads to the brigands of the Abruzzi and black from swarms of swallows rescued across the Apennine Mountains. I saw the lauded sky of ermine and the paltry sky of burlap, and I saw in its greatest moments its hand calmly executing the golden ratio above the housetops.

THERE ARE SINGULAR MOMENTS in Bachmann's texts, such as this excerpt from her early prose piece "What I Saw and Heard in Rome," that reveal how images capture the idiosyncratic and at the same time transmit a collective idea. Here, the singular moment is observed in a Roman sky, oscillating from shades of blue and black to ermine and burlap before executing configurations in keeping with the golden ratio, a mathematical principle documented by Euclid more than 2,300 years ago. In keeping with the practice of emphasizing singular moments, Bachmann's poetics suggest that texts, as modern cultural artifacts, should be inseparable from indelible impressions passed down from one generation to the next. Yet, as Bachmann explains in the first of her highly acclaimed Lectures on Poetics, held in Frankfurt in 1959, "however radiant individual thoughts from an earlier time may come down to us, when we invoke them, we only do so in support of our thoughts today." Experienced as communications from earlier times, Bachmann's imagery is embedded in a generative process in which thoughts from the past are cast as images and images represent signifiers for what is to come.

Uniting objects etched in words with visual connotations and drawing subtle associations, her imagery moves beyond superficial denotations to become a confluence of signifiers both real and virtual. For Bachmann, images inform the postwar aesthetic experience, an experience that can be likened to a situation of beholding, full of novel perceptions that are at once edifying and transformative for the reader. In the first lecture on poetics, she likened the transformative effect of great art to a rupture. As Bachmann described it, the rupture results from a desire to dig down into the substructure of words and language to find new meanings. In turn, these meanings are best expressed as images, which maintain integrity over time, whereas language as a medium submits to the demands of the collective and can easily suffer corruption. Accordingly, art is no longer measured horizontally as a temporal succession of evolving styles, but as a vertical displacement or continual realignment of arbitrary signifiers. Only these can incite an emphatic change of perception and transform the consciousness of the reader. She writes: "In art, there is no progress along the horizontal, but rather the ever-changing rupture of the vertical. Solely the means and techniques applied to art give the impression that we are dealing with progress. In fact, what remains possible is transformation. And the transforming effect that emanates from new works educates us to a new perception, a new feeling, a new consciousness."

Bachmann's transformative approach to the literary arts reveals how eager the author was to redefine the aesthetic experience after 1945. Cognizant of literature's role as a social and cultural agent, she insisted that images, timeless and evocative of eternal truths, differ from the words used to evoke them. At face value, words and language are subservient to time: "Only images, of course, are timeless. Thinking, rooted in time, also succumbs to time. And because it expires, for that very reason our thinking must be new if it is to be genuine and if it is to make a difference." Because images, rather than words, conjure up striking, mostly antithetical associations, Bachmann's tautly woven poems and prose pieces tend to follow contradictory objectives. On the one hand, there is a strong desire to proliferate new forms of the imaginary, calling upon imagery to stimulate unprecedented layers of meaning and comprehension. On the other, there is a tendency to immobilize, even mortify these images, so that they take on the stationary quality of signifiers. The result is a tension between fleeting impressions or visual insights and signifiers frozen in time. This tension characterizes the aesthetic core of Bachmann's Rome text. Balancing a subtle play between a questionable past and an equally questionable present in her evocation of the legendary city, Bachmann's visual rhetoric reinforces the conflict between words with established connotations and images that shatter those connotations.

Turning once again to Bachmann's images of the eternal city, it now seems appropriate that the aesthetic or transformative experience embedded in the text is cast in visual terms, in imagery that is as telling for its author as it is for its readers:

> I have often seen that each builds his house the way he likes, and that no plan brings all the pieces together better than chance and individual taste. But no taste is sufficient to create the spaces, separate areas for sun and shade, and no chance solves the equation in which the weightiness of a wall expresses the weightlessness of a tower. The houses are clad in ancient linen, withered the colors on it.

> Only when light penetrates the porous fabric does the color become apparent to the eye; a brown capable of every transformation.

Blending the weave of the text, seen from an interior position, with the observation of the many hues suffused into the fabric of the signs from an external perspective, Bachmann's Roman vignettes foreshadow her theoretical approach to art in the postwar period. She argues that art should persist in a violent world, after the cataclysms have subsided and an indelible trauma haunts the collective. At the same time, she explores how cultural memory and individual recollection can be encapsulated in a visual rhetoric so uncanny, so searing, that images supplant language to become the preferred agents of truth. Asserting that the visual subverts the jaded words enveloping postwar collectives, Bachmann seeks an absolute or utopian quality that she maintains can only be found in imagery. Likewise, her visual rhetoric captures the many iterations of critical discourse in literary texts.

"On the Trail of Language" ("Auf den Spuren der Sprache"), an early fragment about the impossibility of writing poetry, in which Bachmann argues that "the trail leading to a poem is a trail of language, leading through language, a tissue of words, sentences, pauses," serves to highlight her intentions. Here, language figures as an organic substance, rather than as a creative tool for the writer. Open to interpretation and analysis, language gives rise to the larger questions confronting society, while its allusions amount to little more than self-reflecting riddles. On the one hand, Bachmann asserts that poetry as an art form, which is inherently conducive to visual signifiers, such as metaphors and similes, does not pose riddles. On the other, she argues that language as a tool for expressing art does: "generally, there are not many things that are riddles, with the exception, perhaps, of language. For language does not give us any clue to itself." Insisting that language (medium) and meaning (content) are at odds with one another, in her second lecture on poetics Bachmann articulates a multifaceted approach to poetry. Echoing her other critical writings, she emphasizes once again that literature is made up of words and that words elude us as agents of truth:

> The literature behind us, what is it anyway: a sea of words, cut out of the walls of hearts, and of tragic silences and fallow stretches of words talked to death and stagnant pools of stinking, cowardly silence talked to death; both have always been part of it, language and silence, and of two kinds. And both are always beckoning and enticing. Our share in error is indeed assured, but our share in a new truth—where does that begin?

It appears that Bachmann's exhortation to unearth meaning in language should be equated with her desire for the individual artist and the collective to overcome traditional perceptions of text and context. Indeed, she conjectures that if society does not embrace a literature embodying "a serious and uncomfortable spirit striving for change, then that would be tantamount to a declaration of bankruptcy." Keenly aware of language's flaws, which can subvert even superficial attempts to designate objects in a text, Bachmann gravitates toward images that obviate the insinuations and innuendos fueling language's riddles. At the same time, the tension between image and sign or content and form in Bachmann's texts draws attention to that unspeakable law according to which all cultural memory has been wrought, the *Schandgesetz, nach dem alles angerichtet ist.*

By the same token, Bachmann insisted that reminiscences of past violence jeopardized a tenuous peace in the postwar era. Fearful of the hatred pervading societies after 1945, she argued that traumatic memories propelled mundane experiences of the present into an emotional chasm. Accordingly, she questioned the naive faith placed in poetry, alleging, for example, that "the poem is solitary, has no function, and is in principle of no concern to anyone. A poem, after all, no longer glorifies anything today, and even the faithful have long invalidated it." Programmatic for Bachmann's poetics are the rejection of the literary arts as a purely aesthetic experience and the vacuum confronting the modern subject. As odd as the parallel may seem, literature and the individual share similar fates in modernity, since both find themselves in conflict with the collective—examples in Bachmann's works include the female I in *Malina* or the father figure in "Everything." Nameless, these intentionally generic figures invalidate epistemological labels and, though highly ambiguous, use their anonymity to combat the stock language that breeds stereotypes as well as the disjointed realities confronting postwar societies.

For the purpose of appreciating Bachmann's approach to the rhetoric of the visual, one is well served to concentrate on two aspects that influenced the task of the postwar author and her rite of passage, a journey to a heightened awareness in which art functions both as a victim of the collective experience and as a liberator for the solitary individual. The first aspect is Bachmann's rejection of a "language of innuendo," a language that defies truth and breeds enmity. The second is the sophistication of her visual rhetoric, given her firm conviction that all but the purest of languages can be conscripted to promote cultural repression. The consequence is Bachmann's entreaty to embrace a "beautiful language" in which beauty is wedded to ethics and pure words confront reality with an "epistemological jolt." Of course, Bachmann's repeated call in her critical writings for a language of rupture also equates the "epistemological jolt" to the quandary of the modern writer, who, having lost faith in the fundamental integrity of his medium, eschews the one symbolic order that is both sustained by and expressive of human values. Referring to the plight of the writer, she pronounced:

> We think we all know language, do we not, we use it as a tool. Only the writer does not; he cannot handle it as a tool. It frightens him, is not something he takes for granted. It is there before literature, moving and destined for use in a process that he can make no use of. For him, it is neither an inexhaustible repository of material from which he can draw, nor a social object, the undivided property of all human beings.

With the task of the modern author in mind, let us turn to what Bachmann wrote about Simone Weil in her lengthy radio script on the French activist and mystic, a seminal text on poetics that is included in this section of the volume:

> Simone Weil was not a "literary author." She was not productive. She did not write in order to write and to create something that could stand on its own; rather, for her—despite strong critical and pedagogical impulses—writing was above all an exercise.—An exercise alternating between humility and rebellion and important as long as the distance between "knowing" and "knowing with all one's soul" had not been bridged.

Here, Bachmann's argument hinges on writing as a communicative process embracing intellectual and spiritual aspirations. Her assumption is that language should be commensurate with a peaceful order and that its signs should stimulate both rational and moral commentary, theoretical positions correlating with "knowing" and "knowing with all one's soul." More than a study of poetics, Bachmann's essay on Weil portrays the mystic as living art, an embodiment of affliction and grace due to her relentless advocacy for the improvement of the general living and working conditions of French laborers. Weil's sense of beauty emanates from a belief in social justice and a universal love for all who are in need. Perhaps more than anyone, she personifies Bachmann's uncompromising devotion to beauty as a political and humanitarian force in the postwar era. "To the extent that we are receptive to it, the beauty inherent in anything that has been conceived in purity and lived in purity comes from beauty. Enlightened by it, we behold time and time again what the darkness wants to hide from us: the indestructible face of the human being in a world conspiring to destroy it."

The ethical consequences of this conspiracy are far-reaching for the writer, since any new language is expected to embrace the moral burdens placed on collective experiences of war and its aftermath; specifically, a language that recognizes collective guilt for the butchery at Verdun and the mass murders in Auschwitz. Time and again, Bachmann insisted that there can be no escape from these realities, no opportunity to assuage the darkness of history, no language that justifies the luxury of human forgetfulness. Rather, poetics in the postwar era responds to lost innocence with the commitment to generate new signs expressive of moral integrity. The author, she claims, must "feel beauty," while at the same time responding to a "transformation that does not seek aesthetic satisfaction, either at the beginning or at the end, but a new capacity to comprehend," in order to infuse the aesthetic experience with a moral purpose. The task of finding that purpose, as Bachmann sees it, consists in "remembering with an unremitting concentration that flows back into writing." Even as the poet strives for words to communicate what is happening in the present, cultural memory remains one of the primary inspirations for what enhances or inhibits the poetic experience. In an early prose fragment, "Poem Addressing the Reader" ("Gedicht an den Leser"), poetry assumes its own individuality as an I, contending that an unquenchable love for the reader "has never left me, and now I am searching under the rubble and in the breeze, in icy gales and in the sun, for the words for you, the words that are meant to thrust me back into your arms."

Thinking about Bachmann's poetics and her visual rhetoric, one must also recognize that she was firmly focused on a crisis of representation in modernity. This explains the many correlations between her approach to the exacting language needed for the literary arts, her normative articulations about aesthetic principles, and the rigor of her philosophy. For the philosopher, critic, and poet, the word becomes an obligation to discern a new drumbeat in the march toward addressing cultural and social realities and redressing their flaws. More often than not, realities are beset with murderous intentions and a readiness to repeat a long history of injustices toward humankind. As an antidote for what has gone wrong, art is charged with taking up the gauntlet against injustice and articulating the pain endemic to the human condition, or as Bachmann expresses it: "tortured with poems; the scars still ache in our memory."

Her visual rhetoric is also closely linked to one of her most telling concepts, the playing field, which she appears to have derived from Wittgenstein and cites at the end of her essay on the philosopher, insisting that "he who accepts the rules and joins in the game does not throw the ball beyond the playing field." For an author like Bachmann, the playing field is language itself, a collective sign system rooted in tradition and shackled to old connotations, which a new visual aesthetic wants to sweep away. The capacity to comprehend "a world experienced in pain" relies heavily on the agency of the image and the rhetoric of the visual to achieve its objectives. In fact, as the texts in this section confirm, the visual serves to strip language of its fallacies and give it a new potency, almost in spite of itself.

Pinpointing the central facets of Bachmann's visual rhetoric is no simple task, given that she is fond of combining several layers of meaning, blending images from multiple traditions into signifiers that run counter to linear perceptions. It is almost as though she endorsed the idea expressed in Walter Benjamin's essay "Little History of Photography" ("Kleine Geschichte der Photographie") that the observer should not be fascinated by the object the image captures, but rather by the suggestions of contingency it reveals.[1] Dialectically, this contingency links the image with the beholder's past, present, and future. Dovetailing multiple temporalities, it also serves to incite a heightened situation of beholding. Indeed, the disparity between the presence of the now and the resurgence of a past that has been repressed aptly reflects the transformations impacting media and technology in the postwar era, certainly from a sociocultural perspective. Once derived from immediate sensations, sensual forms quickly adapted themselves to the mediation that the technological eye took on, as cameras amplified visual vocabularies and transitory images in films revolutionized collective viewpoints. This development led to satiation and addiction, as Bachmann noted in the late 1950s: "people today need movies and magazines more than whipped cream." Moreover—and this point is crucial for understanding Bachmann's poetics—emancipated from visual, aural, and haptic modes of signification, modernity subjects communication to the syntax and semantics of rapidly mediated technologies. As we have seen, Bachmann responded to the proliferation of mediated signs in the postwar era with a visual rhetoric that accentuates "a world unveiled and envisioned with precision, a world experienced in pain and extolled and celebrated in happiness."

Contesting the rapid transformation of media and new manifestations of space and time, Bachmann's situation of beholding is also expressive of the complexity of her imagery. The reader is confronted with a constant substitution of sign systems, whether visual or aural, and, all-pervasively, with the cultural scar that is quintessential to a language of insinuations. Removed from their contexts, insinuations inhibit the capacity to think through reality logically and stake a moral claim. Nevertheless, within the sign systems new meanings do arise, clandestinely or surreptitiously at first, but the best of these help to diffuse the proliferation of media and spotlight the unspoken truths underlying postwar cultural memory. Bachmann's insistence on the multifaceted quality or hybridity of her imagery requires her readers to engage with a collective demoralized by the past and in need of new frames of reference. Hence, her images shatter corrupted sign systems and forge paths to a utopian experience of the text as a cultural artifact and moral arbiter.

---

1 See Walter Benjamin, "Little History of Photography," in *Selected Writings Volume 2, Part 2: 1927–1934*, ed. Michael W. Jennings, Howard Eiland, and Gary Smith, trans Rodney Livingstone et al. (Cambridge and London: The Belknap Press of Harvard University Press, 1999), 507–31.

While the thrust of Bachmann's poetics is normative in character, given that she requires art to strive for truth and beauty, the moral thrust of her visual rhetoric attempts to mitigate a reality fraught with deception. In search of potent images, she realigns the paradoxical relationship between the signifier and the signified. To this end, she counsels us to pay close attention to the inner voice of the image, much as she challenges us to question our own cultural contexts, blinded as we may be by a flawed language that obscures cultural memory. For Bachmann, memory is the privilege of art: "if poems turned out to be proof of nothing, then we should still have to cling to the notion that they sharpen the memory," she explains, adding: "I believe that poems are capable of [sharpening memory] and that whoever writes poems inserts formulae into a memory, wonderful old words for a rock and a leaf, linked to or sundered by new words, new signs for reality, and I believe that whoever coins the formulae, tendered as an unsolicited proof of their truth, transports the reader into them with his breath." Alluding here to the potential for poetic recognition or the mnemonics of the word, Bachmann brings an eclectic array of aesthetic concepts into play. First, there is the reference to artistic techniques, implied in coining new formulae that invoke memories of past signs. Second, she associates the formulae with epistemologies of truth. Finally, she closes with the classic notion of the poet as a singer, one who can breathe life into words when reciting them to an audience. In turn, the audience is both inspired and transformed by the spoken word. Hence, the poet's expectations for the postwar era merge new language with old terms, contemporary aesthetics with classical concepts of beauty, and current with past meanings in order to embrace a poetics of the visual that, for Bachmann, is as utopian as it is morally compelling.

What I Saw and Heard in Rome[1]

In Rome, I saw that the Tiber is not beautiful, but mindless of its quays, from which banks emerge that no one lays a hand on. No one uses the freighters bronzed by rust, nor the other boats. The bushes and tall grass are covered with dirt and on the secluded balustrades the workers slumber without moving in the midday heat. Not one has yet to turn over. Not one has ever tumbled down. They slumber where the plane trees cast shade for them, pulling the sky over their heads. But the water of the river is beautiful, muddy green or blond depending on how the light hits it. One should walk along the Tiber and not look from the bridges, which are intended as paths to the island. The Tiberina[2] is inhabited by the Noiantri[3]—us others. That can be understood in the sense that it, the island of the sick and dead, has claimed to be inhabited by us others for all eternity, well-traveled, since it is also a ship and floats very slowly in the water with all of the burdened, in a river that does not perceive them as a burden.

In Rome, I saw that St. Peter's Basilica appears to be smaller than its dimensions and is nevertheless too big. They say that God wanted to have his church on a rock. This now rises above the grave of its saint, which has been laid bare. So it is the saint himself who endangers and weakens his church. Nevertheless the grand festivals still occur boisterously, with ballets in purple under canopies, and in the alcoves, gold replaces wax. *Chiesa granne e divozzione poca.*[4] In their foresight, the poor continue to

1 First published February 1955 in *Akzente* 2, no. 1: 39–43.

2 Island in the Tiber River running through Rome.

3 Noiantri, also known as "Noantri," are both Roman dialect words ("Noialtri" in standard Italian). This word is connected to a Roman and more generally Southern Italian concept of family, neighborhood, country, political party, corporation, mafia district. See Aldo Bonaventura, "L'Italia de Noantri," accessed January 27, 2021, http://aldobonaventura.blogspot.com/2009/12/litalia-de-noantri.html. The word "Noantri" also calls to mind one of Rome's most popular Catholic festivals, held in the Trastevere neighborhood, "Festa de Noantri."

4 Ancient Roman proverb (literally, "big church and small devotion") meaning "the greater the church, the less the piety." See Ariane Huml, *Silben im Oleander, Wort im Akaziengrün: zum literarischen Italienbild Ingeborg Bachmanns* [Syllables in oleander, word in acacia foliage: on Ingeborg Bachmann's literary image of Italy] (Göttingen: Wallstein, 1999), 223. The standard Italian would be: "Chiesa grande e devozione poca." This popular expression is often used to call attention to the disconnect between the big and imposing exterior of many Catholic churches and the inner absence of sincere devotion and prayer by the ordinary people. This proverb is also used in daily settings, when presenting someone with a gift or meal for which the container is big but the actual content is small and insignificant.

ensure that the church does not fall and the one who founded it relies on the footsteps of angels.

In Rome, I saw that many houses resemble the Palazzo Cenci, in which the unfortunate Beatrice lived before her execution. The prices are high and the signs of barbarism are pervasive. On the terraces, tubs of oleander rot in favor of white and red blossoms; they would like to fly away since they cannot compensate for the smell of debris and decay, which makes the past more vibrant than historical monuments do.

In Rome, I saw that the evening crowns the day in the ghetto. But on the day of the Feast of the Atonement, everyone is forgiven for one year in advance. Near the synagogue, the table is set in a trattoria and ruddy little Mediterranean fish, seasoned with raisins and pine nuts, are brought to the table. The elderly remember their friends whose weight was matched in gold; when they were ransomed, the trucks drove up nonetheless, and they never returned. But the grandchildren, two small girls in blazing red skirts and a plump blond boy, dance between the tables and do not cast their eyes from the musicians. "Play some more!" cries the fat boy and swings his cap. His grandmother cracks a smile, and the man playing the violin blanches while skipping a beat.

I saw on the Campo de' Fiori[5] that Giordano Bruno[6] is still being incinerated. Every Saturday, when the stalls around him are dismantled and only the women selling flowers remain, when on the square the stench of fish, chlorine, and rotten fruit ebb away, the men assemble the remaining trash before his eyes, after everything has been haggled over, and set fire to the heap. Once again, smoke rises and the flames whirl in the air. A woman screams and the others scream along with her. Because the flames are transparent in the strong light, you do not see how far they spread and what they strike at. But the man on the pedestal knows and still refuses to recant.

In a Roman bar, I saw and counted: a cat with tiny ears and an almost naked face, white stockings, and a honey-colored vest from happier times; a waiter, who spilled the coffee and let the aperitif glasses spill over; a young boy with an apron tied in the front, who washed the cups and glasses and never got to bed before midnight; guests, who came and went, and one guest, who came again and again, living from small sips of bitterness.

In Rome, I saw the large villas with natural pines and cedars, also box trees, trimmed in the shape of fantasy animals. On top of the Capitol

5 A famous square in Rome, literally "field of flowers."

6 Giordano Bruno (1548–1600) was a Dominican friar, philosopher, mathematician, and astrologer, whose pantheistic teachings were criticized by the Roman Inquisition. Tried and convicted for heresy, Bruno was burned at the stake in the Campo de' Fiori in 1600. In 1889 a statue was erected on the spot where Bruno was executed.

the laurel tree, and the treacherous wild grass in the Forum, and I heard, when the grass assailed the crooked pillars and shattered walls at twilight, the noise of the city, deceptively distant and smooth the gliding of cars.

I saw, where Rome's streets come to an end, the triumphant sky moving into the city, the sky that did not stoop under any gate and that spread itself across the seven hills, blue after raids along Sicily's coasts and full of the island fruits of the Tyrrhenian Sea, unscathed after inroads to the brigands of the Abruzzi and black from swarms of swallows rescued across the Apennine Mountains. I saw the lauded sky of ermine and the paltry sky of burlap, and I saw in its greatest moments its hand calmly executing the golden ratio above the housetops.

I have often seen that each builds his house the way he likes and that no plan brings all the pieces together better than chance and individual taste. But no taste is sufficient to create the spaces, separate areas for sun and shade, and no chance solves the equation in which the weightiness of a wall expresses the weightlessness of a tower. The houses are clad in ancient linen, withered the colors on it. Only when light penetrates the porous fabric does the color appear that we see; a brown capable of every transformation.

In Rome, I saw that everything has a name and you have to know the names. Even objects want to be called by name. The Ludovisi throne[7] did not fall with the last person to be crowned. Pillars of the temple of Venus[8] have remained standing—of this temple and no other. The head of St. Agnes[9] has shrunk, but it has not turned into that of a leather doll. In keeping with many popes, the present pontiff is also carried on the sedan chair, and the papal blessing *urbi et orbi* holds true.[10] The noble houses bear the names: Corsini and Pignatelli, Ruspoli and Odescalchi, Farnese and Barberini, Aldobrandini[11] . . . They still have their names when the homeless put up iron beds and stack water reservoirs on the sarcophagi in a castle in the Campagna.[12] The last descendant of the family moved away long ago. In the city, his rooms have been decorated with

7 The Ludovisi is an ancient sculpted block of marble hollowed at the back and with bas-reliefs on the three outer faces. The throne was discovered on the grounds of the Villa Ludovisi in 1887.

8 The temple to the goddess Venus is thought to have been the largest temple in Ancient Rome.

9 St. Agnes was a virgin-martyr, venerated as a saint in the Roman Catholic Church, Eastern Orthodox Church, the Anglican Communion, and Lutheranism.

10 This Latin phrase meaning "for the city and for the world" indicates that a papal document is addressed to both the city of Rome and the entire Catholic world.

11 Bachmann cites the names of seven noble families, most of which came to prominence and affluence in Rome by striving for the Pontificate or aligning themselves with the Vatican.

12 The Campagna is a low-lying area surrounding Rome.

black brocade; on a black grand piano, he plays blue-blooded chansons. When he hears his name, he is startled. Far removed from him, the animal that did not crave meat, but devoted its flesh to nourish a story that came long before it: the she-wolf.[13]

I saw that whoever says "Rome" is alluding to the world as well and the key to power are four letters. S. P. Q. R.[14] Whoever has the key can shut his books. He can read them from the blazon on the buses driving by, from the cover of a canal entrance. It is the badge identifying fountains and taxable drinks; the sign of the only sovereignty that has governed the city without interruption.

At the railway terminus, I saw that farewells are said more readily than elsewhere. For those who depart leave behind a baggage voucher of longing for those who remain. A vestige of the Diocletian Wall[15] borders on the railway station, and etched against the new floating glass partition three cypress trees emerge clearly in an unequivocal script. The classical is the simplest, and old and new texts signify it equally well.

Whoever throws a coin into the Fontana di Trevi[16] in order to return fears it could be declined. But he can take heart. At night, a boy sits down on the rim of the fountain and whistles, luring the others over. When all have gathered, the boy casts off his clothes and climbs nonchalantly into the water. The moon illuminates the scene as he bends forward shivering and collects the coins. Finally, he whistles again, and all of the currencies melt to silver in his hands. The booty is indivisible under the moon, for the boy has the appearance of a god, as opposed to the others, whose appearance is beholden to shabby garments.

Difficult to see is what lies under the earth: places of water and of death. Steps lead down to cisterns that the wind has drunk up, to well houses arched over by corbels and hollowed out in smooth tuff, to drops of blood that wellsprings have released. The paths dip to the catacombs.

---

13 In Roman mythology, Romulus and Remus are legendary twin brothers, whose story tells the events that led to the founding of the city of Rome and the Roman Kingdom by Romulus. Since ancient times, the image of the twins being suckled by a she-wolf has been a symbol of the city of Rome and the Roman people.

14 S. P. Q. R., signifying Senatus Populusque Romanus (The Roman Senate and People), is an acronym representing the "philosophy" of the Roman Republic. It is frequently used in official Roman inscriptions to designate the will of the Roman state.

15 The walls of the Baths of Diocletian, just across the piazza from Rome's Termini Station, are among the first sights that visitors have of the city's ancient structures.

16 The Trevi Fountain is a fountain in the Trevi district in Rome, designed by Italian architect Nicola Salvi and completed by Pietro Bracci. It is the largest baroque fountain in the city and one of the most famous fountains in the world.

A matchstick is scratched. Its flames stretch toward the emblems. For a brief moment, fish, peacock and dove, anchor and cross, food and drink appear. The match extinguishes rapidly, and those in front of you push upward. In the curve, one person stops and asks: From what directions is the wind blowing?

When I lost my hearing and sight in Rome, the sirocco came, prevailing over the dry wind from across the mountains. Then, the sun wore a shirt and blazed in a false light. It is the time in which misfortunes increase and an unkind word is quickly uttered. For the warm wind has recourse to the desert. Sometimes, it lets it be known by strewing red sand across the dejected city and blowing on it until it becomes insensate. When the sirocco abates, it does so secretly and in the night while we are sleeping obliviously. But in the morning, around three, the dew falls. Who could lie awake then and moisten his lips!

In Rome, I peered from the Protestant Cemetery to the Testaccio[17] and threw in my grief. Whoever struggles to scratch open the earth finds the grief of others underneath. For the cemetery, which seeks shade along the Aurelian Wall,[18] the shards on the Testaccio are not numbered, but few. It holds a big cloud up to its ear like a seashell and hears only one sound. In it have been entered: "One whose name was writ in water," and next to Keats's verses[19] a handful of Shelley's poems. Of Humboldt's little son, who succumbed to malaria, not a word. And of August von Goethe not a word as well. Of the mute painters Karstens and Marées only a few lines remain, a blotch of color, a knowing blue. About the other mute artists, one never did learn anything.

In Rome admittedly, I heard that a few people have bread but not teeth, and that the flies land on the scrawny horses. That to the one much is given and to the other nothing; that the one who pulls too much rips everything to pieces, and only a solid pillar holds the house upright for a hundred years. I heard that there is more time than sense in the world, but that we have all been given eyes to see.

---

17 Testaccio is an artificial hill in Rome created in antiquity from stacked broken clay vessels.

18 After nearly five centuries of unopposed domination, Emperor Aurelian of Rome (270–75 CE) recognized the threat from Germanic tribes near the borders of the Roman Empire, and in 271 CE he decided the city needed a defensive wall to protect it against possible invaders.

19 The complete epitaph on John Keats's tombstone reads: "This Grave contains all that was mortal of a YOUNG ENGLISH POET, who on his Death Bed, in the Bitterness of his heart, at the Malicious Power of his enemies, desired these words to be Engraven on his Tomb Stone: Here lies One Whose Name was writ in Water."

The Love of God and Affliction: The Path of Simone Weil[1]

NARRATOR: After the war, when for the first time French superlatives were heard in Germany to describe Simone Weil, the circles hoping for a "spiritual renewal out of the Christian spirit" hastened to repeat those superlatives;[2] indeed, there were even a few people who knew some of her writings in the original. But it was not until 1953 that two of her books appeared in German, published by Kösel, in a superb translation by Friedhelm Kemp. Their titles were *The Love of God and Affliction* and *Gravity and Grace.*[3] 1953—that meant concern about a "spiritual void" was no longer frequently voiced and widespread demands, such as the one for "spiritual renewal," had been superseded by daily demands. All of the catching up had taken place; everything that was exceptional had been reintegrated into the fabric of cultural life. And, of course, legends surrounding exceptional personalities flourish only so long as their work is barely accessible or so long as their lives remain obscure. The wish to delve into their lives more deeply is what keeps the public's interest and imagination awake.

It has to be assumed that the legend surrounding Simone Weil—that extraordinary individual: professor of philosophy and factory worker, devoutly Christian Jew, critic of the Catholic Church and potential saint—that the legend surrounding such an extraordinary being has also begun to wane now that her books have been translated into various languages and details of her biography made known. The only question remaining is whether such publicity will work to Simone Weil's disadvantage or whether her writings will survive the legend. I believe that they will.

Only very few of Simone Weil's "written works" were published during her lifetime, for the most part essays on current issues that only take

---

1 Simone Weil (1909–1943) was a French philosopher, mystic, and political activist. Weil's essay "L'amour de Dieu et le malheur" appeared as part of the collection *Attente de Dieu* in 1950 and a year later in translation as "The Love of God and Affliction" in the volume *Waiting for God.* The translator Emma Craufurd notes the absence of a satisfactory English equivalent for *malheur*, given that "unhappiness" is "far too weak" and "affliction" fails to carry the "sense of inevitability and doom" of the original. See Simone Weil, "The Love of God and Affliction," in *Waiting for God*, trans. Emma Craufurd (New York: Putnam, 1951), 117. We have cited the published English title here instead of rendering the German translation *Unglück* (unhappiness or misfortune), which Bachmann cites.

2 Praise for Weil went well beyond German intellectual circles to include the likes of André Gide, T. S. Eliot, and Alfred Kazin.

3 "La Pesanteur et la grâce," the title essay of a collection of Weil's writings, appeared in the first French edition in 1947.

on significance within the context of her body of work. After the war, in a newly liberated France, Gustave Thibon, a lay theologian, edited excerpts drawn from the bundle of ten notebooks that she had entrusted to him for publication; in the meantime most of the material has been published by Plon, some of it by Gallimard in Paris.[4]

These ten notebooks contain something that defies definition, in particular, pronouncements and ideas about the so-called "Last Things." Since everything with respect to the "Last Things" is by nature either left to the realm of silence or to a declaration of faith, it is not easy to do justice to Simone Weil's theses. Derived from reason, they flow into a declaration of faith. To do justice to a declaration of faith, let alone to assess it as one would assess scientific propositions and theories, is an impossible task. What is possible, however, is to follow the path leading to that declaration of faith and to trace and record the insights that Simone Weil had in that process as well as the errors to which she succumbed. Finally, it is possible to consider the written document of her efforts, one that owes its luminous quality to an extraordinary intellectual passion and thus possesses a style and stature all its own, as an aesthetic paradigm, even though she herself would surely have rejected such a view; yet, all expression and all communication do devolve to our world and its mundane categories.

Simone Weil was no "literary author." She was not productive. She did not write in order to write and to create something that could stand on its own, rather, for her—despite strong critical and pedagogical impulses—writing was above all an exercise. An exercise alternating between humility and rebellion and important as long as the distance between "knowing" and "knowing with all one's soul" had not been bridged.[5] She was a fanatic believer in precision, in her thought as well as her life, a precision extending equally to the smallest things and to the largest and which was bound to entangle her thought and her life in extreme situations.

1ST SPEAKER: Simone Weil was born in Paris in 1909, the second child of well-to-do Jewish parents. To her older brother, a professor of mathematics at the University of Chicago, she owed her early exposure to literature and science, her exceptional capacity for difficult subject matter. After graduating from the lycée, she studied philosophy with Alain,[6] then enrolled in the École Normale Supérieure and left that institution with

4 The excerpts were published in English as *Gravity and Grace*, trans. Arthur Wills (New York: G. P. Putnam's Sons, 1952), which also includes an introduction by Gustave Thibon.

5 Gustave Thibon, "Introduction," in Simone Weil, *Gravity and Grace*, 5.

6 Émile-Auguste Chartier (1868–1951), commonly known as Alain, was a French philosopher, journalist, and pacifist.

an *Agrégée de Philosophie* (a degree that corresponds to our Ph.D., but only in name, since it is far more difficult to attain). Until the outbreak of the Second World War she taught—with both voluntary and involuntary interruptions—at a variety of secondary schools. From a very young age she participated in French politics, joining the ranks of the extreme left, without, however, becoming a member of any political group. Hers was the party of the poor, the weak, and the oppressed, and she joined that anonymous party in a manner all her own. She took a temporary leave from her teaching position, sought employment under an assumed name as a milling machine operator with the Renault Works, lived with and among the workers, subjecting herself to the same conditions under which the majority of French workers were forced to live at the time. That first experiment was one she was unable to complete. A bout of pleurisy forced her to relinquish her job. The sense of defeat that that period inflicted on her becomes evident in one of her last letters:

WEIL: "I was, as it were, in pieces, soul and body. That contact with affliction had killed my youth. Until then I had not had any experience of affliction, unless we count my own, which, as it was my own, seemed to me to have little importance, and which, moreover, was only a partial affliction, being biological and not social. I knew quite well that there was a great deal of affliction in the world, I was obsessed with the idea, but I had not had prolonged and first-hand experience of it. As I worked in the factory, indistinguishable to all eyes, including my own, from the anonymous mass, the affliction of others entered into my flesh and my soul. Nothing separated me from it, for I had really forgotten my past and I looked forward to no future, finding it difficult to imagine the possibility of surviving all the fatigue. What I went through there marked me in so lasting a manner. . . . There I received forever the mark of a slave, like the branding of the red-hot iron the Romans put on the foreheads of their most despised slaves. Since then I have always regarded myself as a slave."[7]

1ST SPEAKER: When the Spanish Civil War broke out, she joined the Reds, traveled to the Catalan front to help where she could, refusing expressly to engage in armed combat.[8] Once again she had to admit defeat; this time it was an accident that forced her to return to France. Her feet had suffered burns from boiling oil.

In the summer of 1940, as the Germans were approaching Paris, she decided to accompany her parents to Marseilles, but subsequently separated from them to spend a few months in the countryside working as

7 Simone Weil, "Spiritual Autobiography," in *Waiting for God,* 66–67.
8 Weil was not always unwilling to bear arms.

a field hand. Her encounter with the philosopher and lay theologian Gustave Thibon dates back to that period. At night, after her labor in the vineyards, she continued her studies in Greek philosophy and literature as well as Indian philosophy and began to embrace mysticism. A short while later, we find her back in Marseilles. At the suggestion of the Dominican Father Perrin, she lectured on Plato and the Pythagoreans in the crypt of the Dominican monastery. Finally, her parents were able to persuade her to emigrate with them. Together, the family traveled to the United States. But Simone Weil, who had called justice a "fugitive from the camp of the victor,"[9] felt that she belonged in the camp of hapless France. She welcomed the *résistance*, left her more hospitable existence in America within a few short months and went to London to join Maurice Schumann's efforts for the French government in exile. Her desire to be sent on a mission to France was rejected. Because she was Jewish, only the worst could be feared in a country that was being ravaged by the Gestapo. In order to share in the deprivations of the French, she willingly reduced her generous food rations to benefit the refugees. Hunger and overexertion over many years diminished her strength. Following an acute case of pulmonary tuberculosis she had to be taken to a sanatorium and died within a short time, on August 24, 1943, at Ashford, County Kent, before completing her thirty-fourth year. Her last days were not documented. It seems that she was alone there. Her few friends were in France.

WEIL: "The death agony is the supreme dark night which is necessary even for the perfect if they are to attain to absolute purity, and for that reason it is better that it is bitter."[10]

NARRATOR: Having become acquainted with the details of Weil's life, one might think that she was primarily engaged in the political and social struggles of Europe in the years before and during the war—someone with a strong desire to share in the suffering and the struggles of others, ready to assume sacrifice. Seen in that light, her life would be a rare example of benevolence, but, as such, one as invisible and unsung as so many other lives that have been sacrificed.

The integrity of her life should remain intact and speak for itself. Let us speak instead of her teachings, her intellectual legacy, and the manifestations of her thought at the various and highly varied stages of her journey, which she expressly felt called upon to pursue. Although we should not ignore the fact that her calling was a "spiritual" one, we are compelled

9 This phrase calls to mind the book *George Orwell: Fugitive from the Camp of Victory* (1961), by the British Weil scholar and translator, Richard Rees.

10 Weil, "Evil," in *Gravity and Grace*, 127.

to turn our attention to her social and political thought. The driving force of that aspect of her personality was very strong; hence, towards the end of her life she professed:

WEIL: "The observation of social phenomena is an equally effective catharsis as it would be to withdraw from the world, and for that reason it was no mistake for me to concern myself with politics for as long as I did . . ."[11]

1ST SPEAKER: Simone Weil attracted public attention for the first time when, as a professor at Puy, she took up the cause of the workers who were on strike in that region. At the time, she contacted a group aligned with the extreme leftist labor union journal *Révolution prolétarienne* [*Proletarian Revolution*]. More pronounced was the attention she attracted among the workers themselves. People of her sort were held in low esteem in those quarters; she was suspected of belonging to the group of intellectuals whose sympathy for the proletariat was based on a misunderstanding and who were drawn to the fascination of something entirely different from themselves, out of a feeling of insecurity and emotional void. Preoccupied with concrete problems, the workers were not thrilled when intellectuals meddled in their affairs. The encounter with Simone Weil may have been unwelcome to them initially; later it made them ill at ease. What troubled them were her far superior knowledge of socialist theories, her intellectual brilliance, her burning and unalloyed interest in the situation in which French workers found themselves at the time, and her unequivocal advocacy for improving their general condition. Simone Weil did not have an easy time of it. She was very young and not attractive, hardly likable, lacking in charm, unyielding, and deadly earnest. But she was also truthful through and through, tough and unwavering, and she prevailed. She won the men over, who initially shook their heads at her, and ultimately made allies of them. The impression she made on them is best characterized by the tragicomic statement of one of those French workers who, deeply shaken by the news of her death, said:

11 Paraphrase from Simone Weil, "The Great Beast," in *Gravity and Grace*, trans. Wills, 218. The original text reads: "To contemplate the social is as good a way of detachment as to retire from the world. That is why I have not been wrong to rub shoulders with politics as long as I did." This statement by Weil is similarly paraphrased in Thibon, "Introduction," 15.

WORKER: "She was not fit for life; she was too much of a scholar, and she never ate."[12]

2ND SPEAKER: Simone Weil was a "high-strung" person, characterized by an unheard-of cerebral intensity on the one hand and total ignorance with regard to material exigencies on the other. She wanted to force the workers to think, to make them see their situation clearly. For she perceived that the thoughtlessness of the workers was pitted against the thoughtlessness of the employers. She wanted to go to the root of the trouble, and the only flaw in her calculation was her assumption that all human beings had intellectual qualities equal to her own. That assumption did not stem from arrogance, but from naiveté, and she seldom realized that during her intellectual digressions, in which others were invited to participate, she was left to her own devices. According to the many stories related by Madame Thévenon, the wife of one of the leaders of the syndicalist movement, in her memoir of Simone Weil, which describes Weil's personality and ideas at the time in question, it can be assumed that she did not fail to leave an impression on people, despite her awkwardness.

MME THÉVENON: "She was very unassuming, and although her education was so far superior to ours, we could carry on long conversations with her in a sociable vein. She enjoyed our company; she laughed with us, and often asked us to sing—not always the most orthodox stuff. When we were at her home, she would be sitting on the edge of her iron bedstead in her ugly room, in which there was hardly any furniture, reciting Greek verses, which we did not understand but which nevertheless gave us joy, because we felt the joy they gave her. Then, sometimes, there would be an unforgettable smile from her, a look of shared participation in humorous situations; that side of her nature seldom came to the fore, because of the earnestness with which she confronted everything . . ."[13]

2ND SPEAKER: The letters to Perrin were written in the year 1942, before she left Europe, a year before her death. In them, she explains why she cannot become a member of the church.

12 Albertine Thévenon, "Avant-propos," in Simone Weil, *La condition ouvrière* (Paris: Édition Gallimard, [1951] 1976), 9. Francine du Plessix Gray reports that Weil never brought a snack to work and frequently rejected offers to share the bread and chocolate of her fellow employees, in *Simone Weil* (New York: Penguin, 2001), 84.

13 Thévenon, "Avant-propos," 11.

2ND SPEAKER: Because Simone Weil was averse to any kind of conformism and every one of her thoughts breathed the air of freedom, she also triumphed over her environment. Her battle was not for utopia, but for the here and now. She did not believe in an ideal program for the solution to the labor question, but rather in an incremental solution to the problems. She positioned herself squarely in reality or, as she herself would have expressed it, in the "misfortune" to which she knew herself to be an accessory, in any form in which it manifests itself in the world. For her, to think with integrity meant starting with facts.

1ST SPEAKER: We already know from her biography that she gave up the teaching profession for a period and took employment with the Renault Works as a milling machine operator. In those days she kept a "factory journal" from which we would like to cite a few passages to show that, before she arrived at her formulations, she gathered the necessary experience that justified and enabled her to record them. That journal has neither been revised nor filtered; rather, it recorded what she experienced day in and day out with total immediacy. It dealt with the monotony as well as the moral and psychological void that working in large factories breeds in human beings. We also have to take into account the special conditions prevailing in French factories during those years, although we can only draw general conclusions from the many details involved.

2ND SPEAKER: Simone Weil's shift lasted from 2:30 p.m. to 10:00 p.m. That is how the recorded hours should be understood. On a Thursday in the year 1935 she writes:

WEIL: "Going to the shop is extremely painful; each step an effort (morally; returning, it's a physical effort). Am in that half-dazed state in which I am the victim designated for any harsh blow . . . From 2:30 to 3:35, 400 pieces. From 3:35 to 4:15, time lost because of the set-up man in the cap—(he made me do my botched pieces over)—Large pieces—slow and very hard because of the new way the handle of the vice is set up. I turn to the foreman for help—Discussion—Go back to work—Grind off the end of my thumb (there's the harsh blow!)—Infirmary—Finish the 500 at 6:15—No more pieces for me (I am so tired I am relieved!). But they promise me some. In the end, I don't get them until 7:30 and then only 500 (to complete the 1,000). . . . 245 by 8 o'clock. Do the 500 large ones, in a great deal of pain, in 1½ hrs. . . . Free at 9:40. But earned 16.45 F!!! . . . By the time I leave, I'm tired."[14]

14 Simone Weil, "Factory Journal," in *Formative Writings, 1929–1941* (Amherst: University of Massachusetts Press, 1987), 207.

1ST SPEAKER: Three weeks later, again on a Thursday:

WEIL: "Today ruckus at the factory. A female worker was dismissed for spoiling 400 pieces. She has tuberculosis, has a semi-unemployed husband and children (probably by another man), who are being raised by the father's family. Feelings of the other women: a mixture of sympathy and that typical "serves her right," as the little girls in school say. She is said to have been a bad colleague and worker. For an excuse she used the light—because after 6:30 all the lights are doused.—More arguments—Female workers commenting, 'In that bad light I did much harder jobs in my day!'—'She shouldn't have argued with the foreman, she should have gone to the deputy director and told him: I was wrong, but . . .'—'If you want to earn your bread, you've got to do as you're told. If you want to make a living, you've got to be more conscientious.'"[15]

2ND SPEAKER: Undated:

WEIL: "The complete ignorance with regard to the task assigned is extraordinarily demoralizing. There is never a feeling that a product is the result of the effort expended on it. In no way does the worker feel connected to the producer. There is likewise no feeling at all of a relationship between work and income. The activity seems arbitrarily imposed and arbitrarily compensated. The impression is a little bit like being one of those children to whom their mother, in order to keep them quiet, gives pearls to string, with a promise of candy."[16]

2ND SPEAKER: On a Saturday:

WEIL: "Violent headaches, distressed states, afternoon better (but weep at B's . . .)."[17]

2ND SPEAKER: Monday:

WEIL: "LeClerc sends for me. . . . Begins bawling me out because I'm doing these pieces without speaking to him about them. Asks for the number. I bring him my notebook! Looks at it and becomes very kind . . ."[18]

15 Weil, *La condition ouvrière*, 100.

16 Weil, *La condition ouvrière*, 101.

17 Weil, "Factory Journal," 215. According to du Plessix Gray's biography, "B" is the Weil family friend Boris Souvarine. See Gray, *Simone Weil*, 97.

18 Weil, "Factory Journal," 216.

2ND SPEAKER: Wednesday:

WEIL: "Pay: 255F (I was afraid I would hardly get 200) for 81 hrs.
Night: didn't sleep. Terrible headache.[19]

2ND SPEAKER: Undated:

WEIL: "In all other forms of slavery, slavery resides in the circumstances. Here alone it is made part of the work itself.

"Effects of enslavement on the soul."[20]

"The owner of a factory: 'I enjoy this and that expensive luxury and my workmen are miserably poor.' He may be very sincerely sorry for his workmen and yet not form the connection. For no connection is formed if thought does not bring it about."[21]

1ST SPEAKER: Correlations in thought were what Simone Weil endeavored to create in her writings expressly concerned with the condition of the working class, "rationalization," the question of human rights etc., above all in *The Need for Roots: Prelude to a Declaration of Duties Towards Mankind*, which constitutes her political testament.

We cannot discuss each and every one of her texts, but we will try to identify the recurring theme that underlies all of them and to illustrate her principal thoughts.

2ND SPEAKER: Misery—arising from misfortune—takes on various forms. Simone Weil sees the most visible form of misery in the political and social sector, because that kind of misery obstructs any path to freedom for the human being. These lowest forms of misery must be addressed first, with the goal of achieving a social order, a social balance. That is why she addresses the workers in her time off and tries to enlighten them about the causes of their misery, causes that she sees in Taylorism,[22] more precisely, in Taylor's system of the rationalization of labor, a system which, together with Ford's methods (which aim to maximize production) has been implemented in factories more or less successfully. Weil asks what kind of system

19 Weil, "Factory Journal," 217. Bachmann adds the phrase "Entsetzliche Kopfschmerzen" (terrible headache) to Weil's original.

20 Weil, *La condition ouvrière*, 111.

21 Simone Weil, "The Ring of Gyges," in *Gravity and Grace*, 193.

22 A system for the division of labor, first elaborated in Frederick Winslow Taylor's 1911 treatise *The Principle of Scientific Management.*

that might be, even when it is allegedly based on scientific principles, and her answer is as follows:

A calculation is made with respect to the time in which a certain task can be performed, and that period of time is dictated to the workers as a norm. Bonuses, supervision, and dismissal without recourse in the event that the demands are not met are brought into play, in order to motivate the workers to perform optimally. Taylor was very proud of that system because it touched upon the interests of both the employer and the worker, both of whom derived apparent advantages from the system, while the products themselves became cheaper for the consumer. He believed that he had eliminated all social conflicts and created social harmony. The system, as Simone Weil explains, embodies the most perfect form of slavery imaginable. Her belief is that the system has led the workers into total isolation, because the competitive struggle erodes their solidarity. Finally, the division of labor leads to human atomization in the factories and creates the incomparable monotony that generally prevails there. Ford said that monotonous work was not unpleasant for the workers, and he was right about that, since human beings become habituated to nothing more readily than to monotony. According to Weil, that habituation constitutes the beginning of the human being's moral devastation.[23]

That is also why Simone Weil fights vehemently against the use of psychotechnology—still in its infancy at the time, by the way—and why she believes that under the despotism of its calculations (the onset of fatigue, loss of attention after so many hours worked, etc.) enslavement becomes absolute. For a psychotechnician could never calculate and specify the span of time in which an individual worker—and not the abstract worker calculated as a mean—finds a period long or short. Nobody but the worker himself can say that.

1ST SPEAKER: After discussing "internal" problems, she turns to the most comprehensive problem in her essay "La condition ouvrière" [The Labor Condition], to an exclusively national approach to questions of production.

2ND SPEAKER: She starts her analysis with an examination of the product. An automobile, for example, is a product. An automobile can be a variety of things; in our eyes, it is a convenient means of transportation that we can no longer imagine living without. However, cars do not exist

23 Conversely, Weil holds that monotony can be the gateway to grace: "It is when man sees himself as a squirrel turning round and round in a circular cage that, if he does not lie to himself, he is close to salvation." See Simone Weil, "The Mysticism of Work," in *Gravity and Grace*, 234.

solely to travel on the roads, either sooner or later; rather they are also a perennial weapon in the battle among the automotive industries in France, Italy, Germany. Even if, in the interest of the workers, there were a desire to reduce the working hours in the factories of one country, it could not be done. The risk of being crushed by foreign automobile producers would be too great. A ruling could only come about on an international basis and would be tantamount to a uniform reduction in output. Simone Weil says that it is no sign of progress when the statisticians ascertain that production has once more and yet again been increased—on the contrary, it is a regression to the most extreme and terrible form of slavery. This hectic competition is most obvious in the area of arms production, which, needless to say, will not be restricted by any country in the absence of international regulations.

1ST SPEAKER: It is true that Simone Weil's demands, which entertained a high degree of hope of being realized in the thirties, appear almost illusory today. Yet, they have not lost any of their persuasive force. At a time when she could have hardly anticipated how accurate her prognoses were—in regard to Hitler alone, if no other—she wrote:

2ND SPEAKER: If international conventions were to be neglected increasingly, social progress might necessarily be achieved on a national scale. But it would go hand in hand with increasing dictatorial tendencies. In dictatorships, borders are hermetically sealed against foreign products, against contact with people and exchange with citizens from other countries. One can usher in: full employment, higher wages, and in connection with those advancements the growth and expansion of an enormous arms industry.

1ST SPEAKER: But—one way or the other—what remains untouched by all that is the "misfortune" of the worker. Weil calls it mysterious, because that misfortune is compounded by the workers' misfortune at not being able to articulate their misfortune clearly. If they talk about it, they do so in the jargon of people who are not workers. For the most part, the workers' slogans come from non-workers.

2ND SPEAKER: The factory with its atmosphere, so inimitably portrayed by Simone Weil, its rhythm, which arouses the feeling in human beings that they are no longer their own masters, fuels the worker's servitude, giving them the impression of people moving among machines that are constantly in motion. The worker is not "one with himself" in the factory. If the monotony is broken, there is secret resistance. That is true. But the reason for the resistance is that the new labor must be managed and executed just like the old one was. Neither has any connection to the worker. Indeed, the directions are the only element that changes. If one produces ten pieces in one minute, performs ten movements, then it is preordained that in the next minute another ten pieces will be manufactured, another ten movements performed, and so on, up to the next production target. Add to that: the suffering that workers endure outside their working hours, on the way to work and on the way home and on labor-free Sundays. What happens at that time is "chance."

Even a few minutes of respite in the course of the working day, triggered by a malfunctioning machine, are "chance occurrences." The life of the worker is lived between monotony and chance. The circle cannot be broken.

1ST SPEAKER: Misfortune is a mystery, Weil repeats over and over again. Then she makes the surprising assertion that even if working hours and conditions were to improve (and that has happened to some degree in a few countries), misfortune still persists. How are we to interpret that, after her radical demands to eliminate misfortune and create better working conditions? What sort of misfortune is it that Simone Weil has in mind?

2ND SPEAKER: The misfortune is that the worker has no future; for when he "pulls himself up by his bootstraps," he is no longer a worker. A paradox prevails at the core of his existence. A dentist, though he may be starving, is still a dentist after he has become rich; the same is true for any other person with a profession. A worker who succeeds in bringing a factory under his control is no longer a worker but a factory manager.

1ST SPEAKER: There is no way to change that, even if he were to call himself "comrade" or whatever.

2ND SPEAKER: Thus there are many forms of freedom, sad ones and worthy ones, but there is only one form of slavery. What remains to the enslaved, considering the monotony of their days, is the short-lived wish for variety, entertainment; and alongside those loom the temptations: sloth, loathing, *dégout*. Oscillation between meals and work and rest and more work, "eating in order to be able to work" and "working in order to be able to eat,"[24] the absence of a goal, a "finalité," are the attributes of this bare existence.

---

24 Weil, "The Mysticism of Work," 233–34. The quote in its entirety reads: "Work makes us experience in the most exhausting manner the phenomenon of finality rebounding like a ball; to work in order to eat, to eat in order to work. . . .

Simone Weil knows that revolt against social injustice is necessary; its purpose is to limit evil, to bring about some approximation of balance. She calls the promise that workers can wage a successful revolt against their existential misfortune a lie.

WEIL: "Those lies lead to a misuse of the workers' greatest strengths. They promise them a paradise that is impossible. Marx called religion opium for the people. No, the revolution is opium for the people. Revolutionary hopes are a stimulant. All teleological systems are fundamentally flawed."[25]

NARRATOR: In order to understand Simone Weil's next step, it would be necessary for us to grasp her concept of the world. When entering the realm in which she anticipates finding the solution, we are already crossing the outskirts of her faith, and in order to be able to follow her, let us begin by asserting that she believed in God. We will keep the peculiar form of her Christian belief in God in abeyance, her interpretation of "Catholicism" that bordered on heresy, simply by dint of her refusal to join the church as an institution that was not "catholic," not "all-embracing." She perceives the irresolvable misfortune of the worker, his existential misfortune, as a special distinction. A human being without the prospect of focusing his desire on goals, on anything that might be or will be, can only direct his desire toward something that exists.

WEIL: "That something is beauty.[26] Everything beautiful is an object of desire, but one desires that it be not otherwise, that it be unchanged, that it be exactly what it is.[27] What we desire is exactly what we possess. Since

---

If we regard one of the two as an end, or the one and the other taken separately, we are lost. Only the cycle contains the truth."

25 This is a paraphrase of Weil, whose original text reads: "As a revolt against the injustices of society, the idea of revolution is right and proper. But as a revolt against the essential misery of the working condition it is misleading, for no revolution will get rid of the latter. . . . The phrase 'opium of the people' which Marx used appropriately enough to describe religion when it had failed itself, applies essentially to revolution. The hope of a revolution to come satisfies a craving for adventure. . . . The workers' universe excludes purpose." Simone Weil, "Prerequisite to Dignity of Labour," in *Simone Weil: An Anthology,* ed. Sian Miles (New York: Weidenfeld & Nicholson, 1986), 246–47.

26 The wording of this quote from Weil's "Prerequisite to Dignity of Labour" has been altered slightly throughout, although the substance has not, except where otherwise noted. Weil, "Prerequisite to Dignity of Labour," 248.

27 Bachmann's text trims one sentence here, disclosing Weil's example of the object of desire: "One looks with desire at a clear starry night and one desires

the people are compelled to direct all their desires towards what they already possess, beauty is made for them and they for it. The people need poetry the way they need bread.[28] Not the poetry closed inside words: by itself that is no use to them. They need poetry to be the very substance of daily life. Such poetry can come from one source only and that is God. The poetry can only be religion."[29]

2ND SPEAKER: Here, Weil suggests that the worker's fundamental misfortune creates an empty space between the human being and God. The gaze of a human being whose view is unobstructed by any wishes, any goal, need only be raised and in looking up he realizes that nothing separates him from God. The only difficulty would seem to be to get him to lift his head.

1ST SPEAKER: That said, it would be wrong to assume that she attempts to justify the existence of social misfortune, grievances of every sort. We have already said that she advocates for revolt against social grievances, and she actually did so when she supported the French metal workers' strike in 1936 and welcomed the walkout with passionate words. In her eyes, only the existential misfortune of the human being is irremediable, not the attendant circumstances, the accidental misfortune that deprives the human being of the strength to raise his head. Later, she formulates it as follows:

WEIL: "We must eliminate affliction as much as we can from social life, for affliction only serves the purposes of grace, and society is not a society of the elect. There will always be enough affliction for the elect."[30]

---

exactly the sight before one's eyes." Weil, "Prerequisite to Dignity of Labour," 248.

28 Bachmann omits the first part of this sentence ("For other social classes, poetry is a luxury but the people"). Weil, "Prerequisite to Dignity of Labour," 248. In *Gravity and Grace*, Weil intensifies her claim: "the workers need poetry *more than* bread" ("Les travailleurs ont besoin de poésie *plus que* de pain"). Weil, "The Mysticism of Work," 235; our italics.

29 Weil, "Prerequisite to Dignity of Labour," 248. Weil also expresses these ideas in "The Mysticism of Work," 235.

30 Simone Weil, "The Social Imprint," in *Gravity and Grace*, 215. We remind the reader that Weil's English translator opted to render Weil's "malheur" consistently as "affliction"; however, we have opted for "misfortune" as the translation of Bachmann's "Unglück."

2ND SPEAKER: Sentimentality, at any rate, was totally alien to her. That is evident when she characterizes the social and political sector as belonging to the realm of "evil," which is utterly puzzling at first glance.

WEIL: "The social order is irreducibly that of the prince of this world. Our only duty with regard to the social is to try to limit the evil of it."[31]

2ND SPEAKER: Because:

WEIL: "It is the social which throws the color of the absolute over the relative. The remedy is in the idea of relationship. Relationship breaks its way out of the social.[32]

NARRATOR: But with that we have already reached a new phase of her journey. Of course, the stages of her journey overlap, of course—the crystallization of her religious thought is not attained until the final years of her life, while the social and political issues of the thirties remain the soil in which her thoughts are rooted. At the point at which her struggle with misfortune enters its most decisive phases, she feels compelled to bring God into the debate and either renounce or declare allegiance to him. Unlike Pascal, she renounces God, giving allegiance to herself and her love.[33]

Simone Weil's love of God and her journey to God are of a special nature. She is a solitary figure. For that reason, it has not occurred to us to position her in the context of the other Christian intellectuals of her era in France, and it is probably no accident either that she never mentions Péguy, Bernanos, Bloy;[34] it is questionable as to whether she was familiar with them, ignored them, or even viewed them with antipathy. It would hardly be possible to assert that she was interested in the literature

31 Simone Weil, "The Great Beast," in *Gravity and Grace*, 218.

32 Weil, "The Great Beast," 217.

33 Blaise Pascal (1626–1662) claimed in his famous wager that if one believes in God and God exists, the result is infinite gain, but if one believes in God and there is no God, one has lost nothing. Likewise, if one does not believe in God and there is a God, the result is infinite loss.

34 Three French contemporaries of Weil whose writings were influenced by Roman Catholicism: Charles Péguy (1873–1914), French poet, essayist, and editor, whose writings were strongly influenced by Catholicism from 1908 on; Georges Bernanos (1888–1948), French author of Roman Catholic and monarchist leanings, also a soldier in World War I; Léon Bloy (1846–1917), French novelist, essayist, pamphleteer, and poet who underwent a dramatic religious conversion after meeting the aging Catholic author Barbey d'Aurevilly (1808–1889) in December 1868, who then became his mentor.

and philosophy of the twentieth century. Once she mentions Arthur Koestler's *Spanish Testament*,[35] which probably struck her due to its connection with the Spanish Civil War. She mentions Proust and Valéry once, also Joseph Conrad, authors whom she regarded highly. Her true interests lay in very different areas, apart from the social theories that dominated the social and political discourses of the period. They were in Greek literature, Plato above all, and the Pythagoreans. She translated from Greek originals and interpreted the translated texts, because she believed that proto-Christian intuitions were essential to them. It remains an open question, of course, as to whether the Greek concepts of the idea of God were anticipations or whether they appear as anticipations only in retrospect, having been absorbed by or assimilated into Christian concepts. In her encounters with texts, whether they are Greek or those of the mystics, the Upanishads, the Bhagavad-Gita, Shakespeare, or Racine, Simone Weil veers toward fervent love and reverence—while on the other hand she expresses complete rejection for other texts: the Old Testament, Aristotle, Roman-Latin literature for the most part evoke aversion, for Weil must condemn what she cannot love. She only values what is receptive to "revelations," only where they might be found. Often, her criticism appears arrogant, and hardly anyone would be able to share her opinions in every respect. T. S. Eliot is probably right when he says of Weil:

ELIOT: "Certainly she could be unfair and intemperate; certainly she committed some astonishing aberrations and exaggerations. But those immoderate affirmations which tax the patience of the reader spring not from any flaw in her intellect but from excess of temperament. She came of a family with no lack of intellectual endowment—her brother is a distinguished mathematician; and as for her own mind, it was worthy of the soul which employed it. But the intellect, especially when bent upon such problems as those which harassed Simone Weil, can come to maturity only slowly; and we must not forget that Simone Weil died at the age of thirty-three. I think that in *The Need for Roots* [*L'Enracinement*] especially, the maturity of her social and political thought is very remarkable. But she had a very great soul to grow up to . . ."[36]

NARRATOR: For that very reason we will also refrain from paying too much credence to her judgments on one thing or another—not because

35 Record of Koestler's experiences as a prisoner during the Spanish Civil War. Weil experienced the war at the front lines as a partisan of the Reds.

36 T. S. Eliot, "Preface," in Simone Weil, *The Need for Roots: Prelude to a Declaration of Duties toward Mankind*, trans. Arthur Wills (New York: G. P. Putnam's Sons, 1952), vii.

those judgments do not deserve attention, but because we want to keep our focus on her actual journey.

It has become popular today to speak of the "pilgrims in pursuit of the absolute." However, Simone Weil was no "pilgrim." Her journey is a "via negativa," a journey away from God in order to increase the distance between herself and God. And the infinite distance to which she is subjected by embracing extreme "misfortune" is intended to enable her not to confront God as an individual, as a negating factor for anyone in doubt or firm in belief, but to experience divine grace as a creature that has been effaced and is naked. Thus, her many-faceted and multi-layered work becomes a testimony of pure mysticism, perhaps the only one we have been privy to since the Middle Ages. Solely in terms of that aspect, as an inspiration that cannot be comprehended, should her writings be perceived, in order to do them justice.

1ST SPEAKER: A system of a philosophical nature, for instance, is not contained in Simone Weil's writings. Even where the beginnings of a system appear, they are weak; they are strong in their *rapport*—a word difficult to translate into German that suggests building closer relationships. Such *rapport* takes place between Weil's reason and the absent God; for there is no God in everything we see, think, encounter, experience.

WEIL: "God can only be present in creation in the form of absence."[37]

"We have to place God at an infinite distance in order to conceive of him as innocent of evil; reciprocally, evil implies that we have to place God at an infinite distance."

"This world, in so far as it is completely empty of God, is God himself."

"We have to be in a desert. For he whom we must love is absent."

"Nothing which exists is absolutely worthy of love. We must therefore love that which does not exist."[38]

1ST SPEAKER: Simone Weil's sentences already mark the zero point where she perseveres. But she perseveres there not in idleness, but in action and thought. Attention, compliance to "stringent human obligations," accomplishing what is possible, wrestling with the void, the struggles to limit evil—these are the practical and intellectual prerequisites for her connection to "spiritual reality." Because, she says:

37 Translation slightly modified.

38 Simone Weil, "He Whom We Must Love is Absent," in *Gravity and Grace*, 162.

WEIL: "A paralyzed man lacks this perception."[39]

2ND SPEAKER: What must be relinquished unconditionally, however, is anything that deceptively veers away from that zero point: the search for solace, hope, the remedies for suffering; any suppression of the void by delusion.

WEIL: "The imagination is continually at work filling up all the fissures through which grace might pass."[40]

"The imagination, filler of the void, is essentially a liar."[41]

"The past and the future hinder the wholesome effect of affliction by providing an unlimited field for imaginary elevation. That is why the renunciation of past and future is the first of all renunciations."[42]

2ND SPEAKER: The central concepts of the Christian religion, which provide solace to the faithful, are also followed with that same frightening consistency. Thus she reasons: divine mercy consists in the total absence of God's mercy on earth. And the belief in immortality as a prolongation of life only prevents the proper approach to death. It is necessary to deny that belief, for the love of God, because it is not within our power to imagine the disembodied soul.

1ST SPEAKER: Her thinking takes that direction because she wants to avoid one thing, and that is the creation of an imaginary god, another "great beast" that would join the other "great beasts."

2ND SPEAKER: The term "great beast" is one she borrowed from Plato's *Politeia*.[43]

1ST SPEAKER: Among the "great beasts" she counts anything that exerts power and has exerted power.

---

39 Simone Weil, "Training," in *Gravity and Grace*, 177.

40 Simone Weil, "Imagination which fills the Void," in *Gravity and Grace*, 62.

41 Weil, "Imagination which fills the Void," 62.

42 Simone Weil, "Renunciation of Time," in *Gravity and Grace*, 65.

43 *Politeia*, one of Plato's philosophical dialogues, addresses ideals of justice and the democratic state. Weil uses the worship of the Great Beast as a metaphor for the consequences of thinking as a member of the crowd, as opposed to probing truth and grace on a personal level. This reference is explained in the editor's note to Weil, "The Great Beast," 216.

WEIL: "Rome is the Great Beast of atheism and materialism, adoring nothing but itself. Israel is the Great Beast of religion. Neither the one nor the other is likeable. The Great Beast is always repulsive.—The whole of Marxism, in so far as it is true, is contained in the page of Plato on the Great Beast, and its refutation is there too."[44]

"The service of the false God (of the social Beast in whatever form it may be) purifies evil by eliminating its horror. Nothing seems evil to those who serve it, except failure in its service. The service of the true God, on the other hand, allows the horror of evil to remain and even makes it more intense."[45]

2ND SPEAKER: That Simone Weil's most vehement censures of all forms of totalitarianism are immediately associated with her love of God becomes understandable here. Let us single out one point in order to clarify her attitude toward the Catholic Church. With one breath she rejects the God of the Old Testament, along with the great beasts from Allah to Marxism, from the Roman Empire to Hitler.[46] Yet, the divine mission of Israel is also the basis for the New Testament and for the Christian church. It is Eliot's opinion that Weil's rejection of Israel prevented her from becoming an orthodox Christian, that the controversies resulting from that source made conversion impossible. In fact, that might be true—it is evident at any rate that she did not want to convert. She justified her reasons in letters to the Dominican priest, Father Perrin. These contain the most personal and warmest passages she ever wrote, since Perrin was perhaps the only person who gave her the sense of having understood her. In those letters, her brusqueness is transformed into a beautiful, appreciative tenderness. They remind us of one of her most beautiful expressions, which we can apply to Weil herself:

WEIL: "To be ever ready to admit that another person is something quite different from what we read when he is there (or when we think about him). Or rather, to read in him that he is certainly something different, perhaps something completely different from what we read in him. Every being cries out silently to be read differently."[47]

2ND SPEAKER: The letters to Perrin were written in the year 1942, before she left Europe, a year before her death. In them, she explains why she cannot become a member of the church.

44 Weil, "The Great Beast," 219–20.
45 Weil, "The Great Beast," 221.
46 Paraphrased from Eliot, "Preface," viii.
47 Simone Weil, "Readings," in *Gravity and Grace*, 188.

WEIL: "Christianity should contain all vocations without exception since it is catholic. In consequence the Church should also. But in my eyes Christianity is catholic by right but not in fact. So many things are outside it, so many things I love and do not want to give up, so many things that God loves, otherwise they would not be in existence. All the immense stretches of past centuries, except the last twenty[,] are among them; all the countries inhabited by colored races; all secular life in the white peoples' countries; in the history of these countries, all the traditions banned as heretical, those of the Manicheans and the Albigensians for instance; all those things resulting from the Renaissance, too often degraded but not quite without value. Christianity being catholic by right but not in fact, I regard it as legitimate on my part to be a member of the Church by right but not in fact . . ."[48]

2ND SPEAKER: She speaks of the indispensable role of the church as a collective guardian of the dogma, but considers it an abuse of its office to impose its language as a norm on our reason and our love.

WEIL: "This abuse of power is not of God. It comes from the natural tendency of every form of collectivism, without exception, to abuse power."[49]

2ND SPEAKER: In another passage she adds:

WEIL: "In order that the present attitude of the Church should be effective it would have to say openly that it had changed or wished to change. Otherwise, who could take it seriously when reflecting on the Inquisition? My friendship for you, which I extend through you to all your order, makes it very painful for me to bring this up. But it existed. After the fall of the Roman Empire, which had been totalitarian, it was the Church that was the first to establish a rough sort of totalitarianism in Europe in the thirteenth century, after the war with the Albigensians. This tree bore much fruit. . . . It was moreover by a judicious transposition of this use that all the parties that in our own day have founded totalitarian regimes were shaped. This is a point of history I have specially studied."[50]

1ST SPEAKER: It would be unjust, irrespective of her censure of the church, the division of the church that is responsible for the social and political sectors, not to shed light on Weil's deep veneration of the Christian

48 Weil, "Spiritual Autobiography," 75.
49 Weil, "Spiritual Autobiography," 80.
50 Weil, "Spiritual Autobiography," 82.

religion. Christ, to her, was the model of justice, because he was naked and dead. That he healed the sick and raised the dead is in her eyes the smallest part of his mission, the human part of that mission; the supernatural part of the mission is his unfulfilled yearning for human solace, his sensitivity for God-forsakenness. That is a feeling that legitimizes the desire to be like God, not the almighty, but the crucified one for whom God is likewise absent.

2ND SPEAKER: All her thoughts, which she repeatedly and with inner urgency unfolds to Perrin, are accompanied by the question of what needs to be done "now." In one passage she eventually speaks of a contemporary—Maritain[51]—and adopts his demand for a new form of saintliness. To be sure, Maritain—as she asserts—contents himself with an enumeration of those aspects of earlier saintliness that are presently obsolete.

WEIL: "The world needs saints who have genius, just as a plague-stricken town needs doctors."[52]

2ND SPEAKER: And it is her hope that where a need exists, an obligation will also arise.

NARRATOR: It is pointless to explain that the portrayal of a complex oeuvre and the numerous topics that it addresses (without any systematic framework), as well as the portrayal of a life intimately connected to that oeuvre, has to be limited to the study of a few select characteristics, presumably the most important ones. If we are to succeed in illuminating some part of the phenomenon of Simone Weil, then one clarification is still missing. Her first editor—Gustave Thibon, who also knew her personally—provided part of that clarification, based on his concern that her writings would be interpreted in light of the political issues, most assuredly the partisan political distortions that prevailed at the time of their publication.

THIBON: "No faction, no social ideology has the right to claim her. Her love of the people and her hatred of all oppression are not enough to place her among the leftists, any more than her denial of progress and her cult for tradition authorize us to class her on the right. She put the same pas-

51 Jacques Maritain (1882–1973) was a French Catholic Neo-Thomist philosopher who proposed the metaphysics of existence and urged religious involvement in secular affairs.

52 Simone Weil, "Last Thoughts," in *Waiting for God*, 99.

sionate enthusiasm into her political activities as into everything else, but far from making an idol of an idea, a nation, or a class. . . ."[53]

NARRATOR: That is true if, for the sake of completeness, we add that not even the church can claim her as its own. Consistent in her beliefs to the end, she refused to enter any churches during her lifetime.

Nevertheless, it is necessary to interpret Simone Weil's oeuvre in terms of its true political significance, one that extends to the political issues of all ages. Thus it might help us to recognize the "great beast" in any shape in which it appears. Those who do recognize it will no longer serve it, but try to limit the evil that it contains with all their might. The struggle to limit evil becomes a real obligation to society. For Simone Weil that obligation was one that must be fulfilled "under any circumstance," if neighborly love was to remain more than simply an empty word. She only knows universal love and loves those in need of help without asking for their name. National borders that forbid such love must not be allowed to exist. Thus—to give one example—she wanted to go to Russia when the Germans had penetrated deep into Russia, even though she regarded the Soviet state as an evil, a "great beast." That was not possible, but she found sufficient opportunity to prove her readiness. The pain that the persecution and annihilation of the Jews in Germany inflicted on her, the plight of occupied France broke her psyche; the work she performed to lessen the suffering of others did the same to her body.

Her faith in God, which at times seemed impossible in the face of the growing horror, was never broken. The relation in which she placed herself to the absolute was viable. It made love possible in the "worst of all possible worlds," because she denied God's presence in it.

The mystical act of "placing herself in a relation" is something we cannot partake in. It would be absurd to claim that it is possible to participate in it, to profit from it as from a corpus of knowledge. In the strictest sense, that part of Simone Weil's journey is not traversable. It was probably always reserved for the few, and it has always been explored in different ways and will always be explored in different ways.

To the extent that we are receptive to it, the beauty inherent in anything that has been conceived in purity and lived in purity comes from beauty. Enlightened by it, we behold time and time again what the darkness wants to hide from us: the indestructible face of the human being in a world conspiring to destroy it.

---

53 Thibon, "Introduction," 15.

On the Trail of Language[1]

The trail leading to a poem is a trail of language, leading through language, a tissue of words, sentences, pauses, or when spoken: a tissue of words, sentences, pauses, and when spoken well: accented, unaccented. What is in parentheses is also read. "This poem is a riddle to me," someone once said and fell into a pensive state. The poem itself was not the riddle. Essentially, there are not many things that are riddles, with the exception, perhaps, of language. For language does not give us any clue to itself.

But there we already have the apostles of reality and of waxing and waning, who receive and transmit their pronouncements effortlessly.

In that sense, the poem is insoluble, and no acid test will destroy it.

Children and the mentally ill know the pure automatism of language; they do not yet know, or no longer know, what anything means.

One says too little, another too much, we think: he who has the right measure might well possess the measure of language. About the length of the poem, the form of the poem, where expression is no longer fluid, the particles of language collide, rub against one another, burst into flame. Association is not everything. Selection, but selection alone is not sufficient either.

---

1 Undated text fragment, drafted in the late 1950s.

To What End Poems?[1]

A dramatist or a writer of fiction will not be bothered much by the question as to which of his works is closest to his heart; hopefully, it will occur to him that one or the other of his creations provided pleasure or insight to some people or entertained them—if only for a few hours. I have never yet heard that anyone gave thanks to a poem for a fruitful afternoon or evening, although, without doubt, there are still lovers of poetry and people who are capable of being edified. Aside from these, there are the children who are expected to memorize poems by heart, because poems—so it is said—sharpen the memory.

So there is little happiness in a poem. For the person who writes it, almost none that it would turn out right and then again none that it would reach someone. The poem is solitary, has no function, and is in principle of no concern to anyone. A poem, after all, no longer glorifies anything today, and even the faithful have long invalidated it. Glory and faith recoil on the poem itself.

So often today one hears Hölderlin's question profaned: and who needs poets in lean years?[2] Another question, no less legitimate, would be: and to what end poems?[3] What is to be proved and to whom need something be proved? If poems turned out to be proof of nothing, then we should still have to cling to the notion that they sharpen the memory.

I believe that poems are capable of doing that and that whoever writes poems inserts formulae into a memory, wonderful old words for a rock and a leaf, linked or sundered by new words, new signs for reality, and I believe that whoever coins the formulae, tendered as an unsolicited proof of their truth, transports the reader into them with his breath.

How long has it been since we were told: form a word, form a sentence! We were tortured with poems; the scars still ache in our memory. One of those poems started with the line, "I stood upon my country's

---

1 Essay, published without title in *Westermanns Monatshefte* 96, no. 4 (April 1955), 77.

2 Hölderlin, "Bread and Wine," 251.

3 A question borrowed from Siegfried Melchinger's article "Wozu Gedichte? Anmerkungen zu einigen Lyrikbänden" (To what end poetry? Notes on some volumes of lyric poetry), which appeared directly before Bachmann's essay on Heinrich Böll in the August 1952 edition of *Wort und Wahrheit.* Melchinger writes: "Die Dichter, heimatlos, standortlos, und auftraglos geworden, sind gezwungen, die Hölderlin-Frage 'Wozu Dichter?' bescheidener zu stellen: 'Wozu Gedichte?' (The poets, having grown homeless, jobless, and without a place to stand, are impelled to posit Hölderlin's question "To what end poets?" more humbly: "To what end poetry?"). Siegfried Melchinger, "Wozu Gedichte? Anmerkungen zu einigen Lyrikbänden," *Wort und Wahrheit* 8 (August 1952): 618–21.

border. . . ."[4] Who was the I and what was the country referred to? What the borders meant did in fact emerge from the context. For he who accepts the rules and joins in the game does not throw the ball beyond the playing field. The playing field is language, and its borders are the borders of a world unquestioningly seen,[5] a world unveiled and envisioned with precision, a world experienced in pain and extolled and celebrated in happiness.

---

4 Bachmann quotes loosely from Annette von Droste-Hülshoff, who wrote "I stood upon thy country's border" in: "Die tote Lerche" [The Dead Lark], in *Sämtliche Werke* (Munich: Winkler Verlag, 1973), 432.

5 Bachmann alludes to Ludwig Wittgenstein's conception of language as the ultimate boundary of human experience. See "The Sayable and the Unsayable" in this volume.

On the Genesis of the Title "In Apulia"[1]

The titles of poems are rarely discussed. How do we arrive at a title? Do we have the title first, do we search for it last? What happens if we do not find one? I think all lyric poets—and not only lyric poets—have found themselves at a loss at one time or another; recent practice has involved taking a line from the poem in question, one in which the poem seems to culminate, but it should not come as a surprise if readers cling to that line and no longer have much attention left for the other lines of the poem.

In the case of the poem "In Apulia," the title showed up on its own; there was a reason to call it that. Someone to whom I gave the poem to read asked, "You have been to Apulia? Where is that exactly?—I see, I see." Apulia can be found on a map of Italy; it is one of the more obscure parts of the country, an old region, part of Greater Hellas, on the Lombard Way, diverse in its relics, sandstone Baroque in Lecce, Gothic in Trani and Bari, Greek churches in Gallipoli, all of which are grown over today, leaving only a flood of light, peasant land, and a province of small ports, of *frutti di mare*,[2] oyster beds in Taranto; the Germans rarely came this far, although Platen did; classical Italian tours do not lead to that region.

Of course I was in Apulia; but "In Apulia" is another matter, since it dissolves the land into landscape and traces it back to the land that is meant. There are wonderful names for the lands of origin, those immersed beneath the sea and those conceived of in dreams, Atlantis[3] and Orplid.[4] "Apulia" is a wonderful name—I do not think that anyone could bring himself to call it *Le Puglie*;[5] the Italian word misses the mark; it is a geographical name. What a strange manner of expressing it anyway, "in France," "in Sweden," as if the talk were of vessels or their content.

I am not sure whether it was still in Apulia or already in Lucania, when I happened to peer out of the window of a train, into an olive grove, at a vast carpet of poppies extending all the way to the horizon. At moments like this, one lights a cigarette or presses oneself against the wall of the railroad car because someone is trying to squeeze by; but perhaps it was not that unnoticed moment but the one when the word "In" was

1 Unfinished and undated text fragment, drafted 1955.

2 Italian for "fruit of the sea."

3 A fictional island mentioned in an allegory on the hubris of nations in Plato's dialogues, *Timaeus* and *Critias*, where it represents the antagonist naval power that besieges Ancient Athens, the pseudo-historic embodiment of Plato's ideal state.

4 Fantasy island created by the German writer Eduard Mörike (1804–1875).

5 *Le Puglie* is the Italian name for the region, whereas Apulia is of Latin derivation.

written. The process consists of many factors, of writing, of remembering with an unremitting concentration that flows back into writing. The water with which a river flows into the sea does not recall the springs, the tributaries, the banks it has touched, the grass over which it seethed, and the roots and trunks of trees that it swept along.

There are many similes for literary production that suggest themselves for the path from the process to the formula, but only one accurate simile for the process and the formula, the one that coincides in the poem itself.

So let us restrict the discussion to the poem itself.[6]

It consists of five stanzas. The first leads to Apulia. The source of the light is traced. The first two stanzas . . .

---

6 Light pours out its seed beneath the olive trees, / poppies shoot up and start to flicker, / take the oil they need to burn, / and their light will shine forever. // Drums roll without pause in the caverned cities. / Swarms of flies want to feed / on white bread and black lips / and children in the manger. // If only the field's light would pierce the caves, / the poppies could smoke in the lamps, / pain consume them while they sleep, / until their burning was done. // Donkeys rise to carry water over the land. / All hands embroider lace, / glass and pearls for the walls, / a door in the ringing raiment. // Madonnas nurse children, buffalo pass / on their way to green refreshment. / Snake eggs, fish and the blood of lamb— / finally the gifts would suffice. // Stones grind fruit and the vessels at last are burned. / Oil streams down from an open eye, / poppies sink drunken to the earth, / trodden by tarantulas until they die. Ingeborg Bachmann, "In Apulia," in *In the Storm of Roses*, 127.

The Poem Addressing the Reader[1]

What has made us strangers to each other? When I see myself in the mirror and ask, I see myself reversed, a lonely scrawl, and I no longer understand myself. Is it possible that in this awful cold we should have turned away from each other coldly, in spite of the unquenchable love for one other? It is true that I tossed smoldering words at your feet, scorched words, with a loathsome aftertaste, cutting sentences or blunt ones, lacking brilliance. As though I wanted to add to your misery and banish you from my domain with my intellect. Because you came to me with such presumptuous familiarity, sometimes clumsily, demanding an embellishing word; you also wanted to be comforted, and I did not know how to comfort you. Profundity is not my responsibility either.

But an unquenchable love for you has never left me, and now I am searching under the rubble and in the breeze, in icy gales and in the sun, for the words for you, the words that are meant to thrust me back into your arms. Because I am dying for you.

I am not a piece of plain weave, not of the cloth that could simply cover your nakedness, but made of the luster of every fabric, and I want to burst open in your senses and in your mind like the veins of gold in the earth, and I want to shine and glimmer through you when the black blight, your mortality, breaks out in you. I do not know what you want from me. I am not suitable for the anthem with which you might set out to win a battle. I shrink from altars. I am not the mediator. All your transactions leave me cold. But not you. You alone do not.

You are my one and all.

What would I not desire to be in your eyes!

I should like to walk after you when you are dead, turn around after you, even at the risk of changing into a pillar,[2] ring out, move the <re…x a…x> to tears and stir the rock into bloom, draw the scent from every <b…x>.

1 Undated text fragment. Several words in the final line of the fragment are undecipherable.

2 An allusion to Lot's wife, who disobeyed God by glancing behind herself while fleeing the destruction of Sodom and Gomorrah; she was turned into a pillar of salt (Genesis 19:26).

5: Music

Commentary

THE IMPORTANCE OF MUSIC in the life and work of Ingeborg Bachmann can hardly be overstated. Her affinity for music was evident from the beginning and her literary works are in large part indebted to melody, rhythm, and musical form. As a child, she wanted to be a musician, began composing at an early age, and admitted to having "a special relationship to music" as a result of her musical pursuits during her childhood years; she also spoke of her "emphatic belief in music." In her conversations and interviews, she speaks of "music, to which I probably have an even more intensive relationship than to literature,"[1] and tells of writing her first poems as prototypes for her music. A woman of letters composing with words and playing with the idea of musical expression as few writers have, she refers to the process of writing as "composition" and to her sonorous novel *Malina* as an "overture." She inserts a musical score into the novel, at the beginning and again at the end, conspicuously framing the text with a quote from Arnold Schoenberg's atonal song cycle *Pierrot Lunaire* (Opus 21) and signaling the importance of a new kind of language for the novel's narrative.[2] For Bachmann, music was superior to literature or language in its expressiveness: music "helps me by the fact that the absolute is shown in it, which I do not see attained in language, therefore not in literature either."[3] As a timeless element, music's utopian potential is prominent at the end of *Malina*, where it is not the narrator's literary legacy, "The Secrets of the Princess of Kagran" ("Die Geheimnisse der Prinzessin von Kagran"), but her phonograph records that pose the greatest resistance to Malina's rage of destruction: "he tries to break a record, but it doesn't break, it just bends, giving the greatest resistance before it finally does crack."[4]

---

1 Bachmann, *Gespräche und Interviews*, 107.

2 The use of musical notation is not without precedence in modern Austrian literature; Arthur Schnitzler was among the first to incorporate musical scores into his landmark novella, *Fräulein Else*, which appeared in 1924, nearly fifty years prior to Bachmann's *Malina*.

3 Bachmann, *Gespräche und Interviews*, 85.

4 Ingeborg Bachmann, *Malina. A Novel*, trans. Philip Boehm (New York: Holmes & Meier, 1990), 224.

That music was of central importance to the writer resonates not only throughout her literary work, but also in the critical writings included in this volume and in statements by the author as well as by those who knew her. Repeatedly, one encounters the central role of music and musicians in her life and work, particularly her long-term friendship and collaboration with the German composer Hans Werner Henze, who composed incidental music for her radio play *The Cicadas* (*Die Zikaden*, 1955) and for whom she crafted two opera libretti, *The Prince of Homburg* (*Der Prinz von Homburg*, 1958), after Heinrich von Kleist, and *The Young Milord* (*Der junge Lord*, 1964), after Wilhelm Hauff, as well as a ballet scenario for Henze's ballet pantomime, *The Idiot*, after Dostoevsky (1953). Bachmann also provided two poems, "In the Storm of Roses" ("Im Gewitter der Rosen") and "Safe Conduct" ("Freies Geleit"), which Henze set for soprano and orchestra as "Aria I" and "Aria II" in *Night Pieces and Arias* (*Nachtstücke und Arien*, 1957), and a song cycle, *Songs from an Island* (*Lieder von einer Insel*, 1964), which he recast as *Choral Fantasies on Poems by Ingeborg Bachmann* (*Chorfantasie auf Gedichte von Ingeborg Bachmann*, 1967). Moreover, Bachmann's poems have been set to music by the Italian composer Luigi Nono; and her novel was used as the basis for the radio opera *Malina Suite* (1985) by the Austrian composer Otto Brusatti.

The essays on music collected in this volume allow us to experience the breadth of Bachmann's writing in general and the many facets of her affinity to musical expression, from the subtle irony of her parody on musical rituals in the longest piece, "Wondrous Music," to the deep reverence in the shortest one, her tribute to the singer Maria Callas. Bachmann likens the artistry of the great soprano to "the ultimate fairy tale, the ultimate reality that a listener may hope to experience," describing her as a "genuine human being, a stranger to the world of mediocrity and of perfection," who "has always been art, oh art," and "has not sung roles, never, but has lived on the razor's edge."

Similarly, in her essay on Verdi's *Otello* it is the human being that Bachmann singles out for serious analysis, the villain Iago, the only "character of any interest, the driving force of this piece, of this music," in her estimation "the most extreme example of what a human being is capable of." By contrast, she shows a lighter side as she steps back and surveys the various components of what she terms "Wondrous Music" with decided irreverence, poking fun at a long list of bourgeois music rituals: the preparations for a concert, the cloak room, the audience with its many "ears," conductors, singers, ballet, scores, old music, new music, serious and popular music, musical cities, and then, at last, "A Leaf for Mozart" leading to her final rubric, "Music," a solemn coda on the potential for "Wondrous Music" in human lives.

Bachmann's reflections on the two opera libretti she wrote for Henze—"Genesis of a Libretto" on the *Homburg* libretto and "Notes on the Libretto" on *The Young Milord* libretto—as well as her essay "Music and Poetry" ("Musik und Dichtung"), written with Henze and Adorno[5] in mind, are also included in this section of the volume. They highlight the work of the librettist and elaborate on the interrelationship of words and music: "not a decorative environment comprised of sound. But union. The new state in which [words] sacrifice their autonomy and gain a new power of persuasion through music. And music no longer seeks the trivial text as a prompt, but a language in hard currency, a measure on which to test its own value." Here, the poet gives voice to her vision for a utopian alliance of the two arts, "for the moment in which poetry and music have their moment of truth with one another. Together, and inspired by each other, music and word are a provocation, a rebellion, a love, a confession."

In her essay "Music and Poetry," she asks whether the arts "have to go their separate ways at a moment when any missed opportunity would be a rescue forsaken, when any failure to recognize the spirit in a kindred spirit intensifies our unspeakable sadness? Our need for song is there. Does singing need to come to an end?" Of course, music represents a reminder of a lost and irreplaceable utopia, an awareness of a "fundamental transformation" that is not only woven into many of Bachmann's prose works, but is also reflected in her verses. Among many other examples, this awareness is central to the poem she dedicates to Henze, "Enigma" (1967), where music resonates in virtually every phrase as well as in the direct quotes from Mahler's 3rd Symphony, "you should not cry, says the music," and from Alban Berg's "Altenberg Songs" (Opus 4), "nothing more will come."[6]

When reflecting on the process of crafting a libretto in "Genesis of a Libretto" ("Entstehung eines Librettos"), a process as responsive to the peculiar historical moment of the late 1950s as it is to the aesthetic exigencies of the opera genre, Bachmann expresses great reverence for Kleist's drama, *Prince Frederick of Homburg* (*Prinz Friedrich von Homburg*, 1809–1811), and her discomfort at having to abridge it for the opera stage. She reduces the original by two thirds and delivers a libretto that is far more than a mere miniature of the original, altering the drama significantly in response to political as well as formal considerations. Her uneasiness about the glorification of Prussian military values and the triumph of the state over the individual in the play, informed by her reading of Brecht's 1939 sonnet, "On Kleist's Play 'The Prince of Homburg,'" ("Über Kleists Stück 'Der Prinz von Homburg'") directed against the National Socialist misuse of Kleist, resulted in a less than heroic Homburg. Rather, Bachmann's prince is transformed into a poetic,

5 Theodor W. Adorno (1903–1969), German philosopher, sociologist, and composer; leading member of the Frankfurt School of critical theory.

6 Ingeborg Bachmann, "Enigma," in *In the Storm of Roses*, 185.

dreamy, intrinsically "modern" individual confronting a fragile world, where the state is viewed as an absurdity. Through what she terms "small surgical operations," Bachmann aspires to hand the drama over to the music "as intact and undamaged as possible—not to be used by it but rather to provide for a second life in music and with music." Her intervention is justified only for the sake of supporting the musical flow. It is the function of the music, not the libretto, to clarify the spirit of the play and frame her "one wish: that the new music has succeeded in naming [the play's] spirit in a new and adequate way."

Similarly, Bachmann begins her "Notes on the Libretto" ("Notizen zum Libretto"), in which she writes about Henze's opera *The Young Milord*, with reflections on the work of the opera librettist and the necessity for the "subordination of one's own work to the more important work of the composer." She considers her first libretto a failure and recommends the study of "the phenomenon of opera," its "simultaneous progression of contradictory, varying, coinciding textual passages" to librettists. When recasting Wilhelm Hauff's poetic fairy tale, "The Ape as a Human," for the opera stage, Bachmann fashions the innocuous material provided in Hauff's light satire into a black comedy that destroys illusions and warns of concealed dangers in society. Her final libretto bears her unmistakable stamp, and it is not surprising that it was she who initially proposed the piece to Henze as the subject for a comic piece for musical theater. Adapting Hauff's parable, which she describes as "a short didactic story that lost its way and ended up among the fairy tales," she illustrates the dangers inherent in German bourgeois society and, more specifically, in authoritarian characters, pointing her finger at those who follow blindly and thoughtlessly, like spellbound children marching behind a Pied Piper.

Because of its uncommon protagonist, a trained circus ape disguised as an eccentric young Englishman, Bachmann found the tale well suited to the opera stage: "I was also tempted by the idea that the portrayal of the title character is only imaginable in opera, and that only there could it be made credible." Taking liberty with Hauff's language, she parodies the parlance of the early nineteenth century, imbuing it with an array of grotesque proverbs and clichés, meaningless phrases interspersed with quotes from classical German writers. In lieu of Hauff's didactic approach to his material, which was clearly focused on superficial etiquette and manners, Bachmann aims to expose the "distinctive features," the Philistine mentality of lower-middle-class German citizens, particularly the artlessness and smug obtuseness that made Germans prone to fascism. Set around 1830, at the time of the restoration following the European revolutions in 1789 and 1830, Hauff's parable lent itself to a foreshadowing of the perils facing the German territories and their dangerously gullible citizens, who once again might be swayed into following, possibly even imitating yet another trained ape in disguise. Bachmann's libretto is as disquieting as

Kafka's demand that a book be "the axe for the frozen sea within us,"[7] which she cites in her second Frankfurt Lecture. Henze likened the startling change of mood at the end of the opera, when the protagonist is exposed as a trained ape in disguise, to the tipping point in the poems of the great nineteenth-century Jewish German poet, Heinrich Heine, in which an idyllic scene is abruptly undermined by an unexpected turn of events.

For Bachmann, writing was a relentless struggle to find a new language, what she called "true sentences"; and the path to this utopian language was above all through song. At the heart of her writing is her concern—stemming from a deep appreciation of Ludwig Wittgenstein's *Tractatus*—with the limits of language and the boundary between "the sayable and the unsayable." She saw poetic language as a means to transcend these boundaries and to glimpse what she called "the impossible," allowing what Wittgenstein termed "the mystical" to manifest itself. In music Bachmann saw the most powerful metaphor for the quest for truth—thus her understanding of her own writing as "composition," her portrayal of the female narrator in *Malina* striving to create a literary work with the Mozartian title "Exsultate jubilate," and her retort to an interviewer's comment in April 1971 about her novel's lack of social relevance: "I do not write program music."[8] Invariably, Bachmann was deeply moved by the power of the human voice, its ability to unite sound and word into song, into what she considered to be the true essence of all individuals: "It is time to pay respect again to that voice, to entrust our words, our tunes to it, to enable it to reach with a most noble effort those who are waiting and those who have turned their backs. It is time to recognize it no longer as a means but as a placeholder, for the moment in which poetry and music have their moment of truth with one another."

In the case of her novel *Malina*, Bachmann employs music to underscore the absence of a female voice in patriarchal discourse while at the same time signaling the beginnings of a new language and way of writing.[9] In the literary "score" that Bachmann intentionally "composes" as the novel's final dialogue, before the nameless female narrator disappears into the wall, the author provides Italian tempo and pedal markings, such as *senza pedale* (without pedal) and *con sordino* (muted), to accentuate the obstacles to female communication. With these specific marks, the author offers an expressive metaphor for female speech, subject to silence and speechlessness in the space of patriarchal discourse. The narrator's

7 Franz Kafka, Letter to Oskar Pollack, January 27, 1904, in *Letters to Friends, Family, and Editors*, ed. Max Brod, trans. Richard and Clara Winston (New York: Schocken Books, 1977), 15–16.

8 Bachmann, *Gespräche und Interviews*, 95.

9 Bachmann's novel anticipates the theoretical work of French feminist poststructuralists Hélène Cixous, Luce Irigaray, and Julia Kristeva.

speech is governed by Italian expression marks not intended for a female voice, but for an instrument with pedals. Here the marks invoke Ludwig van Beethoven's late piano sonatas Opus 101 through 111, works in which the great classical composer appears to have ventured into a musical language transcending tonal constraints. As such, they offer a glimpse of a new mode of expression, a new musical language, analogous to the quotes in musical notation from Arnold Schoenberg's atonal *Pierrot lunaire* framing the novel.

Beyond the many references to musical works and figures as well as to "composing" her texts as musical works, Bachmann consistently shapes the narrative flow of her signature novel to follow the logic and structure of a musical score. She takes care to break up the coherence of the narrative, its ordered chronological progression and presumed "reality" with sentence fragments and a rich palette of intertexts: quotes from literary and musical oeuvres, woven into a polyphonic fabric of opera, operettas, folk songs, chansons, and film scores that resonate simultaneously and consecutively, together with legends, dreams, letters, dialogues, and truncated telephone conversations, all forming a pastiche of fragmentary pieces of text in the belief that a utopian vision might be glimpsed between the fragments.

Like Hugo von Hofmannsthal, whose Lord Chandos Letter (1902) she quotes at length in the first Frankfurt Lecture, Bachmann is painfully aware of language's shortcomings. The affinity of the two writers is a natural one, since both gave up writing poetry at a relatively early age and both were closely aligned with the musical art. For Hofmannsthal, it was the collaboration with Richard Strauss on the libretti for *Elektra* (1909), *Der Rosenkavalier* (The Knight of the Rose, 1911), *Ariadne auf Naxos* (Ariadne on Naxos, 1912), *Die Frau ohne Schatten* (The Woman without a Shadow, 1919), *Die ägyptische Helena* (The Egyptian Helen, 1928), and, immediately prior to Hofmannsthal's tragic death in 1928, *Arabella* (1933); for Bachmann, beyond her collaboration with Hans Werner Henze, it was turning to a mode of writing that is firmly grounded in song. She closes her essay "Music and Poetry" with a deeply moving tribute to the human voice, one that rings true for her entire work and one that conjures the classical image of the poet as singer, the voice of the text as it is transmitted from generation to generation. "On this darkling star that we inhabit, on the verge of falling silent, retreating from increasing madness, vacating heartlands before abandoning thought and taking leave of so many emotions, who—when it rings out one more time, when it peels out for him!—would not suddenly fathom what that is: a human voice." There can be no greater tribute to Bachmann's affinity for music than the notion of the solitary voice, raised in song to fend off the madness to which our world has succumbed.

Wondrous Music[1]

Preparations

The arena is waiting for savage beasts, but trumpets enter instead, held up by an invisible herd of elephants that modestly take the rear seats. The palm trees that have been squeezed into pots in all of the corridors of the concert hall desire to escape, because a scent divulges to them what was meant to be kept secret.

Many instruments come from forests; their origin can be observed in skin, catgut, and wood. The percussion instruments have practiced making sound on rubbish piles, and the brass has been taught how to resound and blare in the smithies. Hailing from a rough, prehistoric order, all of them now find themselves in the more refined one of the audience.

But the audience also came from the forests. They clap their hands, awaiting the tamer in the crouching cymbal and the pouncing timpani, and it is the audience that actually signals the opening of the battle. They are reminded: *Musicam et circenses*![2]

The musicians have come by tram. They carry sponges soaked in vinegar to press—whenever they think they are not being observed—on their foreheads, which are damp and hot for the duration of the evening.

Playing in the theater at night is even worse.

Wrestling with an instrument for years, exacting obedience from an instrument, and then carrying it into a space that is located a grave's depth below the boards on which, under some pretext, singers perform. Among those who only seem to have died. Raising the lid of the coffin with caution, in order not to unduly frighten the assembly. Not giving one's all right away. Venturing a preparation in the hope of being heard.

Tuning the instruments.

Cloak Room

At the coat-check, the audience straightens up its ears and surrenders its hearing.

---

1 Bachmann's experimental prose text was drafted in the mid-1950s for publication in the *Jahresring*, volume 56/57. Reprinted in an anthology of Bachmann's works in 1964, the text appeared under its ultimate title, "Wondrous Music."

2 Latin for "music and circuses." Play on the Roman saying *panem et circenses* (bread and circuses), which, according to the satirist Juvenal, were the two things needed to keep the populace content.

Audience

Ladies stuffed in taffeta and ladies stuffed in brocade. Naked shoulders, receptive to cascading music, leashed by jealous admirers to pearl necklaces, and untouchable shoulders wrapped in shawls.

The gentlemen with invigorated faces atop ceremonious suits. Black padded shoulders capable of cushioning the most powerful assaults of the orchestra with confidence.

Eyeglasses and opera glasses. For there is supposed to be something to see here.

The readiness to attend an execution with an assured outcome awakens when the violinists tighten the screws on the necks of their instruments and whet the strings with their bows until they start to whine.

The lamentation and mourning in the auditorium bewilder those who pay close attention to the sounds; to those looking up, it is a warning when every second light on the walls is dimmed.

The listeners disperse, take their seats, and collect themselves.

When silence sets in, the hall is evenly furrowed by rows of heads, and in every row the ears of the listeners can be seen growing with curiosity.

Ears

Ears: beautifully coiled snail shells, into which tunes would like to retreat; rest stations for words of love at the twilight hour between six and eight.

Ears: great wings that want to fly away, flapping in the draft, yearning to soar.

Ears: with the puckered edges of shells and built-in distortion devices. Let nothing clamor in their presence!

Ears: with long lobes for rings that dangle and tinkle; purveyors of harmless tunes of brief duration.

Ears: deaf ones, cemeteries of sound with access only in November—for a lament when the ice crunches and the screech owl cries.

Ears: on call, on recall.

Ears: in arousal, with the trace of a modest bite that has set the hammer in motion. Oh, not to have to hear anything! And douse all the lights, because my ear also wants to repose in darkness!

Ears: red ones, fruits of the sea, dragged up from the depths to the light, discolored in a world without a water organ and a cool harmonium.

Ears: curious ones, gatekeepers on either side of a dignified face, listening to rumors as they rise and fade.

Ears: furry ones, ears of hunted hares darting sideways and in flight.

Ears: raised hide, pointed and sharpened by hunters.

Ears: clean ones and unclean ones.

Ears: immersed in the world of danger. Registering shots and hits and the rustling of paper at an inaccessible conference.

Ears: of children and the elderly, in which the first sounds and the last are repeated blissfully until they are remembered.

Ears: shiny ones, made of enamel, created for the barriers of sound, reaching the scream of the stars and the whisper of plants.

Conductors

Conductors have much to answer for. They are not there for the sole purpose of indicating the beat. After all, the whole orchestra looks to them and follows their directions. When the man in tails gives a nod, a violin stops playing; when he lowers an eyelid, the clarinets enter, and the French horns, destined to be kissed, open their mouths when he opens his.

There is one conductor who has memorized the music so well that he can close his eyes when it commences. He leads it through the dark with self-assured hands and does not open his eyes again until all the instruments have become unruly—quite astonished by the commotion that a fortissimo produces.

Another conductor uses a baton. He handles it like a knife, at first neatly and with precision and later with such fury and in such murderous frenzy that the audience becomes frightened the music will end up being carried out of the hall on a stretcher, diced into little pieces.

Then there is a conductor who almost loses control of himself on account of the music. His knees, elbows, and shoulders strain the seams of his suit. He assumes the risk of a tensile test, after the many tensile tests to which the orchestra has already subjected him. (He has memorized all of the musicians' names in order to be able to ward off the obstreperousness of the individuals; but now it is too late, and he is unable to carry the man with the viola along by calling his name.)

One conductor has wrong notes inserted secretly into the musicians' sheet music, so that he is able to stop them with a wave of his hand and make corrections. For he too only has two ears and must pretend that he is listening with twenty.

One conductor operates as a magician. He raises his hands in a conjuring gesture, until the music flashes lightning and thunders. And with a flick of the wrist he makes it fade again. He enjoys creating the impression that he shakes the many sounds that come plummeting out of his own sleeves and then swallows them between his lips, which move in a mute incantation. The audience is just about to catch its breath, but at that moment the auditorium turns bright and cold. All rise, briefly clap their hands, and once again a concert has come to a close.

Only once did a very venerable conductor give cause for complaint. That was when it became apparent that he was conducting his favorite pieces more and more slowly from one performance to the next. But he was already old and had become increasingly frail vis-à-vis the music. "Much too beautiful to be played any faster," he retorted.

There is one conductor who is so famous that he can take the risk of executing what is written in the score. He insists that the instruments gleam, that the musicians do their assigned drills and prostrate themselves before the music, which he calls their supreme commander. If a note sits too loosely, he runs around swearing and raging and screaming, "You blockheads! You bastards!" The interpreter translates only half. But a flute has already been broken on his head, and he need not continue, because the conductor is screaming again. "Your God is worth a damn!" and "My God is alright!"—because some of the musicians speak only English and are weeping. Then he also weeps and wishes just one more rehearsal. The final rehearsal is a test he passes together with all of the musicians before his God, whom he has made their God as well.

Singers

Their tones are the only thing about them that people believe. Not their emphatic strides, their monstrous actions, their smiles, their emotions. Least of all the words, which they draw out and contract as they please, in a legato, a tremolo, a trill.

They rob the listener of his composure, themselves of the confidence in their costumes, which they cannot slip into with a disembodied voice.

Adored singers! Condemned to a programmatic life in the metropolises and the provinces of music; their vocal cords swelled with applause; their tongues paralyzed by hisses; heroes and villains jeopardized by a draft of air; Wagnerian heroines and soubrettes rendered incapable of love by any trace of hoarseness!

Singers loved for a song and scorned for a song!

The day will come when they turn into yellowhammers and conceal the superfluous ballast of their bodies and their brains under their feathers.

Ballet

The choreography diverts attention from the fact that the music is trampled underfoot in ballets. But the dancers have no choice; they are only allowed to touch the music, not the ground.

They overcome the world by replacing it with stage sets, against whose background no nature can ever dispute their poses.

The dancers do not embrace the ballerinas. They make every gesture absolute, because they produce art with their bodies. They appear divorced from all contexts—their locks and smiles draped, their expressions archaic, their bodies accentuated in black leotards. After having overlooked the opening bars, they take off, leap, soar, and land on a chord that is whirled asunder in a pirouette. For a single moment they are, at one and the same moment, the burden and those who cast it off.

Center stage, frozen, the ballerina, the perfect dream of herself, stands in blinding white—on a tone that forgets its pain.

Dance, derived under the premises of autocracy, knows only one you: the music. When it comes to an end, the dancers sink down on one knee, caress it with the tips of their fingers ecstatically, and between their arms that are stretched out in longing, they conceal their faces, which, unnoticed by anyone else, shed their masks.

Scores

First there is the music paper with the horizontal lines; five of them form a road, with road signs, distance markers, signs for stops, no standing zones, and notifications of speed limits. Sometimes there is a great deal of traffic, and the paper is awash with black signs, obedient bumper-to-bumper drivers, and clever breakaways. Here and there, the streets are quiet and empty; merely the one or the other note that has gotten lost, ventured out too far, or lagged behind. The roads lose themselves in another country.

One might also say: music is a language that wants to correspond to a graphic image. The image shows little whips, distended dots stretched out of shape, shadowy curlicues, and strokes, strands pulled by a few dots, and doubly secured strands with many dots, strung up together, thrashing about.

Music is transcribed in accordance with accepted, comprehensible rules, and what is read becomes audible following an incomprehensible structural correlation between those signs and certain sounds.

The graphic image reveals the music to us, but it does not reveal what the music says to us. When we open the scores, we hum as we read them and use our hands for help to underscore movement and rhythm. And yet there is something that the music does not reveal!

Music remains unreal as an image and elapses in the amount of time in which it effectively resounds. But it cannot deliver the signs unless it has first resonated in an inner ear.

It makes a lively leap onto the paper, where, held stationary, it perishes to a sign, and it makes a death-defying leap from the paper into life.

Old Music

The clavicembalo has reached its maturity. You think of autumn in Burgundy and its wine with the sediment of summer. While you are asking yourself how long it may have stood in the sun, it wanders more deeply into autumn, into the biting cold. The crow quill chimes, and ice bursts from a sky that will ultimately be open. What happens is simple. The mood, the randomness are relinquished, and the laws are found.

The world moves back into joint.

Because there is an immutable number of tones under our sky and variation is everything, chaconne and passacaglia insist on making the one theme audible in each and every transformation.

New Music

Accompanied by the anxious encouragement of the older instruments, the vibraphone, which announced its birth with a frail squawk, is maturing.

Once people get used to it, new music ages. Forgotten is the music that no one can get used to. For one standard of the music made by humans for humans is whether it can be remembered. Other standards are applied to music differently from one era to the next.

The creations of every spring and fall are paraded on the catwalks of concert halls, the latest musical fashions with their outrageous or insipid attractions. (A procession of numbers, its pace controlled by the metronome; no longer presented under the shopworn names "Serenada" and "Impromptu," and without the opportune freedom of an "Andante ma non troppo" and an "Allegro assai.")

The musical spies are eavesdropping.

A frill of sound sets the music scene on its ear. A piano effect fails to find favor. A fascinating rhythmic innovation breaks new ground.

The verdicts are: bearable, unbearable . . .

Serious And Popular Music

The weight that encumbers serious music has not yet been determined. It need not be harder to play than popular music, because of that imponderable weight; nor need it be harder to listen to. But it asks to be listened to differently, for what has attached itself to it can, in turn, only be experienced by an experienced feeling.

Feelings assume itinerant forms. They move from a heart into a sound—or into a word or a picture—and resume their initial form in another heart.

In music that is the most serious of all, every sound pays a debt and redeems the feeling from the saddest of forms. It is very rare.

Popular music, of which there can never be enough, is short-lived. Like merchandise in great demand, it is supplied newly packaged and with minute adjustments every year. Everyone catches it in passing, and many people dance to it face to face; it is good for anything and occasionally even good for nothing.

There are hits that become famous overnight and are forgotten from one day to the next, for overnight it is usually necessary to find an antidote to the silence that is on the prowl. There are the wonderful tangos and slow waltzes with which people get to know one another and with which they break up. But much more often, people get to know each other even when no tango is accessible, and very few people have a waltz played for them when they bid farewell to one another. There is hot jazz for the winter and cool jazz for the raging summers, and for the idle evenings all year round there is a movie soundtrack as an accompaniment to kill time.

At times we are roof dwellers and whistle from every roof. At other times we live in cellars and sing to give ourselves the courage to overcome our fear of the dark.

We need music.

A world without sound is a phantasm.

Music Cities

By being called music cities some of our cities are esteemed over others. We must perceive them as cities in which the many compositions played and faded there have become architecture. They are cities with streets in major and minor keys, traffic in three-four and four-four time, rests in green, chromatic stairways, parks full of divertimenti, and above, a sky that is a permanent symphony of colors.

In days long past, sonatas were dedicated to little countesses in music cities, and bishops commissioned musical settings of the mass. Even today, all of the ladies living in the wealthy suburbs still play the piano; the common folk love opera and invent for themselves the songs they need, above all else, to survive. In those cities, the windows are open in the expectation, not that a leaf might flutter in, but that one would flutter out from a music stand and that the coloratura mastered by a housemaid as her day's work would cause a stranger to pause in enchantment.

Those are the cities where the military is beloved for its concert bands and the beggars for the guitar music with which they call attention to their poverty. In matters great and small, hard cash is forever being shelled out for music.

The inhabitants of music cities are represented by two parties: by the claque and the anti-claque, and the deaf and hard-of-hearing, who neither want to align themselves with the right music nor the left, constitute the anarchists.

Music cities have a season, like health resorts—the music festivals. During that period, music is on tap for the many thousands of people who believe their health depends on it and who cannot reside in a music city.

Those who do live in a music city permanently look forward to the end of the season, because then all the unmusical people leave, and the time has come for finger exercises.

A Leaf for Mozart

Don your most beautiful apparel, your Sunday outfit, or your shroud. The lawn has been freshly mown—not only at Mirabell castle.[3] When you observe the Sabbath or lie down to die, call the strings, the brass, the woodwinds, and the tympani. You need not turn the pages for them. The wind, which the lowland plain has let in, will turn them. You feel what sort of wind it is. The great game that was won once before begins again, where the hills have settled around the brown river with its incomprehensible language stemming from the days of creation. You sense what river it is.

Only, you do not want to hear any more stories that tell once again of an angel falling to earth. For the angel never liked harps.[4] (But, so you ask yourself once again, was his origin not compromised with that dislike?)

What would then be the point of these stories?

---

3 The Baroque castle Mirabell was built in 1606 in Salzburg, birthplace of Wolfgang Amadeus Mozart. The young Mozart played music in Mirabell's ballroom with his siblings and father, Leopold Mozart. Mirabell has since come to produce the famous Austrian delicacy named after the composer, *Mozartkugeln*, consisting of chocolate, marzipan, pistachio nuts, almonds, hazelnuts, and praline cream.

4 In Isaiah 14:11–12, the fallen angel Lucifer, banished from heaven for prideful behavior, is condemned with these words: "All your pomp has been brought down to the grave, along with the noise of your harps;. . . . How you have fallen from heaven, O morning star, son of the dawn!" Just as Mozart's music has been connected with heaven in the German psyche, it has also been connected with hell; Goethe, for example, speaks of "the daemoniac spirit of [Mozart's] genius." Johann Wolfgang von Goethe, Conversation from June 20, 1831, in *Conversations of Goethe with Johann Peter Eckermann*, trans. John Oxenford, ed. J. K. Moorhead (New York: Da Capo Press, 1998), 414–15.

"In his baptismal certificate, 'Theophilus'[5] was entered as his last given name."

"As a boy, he fainted when he heard trumpets."[6]

"He wrote that there were no rosy dreams."

"Remind me," he said, turning to his sister, "to write something especially beautiful for the French horn."

"It was a wet and cold December day. He could no longer throw his arms around the empress's neck and kiss her. He said, 'Stay with me tonight and watch me die. I taste death on my tongue.'"[7]

"He could not finish the music and died over the 'Lachrymose.'"[8]

But fallen angels and human beings are full of the same desire, and music is of this world.

The purest, most bitter, and sweetest music is only the perfect variation on the theme circumscribed by the world and left to us.

You hear on which theme.

Music

But what is music?

What is that sound that makes you homesick?

Why is it that in the hours of your death you call the nightingale again and your fever wildly jumps off the chart so that you can see it once more in the tree, on the single bough gleaming in the darkness? And the nightingale says: "Your eyes shed tears when I sang for the first time!" So it thanks you, you who owe it thanks, for it will always remember you for it.[9]

---

5 "Theophilus," like "Gottlieb" and "Amadeus," means "friend of God."

6 Mozart's sister Marianne said that he "grew pale and began to collapse" when confronted with a trumpet. Maynard Solomon, *Mozart: A Life* (New York: Harper Collins, 1995), 64. Seven trumpets herald the apocalypse (and the destruction of Lucifer) in the Biblical book of Revelation 10:7.

7 Mozart is reputed to have said this to Sophie Weber Haibel, not an empress, but his sister-in law. The empress allusion is possibly to Mozart's childhood, when he frequently embraced and kissed royals like Marie Antoinette after performing for them. See Solomon, *Mozart: A Life*, 492.

8 One of many legends surrounding Mozart's death, the *Lacrymosa* story recounts that Mozart asked three friends to sing his unfinished *Requiem* as he lay on his deathbed. At the start of the *Lacrymosa* portion, the composer burst into tears, effectively stopping the rendition, although he did not die until later that evening. See Solomon, *Mozart: A Life*, 493.

9 Bachmann refers to a quote from Hans Christian Andersen's "The Nightingale," spoken by the titular bird to the emperor: "The first time I sang, I brought tears to your eyes—I shall never forget that." Hans Christian Andersen, "The Nightingale," in *Eighty Fairy Tales*, trans. R. P. Keigwin (New York:

You hear its magnificent words and offer it your heart for them. It lays the heart on its tongue, dips it in the stream and sends it through the dark portal toward the one who opens it.

But what is that music that makes you friendly and strong every day? Why do you eat and drink with pleasure again because of it and win over your neighbor as a friend? And what is that music that makes you tremble and takes your breath away, as if you knew that your lover was standing on the other side of the door and you could already hear the key turn in the lock?

What is that music before which your spirit collapses, burnt out and reduced to ashes after having been scorched so many times? What is this bliss and this fright that are granted to the spirit one more time? The curtain is burning, opening onto silence, and a human voice rings out: Oh, joy![10]

What is this chord with which the wondrous music turns serious and leads you into a tragic world, and what is that resolution with which it brings you back into a world of serene delights? What is this cadence that leads into open air?!

What is it that makes your whole being shine when the music comes to an end, and why are you not stirring? What has bent you down so and what has so raised you up?

There are roses on your cheeks, but your lips have turned white as if they had crushed thorns. Your eyes are brimming, but your lashes do not blink.

What is it that you can still hear, since you cannot interrupt me when the music stops?

What is it?!

Answer me!

"Quiet!"

I shall never forget you for it.

Pantheon [1976], 1982), 102. In the story, the Emperor of China welcomes, praises, then rejects the nightingale, only to be revived on his deathbed by its song.

10 A reference to the final word of the last act of Verdi's opera *La Traviata*: "O gioia!"

Music and Poetry[1]

About music, about poetry, about the nature of both, one must speak in asides. The brash talk about them must cease, for what, if not every new creation, could reveal what is genuine change and what remains unchangeable. But sometimes we suspect that something could undergo a fundamental transformation, that nothing remains as it was. And then we have a right to be puzzled once again, to show our perplexity, and to permit ourselves, if we stand aside, to think about associations.

We do not know what it is that, since time immemorial and in every instance, has prompted the one medium to elect the other, why a particular music desired to give a different life to certain words, but it has always happened and, strangely enough, it is still happening today, although the arts seem to have moved away from each other, to have lost sight of one another, and no longer lie in each other's arms as they once did.

After all, we have ceased to search for "poetic content" in music, for "word music" in poetry. To be sure, both arts unfold in time, but how differently each of them is measured: incomparably more rigorous in music, incomparably more lenient in language; even in the chains of a particular meter, the duration of a syllable remains vague, indeterminable. Is it possible, therefore, that music, of which it has been said that it expresses nothing, does not want to express anything, and which seeks communion without rendering itself common, is afraid of losing some of its purity in that company? And what is more: might it be afraid—since it drives the very instruments to the limits of what they are able to do, either treating their peculiarities in new ways or trying to shake them off, wanting to dismiss any hindrance, and gazing at infinity in its search for renaissance and new innocence—that it is obliged to surrender to the human voice with a language that has become insolvent? For the peculiarity of that voice, which has one particular character and no other, is something that no progress can erase.

Language seems unable to measure up to the spiritual demands of music, the voice unable to measure up to its technical demands. It appears, for the first time, that the two arts have a justification to go their separate ways.

The word, banished from music, would know how to make do. We who are engaged with language have experienced what speechlessness and muteness are—our purest states, if you will!—and have returned from no

1 Bachmann's essay on the correlation between music and words first appeared in 1959 in *Musica Viva*, a Festschrift named after the concert series that was founded and directed by the eminent German composer Karl Amadeus Hartmann. A final version of the text appeared in an anthology devoted to Bachmann's works that appeared in 1964.

man's land with a language that we shall carry forward as long as life carries us forward.

But do the arts really have to go their separate ways at a moment when any missed opportunity would be a rescue forsaken, when any failure to recognize the spirit in a kindred spirit intensifies our unspeakable sadness? Our need for song is there. Does singing need to come to an end?

Although we are inclined, more easily than ever before, to concede defeat, to make do, we hold on to the suspicion that a connection can be drawn from one art to the other. There is a passage in Hölderlin that says that the spirit can only express itself rhythmically.[2] For music and poetry have a spiritual measure. They have a rhythm, in the primal sense of the word, the formative sense. That is why they are able to distinguish each other. That is why there is a connection.

And at every turn that music takes is there not a new poetry as well? Does a new neighborliness not bring forth a new kindling? Words, after all, have long ceased to seek the accompaniment that music cannot give them. Not a decorative environment comprised of sound. But union. The new state in which they sacrifice their autonomy and gain a new power of persuasion through music. And music no longer seeks the mundane text as a prompt, but a language in hard currency, a standard on which to test its own value.

Like a stigma, therefore, music clings to the poetry for which it harbors a passion, that of Brecht, Garcia Lorca, and Mallarmé, Trakl, and Pavese, and the older ones, forever connected to the high voltage of enduring presence, that of Baudelaire, Whitman, and Hölderlin (ah, how many could be named!). It is true that they continue to exist by themselves, but they enjoy a precious second life in that union. For like new truths, the old ones may be awakened, confirmed, and swept forward; and any language that professes those truths—German, Italian, French, any!—can be reassured of its participation in a universal language through music.

Music, for its part, enters into a commitment with words that it cannot otherwise profess. It becomes liable, joins in signaling the explicit spirit of the yes and the no; it becomes political, compassionate, caring, and involves itself in our fate. It shakes off its asceticism, accepts a limitation among the limited, becomes assailable and vulnerable. But it need not feel diminished. Its weakness is its new dignity. Together, and inspired by each other, music and word are a provocation, a rebellion, a love, a confession. They keep the dead awake and rouse the living, they precede

2 Quoted in Bettina von Arnim, *Die Günderode* in *Werke und Briefe*, ed. Gustav Konrad, 5 vols. (Darmstadt: Wissenschaftliche Buchgesellschaft, 1959–1963), vol. 1, 393.

the demand for freedom and pursue the unruly into their slumber. They have the strongest intention to have an effect.

It should be possible to pick up a stone like that and clutch it in wild hope until it begins to bloom, as music picks up a word and makes it transparent with the power of sound. It should be possible to express oneself like that, one solitary being through a solitary being, to form an alliance, to lend one another clarity before the world. To take a stand. And, in turn, to render oneself accountable.

For it is time to have an understanding with the voice of man, that voice of a shackled creature not quite able to say how much it suffers, not quite able to sing the heights and depths of that for which the full measure must be taken. There is only this one medium, lacking complete precision, lacking absolute trustworthiness, with its small volume, the thresholds above and below—far from being a tool, a reliable instrument, a successful apparatus. But there is in it an element of unvanquished youth or the harvest of old age, warmth and coldness, sweetness and hardness, every asset of all that is alive. And the distinction: to toil in the service of a futile advance toward perfection!

It is time to pay respect again to that voice, to entrust our words, our tunes to it, to enable it to reach with a most noble effort those who are waiting and those who have turned their backs. It is time to recognize it no longer as a means but as a placeholder, for the moment in which poetry and music have their moment of truth with one another.

On this darkling star that we inhabit, on the verge of falling silent, retreating from increasing madness, vacating heartlands before abandoning thought and taking leave of so many emotions, who—when it rings out one more time, when it peels out for him!—would not suddenly fathom what it is: a human voice.

Genesis of a Libretto[1]

Confronted with the task of transforming the play *The Prince of Homburg* into a libretto, I hesitated.

I admired and loved Kleist. I had read *The Prince of Homburg*, but had seen it staged only once, in French, in Paris, under the direction of Jean Vilar. *Le Prince de Hombourg*. Gérard Philippe gave him splendor, trepidation, humility. He spoke French, was far removed from Prussia, from Germany. One could not help loving the play. But could one still love the play when Brandenburg was once again Brandenburg and the thunderous cannons that called the prince back to life evoked the most dreadful associations?

Belonging to a generation that distrusted not only the nation that had abused its classics politically but also the authors whose works had allowed themselves to be abused, I could not shake off the memory of that poem by Brecht, "The Prince Of Homburg":

O garden in the Brandenburgian sand!
O visions in the steel-blue Prussian night!
O hero prince, whom death can so affright!
Pride of a warrior! Soul of a hired hand!

O backbone broken by a victor's crown!
You won the battle—but weren't ordered to.
Nikki won't hug you now. The Elector's crew
Will fetch the axe and, grinning, cut you down.

And thus we see him then: the mutineer
Cold, sweaty, purified (no doubt) by fear
of death; his laurels crown his agony.
There is his sword, still at his side—in bits.
Not dead, but flat upon his back, he hits
"The dust with Prussia's every enemy."[2]

But was it not Heinrich Heine—no less, and no less passionately, an enemy of servile thought, of inhumanity, and of presumptuous nationalism—who had written in his *Letters from Berlin* in 1822: "It is now certain

1 Bachmann's text was included in the program printed for the premiere of Hans Werner Henze's opera on May 22, 1960, at the Hamburg Opera. Bachmann revised the text for publication in *Melos* and her revision serves as the basis for our translation.

2 Bertolt Brecht, "The Prince of Homburg," trans. Eric Bentley, *Evergreen Review* 4, no. 12 (March/April 1960), 53. This translation of the poem ends with the German quote from the last line of the play: "In Staub mit allen Feinden Brandenburgs!" (To dust with all the foes of Brandenburg!).

that Kleist's play *The Prince of Homburg or the Battle of Fehrbellin* will not be presented on our stage. . . . That play is still a bone of contention in our aesthetic circles. As for me, my vote is that it was written by the genius of poetry himself, as it were . . .!"[3]

So what kind of play is it, having been accused in equal parts of servile thought and of the spirit of freedom? What are the forces that give it life, what imbues it with such ambivalence, and how, finally, are we to interpret it? But explanations and annotations always limp along, and I have only one wish: that new music succeeds in naming its spirit in a new and adequate way.

In this play, the scenes of which are set at night (or at dusk or at dawn), there is great clarity and luminousness, owing to the continuous light shed by language and by a freedom that need not be proclaimed expressly but rather makes itself felt through language. In this play—and this has not, I believe, ever been properly noted—there is not a single scoundrel, not one character capable of a mean act, an intrigue, a villainy. And there is no "fate," nothing incriminating or inexorable. Hence, the prince has to appear to us as the first modern protagonist, fateless, making his own decisions, alone with himself in a "fragile world," and thus close to us in spirit, no longer a hero, a complex "I" and at the same time a suffering creature, an "ineffable human being" as Kleist called himself,[4] a dreamer, a sleepwalker who assumes mastery for himself.

All of the characters in the play are distinguished by peerless candor: the friend Hohenzollern; the Elector's wife, the remarkable Princess of Orange, who orders her regiment into the city to liberate the Prince; the officers, who defy the Elector. All of them—and their actions and their words—are ceaseless testimony to the fact, breathe an air of freedom that may appear self-evident to us, but which, if we think about it seriously, has not yet been breathed in any organized state.

A state organized as described above is Kleist's vision. And the Great Elector, who represents it, is an ideal figure, a ruler who disdains the use of power but also shows scorn for his officers, for whom Homburg's victory is proof that his action was justified. The Prince's tragic concept of justice does not support that proof. However, Homburg, the flawed victor, surrenders to the absurd judgment, because he recognizes the premise on which the Elector passes it—one that does not arise out of power and cruelty. It is precisely at this point, due to the absurdity of both

3 Heinrich Heine, Letter from March 16, 1822, in. *Heine in Art and Letters*, trans. Elizabeth A. Sharp (London: W. Scott, 1895), 134.

4 Heinrich von Kleist, Brief an Ulrike von Kleist, 13.–14. März 1803 [Letter to Ulrike von Kleist, March 13–14, 1803], in *Sämtliche Werke und Briefe*, ed. Helmut Sembdner, 2 vols. (Munich: Deutscher Taschenbuch Verlag, 2001), vol. 2, 729–30.

decisions, that both the Elector and the Prince destroy the heroic world and its specious claims.

What appears in the play as a glorification of legitimacy is not the glorification of that legitimacy (or, better said, illegitimacy) under which we have forever labored in our lands and which led Germany into the abyss, but rather one that has never yet been realized, one that could make the state listen to reason, make justice livable, make candor something more than a risk—one that makes all those things that Kleist knew impossible, and the knowledge of which seared him: "Is truth the object? To the state? A state knows no advantage but that which can be calculated in percentages. It wants to *make use of* truth."[5]

And let us not forget that the same man wrote: "The military life became so hateful to me that by and by I tired of having to help accomplish its purposes."[6] But Kleist went even further, saying that it was impossible to be both an officer and a human being.

It must be feared that this author will never become popular in Germany.

Now that the courage to tackle Kleist had been mustered, I still did not know where to find the courage to abridge, let alone adapt, the text. We have lost the nonchalance with which people used to rewrite great literary works, chopping them up and rearranging them for a libretto (*Othello*, *Falstaff*). It took lengthy deliberations and much encouragement to allay my scruples and to convince myself that respect for a major work need not pervert itself into paralysis before it. What was absolutely necessary was done; the small surgical operations were performed for the purpose of handing the work over to the music as intact and undamaged as possible—not to be used by it but rather to provide for a second life in music and with music.

Guidelines were of little help. But in analyzing the scenes, fanning them out, following an increasingly intimate understanding of the structure, indeed after something like an X-ray image had been produced, it became clear where the text could be tightened up, where abridgments were possible, where more rapid progress or access was permissible. The splendid monologues, the most concise, most concentrated to be found in literature, could all be preserved. What was unavoidable, however, were the following changes: secondary characters, especially those delivering cues, were in some instances combined into one person, or a text was

5 Heinrich von Kleist, Brief an Wilhelmine von Zenge, 15. August 1801 [Letter to Wilhelmine von Zenge, August 15, 1801], in *Sämtliche Werke und Briefe*, vol. 2, 681.

6 Heinrich von Kleist, Brief an Christian Ernst Martini, 19 März 1799 [Letter to Christian Ernst Martini, March 19, 1799], in *Sämtliche Werke und Briefe*, vol. 2, 479.

put in the mouth of another person or of "All" or of "The Officers" or "The Ladies," insofar as a transformation of this nature was compatible with the general sense. More notable was the introduction of a new scene in which the Prince, on his way to the castle to submit his petition to the Elector's wife, sees his grave being prepared by the gravediggers. In the original text he describes that scene to the Elector's wife; in the opera we witness it. The text for Henze's opera was adapted from Kleist's scene between Homburg and the Elector's wife, in which he recounts his experience: "Oh, on the way that led me to your side, / I saw in torchlight where they dug the grave / That on the morrow shall receive my bones! . . ."[7]

It would go too far to enumerate every one of the smaller changes and even the more substantial cuts. Moreover, it seems to me, in a production the effects ought to be decisive and we ought to wait and see how conspicuous they are. To be sure, there would be no justification for this libretto if it presumed to stand on its own. The justification, if there is to be any mention of it, can only come from the music. In the new work, the opera, the composer redeems the diminished, adapted text by lending it a new shape, a new wholeness. Thus, I should consider my work successful if it attracted little notice and were ultimately ignored.

However, I should like to say one more thing about the conclusion, which for the longest time and until the very end caused the greatest problems. The two misgivings that have already been mentioned—the misgiving concerning the text itself and the misgiving concerning any changes to it—were combined here. At first, I tried to forge a finale out of various passages of the text in order to avoid the well-known conclusion ("To arms! To arms! / To war! / To victory! / In dust with all the foes of Brandenburg!").[8] For it was that ending that helped foster misunderstandings and consign Kleist to the thoughtless hordes as a national, patriotic playwright, which he never was. The original ending survived nonetheless, even though I still harbor occasional doubts that the solution is the right one. It has survived, trusting that those who sense the "genius of poetry itself" that fashioned the play will also understand the essence of the work. Those who do understand it will not dwell on the naive operatic apotheosis, which is time-bound and lacks reflection, but will linger in Natalie's grief-stricken words: "Oh, what is human greatness, human fame!"[9]

---

7 Heinrich von Kleist, *The Prince of Homburg*, trans. Hermann Hagedorn, in *The German Classics: Masterpieces of German Literature translated into English*, ed. Kuno Francke, 20 vols. (Albany, NY: J. B. Lyon, 1913–1915), vol. 4, 462.

8 Kleist, *The Prince of Homburg*, 498.

9 Kleist, *The Prince of Homburg*, 469.

Otello[1]

The editors of the Third Radio Network have asked me which opera I would like to see on the program today. If truth be told, the network is limited in its ability to grant a wish, and I understand that, and moreover the network has already broadcast a number of operas that I would have liked to suggest. In the end, I suggested Verdi's *Otello*,[2] which was in fact still available, and that is the work that you will hear today.

That choice requires an explanation, not because *Otello* was still available, but because I am more than satisfied with the choice. The only thing that is not satisfying is the title. The opera ought to be entitled "Iago." That is because it is a much-misunderstood work, in which the title character has, for some reason, been taken seriously for all of these many decades; if no longer a tragedy of jealousy in the end, then at least, it has turned into one of racism.[3] But this opera is only peripherally concerned with all that. There is only one character of any interest, the driving force of this piece, of this music, and that is Iago. The spectator who only sees the villain has never thought about what this piece would signify if there were only a miserable villain, if a few endearing, largely innocent people were destroyed as an outcome of abominable malice. I do not believe that. Iago is no villain, no old-fashioned theatrical felon, but very much more than that; it would be too kind to dismiss him with the words villain and miscreant. Neither is he a fiend, nor the devil, who has always possessed more wit. He is human, but human in a way that we have not yet learned to comprehend, despite the centuries that have elapsed since the play was written. How infinitely silly and foolish *Otello* would be, were we simply dealing with a jealous man and his innocent wife and a foolish, clueless Cassio and Roderigo.[4] This play owes its life to only one figure and has its clandestine motor in that one figure—he is the hero of this play, the anti-hero, whose intelligence and diligence are horrible beyond measure. Not villainous, but reprehensible. His creed (which he would normally keep secret, but in the opera he must come out with it because everything must come out or else it is not an opera) is the most consistent creed that there is for unwavering murderers, that is, for those who possess intelligence. Iago takes human beings apart, beings who are not human to him but dissectible puppets, he makes them suffer and scream

1 Bachmann's text was drafted in the years between 1960 and 1966.

2 Premiered February 5, 1887, and based on the Shakespeare tragedy of the same name (circa 1603). Otello, a jealous husband, is manipulated by his underling Iago and eventually murders his wife Desdemona.

3 The story is set in Venice, where Otello is a black Moor in the predominantly white ruling class.

4 An officer under Othello's command and a Venetian gentleman, respectively. The skill with which Iago manipulates them leads to the play's final tragedy.

and kill; the others are merely human beings, feeble, pitiful, sick, stupid, blind, but Iago is sublime in his frightfulness; he tempts the others into demise. To tempt human beings into death is not villainous, but bestial, if that expression were not too mild. It is human. It is possible to hound human beings to death, but only a human being can do that. And Iago is the most extreme example of what a human being is capable of. Otello's howl, Desdemona's dying, the humiliations and sufferings of the others—those are his prizes.

To no end, one might say, other than self-destruction, are such prizes required.

Hommage à Maria Callas[1]

I have always been amazed that those who heard Maria Callas never got beyond hearing in her an extraordinary voice, subject to every peril. It was probably not merely the voice that was at issue, no, certainly not, at a time when so many excellent voices could be heard. Maria Callas is not a "vocal miracle," she is a long way from being that, or very close to being one. She is the only creative being to have set foot on the opera stage. A being that the yellow press must leave alone, because every one of her utterances, her breath control, her crying, her joy, her precision, her delight in making art, a tragedy that need not be appreciated in the conventional sense, are evident. It is not only her coloraturas, and they are overwhelming, not her arias, not her sense of ensemble that are extraordinary, but her breathing alone, her enunciation. M. C. has a way of enunciating a word for someone who has not completely lost his hearing, out of ennui or snobbery, constantly in pursuit of new sensations on the lyric stage; she will never allow us to forget that there is an I and a you, that there is pain, joy, she is great in hatred, in love, in tenderness, in brutality, she is great in every emotion, and when she misses it, as can undoubtedly be verified in some instances, then she may have failed, but she was never insignificant. She can miss an expression because [she] knows what expression is in the first place.

She has been great ten times or more, in every gesture, every stride, every movement, she has been what reminds some of Eleonora Duse: *Ecco un artista.*[2] She has not sung roles, never, but has lived on the razor's edge instead; she has infused recitatives that seemed stale with new life, no, not new life, she had so much presence that all who composed her roles for her, from Verdi to Bellini, from Rossini to Cherubini, would have seen in her not merely their epitome but far more than that; she is the only person who has rightfully set foot on the stage in recent decades, causing those below to freeze to death, suffer, tremble; she has always

1 Bachmann's draft about the legendary Greek American soprano, Maria Callas (1923–1977), cannot be dated. Presumably, the text was written after January 1956, when Bachmann was first introduced to Callas during a rehearsal of Giuseppe Verdi's *La Traviata* at the Teatro alla Scala in Milan.

2 Italian for "Behold—an artist!" A quote from the third act of Puccini's opera *Tosca*.

been art, oh, art,[3] and she has always been a genuine human being, always the poorest, most stricken, the *traviata*.[4]

She has been, if you remember the fairy tale, the natural nightingale of recent years, of this century, and the tears that I shed—I need not be ashamed of them.[5] So many senseless tears are shed, but those that were bestowed on Maria Callas—those were anything but senseless. She was the ultimate fairy tale, the ultimate reality that a listener may hope to experience.

She has always touched us, traversing indirect routes by way of libretti, by way of characters on whom we must confer love in order to accept them. She has been the lever that turned a world around, toward the listener; suddenly it was possible to hear all the way through the centuries; she has been the ultimate fairy tale.

It is very difficult or very easy to recognize greatness. La Callas—yes, when did she live, when will she die?—is great, she is a human being, a stranger to the worlds of mediocrity and of perfection.

---

3 Bachmann cites Paul Celan's (1920–1970) Büchner Prize acceptance speech of October 22, 1960, "The Meridian" ("Der Meridian"), in which the poet quotes from Georg Büchner's drama of 1835, *Danton's Death* (*Dantons Tod*), where Camille, facing the guillotine, utters the words: "Oh, art!" (Act II, Scene iii). Celan then augments her words: "Art— 'oh, art!'" Paul Celan, "The Meridian," in *Collected Prose*, trans. Rosemarie Waldrop (New York: Routledge, 2003), 41.

4 Italian for "the courtesan." A reference to Callas's role in the Verdi opera of the same name.

5 A reference to the Hans Christian Andersen fairy tale "The Nightingale." Bachmann equates Callas with the natural nightingale responsible for the emperor's salvation, not the impotent, artificial bird. See note 9 to "Wondrous Music" in this volume.

Notes on the Libretto[1]

In January 1956, during the dress rehearsal for *La Traviata* under Luchino Visconti's direction, during a few hours in a cold and creaky theater box in which a rainbow must have emerged over a rain-drenched Milan, the moment in which Italian opera staged a convincing resurrection, my attitude toward opera in general—which extended from condescension to indifference, I am afraid—began to waver and was transformed into an obsessive enthusiasm for the art form, into a relentless passion to see it in a new light and to ultimately comprehend it. In that very same year, I attempted to write a libretto for Hans Werner Henze. It was a failure, as hardly anything could have more miserably failed, and at that time I could not account for the fact that a writer should be unable to accomplish what so many copyists (leaving Da Ponte, Boito, Hofmannsthal aside) had succeeded in doing.

The original libretto (I am not referring to a play that is loaned to the opera stage, whether adapted or not) is far less than a stepchild of literature; justifiably, it has little claim to literature, is not to be measured against literature's criteria, and for that reason it has not been investigated much—it can only be discussed with the composer. The inglorious peculiarity of the libretto, which even Hofmannsthal was unable to overcome completely or did not always master to the benefit of the genre, stems from the fact that it would not occur to anyone to write a libretto the way stage plays, novels, and poems are written, at the writer's initiative and lacking a firm commission. A libretto is written for a composer and his music, tracing the path of the music and its potential, whether already existent or yet to be awakened. Above all, that requires acquiescence and sometimes deception, and inevitably a subordination of one's own work to the more important work of the composer. It will be his work that is presented and displayed to the public. Any flirtation with an autonomy of the text, with authorship as it is understood today, takes its revenge. (In my first libretto, I confused arias with poems, recitatives with dialogues, etc.)

It is certainly possible to produce prose and poetry without being guided by existing literature, but it seems impossible to write a workable libretto without having studied the phenomenon of opera. And by studying I do not mean anything conventionally examinable and learnable, but the observation of the mechanical aspects, such as timing, vocal writing, the progression of scenes, the formation of breaks, inevitably with an eye to what is tolerable in music, the length of its breaths.

1 Bachmann's text was included in the program for the premiere of Hans Werner Henze's opera *The Young Milord* on April 7, 1965, at the Deutsche Oper, Berlin.

For me, the most fascinating and at the same time the most difficult aspects of writing for opera are the words that overlap and the simultaneous progression of contradictory, varying, or coinciding textual passages. For the writer, it is a stimulating peculiarity of opera that more often than not the characters, whether singing in duets or ensembles, do not speak consecutively but with one another, against one another, and next to one another. What seems to be an abstruse feature of opera, utterly artificial, constitutes the superior quality of lyrical theater. In life and prose theater, people are inhibited from yielding to one of the most elemental needs of expression, and no interior monologue can compensate them for what they are prevented from doing together, and when they talk "out of turn," they do greater justice to their mental state than they do by waiting as they have been taught, either in defiance or in agreement. In fact, that is an artificial state of affairs, and opera, in a highly artistic fashion, reinstates the natural one.

The Young Milord was written in a very short time, with insights acquired long ago, and, so I hope, unobtrusive, into the needs of operatic theater. My libretto adopts an idea of Hauff's, little more than a conceit, taken from a short didactic story that lost its way and ended up among the fairy tales. In Alexandria, a young German tells an amusing tale from his native country: "Sire, I am a German by birth, and have been in your country too short a time to be able to entertain you with a Persian tale or an amusing story of sultans and viziers. You must, therefore, permit me to tell you a story of my native land. Sad to say, our stories are not always as elevated as yours—that is, they do not deal with sultans or kings, nor with viziers and pashas, that are called ministers of justice or finance, privy-counsellors, and the like, but they treat very modestly (soldiers sometimes excepted) of persons outside of official life."[2] The essence of the Hauff story not only seemed feasible, but I was also tempted by the idea that the portrayal of the title character is only imaginable in opera, only there could it be made credible.

The language of the libretto is slightly rhythmicized, with cadences borrowed from the era—not to relativize it into historicity but to have a substantial fictional outline such as every play requires, a postulated reality, be it one of today or one of 1830. The time chosen is the period of the restoration. In aiming for something general, one must submit to particulars. Thus, the language may not be true to life; it could never be that, since we do not know how people talked at that time or at any time. It wants to be genuine in its variance, in order to secure a special quality for itself.

2 Wilhelm Hauff, "The Young Englishman," in *Tales of the Caravan, Inn, and Palace*, trans. Edward L. Stowell (Chicago: Jansen, McClurg & Co., 1882), 353.

Comic opera. I could restrict the term even further: German comic opera. If the *Barbiere di Siviglia* is *opera buffa italianissima*, then this opera might disclose to what mentality, to what country it owes its humor and what spirit has sealed its offspring. Therefore, it could not be my intention to suffocate the people of Hülsdorf-Gotha[3] with irony, but rather, not without affection, to let them live and persist in their smug obtuseness, their artlessness, their charm, and other ominous traits that make them suitable for a diabolical experiment.

The comical, more than the tragic, has its distinctive features, and these are national ones.

3 A provincial German town in Thuringia.

6: The Frankfurt Lectures and Other Speeches

Commentary

THE INAUGURAL SERIES OF LECTURES on poetics that Bachmann held at the University of Frankfurt between November 1959 and February 1960 lay claim to a literature that is "sharp with knowledge and bitter with longing." The first in a long line of distinguished writers to hold the lectureship, the young author delivered a nuanced and highly personal assessment of modern literature, focusing on the specific ways that the literary arts can contribute to the restoration of human values following the horrors of World War II. Disillusioned by the deterioration of social, moral, and economic mores since the outset of the twentieth century, Bachmann attributes the cultural decline in the second half of the century to "flawed language," the jaded speech human beings resort to when navigating existential pressures in an increasingly inhospitable and impersonal world. Speaking as a poet, Bachmann argued that it is incumbent upon the literary arts to oppose this negative trend and, at the same time, advocate for the kind of lasting peace that would allow a social utopia to flourish.

Seen from a historical perspective, the five lectures on poetics reference a variety of genres and impulses impacting twentieth-century literary styles, from Symbolism and Impressionism to Realism and Futurism, as well as a host of postwar developments. In the first lecture, Bachmann's appraisal of the questions facing contemporary writers also features a broad range of avant-garde practices, from the "rubble literature" crafted in the immediate aftermath of the war, on the one hand, to Henry Miller's stream-of-consciousness modernism and Samuel Beckett's minimalism, on the other. Her sweeping selection of literary works by Hugo von Hofmannsthal, Franz Kafka, Paul Celan, Italo Svevo, Marcel Proust, and James Joyce, to mention only a few of the many authors woven into the fabric of the lectures, is aimed at reconsidering postwar aesthetic and semiotic categories.

Measured against Bachmann's noteworthy achievements in the lyric genre, the announcement of a series of lectures by one of the most widely recognized poets of the 1950s raised expectations about valuable insights into the shifting parameters of contemporary poetics. At the outset of the second lecture Bachmann admits, however, that "nothing is more intimidating for someone who has written poems than to give an account of contemporary poetry; one's own knowledge is usually less than is expected, and for a long time all of us remain ignorant of what new things are emerging in other countries." Arguing that "poems are not marketable," that "their effect within their respective linguistic areas remains miniscule," she devotes the entire second lecture to a probing discussion of German-language poems by living poets, including verses by Günter Eich, Marie-Luise Kaschnitz, Nelly Sachs, Hans Magnus Enszensberger, and Paul Celan. Bachmann's ethical objectives for postwar literature frame her analyses of these poetic examples, which can be understood as a corrective to the largely positive, ahistorical reception of her own poetic output in the 1950s. Moving beyond literary skill and superficial pleasure, exceptional poetry provides insights into the "horror and beauty" of human existence, and the dignity of her observations serves to redress language's inadequacy in the postwar period. Bachmann affirms how important quintessential perceptions had become in a world confronting inestimable risks, when she asserts:

> A few passages by Günter Eich speak of a discontent with beauty, a discontent with happiness; the whole tension between horror and beauty, the cult of beauty and the cult of horror—which are of course dialectically linked—has given way to another. The poems, as diverse as they are, should not be enjoyed, for they contain insights, as if it were their task in a time of utter linguistic poverty to dispel poverty through utter isolation. From that accomplishment they draw a new dignity, a dignity for which they dare not even strive.

Regardless of genre, coming to terms with great literature requires cultivating the "beautiful word." However, Bachmann insists that the writer approach literature by fixing the "signs within the framework of the limits drawn," making literature "alive again with ritual" and giving it "a gait that it does not receive anywhere else," except, of course, in an exceptional work. At the same time, Bachmann believed that literary truths should not simply acquiesce to the criteria of traditional aesthetics or conventional notions of beauty, clearly the most recognizable of which are the classical balance between form and content. On the contrary, the beautiful word need no longer comply with aesthetic principles, but instead with ethical maxims, suggesting that Bachmann's sights were set on the larger questions facing postwar societies, not only in Europe but also in many other regions of the world. Her aspirations for the literary arts draw particular attention to truths about murderous collectives, their incessant desire to wage war, the erosion of social justice in the course of civilization and an incurable penchant to inflict violence on women and social outcasts. Admonishing contemporary writers to adopt non-literary positions toward the existential questions facing all human orders, she encourages them to espouse vital roles as moral arbiters in the postwar era: "Above all, there are questions for the writer that seemingly lie outside the literary, because their effortless translations into the language of the literary problems we have been exposed to cause us to perceive them as secondary; sometimes we do not even notice them. They are destructive, terrible questions in their simplicity, and where they have not come up in a work, neither has anything else come up."

It is evident from her comments that literary texts cannot exist for themselves, neither as entertainment for the masses nor as *l'art pour l'art* for fellow artists, especially when their capacity for representing social change is central to any moral purpose that they might espouse. Bachmann calls for a radical approach to the artistic process, one that stimulates a shock or a cognitive jolt. Once set in motion, the shock triggers a moral response, which, in turn, redefines the cultural parameters for all literary signs. Ultimately, her objective was to ensure that radical modes of expression invalidate prophecies of an end of poetry in the postwar era.

Although Bachmann was a prominent voice in the first generation of German-language poets following the collapse of the Nazi regime, her status as an Austrian intellectual played an important role in what she believed German literature should represent and in what she viewed as the responsibility of the writer after 1945. Not unlike the majority of other intellectuals associated with Group 47, she felt compelled to develop a literary voice that both invalidated Nazi ideologies and contradicted apologists for an "inner immigration" during the fascist regime. Among the latter were writers who remained in Nazi Germany, but, either critical of or apprehensive about fascism, chose to produce works that contested fascist beliefs in a veiled way and were written "for the drawer" or were kept under lock and key until such time as they could appear without censure.

In a similar vein, Bachmann was obliged to recognize the proscriptive quality in Theodor W. Adorno's dictum that "to write poetry after Auschwitz is barbaric."[1] First pronounced in 1948 and then circulated more widely in a 1955 publication, the dictum underwent much scrutiny by Adorno's followers and critics. Presumably, Bachmann's intimate relationship with the celebrated Rumanian German Jewish poet Paul Celan in the late 1940s stimulated her sensitivity to the conflict between collective memory and the role of art in the post-Holocaust era. Viewed from a non-literary vantage point, convictions about the transformative power

1 Theodor W. Adorno, "Kulturkritik und Gesellschaft," in *Gesammelte Schriften*, ed. Rolf Tiedemann, 20 vols. (Frankfurt am Main: Suhrkamp, 1977), vol. 10.1, *Kulturkritik und Gesellschaft I: Prismen; Ohne Leitbild*, 30.

of the true and beautiful word led Bachmann to confront Adorno's barbarism with literary weapons. Eschewing empty phrases, her critical approach was antithetical to the political rhetoric prevalent in Europe after 1945. Above all, she condemned conservatism and lingering forms of fascism in the sociocultural arena, the declining importance of national entities in the wake of Western European unification, and the ideological pressures posed by the Cold War, as well as the divisive symbolism of the Berlin Wall and the latent threat of nuclear destruction in the aftermath of Hiroshima.

Bachmann's first and fifth lectures conjoin the origin of the literary experience with a justification for a new postwar culture and a yearning for an art form of the future. Her moral aspirations for postwar writers match the drive for perfection outlined in her acceptance speech for the War Blind Prize in October 1959, which opens the section of lectures in this volume. Inaugurated nearly ten years earlier, the prestigious prize recognized outstanding literary achievements in radio plays, one of the most popular genres during the economic transformation of Europe between 1945 and 1960. At the awards ceremony, Bachmann remarked that contemporary literature should guide words into a space in which what might not be readily expressible becomes perceptible, even to those who are blind to the written word.

In essence, she suggested that art should emulate philosophy by challenging the collective with ethical maxims, especially those that expressly indict human malevolence. As an exceptional form of collective communication, literature is charged to balance the adversity of culture and flawed language with "figures of silence," palpable to the human heart long before they can be articulated. Paradoxically, she believed that the more literature was able to bring to light about the innate violence underlying postwar cultures and collective practices, the more certain any redress for society's flaws would be deferred to a later time. Her skeptical assessment of the chasm separating reality and utopia must have been sobering for Bachmann's audience. For, in spite of her passionate endorsement of the quest for all forms of truth, she insisted that human communication falls short of the utopian goals great writers should emulate; and, case in point, the search for truth even falls short of being able to fathom what is meant by "literature" as a term unto itself.

> It is true that we must keep struggling with that word literature, and with literature itself, with what it is and with what we think it is, and often our chagrin at the unreliability of our critical tools will still be great, the chagrin at our nets, out of which it will continue to slip. But let us be glad that it escapes us in the end, for our own sake, so that it remains alive and our lives join with its life in moments when we share our breaths. Literature as utopia—the writer as a utopian existence—the utopian essentials of the works . . .

Because Bachmann's thoughts break off here and remain fragmentary, they epitomize how silence can point to the utopian. Her insight into literature's effectiveness as a cultural agent and the utopian aspirations of the writer was closely aligned with Ludwig Wittgenstein's approach to modes of silence as a medium of truth. Following the philosopher's lead, Bachmann alludes to enigmas deeply embedded within the literary signs. These enigmas arise from the disjuncture between what she describes as the "relationship of trust between I and language and thing" and the memory of an origin that was once recognizable, but has long since become encrusted with cultural residue. Cultural residue impedes the memory process, and memory loss characterizes the collective experience of the postwar era. Defying language's struggle to designate the objects on the page, literature has an obligation to convey what has gone awry with the world order. Accordingly, the writer's greatest inspiration is speechlessness, the purest state in which truth prevails. Bachmann's explanation for this oxymoronic situation hinges on the moral task of the postwar author: for "we who are engaged with language have experienced that speechlessness and muteness are our purest states, if you will, and have returned from no man's land with a language that we shall carry forward as long as life carries us forward."

In her essay "Music and Poetry," also included in this volume, Bachmann observes that the search for truth progresses from the nowhere of speechlessness, before language has had a chance to corrupt human experience or, conversely, be corrupted by it, to an ethos of sound that resounds with the integrity of the human voice. Sounds, and more specifically human utterances, are what connects words and art with a lost origin. In combination, three factors—the spoken word, the text, and the non-literary inspiration of the literary work—are the cornerstones of any endeavor to derive meaning from postwar literary signifiers. Even so, in order to move beyond silence, the author must pursue practical and moral objectives that allow beauty to become decipherable to a wider audience. Bachmann insists on an "obligating impulse," an exogenous position on the part of the writer, something that rises above artistry and outweighs genius—a vocabulary for worldly contexts, or, more specifically, a language for reality:

> Mention has been made of an obligatory impulse that, for the moment, I do not know how to identify other than as a moral one before all morality, an impetus for a thinking that is not initially concerned with direction, a thinking that wants to comprehend and achieve something with language and through and beyond language. Provisionally, let us call it: reality.

Relevant to Bachmann's argument is the idea that beauty can only be a vessel of meaning and an expression of the "real" condition of the world if contemporary artistic experiences are calibrated against comparable past experiences. Correlations between past and present help identify collective truths, providing evidence of "a thinking that wants to comprehend and achieve something with language." Together with the writer's quest for a new intellectual and spiritual impulse, the connection between truth and language charts the spectrum of which the postwar reader should be aware. Essentially, great literature repositions the leading signifiers of a culture, all of which may have been fixed at various times in the past, but which are accorded a renewed exemplariness for the present by a gifted author. Confronted with contemporary works that resonate with past texts, revered as cultural artifacts, the reader negotiates a split perspective. At every juncture in time, there is both a wish to reflect back on an unsullied origin lodged somewhere in a remote past and to anticipate the utopia of an unmeasured and exemplary future: "the wish to link exemplariness back to a beginning obscures another wish, the wish to project something forward, something unmeasured more than a measure, something that, however close we come, can never be attained."

Bachmann's concept of literature as a utopian agent arises from a processual impulse that relies heavily on increasing degrees of artistic acumen or genius. Although introspective creativity propels modern artworks forward, they never attain completion or approach a state of perfection. As such, Bachmann's thinking is reminiscent of the Aristotelian concept of entelechy, with which the classical philosopher characterized the potential of the human soul. In philosophical circles, entelechy is defined as the essence that realizes or makes actual what is otherwise potential. Hence, the impetus for moral perfection in Bachmann's definition of literature is reminiscent of Aristotle's distinction between matter and form, or what is merely potential and what can move beyond potential and achieve fruition. Even if art is devoted to realizing beauty, a visionary form of moral perfection, it can only hope for success when the imperfections of its various articulations are recognized and ever new articulations strive for higher levels of perfection.

> So literature, although and even because it is always a conglomeration of things past and things inherited, always the hoped-for, the coveted, endowed by us out of our inventory in accordance with our desire—so it is a realm of unknown restrictions, both open-ended and forward-looking. At the same time, our desire makes everything that has already formed out of language share in what has not yet been articulated, and our enthusiasm for certain splendid texts is in fact an enthusiasm for the blank page, on which what is yet to be obtained already appears to be inscribed.

In the first of Bachmann's lectures on poetics, she expresses the need for a cathartic experience through literature, even though a moral renaissance poses insurmountable risks for postwar authors. It is important to remember, as Bachmann argues, that it is they who, like Hugo von Hofmannsthal's Lord Chandos, have little or no confidence in language. Bachmann's negative stance is predicated on her argument that language, understood as the primary medium for communicating intellectual, ethical, and cultural values, did not prevent the tragedy of two world wars.

Attempting to channel cultural barbarism by correlating past and future occurrences, Bachmann maintains that postwar German authors subject themselves and their readers to the agony of a world fraught with brutality, a "murder scene" (*Mordschauplatz*). Admittedly, the agony seems justified when Bachmann charges German language and literature with responsibility for the horrors of the past, one that not only involves the crimes of the Nazi terror regime, including the devastation of total warfare and mass genocide, but also, figuratively at least, is sensitive to the culture of violence perpetrated since the beginning of recorded time. According to Bachmann, the integrity of a new language can only be measured in an irrevocable willingness to express guilt for the annihilation of millions of lives and to assume the moral burden for a collective memory steeped in violence.

In the wake of their ritualized gait, language and literature are endowed with an inner dynamic that exposes the reader to the beautiful word and incites the desire to strive for nothing short of a utopian text. At face value, Bachmann alludes to principles championed by the Early Romantics at the close of the eighteenth century, and to the aesthetic writings of E. T. A. Hoffmann, who placed the aptitude for appreciating beauty above the faculty for reason. Beyond any suggestion of aesthetic precursors, Bachmann's advocacy for a new language challenged the historical truths confronting Austria and Germany in the 1950s: on the one hand, Austria's obliviousness to its guilt for not resisting the Nazi terror regime and, on the other, Germany's all-too-rapid self-exoneration from responsibility for its Nazi past in the wake of the "economic miracle." Recognition for Austro-German culpability, for an inexorable trail of historic denial, and for literature's role as a cultural artifact was Bachmann's assurance that literary truth would counter the corruption of human values across the centuries. Reminiscent of Adorno's view, Bachmann believed that art's crusade against barbarism was essential for its purpose after 1945, given the realization that all cultures have inflicted indelible scars on humanity. The effects of this realization weigh heavily on the reception of authors as well as any lasting appreciation of their works:

> How often an author has been dismissed, then acclaimed again, forgotten, and resurrected once again—what works of the masters have been unduly praised or unduly ignored. And we ourselves, of course, are at the center of that process: we disdain, we reevaluate, we treat

> literature on the one hand as a fixture and on the other beat it into shape until it resembles an ideal.

Besides showing an affinity for moral integrity, great literature transcends all ideals and is thus imbued with a specific beauty, the beauty of the true word, a dream state that redeems humankind from cultural decay and the flawed language that erodes the fabric of the collective order. Here, correlations between Friedrich Nietzsche and Bachmann can be observed. Like Bachmann, Nietzsche expressed a pessimistic view of modern society, arguing that mass culture tends to promote conformity and mediocrity, even going so far as to proclaim that "we belong to a period of which the culture is in danger of being destroyed by the appliances of culture" in *Human, All Too Human* (*Menschliches, Allzumenschliches*, 1878).[2] According to Nietzsche, individuals need to overcome the self-serving manifestations of mass culture, since by rising above egotism, mediocrity, and uniformity, society sustains higher, brighter, and healthier principles. In *The Birth of Tragedy* (*Die Geburt der Tragödie*, 1872), Nietzsche characterizes the heroes of classical Greek tragedies as isolated beings, juxtaposed to the Greek chorus or what presumably correlates to the faceless masses in modern collectives.[3] Bachmann embraced the philosopher's view of the fragile nature of the individual within the modern collective order, asserting that subjects are obliged to develop sophisticated methods of self-observation as they struggle to free themselves from the cultural impediments of postwar societies. Conscious of their precarious status, individuals find themselves torn between intimate subjectivity and public objectivity. Irrespective of any attempt to garner personal insights and gain a deeper awareness of the perils that weigh heavily on all forms of being, the I has forfeited its exemplary quality in modernity.

Reflecting on that realization, Bachmann analyzes the dislodgement of the I in modern literature in her third lecture, asserting that it once "starved, suffered, thought, felt" in its own inimitable way. In the past, one could even measure one's own subjective status by comparing it to the I in great literature. Subsequent to Romanticism in the early nineteenth century, or perhaps more decisively, since the reception of Kafka and Proust in the twentieth, cultural obstacles impacting the author and the I have eroded the status of the subject, giving rise to "the fictitious, the hidden, the reduced, the absolute lyrical, the I as a conceptual figure,

---

2 Friedrich Nietzsche, *Human, All-Too-Human*, trans. Helen Zimmern (Edinburgh and London: Foulis, 1910), §520, 362. Originally published in 1878 and republished in a revised form in 1886, *Human, All Too Human* is Nietzsche's first book in the aphoristic style that would come to dominate his writings, presenting a variety of concepts in short paragraphs or sayings.

3 Friedrich Nietzsche, *The Birth of Tragedy Out of the Spirit of Music*, trans. Shaun Whiteside, ed. Michael Tanner (London: Penguin, 1993), 43–45.

an acting figure, an immaterial I or one thrust into the material." Quoting passages from Henry Miller, Italo Svevo, Céline, and Samuel Beckett, Bachmann demonstrates in the third lecture that a variety of I concepts has been tested in modern literature and that, for example, an abyss exists between the I in Goethe and the I in the prose works of the Italian novelist Italo Svevo: "the first transformation that the I has undergone is that it no longer resides *in* the story, but rather now the story resides *in* the I. That is to say: only as long as the I itself remained unquestioned, as long as we trusted it to know how to tell its story, the story was also guaranteed by it and likewise the I itself was guaranteed as a person. Since the I has been dissolved, the I and the story, the I and narration are no longer guaranteed." Bachmann devotes the third lecture to her conjectures about the phenomenon of the "I, about its sojourn in literature and consequently about the dealings of the human being in literature," crediting the I with a quintessential resilience spanning the chronicle of humankind, "for there is no final pronouncement" about representing forms of subjectivity.

On the one hand, the I is couched in the framework of a philosophical grammar, one that resonates with Wittgenstein's approach to the language of the subject in the *Tractatus* and with comparable facets of the Neopositivist tradition. On the other, Bachmann's "I without guarantee" alludes to the Aristotelian premises of ever-improving perfectibility incorporated into her War Blind Prize acceptance speech. Once on a trajectory to achieve perfection or truth, the I comes to realize that the state of perfection is as desirable as it is elusive. By the same token, an implicit analogy to Goethe's philosophy of perfection can be surmised here. Harking back to the monumental author of the German classical tradition, two important aspects are noteworthy. The first involves Goethe's respect for the existential entitlement of the human voice, and the second is his belief in palingenesis or reincarnation. In postwar literature, multiple iterations or reinstatements of the I are given a privileged focus. Bachmann even goes so far as to suggest that the modern I is the "placeholder for the human voice." What separates the I from the collective and ensures its individuality as a moral force is its capacity to raise its voice in protest, on the one hand, and to call on the authority of beauty, on the other. As fragile as the I may have become in the twentieth century, its virtue lies in its capacity to convey indignation in works of genius.

Citing Adorno's literary theories, which are arguably as influential for Bachmann's thinking as Nietzsche's critical philosophy and the logic of the Vienna Circle, Bachmann concludes that the correlation between abstract terms and spoken words precedes the process of putting signs to paper. Because humankind is prone to utterances, the conviction is that language should be informed by deeper meanings transcending the trivial conventions of routine communication. Bachmann also moved beyond the sphere of the signs on the page, since she was determined to unite written inscriptions with allusions to sound. Although the two media entail competing maxims—written inscriptions as words codified on the printed page and the vitalism of spoken words exemplifying life forces—weaving them together helped to substantiate an aesthetic realignment after 1945.

The existential perils afflicting the modern I detailed in the third lecture are counterbalanced in Bachmann's fourth lecture, which focuses on the aura of names: "an aura that is indebted to music and language, to be sure, but when the name has it, once it has such radiance, then it seems that it sets itself free and takes on a life of its own. A name is all it takes to be in the world." Even though Bachmann concedes that names in contemporary literature have either persevered or been lost, an auratic quality can still be experienced in literary appellations, whether they affirm Thomas Mann's ingenuity in lending his literary figures unforgettable identities indelibly linked to their names, or whether modern protagonists have been reduced to a single initial in Kafka's momentous prose fragments. Bachmann explains:

> Yes, it is so natural for us to keep company with them in conversation or in thoughts, we are so at ease with them that we do not ask even once why their names are in the world, as if someone had been christened with a better name than we with ours, as if a christening had taken place, albeit one without the benefit of holy water, one without a formal entry in a registry—as if a naming had taken place that is more decisive and of greater privilege in which the living have no part. These names are branded onto imaginary beings and stand in for them at the same time. They are lasting and so connected with these beings that, when we borrow them and name children after them, those children spend their lives with that allusion, as if they were wearing a costume: the name remains more strongly tied to the invented figure than to the living one.

One can only admire how thoroughly Bachmann pondered the crisis of the modern individual and postwar representation, given the close correlation between her poems, her theoretical approach to art, the burden of authorship after the war, and the archaeological layering in her prose works. "Language," applying the theories developed by Walter Benjamin to Bachmann's quest, "is the highest application of the mimetic faculty . . . in other words: it is to writing and language that clairvoyance has, over the course of history, yielded its old powers."[4] In both cases, for the German Jewish critic of modern culture and media, who ended his

4 Walter Benjamin, "Doctrine of the Similar," trans. Knut Tarnowski, *New German Critique* 17 (1979): 68.

life abruptly in the political turmoil of Europe at the outset of the war, as well as for the Austrian poet and European intellectual who turned her back on her poetic talent following the Frankfurt Lectures to pursue new ventures in prose, the capacity to perceive what is not obvious or to comprehend what lies beyond the tangible is pivotal. Accordingly, Benjamin considered texts as archives, mimetically coded repositories of cultural memory, which allow us to read the signs with heightened clarity.[5] For Bachmann, the mimetic function also resided in literary texts, since they are the best vehicle to refute corrupt intentions and defy flawed language in the interest of infusing a utopian spirit into the collective experience.

Alluding to a line from Georg Büchner's drama *Danton's Death* that Paul Celan cited with chilling effect in his acceptance speech for the Büchner Prize—"but literature, always literature . . ."—Bachmann cements her central thesis that a utopian spirit infuses the overarching goal of the postwar author. In any case, specific signs from the past press forward into the present, where they take on a new capacity to signify truth and thus facilitate insights into the utopian premises crucial for redeeming the concept of great literature. "If the works themselves did not contain those utopian premises, then literature, in spite of our sympathies, would be a graveyard. The only thing left for us would be to lay wreaths. In that case each work would have been displaced and improved by another, each buried by a subsequent one."

These utopian premises are clearly echoed in Bachmann's Wildgans Prize acceptance speech delivered in 1972, the final year of her life. There, the convictions expressed in the Frankfurt Lectures more than a decade earlier are moderated by Bachmann's assumption that authors become immaterial to their work. Commenting on her isolation when writing, she hopes that her works establish a lasting relationship with her readership, while the creative process itself is little more than damnation for the author. Undoubtedly, in the Frankfurt Lectures she remained faithful to the untenable position of the I; however, the Wildgans Prize speech no longer targets the I within the story, but rather the I crafting the story or the author herself:

> An I that takes in, puts out, and is transformed, one transformed through the writing process, is another matter. And as for the issues of the day, I only have to say that the writer must write them away, must subvert the issues of his time, may not allow himself to be corrupted by the empty phrases with which these issues are forced upon him. A writer must destroy the phrases, and if there are recent works that endure, then it will be the few that do without empty phrases.

5 Benjamin, "Doctrine of the Similar," 67–68.

Subsuming the signs of the world into the process of writing, the authorial I is as much without guarantee as the personal I in the work itself. "The author must destroy the phrases," even when that lofty ambition equates to self-destruction. The thought is disquieting, yet it is perhaps the most telling statement about Ingeborg Bachmann's ambition to locate truths in postwar German literature. Accordingly, the lectures provided in this section maintain their significance as a testament to Bachmann's struggle to overcome the "empty phrases" of the postwar period and recognize the integrity of great literary artifacts deemed worthy of transmission from one generation to the next.

Truth is Within Human Reach[1] (Acceptance Speech for the Radio Play Prize of the German Union of the War Blind)[2]

The writer—and that is in his nature—wants to make himself heard. And yet it seems like a miracle to him one day, when he senses that he is capable of producing an effect—all the more so when he can say little to console those who are as much in need of consolation as anyone can possibly be, injured, wounded, and filled with that great furtive pain that distinguishes us as a species from all other creatures. It is a terrible and incomprehensible distinction. If it is true that we must endure it and go on living with it, then what form could consolation possibly take and of what use could it be? In that case, reproducing it through words—in my opinion—is bound to be inadequate. Whatever form it might take on would be too insignificant, too paltry, too provisional.

That is why it cannot be the task of the writer to deny pain, to conceal its traces, to pretend that it does not exist. On the contrary, he must acknowledge its reality and, once again, in order to enable us to see it, make it real. For all of us would like to be able to see. And that furtive pain sensitizes us to many experiences, but more specifically to the experience of truth. When we reach that state, the lucid, afflictive moment in which our pain bears fruit, we say quite simply and fittingly: my eyes have been opened. We do not say it because we have perceived the external reality of an object or event, but because we have grasped something, although we may not be able to perceive it. And that is what art ought to bring about: that our eyes, in this sense, be opened.

The writer—and that, too, is in his nature—focuses his entire being on a "you," on the human being to whom he would like to convey his experience of humankind (or his experience of objects, of the world, of his era, yes, of all that as well!), but especially his experience of the human being that he himself or the others may be and in those circumstances in

1 Bachmann's title, "Die Wahrheit ist dem Menschen zumutbar," has remained difficult to render adequately in English. It implies that a human being can be expected to face the truth, an aspect reflected in Jan Van Heurck's 1993 translation of Christa Wolf's essay on Bachmann's prose, "Die zumutbare Wahrheit," as "The Truth You Can Expect." See Christa Wolf, "The Truth You Can Expect," in *The Author's Dimension*, University of Chicago Press, 1995: 99–109; also published in *The German Library* 94 (New York: Continuum, 1998), 101–12 with an editor's note proposing a "better" translation: "The Truth One Can Face."

2 In 1950, the German Union of the War Blind began awarding annual prizes to a single outstanding radio play. Bachmann was awarded the prize in 1958 for *The Good God of Manhattan*, and delivered this speech in Berlin on May 17, 1959.

which he himself and the others are most completely human. Extending all of his feelers, he gropes for the shape of the world, for the traits of humankind in this era. How do human beings feel, and what do they think, and how do they act? What are their passions, their vexations, their hopes . . .?

When, in my radio play *The Good God of Manhattan*, all questions come down to the one of love between man and woman and what it is, what course it takes, and how little or how much it can be, one might say: But that is a borderline case. But that goes too far . . .

A borderline case is embedded in each and every situation, however, even in the most commonplace one of love, one that we can detect upon closer scrutiny and one that we should perhaps always endeavor to detect. For in everything that we do, think, and feel we would sometimes prefer to go to extremes. Within us, a wish stirs to transcend the boundaries that have been set. Not to retract what I have said, but to amplify it more clearly, I should like to add: I am certain that we must remain within the given order, that there is no escape from society, and that we must test ourselves against one another. Yet, from within those limits, our eye is fixed on the absolute, the impossible, the unattainable, be it of love, of freedom, or of any pure entity. In the interplay of the impossible and the possible we expand our possibilities. That we initiate the relationship of tension through which we are able to grow, that, I believe, is what matters; that we orient ourselves toward a particular goal, which, without question, recedes once again into the distance every time we approach it.

As the writer attempts to encourage others to encounter the truth by representing it, so do others encourage him by letting him know, either by praise or censure, that they demand the truth from him and desire to reach the point where their eyes have been opened. The truth is within human reach after all.

Who, if not those among you who have met with a grave misfortune, could better testify that our power reaches farther than our affliction, that a person deprived of many things is capable of pulling himself up again, that it is possible to exist in disillusionment, that is to say without illusion. I believe that human beings are permitted one sort of pride—the pride of one who does not give up in the dark imprisonment of the world and never ceases to keep an eye on what is just.

A festive break between projects, like this one today, is at the same time a moment for reflection; insofar as it is my moment for reflection, I ask you to spare me the many questions that you might reasonably pose at this time and to which nothing but new works and literary endeavors can hope to provide answers. This is the time to thank you for the honor you are conferring on me today. Because in saying thanks it never seems fitting to do so only in general terms, let me convey my gratitude to the institutions that have often been the first to make my work and that of so many authors possible or at least easier through their generosity, the German broadcasting networks; beyond that, to the listeners I have found, the unidentified, whose names I do not know; but above all to the war blind, who even more than anyone else lend their ears to the word and who, as a worthy authority, are conferring this prize.

I thank you.

The First Frankfurt Lecture: Problems of Contemporary Literature I. Questions and Pseudo-Questions

Ladies and Gentlemen,
The curiosity and interest that have led you to this hall is something I believe I know. It stems from the desire to hear something about the things that concern us, such things as judgments, opinions, and deliberations about objects that in themselves, in their existence, should be enough for us. Hence, something weaker, for everything that is said about works is weaker than the works. That is also true, I believe, for the greatest products of criticism and for what from time to time has basically and fundamentally wanted to be said and wants to be said over and again. It is said as an orientation, and we insist on hearing it for the sake of orientation. Not least of all, writers themselves have always shown the greatest interest in the testimony of other writers, in diaries, work journals, correspondence, and theoretical statements, lately increasingly more in the disclosure of "trade secrets." Thirty years ago, the Russian writer Mayakovsky informed his readers that they had the right to demand that writers not take the secrets of their trade to the grave.[1] Well, that danger hardly exists anymore today. Poets, especially, are not sparing with pronouncements. (There is no absolute consensus, however, even among poets: a poem is made,[2] a poem is intuited, brewed, built, assembled.)

Be that as it may, you will be amply enlightened, and you may even become privy to secrets that are really no secrets at all. As much curiosity as there is—so much disappointment is possible, and all this may serve temporarily as an apology for the false hopes that you are presently entertaining and that I entertain when I summon up the courage to believe that, albeit nothing can be taught from this podium, perhaps something

1 Vladimir Mayakovsky (1893–1930), *How Are Verses Made?*, trans. G. M. Hyde (London: Jonathan Cape, 1970), 12: "You're right to demand of poets that they shouldn't carry with them to the grave the secrets of their skill."

2 Reference to Gottfried Benn (1886–1956): "Very seldom does a poem simply emerge; a poem is made." See Gottfried Benn, "Probleme der Lyrik" [Problems of lyric poetry], in *Essays, Reden, Vorträge*, Vol. 1 of *Gesammelte Werke in Vier Bänden*, ed. Dieter Wellershoff, 4 vols. (Wiesbaden: Limes, 1959), 495. Benn's lecture, which was held at the University of Marburg in August 1951, essentially reiterates the formalist precepts of early-twentieth-century modernism. Along these lines, Benn quotes Hugo von Hofmannsthal's "Words are everything" and Mallarmé's "A poem does not arise from feelings, but from words." Benn, "Problems of Lyric Poetry," in *Selected Poems and Prose,* trans. David Paisey (Chicago: Carcanet Press, 2013), 452. See also Marjorie N. Smith, "An Annotated Translation of Gottfried Benn's 'Probleme der Lyrik.'" (MA diss., Southwest Texas State University, 1970).

can be awakened—a cognition of the despair and hope with which some few—or are there already many?—put themselves and new literature on trial.

"Questions of contemporary literature"—this title was chosen for a first series of lectures, and when I wanted to begin working, almost incapable of finding a starting point for this endeavor until very recently, which seems a bit uncanny to me, I gave even more thought to the title. Should questions be dealt with here that have already been asked, which ones for that matter, and asked where and by whom? Or should answers be given? Do you know the authorities, do you believe in those who dispense questions and deliver answers?! And above all, what questions could they be! Should we deal with the sort of questions that the daily press raises now and then in its literary supplements, or the ones that are discussed at academies and conferences, or should we, in an even more progressive mood, be concerned about radio surveys or those in the literary crossword puzzles at Christmas? To name just a few: "Should the material be treated coldly?"[3] "Is the psychological novel dead?" "Is chronology in the novel still possible in the age of the theory of relativity?" "Must new literature be so arcane?" "Dramaturgy on a case-by-case basis."

Or should the less noisy, less attractive questions, such as are posed in literary criticism, be taken into consideration? May one venture, untrained, without expert knowledge, to seek help there? There, life preservers have been supplied—sensitive interpretation, historicism, formalism, socialist realism. Who would not like to be saved, and at no one's expense! Psychology, psychoanalysis, existentialist philosophy, sociology offer their services, have questions to pose to literature. Everywhere profundity, positions, points of view, mottoes, fact sheets, catchwords derived from intellectual history, according to which something can be determined—and how it is to be found? The key word is missing for the one who has to step forward at this moment and who feels all the works, the ages lying behind him, even the most recently created, the most recently past, and lacking erudition, fears that he will have to withdraw to a small number of his own experiences with language and those shaped entities that have been earmarked as literature. And yet, experience is indeed the only teacher. However insignificant it may be—perhaps it will not give any worse counsel than knowledge that has passed through so many hands, often used and abused, spent and idling, not revitalized by any experience.

3 Allusion to Benn's statement that the bearer of art "is cold, the material must be kept cold." Gottfried Benn, "Soll die Dichtung das Leben bessern?" [Should poetry make life better?], in *Essays, Reden, Vorträge*, 587. A single paragraph from this text is translated into English in "Should Poetry Improve Life?," in *Selected Poems and Prose*, 459

Above all, there are questions for the writer that seemingly lie outside the literary, because their effortless translations into the language for the literary problems we have been exposed to cause us to perceive them as secondary; sometimes we do not even notice them. They are destructive, terrible questions in their simplicity, and where they have not come up in a work, neither has anything else come up.

When we look back on the past half century, on its literature with the various periods—Naturalism and Symbolism, Expressionism, Surrealism, Imagism, Futurism, Dadaism, and some specimens that do not want to fit into any chapter—then it seems to us as if literature were developing in the most wonderful way, despite its contradictions, just as always, in times past: first *Sturm und Drang*, then Classicism, Romanticism and so on. There are few major difficulties in coming to an understanding about that. Only the present leaves something to be desired, one does not quite see how it is developing, where it wants to go, nothing is clear anymore, not even the direction or directions can be specified reliably. What happens to us is the same as what happens with contemporary history. Because we are too close to it, we do not have a clear view of anything. Not until the empty phrases of an age disappear do we find the language for an age and does representation become possible. Even of today's empty phrases, we only take notice of the most violent. If we had the word, if we had language, we would not need weapons.[4]

As far as literature is concerned, I need only remind you of what people were talking about most in past years and what they are talking about at present. On the one hand, you hear the lament about the loss of the center, and the labels for these literary products without a center[5] read: alogical, too calculated, irrational, too rational, destructive, anti-humanistic—thus all conceivably negative characterizations. On the other hand, modern literature's proponents employ a vocabulary that resembles the other one to a great degree. The negative characterizations are adopted voluntarily, or new ones created, so, thank heavens, they say, and yes, let us welcome it, the alogical, the absurd, the grotesque, the anti-, dis- and de-, destruction, discontinuity, there is the anti-play, the anti-novel; there has not yet been any talk of the anti-poem; perhaps it is yet to come. More sedate, more traditional products are running alongside all of this, accompanied by traditional criticism that puts great store in terms like:

4 Variation of the 1921 quote by Karl Kraus: "If humanity had no empty phrases, it would need no weapons." Karl Kraus, "Zur Sprachlehre" [On Grammar], *Die Fackel* (June 1921) 572–76, in *Die Fackel*, vol. 8, 12.

5 Allusion to Hans Sedlmayr's 1948 book *Verlust der Mitte: Die bildende Kunst des 19. und 20. Jahrhunderts als Symptom und Symbol der Zeit* (The loss of the middle: The fine arts of the 19th and 20th centuries as symptom and symbol of the times).

the formed, the creative, the essential. You can add to these labels as you like. And sometimes we even come across words from that agitated time right after the war so suffused with hope, words like clear-cutting, point zero, calligraphy, the existential, conditions of being, the foreground and background, and our generation was the first to witness the kindling of the battle between politically engaged literature and *l'art pour l'art*, this time as a result of the political catastrophe in Germany and related catastrophes in the ravaged neighboring countries, nurtured by the presentiment of new catastrophes to come.

Thus one has the choice, and would only need to express enthusiasm about the one, disgust about the other, and join the side that is more appealing. Perhaps you ask yourselves from which position you will be forced to take part in the drama of the battle, or whether you would even prefer to content yourselves with a neutral, objective observation—in order to please everyone and not offend anyone. For every writer finds himself in a tangled situation; whether he likes to admit it or not, he lives in a network of favor and disfavor, and it is impossible to be blind to the fact that literature today is a commodity market. But those are not my words and not even contemporary; they are in fact Hebbel's, Friedrich Hebbel's,[6] written in the year 1849. In this respect, the times have not changed all that much.

But let us discard both partiality and neutrality and try a third path: an obstacle-laden extrication from the Babylonian confusion of languages.

The first of the questions that I spoke to you about and that concern the writer deals with the justification of his existence. Of course, the individual who writes, tempted and invigorated by his talent, is seldom aware of it immediately; indeed, often he is not aware of it until later. Why write? To what end? And for what, since there is no longer a commission from a higher authority, no longer any commission, none to deceive us any longer. To what purpose should we write, for whom should we express ourselves, and what should we express to the people, in this world? The writer who is more addicted to knowledge, meaning, and sense than the others, can he pass muster with any single explanation or interpretation, with a mere description, no matter how exact it may seem to him? Is not his evaluation through language—and he is always evaluating, with every denotation he evaluates objects and people—completely indifferent, or misleading, or reprehensible? And the commission, if he does dare to give it to himself (and in these times only he can give it to himself!), is it not arbitrary, biased, does he not always, however much he may exert himself, fall short of the truth? Is not every act one of hubris, and does he not constantly have to distrust himself, each of his words,

6 Christian Friedrich Hebbel (1813–1863) was a German poet and dramatist.

each of his objectives? It is disturbing that this question has long been exclusively of biographical interest to those who were concerned with literature and its victims. For when one begins to speak about the "end of literature" and weighs such a possibility with rapture or with rancor, as if it were literature itself that wanted to come to an end, or as if this end were its ultimate theme, then one cannot ignore the place where one of its preconditions has always been: in the writers themselves, in their agony over their inadequacy, in their feelings of guilt. Tolstoy condemned art in his last years, scorned himself and all geniuses, accusing himself and the others of every act of devilry, of arrogance, of sacrificing truth, love, and howled his spiritual and moral defeat into the world.[7] Gogol burned the sequel to the *Dead Souls.*[8] Kleist burned *Robert Guiscard*, deemed himself a failure after that, and ended up committing suicide.[9] One of his letters contains the sentence: "A great need has arisen in me, which if I do not fulfill, I shall never be happy, and that is to do something *good.*"[10] And what does Grillparzer's and Mörike's silent refusal to continue writing mean? The external circumstances can hardly serve as an explanation. And Brentano's flight to the bosom of the Church, his revocation, his rejection of all the beautiful things that he had written? And all these revocations, the suicides, the lapses into muteness, the madness, silence upon silence out of a sense of sinfulness, of metaphysical guilt, or of human guilt, culpability before society as a result of indifference, of insufficiency. Already, we encounter all kinds of inadequacy before the time that we must concern ourselves with. In our century, these plunges into silence, the motives for them and for the return from silence thus seem to me to be of great importance for the understanding of the achievements in language that precede or follow that silence, given that the situation has become even more critical. For the first time now, the questionable nature of the writer's existence is being confronted by a precariousness of the

---

7 See Leo Tolstoy, "My Confession," in *My Confession, Dogmatic Theology, My Religion, On Life*, vol 7 of *Works*, trans. and ed. Leo Wiener, 24 vols. (Boston: C. Page, 1904), 9–10. Also Stefan Zweig's summary of these ideas in Tolstoy's voice in his *Master Builders: A Typology of the Spirit*, trans. Eden and Cedar Paul (New York: Viking Press, 1939), 852.

8 In 1845, Nikolai Gogol burned his manuscript of the second part of *Dead Souls*, but soon began to rewrite it. Shortly before his death in 1852, he burned everything he had written of the second and third parts. Only fragments remain of the second part.

9 After repeatedly destroying his work in the early stages, Kleist finally burned his nearly completed tragedy *Robert Guiscard: Duke of the Normans* (*Robert Guiskard: Herzog der Normanen*) in Paris in October 1803.

10 Heinrich von Kleist to Wilhelmine von Zenge, October 10, 1801, in *An Abyss Deep Enough: Letters of Heinrich von Kleist* (New York: E. P. Dutton, 1982), 130. Translation slightly altered.

whole situation. The realities of space and time are dissolved; reality constantly awaits a new definition because science has completely converted it into formulas. The relationship of trust between I and language and thing is badly shaken. The first document that addresses the self-doubt, the despair about language, and the desperation over the overwhelming alien force of things that can no longer be grasped in one universal notion is the famous *Letter of Lord Chandos* by Hugo von Hofmannsthal. This letter[11] coincides with Hofmannsthal's unanticipated turning away from the pure, magical poems of his early years—a turning away from aestheticism.

"But earthly concepts, my excellent friend, tend to withdraw from me in just the same way. How shall I attempt to describe for you these singular spiritual torments, the sudden upward rushing of branches of fruit above my outstretched hands, the welling back of gurgling water from my thirsty lips?

"My case, in short, is this: I have utterly lost my ability to think or speak coherently about anything at all.

"At first it only gradually became more difficult for me to discuss any loftier or more general topic, and in so doing to take into my mouth the words that everyone is in the habit of using without thinking. I felt an unaccountable discomfort whenever I simply tried to pronounce the words 'spirit,' 'soul,' or 'body.' I found myself inwardly incapable of expressing an opinion about affairs at Court, the issues before Parliament, or what you will. And not out of any sense of discretion, mind you, for you know that I can be frank to the point of flippancy; but rather because the abstract words that the tongue necessarily shapes when passing any kind of judgment simply fell to dust in my mouth like decaying mushrooms."[12]

And further:

"Little by little, this infection then spread like some insidious rust. Even in the most prosaic, everyday conversation, all of those opinions that one tends to produce with somnambulant assurance struck me as being so suspect that I finally had to refrain from taking part in such exchanges altogether. Only with great effort could I contrive to hide the unaccountable rage that filled me whenever I heard comments like: this matter turned out well for this person or badly for that one; Sheriff N. is a wicked man, Pastor T. a good one; Farmer M. is to be pitied, for his sons are wastrels, while some other one is fortunate in having such frugal daughters; this family is making quite a name for itself, but that one has

11 The text is in the form of a letter, dated August 1603, from a writer named Lord Philip Chandos (a fictional character) to Francis Bacon; in it, Chandos details a profound crisis of language.

12 Hugo von Hofmannsthal, *The Lord Chandos Letter*, trans. Russell Stockman (Marlboro, VT: The Marlboro Press, 1986), 18–19.

had its day. All of this seemed so indemonstrable to me, so false, so hopelessly full of holes. My intellect forced me to examine at curiously close range all of the things that surface in such conversation. Just as I once saw a bit of this skin of my little finger in a magnifying glass, and found it to resemble a huge field full of ridges and hollows, so it was for me now in my encounters with men and their conduct. I could no longer comprehend them with the simplifying glance of habit. Everything fell into fragments for me, the fragments into further fragments, until it seemed impossible to contain anything at all within a single concept. Disjointed words swam about me, congealing into staring eyes whose gaze I was forced to return; whirlpools they were, and I could not look into them without dizziness, their incessant turning only drew me down into emptiness."[13]

Though dealing with very different ordeals, *Malte Laurids Brigge* by Rilke,[14] several novellas by Musil, and Benn's *Rönne, Notes of a Physician* bear witness to similar experiences. And yet, one should not think of correspondences in literature here, but must keep in mind that we are speaking of a phenomenon of individual revolutionary impulses here. It is always assumed that things are in the air. I do not believe that they are simply in the air, that everyone can grasp them and take possession of them. For a novel, experience is *made* and not picked out of the air. Only those people who have had no experience of their own pick it out of the air or take it from others. And I believe that where these wherefore-and-why questions, which are always new and do not spare anyone, and all the related questions (even those of guilt, if you will) are not raised, where no skepticism and thus no true sense of the problematic is present in the producing agent himself, no new literature will come into being. It may sound paradoxical because we were just talking about falling silent and not saying anything as a result of the personal dilemma that the writer has with himself and his reality—a dilemma that has merely taken on other forms today. Religious and metaphysical conflicts have been replaced by social, interpersonal, and political ones. And for the writer, all of them enter into a conflict with language. The really great achievements of these last fifty years that have shed light on new literature did not result from a desire to experiment with styles, to express oneself in this or that fashion, because one wanted to be modern, but rather they came into being at the point at which, prior to every insight, there was a new way of thinking that triggered the impetus like an explosive—where, in advance of every moral that could be formulated, there was a moral impulse significant enough to grasp and formulate a new ethical stance. In this respect I do

13 Hofmannsthal, *The Lord Chandos Letter*, 20–21.

14 *The Notebooks of Malte Laurids Brigge* (*Die Aufzeichnungen des Malte Laurids Brigge*, 1910) is the only novel written by the Austrian poet Rainer Maria Rilke (1875–1926).

not believe that we have the problems today that people are trying to talk us into, and we are unfortunately all too easily seduced to participate in idle talk. Nor do I believe, after ever so many formal discoveries and adventures were made in this century (above all at the beginning of this century), that there is nothing left for us to do but write epigonic works, if we do not write even more surrealistically than the surrealists and even more expressionistically than the expressionists, and that there is nothing else we can do but make use of the discoveries of Joyce and Proust, of Kafka and Musil. For Joyce and Proust and Kafka and Musil did not use any previous, ready-made experiences either, and what they did use, and what can surely be ascertained in seminar papers and dissertations, appears as the least significant thing about them in any case, is superficial, or has already been absorbed. When those earlier assessments of reality, those once-new ways of thinking are borrowed blindly, the result can only be an imitation and a weaker reiteration of the great works. If this were the only possibility: to continue, to carry on, and to experiment without experience until it appears to be worthwhile, then the accusations that are often raised against younger writers today would be justified. But there already seems to be trouble in the air. Night comes before the day and the fire is set at twilight.

A new language is what responds to reality where a moral, epistemological jolt has occurred, and not where one attempts to make language new by itself, as if language itself could drive knowledge home and reveal an experience one has never had. Where it is only manipulated to produce a novel feel, it soon takes revenge, unmasking the intention. A new language must have a new gait, and it has this gait only if a new spirit inhabits it. We think we all know language, do we not, we use it as a tool. Only the writer does not; he cannot handle it as a tool. It frightens him, is not something he takes for granted. It is there before literature, moving and destined for use in a process that he can make no use of. It is neither an inexhaustible repository of material for him, from which he can draw, nor the social object, the undivided property of all human beings. For what he wants, and wants with language, has not yet proven its value. He must fix its signs within the framework of the limits drawn for him and make it alive again with a ritual, give it a gait that it does not receive anywhere else except in the literary work of art. Here it may certainly allow us to take notice of its beauty, to feel beauty, but it responds to a transformation that neither firstly nor lastly strives for aesthetic satisfaction, but rather for a new capacity to comprehend.

Mention has been made of an obligatory impulse that, for the moment, I do not know how to identify other than as a moral one before all morality, an impetus for a thinking that is not concerned with direction initially, a thinking that wants to comprehend and achieve something with language and through and beyond language. Provisionally, let us call it: reality.

Once this direction has been taken, and it is neither a question of a philosophical nor of a literary direction, then it will be a different one every time. It led Hofmannsthal to a different place than George, it was a different one again for Rilke, a different one for Kafka. Musil was destined for a completely different one than Brecht. Setting this course, being catapulted into a trajectory in which there is flourishing and ruin, in which nothing accidental in words and things is accepted anymore . . . Where this happens, I believe, we have greater assurance of the authenticity of a poetic phenomenon than when we search their works for fortuitous traits of quality. The quality is indeed variable, subject to discussion, and can even be denied now and then. Occasionally, a poem by a mediocre writer also has quality; a good story, an engaging, intelligent novel can be found. There is absolutely no lack of craftsmen, not even today, and there are chance hits or oddities, far-fetched works on the fringe that can become dear to us personally. And yet it is only a direction, the continuous manifestation of a recurring central issue, an unmistakable world of words, forms, and of conflict, that is capable of causing us to see a writer as inescapable. Because he has direction and maintains that trajectory as the only possible one among many, at the same time agonizing under the onus of having to make the entire world his own, and guilty in his presumption of defining that world, he is truly present. Because he asserts of himself that "I am inevitable," and because he cannot elude himself, his mission is revealed to him. The more he begins to know about it and the clearer it becomes to him, the more his works are accompanied by an implicit or explicit form of theoretical vigilance. We often hear it said that Rilke was a great writer, but that the world-determining and ideological content of his writings should not concern us at all, as if it were detachable, more precisely a detrimental embellishment, an extra. Of sole significance is the single successful poem or even the line. We hear it said that Brecht was a great writer, altogether one of our greatest dramatists, but one must politely forget or vehemently regret that he was a communist. Barbarically put: the main thing is that the beautiful words are there, the poetic quality, that is good, we find that appealing, especially the plum trees and the little white cloud.[15]—Hofmannsthal's overexertion when attempting to revive the destabilized intellectual tradition of Europe in his work, at a time when this very tradition had given way to a vacuum, appears to many as a futile effort; and yet without the fictive references his theater would not have become possible, nor would judgment have been able to create order in his essays.—In the final volume of *Remembrance of Things*

15 Reference to Brecht's poem, "Remembering Marie A.": "It was a day in that blue month September / . . . / Above us in the shining summer heaven / There was a cloud my eyes dwelled long upon / It was quite white and very high above us / . . ." Brecht, "Remembering Marie A.," 35.

Past, Proust anchored the entire work almost in one theory, reflected on the genesis of the work, gave it a justification, and one might well ask, to what end? Was that necessary? I believe it was. And why, I once heard someone ask, did Gottfried Benn not spare us his formulation of a radical aestheticism, that conception of his world of expression,[16] those fanatic markers: intoxication, intensification, monologic I. But would it have been possible by other means for him to let those few poems emerge that the questioner wanted to acknowledge?—Do the essayistic passages in Musil's *Man Without Qualities* not have their place in the work? Is it possible to imagine the book without the construction of a doomed utopia or the search for a "clear-sighted mysticism"?[17] Is it not precisely all of the thought experiments that transform the book into what it is?

I do not mention all this in order to make it impossible to judge the individual writers and their mistakes, their partialities, but rather as a reminder, when someone asks himself today, disoriented, just how the new is to be acknowledged as well as the appearance of a real writer and of literature in general. It will be recognizable by a new comprehensive definition, the endorsement of a law, by the secret or explicit rendering of inexorable thoughts.

Only images, of course, are timeless. Thinking, rooted in time, also succumbs to time. And because it expires, for that very reason, our thinking must be new if it is to be genuine and if it is to make a difference.

It would not occur to us to cling to the ideological world of Classicism or of any other epoch, since it can no longer be decisive for us; our reality, our quarrels have become different ones. However radiant individual thoughts from an earlier time may come down to us, when we invoke them, we only do so in support of our thoughts today. It should also not occur to us to believe that everything has already been accomplished because fifty and forty years ago a few great minds appeared on the scene. It is not beneficial to leave the thinking to them, as if they were our fixed stars. It is no use to prop oneself up on the admirable works that have been created in the last few decades. All we can learn from this is that we are not exempt from making the same dangerous appearance. In art, there is no progress along the horizontal, but rather the ever-changing rupture of the vertical. Solely the means and techniques in art make the impression that we are dealing with progress. What is possible, however, is in fact transformation. And the transforming effect that emanates from new works educates us to a new perception, a new feeling, a new consciousness.

16 Reference to Benn's 1949 book of essays and aphorisms, entitled *Ausdruckswelt* (World of Expression).

17 Musil, *The Man Without Qualities*, 2:1184.

When it seizes a new possibility, art gives us the chance to experience where we stand or where we should be standing, how things are going and how they should be going. For its designs do not emerge in a vacuum. Surely no one believes anymore that writing takes place beyond the historical situation—that there is even one writer whose point of departure is not determined by the circumstances of his times.[18] In the most fortunate instance, he can succeed in two things: in being a representative, in representing his time, and in presenting something for which the time has not yet come. Admittedly, even if the anxious grasping for straws, the intellectual clinging of those only capable of receiving are to no avail, there are triggers to ignite the mind from afar. For an entire generation it was Nietzsche, from whom a spark flashed to André Gide, to Thomas Mann, Gottfried Benn, and many others. For Brecht it was Marx, for Kafka, Kierkegaard. Joyce was ignited by Vico's philosophy of history,[19] and there were Freud's countless impulses, and most recently Heidegger has been an influence.

How something new could possibly ignite? It is difficult to say. The specialists, the experts are multiplying. The thinkers are in short supply. Perhaps Wittgenstein will have an effect, maybe Ernst Bloch. Pure speculation.

Art as a force for change . . .? "Change," if anything, that is the question that belongs among those crucial, doubt-ridden, awful questions. What do we mean by change and why do we want change through art?! For we surely do want something from it! Art has already moved so many times, from the house of God to the house of ideals, from *House Beautiful*[20] to the *bateau ivre*,[21] and then to the gutters, to naked reality, as it was called, and then again to the house of dreams and to the temples with hanging gardens,[22] and on again to the pseudo-mystical, stale air of "blood and soil,"[23] and on to the house of humanity and to

18 Bachmann echoes Celan's 1958 speech here: "For the poem does not stand outside time." Paul Celan, "Speech on the Occasion of Receiving the Literature Prize of the Free Hanseatic City of Bremen," in *Selected Prose*, trans. Rosmarie Waldrop (Riverdale-on-Hudson, NY: The Sheep Meadow Press, 1986), 34.

19 The Italian Giambattista Vico (1668–1744) maintained that each period in history has its own character and identity, and that certain periods repeat themselves in the same order throughout history.

20 Reference to a popular American magazine about home design and decoration, published 1896–1938, 1939–1942, and 1973–present.

21 Reference to Arthur Rimbaud's 1871 poem "Le bateau ivre" ("The Drunken Boat").

22 Reference to Stefan George's 1895 cycle of poems *Das Buch der hängenden Gärten* (The Book of the Hanging Gardens).

23 Nazi catchphrase, referencing an ideology that focuses on ethnicity based on two factors, descent blood (of a folk) and territory.

the house of politics. As if it had no place of rest, as if it were meant for all time to have no shelter to call home. For a while, it receives commandos and bows to them, and one day it begins to listen to new ones. That is its particular progression, its advance.

And the writer who wants to bring about change, how much is he free to do and how much not? That, too, is the question. There is a drama for him that has only become totally manifest in our time: Because he has the collective misfortune of human beings and of the world in view, it seems as if he were sanctioning that misfortune, it seems as if he were failing to achieve the desired effect. Because he allows his gaze to take in the entirety of misfortune, it seems permissible that the changeable not be changed. He is seen foaming at the mouth, and he is applauded. Nothing stirs, only that fatal applause. And I suspect that through the many playful shocks that have been inflicted upon audiences for years a conditioning has taken place, a numbing or an addiction, similar to a drug, to being shocked a little. Only the utmost earnestness and the struggle against the abuse of the original and the grave experiences of pain could help us to awaken audiences from their fantastic lethargy. "Workers need poetry more than bread"[24]—Simone Weil once wrote this moving sentence, a wish to be sure. But people today need movies and magazines more than whipped cream, and the more discriminating (and we too belong to that group, as you know) need a slight shock, a little Ionesco or Beatnik howling,[25] lest they lose their appetite for everything altogether. Poetry as bread? That bread would have to crunch between our teeth and reawaken our hunger before it appeases it. And that poetry will have to be sharp with wisdom and bitter with longing in order to awaken people from their slumber. We are indeed asleep. We are sleepers simply for fear of having to become aware of ourselves and our world.

Our existence today lies at the intersection of so many disjointed realities, laden with the most contradictory values. Within your four walls you can cultivate a domestic happiness of the patriarchal style or a libertinage or whatever you want—outside you spin in a functional world of utility that has its own ideas about your existence. You can be superstitious and knock on wood, but the reports on the status of research and of armament are also reassuring with respect to the protection of your security and freedom. You can believe in the immortality of your soul and issue a report on your own spiritual condition, but on the outside you confront a different situation. There the tests decide, the authorities and business; there you are written off as sick and written up as healthy, classified and

24 Weil's quote reads: "Workers need poetry more than bread. They need that their life should be a poem." Weil, "The Mysticism of Work," 235.

25 Reference to the 1956 poem "Howl" by Alan Ginsberg, a member of the Beat Generation, which gloried in the defiance of convention.

evaluated. You can see ghosts or values, at any rate there are plenty of both. And you can entrust yourself to all of them at the same time, only if you know how to keep everything neatly separate in practice. Here inwardness and meaningfulness, conscience and dream—there utilitarian purpose, meaninglessness, cliché, and speechless violence. Do not ground your thinking on *one* principle, that is dangerous—ground it on many principles.

As things stand, overwhelming consensus has brought us to the point of allowing a condition to arise that Hermann Broch once castigated with a furious sentence. Now his words hold true, now that point has come: "Morals are morals, business is business and war is war and art is art."[26]

If we sanction this "art is art," if we accept his scorn here as representing the whole—and if the writers condone and promote it out of a lack of earnestness and the deliberate dissolution of communication with society, communication that is always endangered and therefore in need of renewal—and if society withdraws from a literature that embodies a serious and uncomfortable spirit striving for change, then that would be tantamount to a declaration of bankruptcy.

Merely to make the artistic enjoyment of a few intricate works possible, to stimulate the appreciation of art—this precautionary measure against art, rendering it harmless—cannot be the purpose of this lectureship. Under these meager auspices, we would not have anything more to say to one another. Neither art to human beings, nor human beings to art. Then there would no longer be a need for any more questions.

But let us ask them nonetheless. And let us ask them from now on in such a way that they become binding once again.

---

26 Broch's quote reads: "War is war, l'art pour l'art; in politics there are no qualms. Business is business—all this proves it exactly . . . all this is the mindset of these times." Hermann Broch, *The Sleepwalkers: A Trilogy*, trans. Willa and Edwin Muir (New York: Vintage, 1996), 448.

The Second Frankfurt Lecture: On Poems[1]

Ladies and Gentlemen,
A start has been made, and the foundations for the first misunderstandings have been laid. In the beginning, beginning seems hardest—but once we have begun to talk and said a few things out loud, then continuing on turns out to be even more difficult. That is why I want us to set out on an excursion rather than engage in a learned investigation and try, as we roam, to bend down for a word, to pick up a word that was dropped at the start.

Nothing is more intimidating for someone who has written poems than to give an account of contemporary poetry; one's own knowledge is usually less than is expected, and for a long time all of us remain ignorant of what new things are emerging in other countries. We usually learn about them with a delay of one to two generations; we are familiar with Eliot, Auden, and Dylan Thomas is someone we might know only because he is dead, that legendary drinker; we know Apollinaire, Éluard, Aragon, René Char as the most recent of the French poets; among the Italians we are just beginning to recognize Ungaretti and Montale, the Russians Blok and Mayakovsky, and, finally, thanks to a questionable political tempest in a teapot, Pasternak, and that is not only because poems are less often translated. Even if we have mastered another language or several of them and make an effort to keep an eye on developments beyond our borders, there is still a dimming of our vision for poetry in the present. Where poems have a new expressive intensity, that intensity is so intimate to each individual language that it does not readily manifest itself in more public forms of literature, such as in novels, in plays. There is hardly a new novel, a new play in Paris or New York or Rome about which we are not rapidly informed, hardly one that we will not soon be reading, that we will not be compelled to see soon. But on top of all that, poems are not marketable and their effect within their respective linguistic areas remains minuscule even if in some countries—Germany among them—the strongest talents at present are reported to be among the lyric poets. Whether that assertion holds true is not the question—the coin has a flip side, a less friendly one, for nowhere does dilettantism run more rampant than in lyric poetry, and nowhere is it harder for most readers, or writers, to decide whether or not this or that author has actually "got what it takes." And the unkindest opinion of some would have it that no volume of poetry has any effect in

1 Held at the University of Frankfurt on December 9, 1959, the second lecture remains the most difficult to reconstruct of the five. Bachmann chose not to include the lecture on poems in April 1960 when she recorded the lectures for Radio Bavaria in Zurich. The title is not original.

our lands other than to encourage another twenty young people to write poems as well.

What I am more concerned about is the question of whether limiting myself to exclusively discussing German poems of the recent past constitutes a fault. I do not think so, not in the present case, for their first claim, after all, is to be noticed here and by us; their novel concepts, what is new about them wants to find acceptance, first of all, in their own language.

Do not expect, however, to be introduced to all the new poets that there are—what would that accomplish? Enough essays exist in which they are listed, one after the other, divided into nature poets and consciousness poets and God knows what else, with examples. There are anthologies, and poems printed in every monthly journal, and there are volumes of poetry that can be found in libraries. There, you can inform yourself. I am in no position to present each and every one of them to you, with a label, and add an appropriate comment.

All right then, excursions . . .

Günter Eich: "Examine Your Fingertips."

> Examine your fingertips—have they changed color yet?
> One day it will come back—the exterminated plague.
> The postman will throw it with a letter into the rattling mailbox,
> it will lie with a ration of herring on your plate,
> the mother will offer it to her child as her breast.
>
> What shall we do when not a soul
> who knew how to handle it is still alive?
> Whoever is good friends with horror
> can wait for its visit in peace.
> We prepare again and again for happiness
> but it does not like to sit in our easy-chair.
>
> Examine your fingertips! When they turn black,
> It is too late.[2]

This poem is by Günter Eich. Now, I hope that none of you, if that is even likely, would want to raise his hand troubled by the question: What does the poet want to tell us here? What observations are we then capable of making? What could come of our engaging with this poem? First, I should like to assume that this poet conceived of himself, of his project, differently than the poets one or two generations before him. It is hardly possible to imagine him as a prophet or as an artist, but as a magician, as . . .; there is

2 Günter Eich, "Examine Your Fingertips," in *Günter Eich*, trans. Teo Savory (Santa Barbara, CA: Unicorn Press, 1971), 14.

nothing overbearing, nothing presumptuous in his conception of himself, for a conception always manifests itself through the work; the aspiration, the stance, always announces itself. A change can be observed here, something has occurred here, a change in the position of the creator himself. And yet, despite the renunciation of so many . . ., this is not an abdication, a retreat, even though the position from which the voice speaks has been moved into a fatal solitude, not self-chosen, not disdainful, but dictated by a society in the midst of society, a site that is fraught with unnamed peril and in which staying awake has been made difficult for the one who must, can, wants to stay awake. A person on a vigil is speaking, a person sleeplessly exposed, dwelling in our midst . . .

> "When the window is open
> and the horror drifts into the room—
> ....
>
> The two-headed child
> —while one head is asleep, the other one screams—
> screams across the world,
> filling the ears of my love with terror . . ."[3]

The vocabulary of reality is simple, focusing on windows, fields of rubble, refuse, a freight train, rain, rust spots and oil slicks, a thermos for coffee, a bakery, a factory, a subway: the world is questioned, but not in excess. The only one questioned in excess is the poem's I, pursued, warned, and asked to pass on warnings.

Ladies and gentlemen, any talk of sacred chant, a mission, a select community of artists is utterly out of the question today. Deliberately invoking an extreme, I am requesting permission to cite a word of affirmation from the circle around Stefan George: "We nurture a proud faith that for these years we have not only gathered the greatest harvest that in a certain field of human achievement an entire federation of peoples was capable of producing, but we also hope that we have smoothed the paths for those who are still growing and on their way, that they may tread them to stride on to the discovery of ever purer heavens of art."[4]

Those "pure heavens of art," however, as significant as their beginnings were, could not hold up, and those spirits who understandably rose up against a banal naturalism in their day and whose accomplishments we shall not forget, lived long enough to witness the collapse of their heavens

3 Günter Eich, "Moment in June," in *Contemporary German Poetry: An Anthology*, trans. Gertrude Clorius Schwebell (New York: New Directions, 1964), 53–55. Bachmann omits 11 lines in the middle of the poem.

4 Stefan George, *Blätter für die Kunst* [Leaves for Art] (Berlin: Verlag Georg Bondi, 1899), 24.

of art. Expressionism dealt the first counterblow, and under the impact of the First World War human voices were raised, only to fade and wane again. And new aesthetic upheavals were to follow; of these we shall also have to speak, because, while they led to breakthroughs in language and discoveries of a new reality, the aftereffects of which are still felt today, they have nonetheless been discredited in the worst way.

In saying this, I am also thinking of Surrealism with its concept of beauty. It was stipulated that beauty be full of terror, breathtaking, and demonically enigmatic; Surrealism was to familiarize us with death, and in the Second Manifesto, André Breton, the spokesman of the new poetry, wrote that Surrealism was not an artistic school; on the contrary it aspired to total disobedience, rank sabotage; everything had to be done to annihilate the ideas of family, of fatherland, of religion—so far, so good, that was an impressive outburst—but then came the postscript: what Surrealism strove for above all was nothing other than violence. And: "The simplest Surrealist act consists of dashing down into the street, pistol in hand, and firing blindly, as fast as you can pull the trigger, into the crowd."[5] To be sure, the Surrealists did not put that directive into practice. On the contrary, as you may also remember, all those writers, those painters, were berated, ostracized, threatened in their very existence under the German dictatorship. And yet there remains an unresolved residue, a suspicion that in their radicalness the victims, without suspecting what they were doing, allowed their language to confront the language of violence. Of course Surrealism possessed spirit, the anti-bourgeois, it seriously wanted to shock the public, but it had nothing in common with the actual practice of murder that was later launched from quite another quarter.

The proclamations of beauty issued by the Futurists were far more questionable, though they were understandable as a forward thrust, an ardent desire to embrace the world of technology and to recognize it in its beauty and in nothing but its beauty. Deeply passionate, Marinetti was the first to shout: "We say that the world's magnificence has been enriched by a new beauty; the beauty of speed. A racing car whose hood is adorned with great pipes, like serpents of explosive breath—a roaring car that seems to ride on grapeshot—is more beautiful than the *Victory of Samothrace*."[6]

The Futurist manifesto, which subsequently appeared at the outbreak of the Ethiopian Colonial War, proclaims: "For twenty-seven years we

5 André Breton, "Second Manifesto of Surrealism" in *Manifestoes of Surrealism*, trans. Richard Seaver and Helen R. Lane (Ann Arbor: University of Michigan Press, 1969), 125.

6 Filippo Tomasso Marinetti, "The Founding and Manifesto of Futurism" in *Marinetti: Selected Writings*, ed. R. W. Flint, trans. R. W. Flint and Arthur A. Coppotelli (New York: Farrar, Straus, and Giroux, 1972), 41. Bachmann cites the fourth point of the manifesto.

Futurists have rebelled against the branding of war as anti-aesthetic . . . Accordingly we state: . . . War is beautiful because it establishes man's dominion over the subjugated machinery by means of gas masks, terrifying megaphones, flamethrowers, and small tanks. . . . War is beautiful because it enriches a flowering meadow with the fiery orchids of machine guns. War is beautiful because it combines the gunfire, the cannonades, the cease-fire, the scents, and the stench of putrefaction into a symphony. War is beautiful because it creates new architecture, like that of the big tanks, the geometrical formation flights, the smoke spirals from burning villages, and many others. . . . Poets and artists of Futurism! . . . remember these principles of an aesthetics of war so that your struggle for a new literature and a new graphic art . . . may be illumined by them!"[7]

So this is what *l'art pour l'art* may ultimately lead to. The reversal was formulated clearly enough here.

Please do not consider me too narrow-minded for insisting on that question, on questions of responsibility in art, and for bringing them into focus. Let us, in fact, take yet another step. I do not regard it as accidental that Gottfried Benn and Ezra Pound, whom a number of our young poets will have to discover for themselves, an American with the most confused notions about revitalization and a renaissance of the Renaissance—that for those two poets—and they are poets, no doubt about it—it was but one small step from the pure heavens of art to consorting with barbarism.[8]

But there is a maxim that Karl Kraus could never get over and that one never tires of highlighting: "All of the merits of a language are rooted in morality."[9] And that does not mean conventional wisdom, nothing that can be liquidated like bourgeois or Christian morality, no moral code, but that preliminary region in which every new writer has to establish the measure of truth and lies all over again. A moment ago these words were spoken: "War is beautiful because thanks to the gas masks, the flame throwers . . . and so on."

Here is a recent poem that also has a gas mask in it; it is taken from a collection of love poems, and now note the different aura that surrounds the objects and that signals the destruction of an absolute, feverish aesthetic.

7 Bachmann takes this quote, which appears in Marinetti's *Manifesto on the Ethiopian Colonial War*, from Walter Benjamin's epilogue to the second edition of his essay "The Work of Art in the Age of Mechanical Reproduction," in *Illuminations: Essays and Reflections*, ed. Hannah Arendt, trans. Harry Zohn (New York: Harcourt, Brace, and World, Inc., 1968), 243–44.

8 An allusion to the fascist and anti-Semitic leanings of Pound and to Benn's initial endorsement of National Socialism in the early years of the Third Reich.

9 Karl Kraus, "Sprachlehre" [Grammar], in *Die Fackel* (October 1925) 697–705, in *Die Fackel*, vol. 8, 92. Bachmann ends the sentence in a period where Kraus has an exclamation mark.

"The Frog Prince Bridegroom," by Marie Luise Kaschnitz:

How ugly he is
Your bridegroom
Mistress Life

With a gas mask for a face
A cartridge belt for hips
A flame thrower for a hand

Your bridegroom the frog prince flies with you
(Wheels spinning in all directions)
Over the houses of the dead

Between Doomsday
And Doomsday
He eases himself
Into your body

In the darkness
All you touch is
His damp hair

Only when it dawns
Only when
It dawns
Only when

Do you discover his
Sad
Beautiful
Eyes.[10]

Only the eyes are said to be beautiful here, the sad eyes; sad precedes the word "beautiful." And in the beginning, all that is said about the man with the flamethrower, the cartridge belt, the man with a claim to dominance is: "How ugly he is / Your bridegroom . . ."

The determinations that have been made here are new, new definitions, also for poetry.

In Sweden, at this time, the oldest living German female poet, Nelly Sachs, pens a word that is meant for the young, pointing out what they are doing as well as what they should be doing. The subject is a young man, without a compass, at odds with all the heavenly lights:

10 Marie Luise Kaschnitz, "The Frog Prince Bridegroom," in *Selected Later Poems of Marie Luise Kaschnitz*, trans. Lisel Mueller (Princeton, NJ: Princeton University Press, 1980), 17.

From the rocking chairs
of settled generations
he repels himself

beside himself
with the fire helmet
he wounds the night.[11]

("To you that build the new house,"[12] remembering what ground we are building upon, upon how many graves, places of infamy, and at the same time the challenge not to sigh, not to weep the minutes away, but our walls and our tools will be as receptive as Aeolian harps.)[13]

But here the prophetic and the psalmodial are not to be mistaken for the prophecy of art; this is not a gesture but a motion born of the experience of suffering. And would it be acceptable otherwise? Have we not become, almost to the point of excess, very sensitive to and sober about and dismissive of the language of rapture, on the one hand, and the conservative semantics of the Biedermeier,[14] on the other, the affectation of morbidity and the affectation of salubrity? Have we not reached the point where we will no longer allow anyone to fascinate us? Is this not perhaps the only demand that we still have: to bring about a new law between language and the human being?

And were we not to make use of this law or to make use of none, and want to take a path through the errors and harbored truths or opt to take none?

The literature behind us, what is it anyway: a sea of words, cut out of the walls of hearts, and of tragic silences and fallow stretches of words talked to death and stagnant pools of stinking, cowardly silence talked to

11 Nelly Sachs, "Without Compass," in *The Seeker and Other Poems*, trans. Ruth and Matthew Mead and Michael Hamburger (New York: Farrar, Straus, and Giroux, 1970), 303.

12 Reference to Nelly Sachs' poem of the same title, "To you that build the new house," in *O the Chimneys: Selected Poems, including the verse play, Eli*, trans. Michael Hamburger (New York: Farrar, Straus, and Giroux, 1967), 5–6.

13 An Aeolian harp plays random notes and harmonies when the wind hits its strings.

14 "Biedermeier" denotes a range of artistic styles, from utilitarian simplicity to clumsy tastelessness, that flourished in the fields of literature, music, the visual arts, and interior design from 1815 to 1848. At a time of official censorship, Biedermeier writers—most notably Droste-Hülshoff, Chamisso, Mörike, and Müller—avoided political subjects in favor of historical fiction and depictions of country life. In contrast to the impassioned rapture of Kaschnitz and Sachs, their language is characterized by unimaginative, dutiful piety and homey contentment (i.e., "Glück im Winkel").

death? Both have always been part of it, language and silence, and of two kinds. And both are always beckoning and enticing. Our share in fallacy is indeed assured, but our share in a new truth—where does that begin?

How, since we are here to speak of new poems, does a poem begin to have a share in it?

Enzensberger:

The wolves defended against the lambs

should the vultures eat forget-me-nots?
what do you want the jackal to do,
cut loose from his skin, or the wolf? should
he pull his own teeth out of his head?
what upsets you so much
about commissars and popes?
why do you gape at the fraudulent TV screen
as if someone just slipped you the shaft?

and tell me who sews the ribbons
all over the general's chest? who
carves the capon up for the usurer?
who proudly dangles an iron cross
over his rumbling navel? who
rakes in the tip, the thirty pieces
of silver, the hush money? listen: there
are plenty of victims, very few thieves: who's
the first to applaud them, who
pins on the merit badge, who's
crazy for lies?

look in the mirror: squirming,
scared blind by the burden of truthfulness,
skipping the trouble of learning, abandoning
thought to the wolves,
a nose ring your favorite trinket,
no deception too stupid, no comfort
too cheap, every new blackmail
still seems too mild for you.

you lambs, why crows would be
nuns stacked up against you:
all of you hoodwink each other.
fraternity's the rule
among wolves:
they travel in packs.

blessed are the thieves: you
ask them up for a rape, then
throw yourself down on the mouldy bed
of submission. moaning
you stick to your lies. you'd love
to be torn limb from limb. you
won't change the world.[15]

"You won't change the world." True. And what about the poem itself? What is its effect? Is it not possible that because such a poem makes us unhappy, because it succeeds in doing so, and because there are new poets who can make us unhappy, there is in us a jolt too, an epistemological one, under the impact of which we can follow the one that is taking place. There is such a wonderful letter of Kafka's, one about the demands he places on a book:

"If the book we're reading doesn't wake us up with a blow to the head, what are we reading it for? So that it will make us happy . . .? Good Lord, we probably would be perfectly happy if we had no books, and books that make us happy we could write ourselves if we had to. . . . A book must be the axe for the frozen sea within us. That is my belief."[16]

Perhaps you have been wondering for a while why I have not said anything about the new forms and barely touched on the new language in the new poems. In connection with this poem I should like to attempt it after all, in a roundabout way. A while ago, two books were published, written not, in fact, by a literary historian but by an outsider. I am referring to *The World as a Labyrinth* [*Die Welt als Labyrinth*, 1957] and *Mannerism in Literature* [*Manierismus in der Literatur*, 1959], two studies by Gustav René Hocke.[17]

Those books also discuss the authors I have mentioned today, besides many others, with examples, and the argument goes something like this: The provocative formal and thematic phenomena that we have been observing in literature, but also in the other arts, since approximately 1850 are not new; this is not their first appearance, since there has always been a clandestine tradition of modernism. The linguistic feats of daring and the "vices of thought," as they are called, occurred for the first time

15 Hans Magnus Enzensberger, "the wolves defended against the lambs," in *Poems of Hans Magnus Enzensberger*, trans. Jerome Rothenberg (Harmondsworth: Penguin Books, 1968), 23–24.

16 Kafka, Letter to Oskar Pollack, 15–16.

17 Gustav René Hocke (1908–1985) was a German journalist, author and cultural critic, who published a notable study of mannerism, in which he argues there is a continual resurfacing of mannerist tendencies in European art.

in the Hellenistic era; they were of Greco-Oriental origin. The second revolution took place in the middle of the sixteenth century and came to an end in the middle of the seventeenth century. In literature, the most recent one occurs with the emergence of Baudelaire. Those three epochs are subsumed under the generic term "Mannerism," to denote the anti-Classical constant in European intellectual history. Poets during those periods want to be "modern." They are characterized in the following fashion: They shun immediacy, love obscurity, allow sensuous imagery only in veiled, abstruse metaphors; an intellectual sign system is employed to capture the real or the super-real; the poets are drawn to the peculiar, to the exclusive, to extravagance; their works are enigmatic, hieroglyphic, and thus elude the aesthetic control that is consistent with Classicist criteria. I do not want to provide any more than that imprecise outline, and I can only recommend that you read those two studies, even at the risk of your detecting "Mannerism" in anything and everything for a while and in your astonishment forget objective judgment. But, with its significant findings, this very stimulating book has provoked truly curious reactions. For it is true that some drops of bitterness have inevitably been splashed on the new linguistic parade grounds, on the metaphor labs, and on the nuclear fission of words; because someone beat you to it, be it in 1600 or in 1910. A few centuries ago a man by the name of Athanasius Kirchner,[18] so we learn, devised a metaphor-producing machine to allow the perfect image to emerge from a void. Abstract tendencies have come around again for the third time at any rate; Lettrism, which Isidor Isou[19] inaugurated in Paris a few years ago as the logical last stage to break open the alphabet, to conjure existence by means of a few newly added letters as well as by means of sound rhythms, already had a precursor in the third century. And then there was Hugo Ball,[20] who wrote Lettristic poems in the first Dada year in Zurich, albeit with a different intention, i.e., a polemical one. So that seems to make many people a little sad, those who contend that the revolutions, the acquisition of virgin territory in literature, are to be primarily found in formal experiments and who sometimes overlook that those changes can only be accomplished in the wake of a new mode of thinking. But let us wait and see.

On the other hand, however, the discovery of "Mannerism" was manna from heaven for many critics, because, at last, a few criteria were

18 Athanasius Kirchner (1602–1680) was a German Jesuit scholar and polymath who published around forty major works, most notably in the fields of comparative religion, geology, and medicine.

19 Isidor Isou (1925–2007), Romanian-born French poet, film critic, and visual artist, was the founder of Lettrism, an art and literary movement which owed inspiration to Dada and Surrealism.

20 Hugo Ball (1886–1927) was a German author, poet, and one of the leading Dada artists, who was a pioneer in the development of sound poetry.

made available to judge new literature, the verbal potpourri as well as the true power of words. Thank heavens everything has already transpired; nothing is new; no need to be startled at encountering a metaphor like "black milk,"[21] since Marino (sixteenth century) already references "red snow."[22] Everything has already occurred; at last you understand it, and to understand everything means to forgive everything. Or, if you belong to another type, the censorious type, the message is: That has been done before, so it is no longer interesting, has been done better before; it is a weak imitation, plagiarism; the Surrealists could do it too, and better, the *poètes maudits*[23] could do it too, and better; the earlier ones, of course, and better still—think of Marino, of Góngora, think of, think of.

But to whom should we decide to turn when we reflect on this poem once again? Is its author a Mannerist? There are poems in which words occur such as "manitypist," "stenocure," well yes (but to what end—that is precisely the question!),[24] and if we sat down with an anthology of more recent authors, we should soon see through the surface, as long as we limited ourselves to the formal aspects, staring at the metaphors, at the similarities, at participating in an anonymous reservoir of words, at familiarity with certain voguish prescriptions, indeed, we should easily see through everything to see what is behind everything. And yet, the most important thing would remain hidden, and that would be the question of whether we were dealing with mere handicraft and with affectations, with finger exercises or with only temporarily unsuccessful beginnings, and it would remain unclear as to whether someone is actually out seeking prey and falls prey to language, falls prey to truth, where the inimitable devours the imitable. For everyone, indeed, shares in the voguish—I think almost everyone—and we feel that very clearly too, whenever we pick up older works that have long been established in their eminence,

21 The metaphor "black milk" begins Celan's poem "Death Fugue" ("Todesfuge"). Paul Celan, "Death Fugue," in *Poems of Paul Celan*, trans. Michael Hamburger (New York: Persea Books, 1988), 61–63.

22 Giambattista Marino, *Adonis: Selections from L'Adone of Giambattista Marino*, trans. Harold Martin Priest (Ithaca, NY: Cornell University Press, 1967), 77.

23 Literally "damned poets," the term originates with Verlaine and refers to the figure of the poet or artist "damned" by society and fated to a tragic, often brief life as an irreconcilable outsider. Primary examples include Baudelaire, Rimbaud, and Verlaine.

24 Bachmann makes reference here to the title of her own essay, "To What End Poetry?" in this volume as well as to Siegfried Melchinger's original question "Wozu Gedichte? Anmerkungen zu einigen Lyrikbänden." The terms "manotypist" and "stenocure" are found in Hans Magnus Enzensberger's poem "bildzeitung," in *verteidigung der wölfe* (Frankfurt am Main: Suhrkamp, 1963), 80–81.

that a time-bound vocabulary, that time-bound figures survive only in a stable and stronger context.

But why—you may still be uncertain about this—did I happen to pick those particular poems, and what are they supposed to demonstrate? Perhaps the good disposition of those authors. That assumption, after all, would not be too far fetched. But what is meant by "disposition," and who does not claim to have it? Liberally and peacefully disposed, and from there it is not far to compassionate, but compassionate towards whom? And if the radical cast of any aestheticism has left us with one certainty that is binding, then it is the knowledge that a good principle is still a far cry from a good poem. I do not know whether it was really as necessary as some people—Benn among them—believed to drive this home to the Germans time and time again, because, being as receptive as they were to "rhapsodies"[25] and "mood pieces," they did not really acknowledge it after all. All right, then, let us say it once more, even though, thinking of the young people who have published poems in the last ten, fifteen years, one gets the feeling that hardly anyone has pandered to popular demand. More tedious, to be sure, are the demands of some critics with their diagnoses and prognoses, those who habitually see everything in crisis, and a call is issued to overcome the crises, and of late, it has been Mannerism that had to be overcome, and with it the crisis of the novel, the crisis of the theater—everything is to be overcome or integrated into something. But if you really think about those sentences, you begin to become stubborn: Who, then, is in fact to be overcome by whom? You can overcome an adversary or a pain or a weakness, but a crisis of the novel or one of culture or one of those abstract conceptual monstrosities, that is something no one can overcome. The determinations that are made are good, often have merit, but the questions that cling to them are poorly posed, practically weightless, and only serve to crowd out the small circle of real questions that might be posed at all. But the sting of those questions, of which I tried to impart an idea to you in the previous lecture, is something that only the individual comes to feel, and the one who has been more deeply moved from afar by a few words than by a whole assortment of problems, and one of those words—words that do not ask to be overcome either—is this one, for instance, by Bertolt Brecht:

"What kind of times are these, when / A conversation about trees is almost a crime, / Because it implies silence about so many horrors?" That

25 In his "Problems of Lyric Poetry," Benn sets out to illustrate the characteristics of modern poetry by listing counterexamples to modern style. His first counterexample is what he calls *Andichten*, or a rhapsodic, gushing manner. Gottfried Benn, "Probleme der Lyrik,", 503.

is probably also why "those born later"[26] are a little reluctant to display their concern with form, with expression, with power of perception, a concern that is as torturous as ever.

A few passages by Günter Eich speak of a discontent with beauty, discontent with happiness; that whole tension between horror and beauty, which are of course dialectically linked, the cult of beauty and the cult of horror, has given way to another. The poems, diverse as they are, cannot be enjoyed, but they contain insights, as if in a time of utter linguistic dearth, out of utter isolation they had to accomplish something to lessen the need. From that accomplishment they draw a new dignity, a dignity for which they dare not even strive.

Beside themselves, they wound the night with their fire helmets.

That is also true, to a great degree, of the poet about whom I want to speak last: about Paul Celan. He first stepped into our midst with an epitaph, his "Death Fugue," and with brightly shining dark words that went on a "journey to the end of the night."[27] And the I in these poems also renounces a forced design, renounces that usurped authority, and acquires authority by asking nothing for itself but this: "Render me bitter, number me among the almonds, count me in . . . what was bitter and kept you waking. . . ."[28]

But I have brought his most recent volume of poems with me, *Speech-Grille*, because it enters new territory. The metaphors have completely disappeared; the words have shed every disguise, every veil, no word drifts to the next anymore, enrapturing another. After a painful turn, an ultimate harsh testing of the relations between word and world, new definitions are found. The poems are entitled "Matière de Bretagne" or "Embankments, Waysides, Desolate Spots, Rubble," or "Sketch of a Landscape," or "Rubble Barge."[29] They are uncomfortable, probing,

---

26 Here Bachmann cites from Brecht's 1934–38 poem, "To Those Born Later" ("An die Nachgeborenen"). Bertolt Brech, "To Those Born Later," trans. Naomi Replansky, in *Poems 1913–1956*, 318–20. Translation slightly altered.

27 Bachmann uses the title of Louis-Ferdinand Céline's deeply pessimistic novel *Journey to the End of the Night* (*Voyage au bout de la nuit*), published in 1952, as a metaphor for the brilliantly dark language of Celan's "Death Fugue."

28 Bachmann cites Celan's "Count Up the Almonds" ("Zähle die Mandeln"). Paul Celan, "Count Up the Almonds," in *Selected Poems and Prose of Paul Celan*, trans. John Felstiner (New York: W. W. Norton, 2001), 49. The translation of the original reads: "Count what was bitter and kept you waking, / count me in too . . . Render me bitter. / Number me among the almonds." Bachmann omits 11 lines.

29 "Matière de Bretagne" and "Sketch of a Landscape" ("Entwurf einer Landschaft") are printed in *Selected Poems and Prose of Paul Celan*, 109 and 115; "Rubble Barge" ("Schuttkahn") in *Poems of Paul Celan*, 127; and "Train-Tracks, Roadsides, Vacant Lots Rubble" ("Bahndämme, Wegränder, Ödplätze, Schutt"),

dependable, so dependable in naming things that the message must be: This far but no farther.
Poem: [][30]

But suddenly, thanks to rigorous restraint, it has once again become possible to say something, very directly, without encryption. It has become possible for someone who says of himself that, wounded by reality and in search of reality, he goes toward language with his very being.[31] At the end of the long poem "Stretto," such a sentence shines forth, and I should like to close with it—and just explain in advance, so that you understand the word "star" properly, that to Paul Celan the stars are "human work," that human work is what is meant.

A
star
may still give light.
Nothing,
nothing is lost.[32]

in *Poems of Paul Celan*, trans. Michael Hamburger (New York: Persea Books, 1988), 194.

30 Bachmann originally read a poem here, the identity of which is unknown.

31 Bachmann cites the closing words from Celan, "Speech on the Occasion of Receiving the Literature Prize of the Free Hanseatic City of Bremen," 35. Translation altered.

32 Paul Celan, "Stretto" ("Engführung"), in *Selected Poems and Prose*, 119–31. The quoted passage of this final poem in the collection *Speech-Grille* is not "at the end of the long poem," but followed by five short stanzas.

The Third Frankfurt Lecture: Concerning the I[1]

Ladies and Gentlemen,
I would like to speak about the I, about its sojourn in literature and consequently about the dealings of the human being in literature, to the extent that it proceeds with an I or its I or hides behind the I. And some of you will probably wonder: how could one hide behind the I; it is surely the least hidden, and so unambiguous—I—we could even manage that ourselves, to speak in a straightforward manner about ourselves, without pretense.

"I am telling you"—when I say that to an individual person, then it seems to be quite obvious which I is voicing itself there and what is meant by the sentence in which the I appears, as well as who it is that is saying something. But the minute you stand up here alone and say to the many seated below, "I am telling you," then the I changes unexpectedly. It eludes the speaker, becoming formal and rhetorical. The person who utters it is no longer certain that he can assume responsibility for the "I" that has emanated from his lips, that he can cover for it. For how is he to show proof of this I if his mouth only keeps on moving, bringing forth sounds, but his most banal identity can no longer be guaranteed? Those sitting below only hear a recited I and no longer perceive it very distinctly. So if you, a few hundred people, usually individuals but at this juncture a crowd, pick up an I that is as distant as the sky—and that can be only as far as ten meters, and as distant as the sky can be equivalent to the physical disappearance of the speaker or his invisibility if he only makes himself heard, for example, over the radio or with the help of a microphone—then nothing more than a sentence remains, transmitted to you via a loudspeaker or a piece of paper, a book or a stage, a sentence from an I without guarantee.

I without guarantee! For what is the I, what could it be?—a star whose position and trajectories have never been completely determined and whose core has not been comprehended in its composition. That could be: myriads of particles composing the I, and at the same time it seems as if the I were nothing, the hypostasis of a pure form, something akin to an imaginary substance, something that refers to a dreamed-up identity, a code for something that takes more pains to decipher than the most secret of orders. But there are researchers and writers who do not

1 The exact date on which Bachmann held the third of five lectures has never been firmly established; with respect to the dates of the other lectures, which have been verified, it must have been between December 9, 1959, and February 10, 1960. The title of the lecture, "*Das schreibende Ich,*" (literally "The writing I") is derived from Hans Henny Jahnn's (1894–1959) unfinished novel, *Shoreless River.*

give in, who want to seek it out, examine it, dig to the bottom of it and give it substance, and who are driven crazy by it over and over again. They have made the first person their field of experimentation or have made themselves the field of experimentation for the first person. And they have thought of all the I's of the living and the dead and of phantom figures, the I of the people next door and Caesar's I and Hamlet's I, and all of this is not yet consequential because it is not yet universal. For that very reason, we should also think of the I of psychologists, of analysts, the I of philosophers as a monad or as part of a greater whole, as an empirical control station or as a metaphysical quantity. All these experts assure themselves of their I: they flood their lights all over it, touch it, mutilate it, and smash it to pieces; they evaluate it, divide it up, draw circles around it.

I once saw a small child that had been pressured by its mother to admit that it had done something naughty. It was obstinate at first and may not have even known what was expected of it. "Say that you did it," the woman demanded again and again. "Say: I did it!" And suddenly, as if it had seen the light or was tired of remaining mute and resistant, the child said: "I did it," and then right away again and quite pleased with the sentence or rather the decisive word: "I did it, I, I, I!" The child did not want to stop at all and kept screaming and squealing, ultimately writhing from laughter in the woman's arms like an epileptic. "I, I, did it, I!" It was a peculiar scene, because at that moment an I was discovered and at the same time unmasked, its meaning and its lack of meaning, and a reckless pleasure at the discovery of the I in the first place, enough to drive a person mad as he might never go mad again when forced to say I, once the word has long been taken for granted, even worn out, a habitual term that degrades everything it is used to signify, from one instance to the next.

But one day when we say I again in an unusual situation, we feel, more than in that early state: uneasiness, astonishment, horror, doubt, uncertainty.

I do not know if there is a study of the I and the many I's in literature. I do not know of any, and although I am not in a position to conduct an orderly, let alone exhaustive examination, I think that there are many I's here and that there is little consensus about the I—as if there should not be a consensus about human nature, but merely a continuity of new strategies. It emerges early on and becomes more and more fanciful and fascinating in the literature of the last few decades. As if a carnival had been arranged for the I in which it can confess and deceive, transform and betray itself, this I, this Nobody and Somebody, in its fool's attire.

The I is unproblematic for us when a historical person, a politician for example, a statesman or a military leader comes forward with his I in memoirs. When Churchill[2] or de Gaulle[3] delivers a report or passes judgments on to us, then we demand this I of them, and we demand of this I that it be identical with the author. This I is only interesting to us in connection with the Winston Churchill who held office from . . . to, the decisive I in reflection, his actions in reflection, which may be assumed to be familiar, and, for all I care, formative years and private matters aside, but only because Churchill's historical role demands the naïve affirmation of his I. And "naïve" does not refer to the literary quality of this or a similar author, but rather to the way the I is treated, the naïve character prescribed for it. The role of the Churchillian I in his books is Churchill, the statesman.

The I-role, as I have attempted to describe it here, applies to all literature of this kind, from antiquity to the present, and it applies to works from the highest levels, those worthy of being called literature, to the lowest and most disreputable. The critical and demanding reader accepts this self-assured, unbroken I in celebrated memoirs with the same assurance with which a stultified, disoriented readership devours the dregs of memoir literature by the hundreds today, allowing itself to be enthralled by the I's of SS generals, gangsters, and spies. For the I of the agents, those acting in the simplest roles (of recent and contemporary history), is the most convincing, most accessible; it does not need to provide any further identification, it will be believed and listened to, because the deeds or misdeeds of the author were of consequence to society.

Yet this simplest role is not an option for the majority of writers, and I would like to speak specifically about these, about their I's, which only appear to us as unquestioned and identical when we are very young. Who among us has not, at age sixteen, encountered an I in a book, in a poem, seemingly the author himself, and we almost became that I as well, for the I was you and that you the I, that is how blurred all boundaries were in our initial gullibility and enchantment: there was not even an exchange of

2 Sir Winston Churchill (1874–1965), British Prime Minister during the Second World War, whose memoirs can be found in several books published from 1908–49. His *The Second World War* (6 vols., 1948–54) is considered his autobiography, for which he received the Nobel Prize for Literature in 1953.

3 Charles de Gaulle (1890–1970), Brigadier general and leader of the provisional government of France during the Second World War, called for French resistance against the German occupation of his country and organized French support for the Allies. In 1958 he became president of France and established the Fifth Republic, which still endures. This means he had only been president for about one year at the time Bachmann held the Frankfurt Lectures. Writings include *The Edge of the Sword* (*Le Fil de l'Épée*, 1944, trans. 1960), *War Memoirs* (*Mémoires de Guerre*, 1954–59, trans. 1955–60), *Memories of Hope* (*Mémoires d'Espoir*, 1970, trans. 1971).

roles because we did not perceive a role. Here was quite simply an I on the page, and that seemed so simple. This I, let us assume, starved, suffered, thought, felt, and we ourselves did all of this too; it was strong or weak, magnificent or pitiful, or everything mixed together, and we succeeded in all of that at the same time, for a couple of hours or for a month. And then other books and other poems came, with them other I's, and they managed to occupy our own I again and again. But the invasions did not prevent us from becoming totally different I's and from confronting the alien I's of the books, viewing them more sharply and distancing ourselves from them. And after the dissolution of this union with the I's, we came to a new revelation. We noticed the instances of interference between author and I, and, finally, we were cognizant of all imaginable I's in literature, the fictitious, the hidden, the reduced, the absolutely lyrical, the I as a conceptual figure, an acting figure, an immaterial I or one thrust into the material.

Nevertheless, I would like to begin with the simplest and at the same time most arresting I, although it hardly seems possible, after what was said earlier, that an author (unless he is a historical figure) introduces his I to us, furnished with his own name and all his dates. As if he were credible, as if his existence were of interest to us without invention, as if it were possible to project one's own person, one's own life into a book without alteration. Such an I—that is, such a furious, breakneck attempt at saving oneself the trouble of conceiving of the I—is a feat that can be marveled at in the books of Henry Miller.[4] Better yet, in the outcast of modern French literature, Louis Ferdinand Céline.[5] It is irrelevant and defies examination as to whether the books of Henry Miller and Céline are purely autobiographical. What interests us above all else is the attempt to do without inventing the I. It is an attempt that appears dilettantish and would spell disaster for any less gifted writer, although at times it proves disastrous for Céline and Miller, especially for Miller.

In Céline's novel *Journey to the End of the Night*, events, experiences, and encounters with the I are related to us as belonging to the author.

---

4 An American writer, Henry Miller (1891–1980) was known for breaking with existing literary forms, developing a new sort of semi-autobiographical novel that blended character study, social criticism, philosophical reflection, explicit language, sex, surrealist free association, and mysticism.

5 The pen name of Louis Ferdinand Auguste Destouches (1894–1961), Louis-Ferdinand Céline was a French novelist, pamphleteer and physician. He developed a new style of writing that modernized French literature. Céline attacked what he considered to be the overly polished, "bourgeois" French of the *académie*. His most famous work is his 1932 novel, *Journey to the End of the Night*. His works had an influence on a broad array of literary figures who followed, not only in France but also in the Western World; this includes authors associated with modernism, existentialism, black comedy and the Beat Generation.

The writer and welfare doctor Céline introduces himself as a welfare doctor, calls himself Ferdinand, was on the front during the First World War, then in the colonies, then in New York, and later opens his practice in a Parisian suburb. His hero, the I, goes by the same name, shares the same experiences. Céline insists on the matter of fact and does not allow us to draw a line between author and I. Because the author Céline is identical with the novel's hero Céline (just as the author Miller is identical with the novel's hero Miller), the I cannot be influenced; the material cannot be fabricated. All occurrences are accidental to the point of excess; for the life of the individual, however interesting and rich or even significant it may seem to him or to others at times, is completely meaningless in those instances where no selection has been made and where the ordering of the raw material "life" has been dispensed with. It appears meaningless to the reader. That Miller's and Céline's narrating I can hold up is only due to the fact that they adopt a language that replicates their chaos at an intensified level. They talk, talk, and talk until their lives dissolve into language. And Céline produces noise and shouts and polemicizes and rages in his jargon until his stories of misery, which would otherwise not be of interest to anyone, represent, in this stream of language, the misery of all poor people:

"I, too, was thinking of my future, but in a kind of delirium, because my constant companion was a muted fear of being killed in the war or of starving when peace came. I had a death sentence hanging over me, and I was in love. It was worse than a nightmare. Not far, less than seventy miles away, millions of brave, well-armed, well-trained men were waiting to kill me, and plenty of Frenchmen were also waiting to pump me full of lead, if I declined to be cut into bloody ribbons by the enemy.

"A poor man can be hounded to death in two main ways, by the absolute indifference of his fellows in peacetime or by their homicidal mania when there is a war. When other people start thinking about you, then it is to figure out how to torture you, that and nothing else. The bastards want to see you bleed, otherwise they're not interested!"[6]

And another passage:

"So there was no law against people shooting at people they couldn't see! And there was no mistake! It was one of the things you could do without anyone reading you the riot act. In fact, it was recognized and probably encouraged by upstanding citizens, like the draft, or marriage, or hunting! . . . No two ways about it. I was suddenly on the most intimate terms with war. I'd lost my virginity. . . . Oh! What wouldn't I have given to be in jail instead of here! What a fool I'd been! If only I had had a little foresight and stolen something or other when it would have been

6 Louis-Ferdinand Céline, *Journey to the End of the Night*, trans. Ralph Manheim (New York: New Directions, 1983), 67–68.

so easy and there was still time. I never think of anything. You come out of jail alive, out of a war you don't! The rest is blarney."[7]

The book becomes a distress call, and the distress makes him call out, in the colonies, in America, in the Parisian suburb. Destitute is the word for him, again and again.

"My weariness increased at the sight of those endless house fronts, that turgid monotony of pavements, of windows upon windows, of business and more business, that chancre of the world, bursting with pustulent advertisements."[8]

Miller has a more difficult time of it with his hero, the writer Miller, and more specifically every single time the author fails to see through himself as the trustworthy but confused autodidact and regales us for many pages, as in the novel *Plexus* for example, with his enthusiasm for Benn,[9] Dostoyevsky,[10] or Spengler.[11] He is able to interest us in his most banal experiences, but not in his intellectual development, the books he has read, his thoughts, for superfluous matters may be narrated in a book, but no superfluous thought may be articulated.[12]

Thoughts, noted in a diary, are acceptable, but not when a figure in a novel is burdened with them without any further consequences. For the I of the diarist, of an author, has a different capacity to carry on and endure. It is an I that, as André Gide[13] does, might note that Jammes came to visit, that a trip is being planned. It can record which books have

7 Céline, *Journey to the End of the Night*, 10. Bachmann quotes the first and second sentences in reverse order.

8 Céline, *Journey to the End of the Night*, 176.

9 Gottfried Benn (1996–1965) is discussed more extensively in the first two Frankfurt Lectures in this volume.

10 Fyodor Dostoevsky (1821–1881), Russian existentialist author known for the psychological and philosophical aspects of his novels, two areas that Bachmann had studied.

11 Oswald Spengler (1880–1936), German philosopher and historian, who maintained that, like people, cultures went through maturity cycles (birth, youth, maturity, decline, death). This led him to write his most famous work, *Der Untergang des Abendlandes* (The Decline of the West, 2 vols., 1918/22, trans. 1926/28).

12 A sentence by Musil resonates here: "It is my view that narrated episodes *can be* superfluous and present only for their own sake, but not ideas. In a composition I place unpretentiousness above so-called wealth of ideas, and in the case of this book there should be nothing superfluous." Cited in the editor's "Afterword" in Musil, *The Man Without Qualities*, 2:1767.

13 Reference to the journals of French writer André Gide (1869–1949) from the years 1899–1949, published in German from 1948–1936. Gide traveled through Algeria with the French poet Francis Jammes (1868–1938) and recorded their progress in his journals. See André Gide, *The Journals of André Gide, 1889–1949*, trans. Justin O'Brien (New York: Vintage Books, 1956).

been read, which might be read. It speaks of thoughts, of headaches, of the weather, and in the next moment can express an opinion about the political or literary condition. Although the I of the diarist might appear to act without choice, it is by nature selective. For the I does not figure as the entire André Gide, but rather it poses, and I do not use that word disparagingly, as the writer Gide.

The I of a diary is also peculiar in that it does not need to create the figure I, any more than the I of a letter. It has no choice but to enter the text as I. It also does not need to move anything forward; it is not burdened with contexts. It progresses step by step or by leaps. It can interrupt, touch everything and then let everything be again. This I does not enter the text as life, not as a three-dimensional entity. It sounds like a contradiction, for is the diary form not considered the most subjective, most immediate genre? And yet, in spite of all its subjectivity, in spite of the intimate expression and communication, it conceals the person. In diaries, it is "I" and "I" again, and in an inexplicable way the author is removed and has found refuge behind the grammatical form, the obligatory first-person form.

Of necessity, the diary is in the first person. The novel and the poem are not, and because novel and poem have a choice, have other possibilities, they have many options for the I at their disposal, many I-problems. Only in these two genres do we encounter the wish for the destruction or removal of the I or for a new conception of it. I would almost go so far as to maintain that there is no novel-I or poem-I that does not owe its existence to the claim: I speak, therefore I am.[14] This argument is intended to suppress the question that often arises for the writer when the text is not in the I-form: Who is actually speaking here? Who knows this and that about the figures? Who directs them? Who makes them come and go and by what right? And who chooses what is to be narrated? An understandable question that drove uncompromising examples of naturalism into a corner half a century ago and caused them to demand even greater, painstaking objectivity, and today a few young novelists in France are writing behaviorist prose, prose that exhausts itself in the description of behavior and objects in order not to subject itself to suspicion.

But back to the I.—There is a book, written some time ago, that begins with a scene among travelers in a train compartment.[15] It is narrated by an I about whom we know little more. We do not know: is it

14 "I speak, therefore I am" (Ich spreche, also bin ich). Play on French philosopher René Descartes's famous statement "I think, therefore I am" made in his *Discourse on Method* (*Discours de la Méthode*), first published in French in 1637.

15 Leo Tolstoy, *The Kreutzer Sonata*, trans. Aylmer Maude, in *Short Novels*, 2 vols., (New York: Modern Library, 1966), vol. 2, *Stories of God, Sex, and Death*, 114–212.

the author or the I posited by the author? This I tells of a conversation among fellow travelers about marriage, which suddenly turns into a confrontation that escalates to the point of impropriety, as the text calls it—through the intervention of an older grey-haired gentleman.

"'I see you have found out who I am!' said the grey-haired man softly, and with apparent calm.

"'No, I have not had that pleasure.'

"'It is no great pleasure. I am Pózdnishëv, in the life of whom that critical episode occurred to which you just alluded; the episode when he killed his wife,' he said, rapidly glancing at each of us."[16]

And two pages later when the narrator is alone with the grey-haired man, he continues:

"'Well then, I'll tell you. But do you really want to hear it?'

"I repeated that I wished it very much. He paused, rubbed his face with his hands, and began: . . ."[17]

The confession that follows is known to us under the title *The Kreutzer Sonata* by Leo Tolstoy.

I wanted to present the beginning to you, because what we have here has become a classic model of the modern first-person narrative, indeed of the double first-person narrative. An I is introduced in the action of the frame as an excuse to listen to another figure, the important I, thus allowing the confession to be transmitted in a confidential manner.

There is an even more interesting variant of the first-person narrative: it occurs when an editor-I is created as a pretext to camouflage or circumvent the crucial I in the book. Dostoyevsky used this variant for fear of censorship. His I appears twice in *The House of the Dead*, claiming to be an editor who met a certain Alexander Petróvitch Goriántshchikov, who spent ten years in Siberia as a prisoner convicted of murdering his spouse. After the prisoner's death, the narrator says he found a notebook with the details of the lives of the prisoners—but we know today, of course, that Dostoevsky was disguising himself, that he himself was a prisoner in Siberia and for other reasons. As the editor he writes cautiously in the preface:

"It was a disconnected description. . . . I read these fragments over several times, and was almost convinced that they were written in a state of insanity. But his reminiscences of penal servitude—'Scenes from the House of the Dead' as he calls them himself somewhere in his manuscript—seemed to me not devoid of interest. I was carried away by this absolutely new, till then unknown, world, by the strangeness of some

16 Tolstoy, *The Kreutzer Sonata*, 123. Bachmann is quoting here from the German translation by Arthur Luther, *Die Kreutzersonate* (Wiesbaden: Insel, 1957), 16.

17 Tolstoy, *The Kreutzer Sonata*, 124.

facts, and by some special observations on these lost creatures, and I read some of it with curiosity. I may, of course, be mistaken. To begin with I am picking out two or three chapters as an experiment—the public may judge them."[18]

The subterfuge that Dostoyevsky was forced to use gave birth to an artistic device that would remain interesting, even if its source had long been forgotten.[19] This obvious staging, this "I may, of course, be mistaken" and "to begin with, I am picking out two or three chapters as an experiment"—how often do we encounter this in the novel to the present day! Its effect is never lost on us; it makes us curious. We like to puzzle over the game of hide and seek with an I that has to remain clandestine in order to reveal itself more effectively.

The situation is not all that different with Italo Svevo[20] in his novel *Zeno Cosini.*[21] A physician, a psychoanalyst, publishes the journals of his patient Zeno Cosini, a Trieste merchant, out of callousness. The journals owe their existence to the fact that the patient, who did not take psychoanalysis seriously and did not feel like lying down on the couch, wanted to examine his life on his own initiative. However, with Italo Svevo we have returned to the twentieth century and to an I that not merely narrates in the hope of a personal catharsis (as in the earlier confessions of the Russian narrators, for example), but for whom the I has already become uncanny. In fact, the Italian title reads *La coscienza di Zeno—The Consciousness of Zeno.*[22] And the principal question of this book is none other than "Who am I?" It is true that we apparently follow little more

18 Fyodor Dostoyevsky, *The House of the Dead*, trans. Constance Garnett (London: W. Heinemann, 1967), 5.

19 In fact, framing devices, such as doubling the first-person narrator, have been used for hundreds of years, from Giovanni Boccaccio's (1313–1375) *Decameron* and Geoffrey Chaucer's (1343–1400) *Canterbury Tales* to Mary Shelley's (1797–1851) *Frankenstein.*

20 Italo Svevo (1861–1928), pseudonym of Ettore Schmitz, Italian novelist, whose stream-of-consciousness writing is considered a forerunner to the modern psychoanalytic novel. Svevo is often compared to Proust and Joyce, by whom he was greatly admired.

21 Bachmann cites the German title of Italo Sveno's novel here, *Zeno Cosini.* The Italian title of his novel, as she goes on to say, is *La coscienza di Zeno*, published in English as *Confessions of Zeno*, trans. Beryl De Zoete (New York: Vintage Books, 1958).

22 Bachmann renders the title of Svevo's novel literally as *Zenos Bewusstsein* (Zeno's Consciousness). However, *coscienza* can mean both "consciousness" and "conscience," and the title is generally translated as Zeno's Conscience, although the title of the published translation is *Confessions of Zeno.* Unlike many of the other novels Bachmann cited, of which she refers only to the German title, the Italian title, *La coscienza di Zeno,* suggests the search for the ego more strongly than any of the above-mentioned translated titles.

than the process of maturation of an ordinary person from his childhood on, learning of his first surreptitious attempts at smoking, of his dissolute days as a student until the death of his father, of his unhappy love for Ada and the grotesque engagement to her ugly sister, of his infidelity, which in no way disturbs their bourgeois family life, of the establishment of a business firm, the outbreak of the First World War, which finally gives Zeno Cosini, who has apathetically lived one day at a time, the opportunity to take "action," for racketeering. This empty existence, which evidences a Chaplinesque quality,[23] the fantastic comedy of all these inconsequential, undramatic events, receives its significance from the illumination of this I. This hypochondriac Cosini, who is searching for his sickness and fails to find it, who is searching for truth and fails to find it, who can narrate his life in one manner, but also in quite another, calls out:

"A written confession is always mendacious. We lie with every word we speak in the Tuscan tongue! If only he [and here he means the psychoanalyst] knew how we tend to talk about things for which we have the words all ready, and how we avoid subjects that would oblige us to look up words in the dictionary! That is the principle that guided me when it came to putting down certain episodes in my life. Naturally it would take on quite a different aspect if I told it in our own dialect [here he means the dialect of Trieste]."[24]

What Italo Svevo's I allows us to discover, and what possibilities it broaches, has scarcely been understood so far. It is an I that has, as yet, barely been made use of or exploited, that parades around in the fool's garb of a Trieste slouch, good-for-nothing, dishonest, addicted to the truth, very direct and the next moment laughing at us, because what we believe to be his face is a wishful face in one instance and a mask in the next, and then again his true face suddenly surfaces after all. This I is already totally unclear about his denseness, his characteristics, and it will not be too long before another writer comes and explicitly establishes his "Man Without Qualities."[25] And because Svevo's tragicomic hero runs from doctor to doctor, taking one cure after another, and is driven by psychoanalysis into his adventure in recollection, in which he deceives the physician and ultimately prevails in his own totally original way, Svevo's

---

23 Reference to Charlie Chaplin (1889–1977), the famously bumbling silent film comic, whose little moustache, derby hat, cane, baggy pants, large shoes, and bow-legged walk made him famous as "The Little Tramp."

24 Svevo, *Confessions of Zeno*, 368. The bracketed elucidations within the quotation are supplied by Bachmann.

25 Robert Musil wrote his seminal four-volume, but incomplete work *The Man Without Qualities* between 1914/1920 and 1942. Bachmann references his work also in the First, Fourth and Fifth Frankfurt Lectures in this volume.

more famous friend and admirer James Joyce[26] was able to write that he found the treatment of time in the novel especially interesting.[27] And indeed, Italo Svevo's I enables an approach to time that has to be counted among the pioneering literary achievements of this century.

He himself says: "The past is forever new: it changes constantly as life progresses. Parts of it that seemed to have sunk into oblivion emerge again while others, in turn, fade because they are less important. The present directs the past like the members of an orchestra. It needs those tones and no others. Thus at one moment the past seems long and at another short. Now it rings out, and now it falls silent. Only that part of what has passed affects the present that is ordained to illuminate it or to obscure it."[28]

For that very reason, I also believe that deep chasms lie between the I of the nineteenth century (or even the I of Goethe's *Werther*, who was truly one of the outstanding instances of an I, an I as the single authority illuminating the action)—that is to say between the old I—and the I in a book like *Coscienza di Zeno*, and again deep chasms between this I and the I of Samuel Beckett, to which we shall turn in a little while. The first transformation that the I has undergone is that it no longer resides *in* the story, but rather now the story resides *in* the I. That is to say: only as long as the I itself remained unquestioned, as long as we trusted it to know how to tell its story, the story was also guaranteed by it and likewise the I itself was guaranteed as a person. Since the I has been dissolved, the I and the story, the I and narration are no longer guaranteed. Neither the reader nor the author Italo Svevo would be willing to vouch for Zeno Cosini's I. And yet, due to the loss of confidence, the I has suddenly developed an advantage. The innovative treatment of time that Svevo's I made possible, and with it the new treatment of the "material," is but one trailblazing example. The fulfillment of the technique was realized in Marcel Proust's novel *Remembrance of Things Past*.[29] When

26 James Joyce (1882–1941), famous Irish novelist instrumental in bringing publicity to Italo Svevo's novels, which he greatly admired.

27 In a letter to Svevo on January 30, 1924, Joyce wrote: "At the moment two things interest me. The theme: I would never have thought that smoking could dominate a person in that way. Secondly: the treatment of time in the novel." In *Selected Letters of James Joyce*, ed. Richard Ellmann (New York: Viking Press, 1975), 299–300.

28 This is from Svevo's epilogue to *The Confessions of Zeno Cosini*, which is not found in the English edition. Bachmann quotes from the epilogue to the German edition: Italo Svevo, *Zeno Cosini*, trans. Piero Rismondo (Reinbek: Rowohlt, 1959), 467.

29 Bachmann uses the German translation of Marcel Proust, *Auf der Suche nach der verlorenen Zeit*, trans. Eva Rechel-Mertens (Frankfurt am Main: Suhrkamp, 1958).

Proust deploys his I and sends this hardly novelistic I on its quest, when he saddles it with a huge novel, then he entrusts the main role to it not as a person, let alone as an active character, but rather as a consequence of the I's gift of remembrance—because of this single quality and no other. The I that only accomplishes exemplary feats as a witness is no longer interrogated, induced to speak in the old sense, made to confess, but instead it comes into being because it was present at all the scenes of the action—in Combray, in Balbec, in Paris, in the residence of the Countess of Guermantes, in the theater, at all the locales of what does and does not transpire—thus because it was present at all of the scenes of the action and is forced by that murderer, time, to move on and forget and can only suspend time when a smell, a taste, a word, a sound brings back what is past—places and figures—back into what the I itself has experienced and what has been related to it. It is indeed a peculiarity of Proust's novel that the I vanishes for long stretches. The entire Swann book and a few other parts appear to have been afforded independence and are in the third person. And yet it is the I that enters, taking it upon itself to descend into time and conquering a previously unattained depth of memory. At the end of the first book, the I justifies the Swann book that follows in these words:

"And so I would often lie until morning, dreaming of the old days at Combray, of my melancholy and wakeful evenings there; of other days besides, the memory of which had been more lately restored to me by the taste—by what would have been called at Combray the 'perfume'—of a cup of tea; and, by an association of memories, of a story which, many years after I had left the little place, had been told to me of a love affair in which Swann had been involved before I was born; with that accuracy of detail which it is easier, often, to obtain when we are studying the lives of people who have been dead for centuries than when we are trying to chronicle those of our own most intimate friends, an accuracy which it seems as impossible to attain as it seemed impossible to speak from one town to another, before we learned of the contrivance by which that impossibility has been overcome. All these memories, following one after another, were condensed into a single substance, but had not so far coalesced that I could not discern between the three strata, between my oldest, my instinctive memories, those others, inspired more recently by a taste or 'perfume,' and those which were actually the memories of another, from whom I had acquired them at second hand—no fissures, indeed, no geological faults, but at least those veins, those streaks of colour which in certain rocks, in certain marbles, point to differences of origin, age, and formation."[30]

30 Marcel Proust, *Swann's Way*, in *Remembrance of Things Past*, trans. C. K. Scott Moncrieff, 3 vols. (New York: Random House, 1981), vol. 1, 203.

But where this I, this Marcel, comes closest to being what we usually imagine to be a novelistic I, for instance in the book *The Captive*, which tells of his love for Albertine, it is never the intimate that fascinates, never the confession—for this I specializes in entering each of its encounters into a totality of experience and illuminating them in a very steady light of discovery. Characteristic of this transmittal of I-communications in Proust, of the dissolution of the subjective into the objective, are sentences like the ones that relate to his love for the Duchess of Guermantes:

"And at once I fell in love with her, for if it is sometimes enough to make us love a woman that she looks on us with contempt, as I supposed Mlle. Swann to have done, while we imagine that she cannot ever be ours, it is enough, also, sometimes that she looks on us kindly, as Mme. de Guermantes did then, while we think of her as almost ours already."[31] This "And at once I fell in love with her" is immediately recovered in the following we-sentences, in sentences of perception.

Surely you understand that I only want to give you a few hints with respect to the I; indeed, there would be so much more to say about a single I like that of Proust's that one regrets having to leave it so quickly, this I with its special faculty of perceiving, which only appears as exceptional in our day-to-day experience. Ernst Robert Curtius writes about this kind of perception:

"It [he means this kind of perception] is situated at that threshold where the normal, conscious waking state merges into other states of consciousness. It coincides with what the psychology of mysticism, in a precisely defined sense, terms 'contemplation': an attitude that produces a real connection between the seer and the seen."[32]

The Proustian I is everything imaginable, but in any case, to itself, as an instrument, it is not enigmatic. It keeps calm and trusts its ability to grasp things. In its search of lost time[33] it assumes the task of transmitting an insight that, since it does not produce partial results, is the reconstruction of our entire mode of experiencing and therefore a "summa."

An enigmatic I that does not lead to the depths of time but into the labyrinth of existence, to the monsters of the soul, was created in a German novel, Hans Henny Jahnn's *Shoreless River*.[34] The hero, Gustav

31 Proust, *Swann's Way*, 136.

32 Ernst Robert Curtius, *Französischer Geist im zwanzigsten Jahrhundert* [French spirit in the twentieth century] (Bern: Francke, 1952), 320. The parenthetical reference at the beginning of this quotation is supplied by Bachmann.

33 The title of Proust's novel in seven volumes *À la recherche du temps perdu* (1913–27) has been rendered in English as both *Remembrance of Things Past* by C. K. Scott Moncrieff, 1922–31 and *In Search of Lost Time* by Lydia Davis, 2002.

34 Hans Henny Jahnn's, *Fluss ohne Ufer* (Shoreless River) trilogy consists of: I *Das Holzschiff*, 1949 (The Ship); II *Die Niederschrift des Gustav Anias Horn II* (1949/50, The Record of Gustav Anias Horn II); part III of the trilogy appeared

Anias Horn, having completed his forty-ninth year, writes for himself, looking to no one, keeping a wary eye on his I, in constant despair about tracking down the clues about his past, together with an unsolved crime of which he is himself guilty. It is not the elements of the plot in their unbridled growth and proliferation that are of consequence, but the situation of the writer who narrates to no one, and who, by refraining from lies and convention, transforms himself into his own judge. However, because the I is not a known quantity for Hans Henny Jahnn, but rather an enigma, because it is constantly changing and because how it once was and who it used to be can no longer be discerned, this I, flowing, transitory, constantly renewing itself in a turbulent sea, seems to regard its difficulties as insurmountable. A constant of being, which would enable us to hold it responsible and to judge it, cannot be found. Its yearning for precision is its only outstanding quality, and that quality goes far enough that the I makes contact with people who can provide clarity about certain details of the past. With that, the past flows into the present, and Horn encounters the person who will ultimately murder him. Horn is obsessed with the idea: "I am on trial here; everything that is happening is a measure of the court, and the object of the investigation and of the verdict is my life. There is no escape."[35]

And the longing of his I expresses itself thus:

"In this unreliable world there ought to exist something reliable for me—the image of our fate and our actions ought not to be the subject of distortion."[36]

The I suffers because it no longer possesses any determinate personality. It is cut off from every connection, every context in which it could be determined as such. It discovers itself as the mere instrument of a blind process. "I am standing on the vulnerable place of an individual, a heretic who is trying to think—one who knows that he is dependent on the movements and the measures of his era, one whose ears ring with the words that are spoken, taught, professed, the words according to which judgments are pronounced, according to which deaths are died—and one who no longer believes in them. One who no longer believes in electric power plants, coal mines, oil wells, iron lodes, blast furnaces, steel mills,

---

posthumously in 1961 as *Epilog* (Epilogue). Only the first novel has appeared in English translation: Han Henny Jahnn, *The Ship*, trans. Catherine Hutter (New York: Scribner, 1961).

35 Hans Henny Jahnn, *Die Niederschrift des Gustav Anias Horn II* (The Record of Gustav Anias Horn II), Part II of *Fluss ohne Ufer* (Shoreless River) in *Romane III*, vol. 3 of *Werke und Tagebücher in sieben Bänden* (Hamburg: Hoffman & Campe, 1974), 350.

36 The editors have consulted the Albrecht-Göttsche edition of Bachmann's *Kritische Schriften*, which notes that this quotation is "nicht nachgewiesen" (not verified); and the present editors too are unable to verify the references.

tar products, cannons, moving pictures, and telegraphy—one who suspects a fallacy."[37]

This is an I that seeks, finds and judges itself before the void. It can only grasp its tragic situation as doom, yet it still knows something that Jahnn terms "fate."

None of this holds true anymore for the last I about which I would like to speak, for the I of Samuel Beckett.[38] In his last novel, *The Unnamable*, he delivers a monologue without beginning or end, in a hopeless quest for himself. This I, Mahood, no longer experiences anything, no longer knows any stories; it is a being that consists of nothing more than head and torso, an arm and a leg, that lives in a flower pot, tries to concentrate, to think, just to keep on thinking in order to ask questions—but *what*, that is already the question!—thus to keep himself alive by questioning. Not only are personality, not to mention identity, the immutable qualities of its being, history, milieu, and the past lost to it, but its quest for silence threatens to extinguish, to annihilate it. Its trust in language is so fractured that the customary questioning of I and world have become moot. I said at one point earlier that the narrating I initially inhabited the story that surrounded it, and that later, in Svevo and Proust, the stories have come to inhabit the narrating I, in other words that a repositioning has taken place. Beckett finally commits the liquidation of content as such.

"And man, the lectures they gave me on men, before they even began trying to assimilate me to him! What I speak of, what I speak with, all comes from them. It's all the same to me, but it's no good, there's no end to it. It's of me now I must speak, even if I have to do it with their language, it will be a start, a step towards silence and the end of madness, the madness of having to speak and not being able to, except of things that don't concern me, that don't count, that I don't believe, that they have crammed me full of to prevent me from saying who I am, where I am, and from doing what I have to do in the only way that can put an end to it, from doing what I have to do. How they must hate me! Ah a nice state they have me in, but still I'm not their creature, not quite, not

37 Here, the Albrecht-Göttsche edition of Bachmann's *Kritische Schriften* cites "1:150," but the present editors have also been unable to verify this reference.

38 Samuel Beckett (1906–1989), Anglo-French novelist and playwright, who wrote primarily in French and translated his own works into English. Lacking such traditional literary fundamentals as plot, setting, and character, Beckett's novels and plays serve to demonstrate the meaninglessness and futility of existence and consequently fall under the genre "literature of the absurd." He published a major study of Proust in 1931, which may have influenced his radical portrayal of the ego. He was awarded the Nobel Prize for Literature in 1969 and his *Collected Works* appeared in 1970.

yet. To testify to them, until I die, as if there was any dying with that tomfoolery, that's what they've sworn they'll bring me to. Not to be able to open my mouth without proclaiming them, and our fellowship, that's what they imagine they'll have me reduced to. It's a poor trick that consists in ramming a set of words down your gullet on the principle that you can't bring them up without being branded as belonging to their breed. But I'll fix their gibberish for them. I never understood a word of it in any case, not a word of the stories it spews, like gobbets in a vomit. My inability to absorb, my genius for forgetting, are more than they reckoned with. Dear incomprehension, it's thanks to you I'll be myself, in the end. Nothing will remain of all the lies they have glutted me with. And I'll be myself at last, as a starveling belches his odorless wind, before the bliss of coma."[39]

Beckett's I loses itself in a mumble, and it is even suspicious of its own mumbling, but the urge to talk persists nevertheless; resignation is impossible. Even though it has retreated from the world because it was abused by it, humiliated and robbed of all content, it cannot retreat from itself, and in its paltriness and neediness it is still a hero, the hero I with its heroism from time immemorial, the courage that remains invisible in it, and that is its greatest virtue.

". . . I'll go on, you must say words, as long as there are any, until they find me, until they say me, strange pain, strange sin, you must go on, perhaps it's done already, perhaps they have said me already, perhaps they have carried me to the threshold of my story, before the door that opens on my story, that would surprise me, if it opens, it will be I, It will be the silence, where I am, I don't know, I'll never know, in the silence you don't know, you must go on, I'll go on."[40]

Those are the last dismal utterances of the I in literature that we know of, although we obstinately say "I" every day and with the true ring of conviction, under the condescending smile of the "It" and "One," of the anonymous authorities that ignore our I's as if no one were talking. Nonetheless, will literature not bring forth time and again the I, in spite of its indeterminable quantity, its indeterminable position, commensurate with a new position, supported by a new word? For there is no final pronouncement. It is the miracle of the I that, wherever it speaks, it is alive; it cannot die—whether it is defeated or in doubt, without credibility and mutilated—this I without guarantee! And if no one believes it,

---

39 Samuel Beckett, *The Unnamable*, trans. Samuel Beckett (New York: Grove Press Inc., 1958), 50–51.

40 Beckett, *The Unnamable*, 179. In Beckett's own English translation, there is an added phrase: ". . . . . . you must go on, *I can't go on.* I'll go on" (emphasis added). However, neither the original French version nor Bachmann's quote contains this added phrase.

and if it does not believe itself—we must believe it, it must believe itself, the moment it opens its mouth, the moment it starts to speak and separates itself, whoever it may be, whatever it may be, from the uniform chorus, the silent gathering. And it will have its triumph, today as ever—as a placeholder for the human voice.

The Fourth Frankfurt Lecture: Names[1]

Ladies and Gentlemen,
In recent weeks you have had the good fortune here in Frankfurt to become acquainted with Alban Berg's opera *Lulu*, and it is probably true for many of you, even for those who have not been able to see and hear it, that you are unable to imagine not having the name "Lulu," the name of this creature of Wedekind, the writer, and Berg, the composer.[2] It is eternally anchored in your consciousness, this name with an aura, an aura that is indebted to music and language, to be sure, but when the name has it, once has such radiance, then it seems that it sets itself free and takes on a life of its own. A name is all it takes to be in the world. There is nothing more mysterious than the luminescence of names and our clinging to names of this sort; and not even a lack of familiarity with the works prevents the triumphant existence of Lulu and Undine,[3] of Emma Bovary[4] and Anna Karenina,[5] of Don Quixote,[6] Rastignac,[7] Green Henry,[8] and Hans Castorp.[9] Yes, it is so natural for us to keep company with them in conversation or in thoughts, we are so at ease with them

1 The radio broadcast of this lecture, on April 27, 1960, was entitled "Der Umgang mit Namen" (Keeping Company with Names), a title difficult to render in English, as it carries the meanings "dealing with names" as well as "closely associating with names." This is also the title of the lecture in the 1978 edition of Bachmann's works. The version provided here is based on a reconstruction of the original lecture held in Frankfurt on February 9, 1960.

2 Based on two plays (1903–5) by Frank Wedekind (1864–1918), Berg's second opera *Lulu* (1937) chronicles Lulu's careers, sexual experiences, and eventual murder in late-nineteenth-century Vienna.

3 The water sprite Undine is featured in a number of literary and musical works, notably Bachmann's 1961 short story "Undine Goes" in *The Thirtieth Year: Stories by Ingeborg Bachmann*, trans. Michael Bullock, with an introduction by Karen Achberger (New York: Holmes & Meier, 1987), 171–81. Also published in English as "Undine's Valediction," trans. Lilian Friedberg, *Trivia: A Journal of Ideas* 22 (1995): 103–11.

4 Adulterous title character of Gustav Flaubert's novel *Madame Bovary* (1856).

5 Tragic title character of Leo Tolstoy's realist-modernist novel *Anna Karenina* (written 1873–76).

6 Title character, and caricature of a questing knight, in Miguel de Cervantes' two-part mock romance *El Ingenioso Hidalgo Don Quixote de la Mancha* (*Don Quixote*) (1605 and 1615).

7 A main character in several novels and novellas by Honoré de Balzac, including *Le Père Goriot* (1835), an adaptation of Shakespeare's *King Lear*.

8 Title character of Gottfried Keller's eponymous novel (1854/55).

9 Main character of Thomas Mann's novel *Der Zauberberg* (1924; *The Magic Mountain*, 1927).

that we do not ask even once why their names are in the world, as if someone had been christened with a better name than we with ours, as if a christening had taken place, albeit one without the benefit of holy water, one without a formal entry in a registry—as if a naming had taken place that is more decisive and of greater privilege in which the living have no part. These names are branded onto imaginary beings and stand in for them at the same time. They are lasting and so connected with these beings that, when we borrow them and name children after them, those children spend their lives with that allusion, as if they were wearing a costume: the name remains more strongly tied to the invented figure than to the living one.

Because in fortunate instances literature has been successful in naming and the christening was possible, the problem of naming and the question of a name are something quite momentous for writers, and not only in reference to characters, but also to places, to streets that have to be recorded on this extraordinary map, in this atlas, which is made visible only in literature. Only in a few places does this map coincide with the maps of geographers. To be sure, there are places recorded on it that a good student would recognize, but also others that no teacher knows, and all of them together result in a network that reaches from Delphi[10] and Aulis[11] to Dublin[12] and Combray,[13] from the Rue Morgue[14] to Alexanderplatz,[15] and from the Bois de Boulogne[16] to the Prater:[17] the des-

10 Ancient Greek home to a major oracle; associated in Greek mythology with Apollo and the Muses.

11 Port city and home to the temple of Artemis; site of the supposed sacrifice of Iphigenia in Homer and Euripides.

12 Ireland's capital city; setting of James Joyce's novel *Ulysses* (1922) and his short-story collection *Dubliners* (1914).

13 The narrator's childhood hometown in Proust's *Remembrance of Things Past.* Combray was based on the small French town of Illiers, now called Illiers-Combray (in memory of Proust), where the author spent many of his Easter holidays.

14 Fictional French street; the setting of Edgar Allan Poe's gothic short story "The Murders in the Rue Morgue" (1841).

15 Famous square in Berlin; the setting of Alfred Döblin's novel *Berlin Alexanderplatz* (1929).

16 Famous park in Paris, after which Robert Bresson's film *Les Dames du Bois de Boulogne* (1944, The Ladies of the Bois de Boulogne) was named.

17 Amusement park in Vienna; backdrop for Arthur Schnitzler's plays and narratives, as well as Christopher Isherwood's novel *Prater Violet* (1945). Like Bachmann in *Malina*, Schnitzler included musical notation in his 1924 stream-of-consciousness monolog, *Fräulein Else.*

ert of T. E. Lawrence[18] and the sky traversed by Saint-Exupéry[19] are also among them, but many deserts are not, much fertile ground is not—they cannot be found here. And there are places on it, some of them numerous times, Venice probably a hundred times, but always a different Venice, the Venice of Goldoni[20] and of Nietzsche,[21] the one of Hofmannsthal[22] and the one of Thomas Mann;[23] and there are countries that can hardly be found on atlases for purchase, Orplid[24] and Atlantis,[25] and others that do exist, like Illyria,[26] but it does not coincide with Shakespeare's Illyria; and, of course, we can find France and England and Italy and whatever the countries are all called! But let us look for the France that we have in mind, let us take a trip—we will not get there, since we have either been there all along or not yet. It is inscribed in a magical atlas, true, much truer, and there the Neva borders on the Seine,[27] and the Pont du Caroussel of Balzac[28] and the Pont Mirabeau of Apollinaire[29] span the Seine, while the stones and the waters are made out of words. We shall never set foot on them, never on this Pont Mirabeau, and we will

18 British scholar, soldier, and memoir writer; fought for Arab independence in the Middle East from 1917 to 1919; popularized by the highly acclaimed British film *Lawrence of Arabia* (1962).

19 Military pilot and author of the children's fable *Le Petit Prince* (The Little Prince, 1943).

20 Venetian dramatist Carlo Goldoni featured his home city in *Il Campiello* (The Little Square, 1756), among other plays.

21 The German philosopher Friedrich Nietzsche traveled to Venice frequently and wrote a lyrical poem, "Venice," about the city.

22 In addition to stories about Venice, the Austrian poet and dramatist Hugo von Hofmannsthal, published *Das gerettete Venedig* in 1905. The play appeared in English as *Venice Preserved, A Tragedy in Five Acts* in 1915.

23 Mann's novella *Death in Venice* (*Der Tod in Venedig*, 1912) was, in part, inspired by the author's personal experiences in Venice.

24 A mythical island conceived by the German author Eduard Mörike and his friend Ludwig Bauer when they were boys. Mörike's novel *Maler Nolten* (Nolten the Painter, 1832) contains the verse play *Der letzte König von Orplid* (The Last King of Orplid).

25 Mythical island of Greek legend.

26 A region renowned for piracy, conquered by the Romans, and located in what is now Slovenia and Croatia. It is also the setting of Shakespeare's *Twelfth Night*.

27 The Neva is actually located in Russia, whereas the Seine runs through northern France.

28 Parisian bridge; also the name of a poem by Rainer Maria Rilke (1875–1926), not Honoré de Balzac (1799–1850).

29 Parisian bridge; also the name of a 1913 poem by Guillaume Apollinaire (1880–1918).

never experience the snowy Russia that the Twelve of Alexander Blok[30] roamed. But on the other hand: on all our journeys, where have we actually been? In the brothel of Dublin[31] and on the Blocksberg,[32] on the Finnish estates of Mr. Puntila[33] and in the salons of Kakania[34]—there, perhaps, have we truly been.

Our names are so accidental and a sense of namelessness with respect to ourselves and to the world befalls us regularly. That is why there is a need for names, character names, place names, names in any case. But it is nevertheless surprising, and who would not at times like to exclaim with Hamlet:

> "And all for nothing!
> For Hecuba!
> What's Hecuba to him, or he to her,
> That he should weep for her?"[35]

Yes, what are Lulu and Julien Sorel[36] to us, Manon[37] and the Boy Eli?[38] Are they only surrogates or allusions? The way that one alludes to Hecuba and Hecuba, in turn, alludes to a third person. Are they placeholders? Or something more?

For it seems to me that the loyalty to those names, character names, place names, is about the only loyalty that people are capable of.[39]

---

30 Reference to Alexander Blok's (1880–1921) 1918 poem *The Twelve*, considered one of the first great poems of the Bolshevik Revolution.

31 Another reference to Joyce's 1922 novel *Ulysses.*

32 Reference to two scenes in Goethe's *Faust*: Walpurgis Night in part I (1808) and Classical Walpurgis Night in part II (1832).

33 The main character in Bertolt Brecht's 1940 play *Mr. Puntila and His Man Matti (Herr Puntilla und sein Knecht Matti)*, written with Finnish author Hella Wuolijoki.

34 Pejorative term for the declining Austro-Hungarian Empire in Musil's unfinished novel *The Man Without Qualities.*

35 Hecuba was the wife of King Priam of Troy in Greek mythology, here referenced through a quote from Shakespeare's *Hamlet*, II.2.

36 The main character of Stendhal's famous 1830 novel *Le Rouge et le Noir* (The Red and the Black).

37 Title character of a novel by Abbé Antoine François Prévost d'Exiles, *Manon Lescaut* (1731), Jules Massenet's opera *Manon* (1884), and Giacomo Puccini's opera *Manon Lescaut* (1893).

38 Character in the verse mystery play *Eli* (1951) by Nelly Sachs (1891–1970).

39 The idea of names as placeholders for objects was under intense philosophical debate at the time Bachmann studied philosophy. Gottlob Frege, Bertrand Russell, Ludwig Wittgenstein, and others were continuously debating the ontological status of names and the object named. In the following paragraphs, Bachmann seems to identify with the notions expressed by Martin Heidegger,

Our memory is structured in such a way that we forget the names of the living; after fifteen years we hardly remember what the names of our school friends were; the addresses that we once knew by heart escape our memory; or a part of a name slips from memory, the correct spelling; one day we are confronted with a mistaken identity. And this dimming of memories: back then, was that in Parma or in Piacenza? —No, in Pavia, or was it? Little is immune from this passing away of names, the names of those who were closest to us or the names that have been anchors for incidents and coincidences.

What we hoped to be able to forget, however, back in our early school years, annoyed when Odysseus and Wilhelm Tell were forced upon us once again; and although we swore we would forget them like the chemical formulas that we did indeed forget, we did not forget them, and our impression of them, vivid or rudimentary, is more durable and justifiable than that of living people. Our involvement with them is interminable.

We really are involved with them; and, for our purposes, the world is also populated by them.

Not long ago a painting by Monet, the *Water Lilies*, was destroyed by fire in a New York museum. I once had the opportunity to view it, and when the news appeared in the newspapers I could not stop thinking: where have the *Water Lilies* actually gone?[40] This disappearance, obliteration is not possible; our memory still retains them, wants to hold on to them, and we want to talk about them, so that they remain with us, for this destruction is so very different from the dying of all the water lilies in all of the lakes. And yet the fire was only negligible in comparison with the many kinds of destruction that we encounter in wars. Or what about the burning of the library of Alexandria,[41] which we are still talking about, after two thousand years, as though our houses and cities had not been destroyed by conflagrations in the meantime? We still keep thinking about it, faithfully, in the face of so much faithlessness. Whether this loyalty is to be sanctioned—along with the tears for Hecuba—we do

---

about whom she wrote her doctoral dissertation. Heidegger argues in his introduction to *Being and Time* titled "Existence and Being" that "Poetry is the establishment of being by means of the word." See Martin Heidegger, *Existence and Being*, trans. Ralph Manheim (New Haven, CT: Yale University Press, 1959), 281.

40 A *New York Times* article from April 16, 1958, reads: "The Museum of Modern Art was damaged by a three-alarm fire yesterday. . . . But only six paintings were destroyed or damaged. . . . The two items most severely damaged were French Impressionist paintings of water lilies by Claude Monet."

41 Containing as many as seven hundred thousand scrolls, the ancient Library of Alexandria was destroyed in two fires, the first in the third century CE and the second in 391 CE.

not know. We are transmissible and have to carry forward what is best. Thus it seems to have been decreed.

In contemporary literature, several things that give cause for consideration have happened with respect to names, a deliberate weakening of names and an inability to convey names, although names continue to exist and, notwithstanding, sometimes even strong ones. And we shall speak of both, of the perseverance of names and of their atrophying, of their imperilment and of the reason for it.

As Kafka's novels and stories became more and more famous, K. and Joseph K.[42] became famous with them, two figures who are not only scarcely discernible as characters in a novel in the conventional sense, but are already diminished in their appellations, furnished more with a cipher than with a name. To be sure there is a striking connection between this denial of a name on the part of the author and the denial of everything that could entitle K. to bear a name. Origin, milieu, specific qualities, everything binding, every chance to infer something about K. has been eliminated from the figure. Certainly, you are familiar with the consequences of Kafka's inspired manipulation. The enthusiasm for Kafka has given us an entire literary style, stories and novels in great numbers in which the heroes are called A. and X. and N., unsure as to where they come from or where they are going, living in cities and villages, in countries where no one is able to find his way, not even the author himself. Only general designations are to be found there, the city, the river, the authorities, trials, encirclements that are to be understood as parables, but for what? They can be applied to each and every thing. We should not be totally dismissive of the epigones, however, for some of them must have grasped one thing, consciously or unconsciously—namely, that it is not so easy to name something today, to give names to things, that our trust in imparting names has been shattered, that there is in fact a difficulty here, that even the other authors who continue to name naïvely are seldom successful in bestowing us with a name, a character bearing a name that is more than an identification tag—one with such conviction that we accept it unquestionably, remembering it and repeating it to ourselves, one with which we are willing to initiate a relationship.

Yet how consistently Kafka himself, unlike his imitators, handles his names, can be demonstrated with the following example from his novel *The Castle*. I would like to show with what precision he leads us into uncertainty and imprecision!

---

42 Joseph K. is the main character of Kafka's (1883–1924) novel *The Trial*, and K., as extensively discussed later in this lecture, is the central figure of his novel *The Castle*.

A land surveyor, K., enters the village, presumably as an employee of the Castle. A short time later, his assistants also arrive and the following scene ensues:

"'You're a difficult problem,' said K., comparing them as he had already done several times. 'How am I to know one of you from the other? The only difference between you is your names, otherwise you're as like as . . .' he stopped, and then went on involuntarily, 'you're as like as two snakes.' They smiled. 'People usually manage to distinguish us quite well,' they said in self-justification. 'I am sure they do,' said K., 'I was a witness of that myself, but I can only see with my own eyes, and with them I can't distinguish you. So I shall treat you as if you were one man and call you both Arthur, that's one of your names, yours, isn't it?' He asked one of them. 'No,' said the man, 'I'm Jeremiah.' 'It doesn't matter,' said K. 'I'll call you both Arthur. If I tell Arthur to go anywhere, you must both go. If I give Arthur something to do, you must both do it, ...'"[43] However, we shall see that K.'s ignorance will lead to retaliations, for he does not possess the right to deny names.

K. himself is in a very awkward predicament when the call from the Castle finally comes and he must respond.

K. hesitates to give his name. K.'s hesitancy makes the man impatient. "Who's there?" he repeated, adding: "I should be obliged if there was less telephoning from down there, only a minute ago somebody rang up."[44] K. ignores this remark, but identifies himself falsely with impulsive resolve as an assistant to the land-surveyor. Pressed more urgently as to which assistant he is, K. finally reveals his first name and says: "Joseph." "He was a little put out by the murmuring of the peasants behind his back, obviously they disapproved of his ruse."[45]

On the telephone he is contradicted. It is known that the assistants are Arthur and Jeremiah. K. continues to lie, claiming to be the old assistant who came after the land-surveyor. "'No,' was shouted back. 'Then who am I?' asked K. as blandly as before."[46] And after a pause, the voice on the telephone concedes what he wanted to hear, that he is indeed the old assistant.—Essentially, an ominous beginning has been made with this call; hiding behind another person, he can only ask when his master, which means he himself, would be allowed to enter the Castle. And the answer is: Never!

K. does not deign to call Jeremiah "Jeremiah" until the latter becomes dangerous, when Arthur has run away and is working against him in the

---

43 Franz Kafka, *The Castle*, in *The Penguin Complete Novels of Franz Kafka*, trans. Willa and Edwin Muir (Harmondsworth: Penguin Books 1983), 196.

44 Kafka, *The Castle*, 198.

45 Kafka, *The Castle*, 198.

46 Kafka, *The Castle*, 198

Castle, but that is too late, since Jeremiah, as he discovers, has taken Frieda away from him, the woman K. wanted to have become dependent on him, because she was the mistress of the purportedly powerful Klamm of the Castle. In a conversation about Klamm, incidentally, when K. questions the landlady, also a former mistress of Klamm's, he receives a characteristic answer: "The landlady remained silent, and only looked K. up and down with a considering stare. At last she said: 'I'll try to listen quietly to what you have to say. It's better if you speak frankly and don't spare my feelings. I've only one request. Don't use Klamm's name. Call him "him" or something, but don't mention him by name.'"[47]

If, however, the use of the name is still unequivocal in the case of Klamm—even though only his name haunts the book and K. can observe him only once, dimly, through a peephole, and although the landlady can only preserve a photo of the messenger who once summoned her to Klamm—then the confusion of names becomes complete once a person from the Castle in a higher position has appeared physically and cast a shadow, as if the eradication that Kafka desired were to be replicated by the treatment of the names. At the beginning of his stay, K. comes across the name of a civil servant: Sordini. Someone explains:

"'I can't comprehend how even a stranger can imagine that when he calls up Sordini, for example, it's really Sordini that answers. Far more probably it's a little copying clerk from an entirely different department. On the other hand, it may certainly happen once in a blue moon that when one calls up the little copying clerk Sordini will answer himself. Then finally the best thing is to fly from the telephone before the first sound comes through.'"[48]

K. believes that Olga is talking about Sordini when she tells him the story of her sister Amalia, who refused the official's indecent proposal and whose entire family has been struggling ever since to restore its position in the village: "'There's a great official at the Castle called Sortini.' 'I've heard of him already,' said K., 'he had something to do with bringing me here.' 'I don't think so,' said Olga, 'Sortini hardly ever comes into the open. Aren't you mistaking him for Sordini, spelled with a "d"?' 'You're quite right,' said K., 'Sordini it was.' 'Yes,' said Olga. 'Sordini is well known, one of the most industrious of the officials, he's often mentioned; Sortini on the other hand is very retiring and quite unknown to most people. . . .'"[49] The story follows, and later we are suddenly told: "'Klamm's notorious for his rudeness, he can apparently sit dumb for hours and then suddenly bring out something so brutal that it makes one shiver. Nothing of that kind is known of Sortini, but then, very little

47 Kafka, *The Castle*, 250.
48 Kafka, *The Castle*, 319.
49 Kafka, *The Castle*, 328.

is known of him. All that's really known about him is that his name is like Sordini's. If it weren't for that resemblance between the two names, probably he wouldn't be known at all. Even as the Fire Brigade authority apparently he's confused with Sordini, who is the real authority, and who exploits the resemblance in name to push things onto Sortini's shoulders, especially any duties falling on him as a deputy, so that he can be left undisturbed to his work. . . .'"[50] The anonymity of persons or their relative anonymity thus corresponds to the variations or secrecy of names. The one determines the other.

And for that very reason it is no longer surprising to read K.'s grotesque conversation with the teacher regarding the Count of the Castle: "But K. would not be put off and asked again: 'What, you don't know the Count?' 'Why should I?' replied the teacher in a low voice, and added aloud in French: 'Please remember that there are innocent children present.'"[51] This "please remember that there are innocent children present," as if the harmless inquiry about a person were something obscene or criminal, is unparalleled.

The fact that simple, homely names are also to be found in Kafka, for instance the girls' names Frieda, Olga, also family names like Gerstaecker and Lasemann in all their artlessness and insignificance, only diverts attention from the increasingly impracticable question of names. Indeed, the hero, K., in a moment of genuine insight, tells himself that he would have to become inconspicuous like those Gerstaeckers and the other village inhabitants in order to find his peace in the village. Max Brod reports that on his deathbed, K. was to learn that he would be permitted to live and work in the village, although he had no legal claim to do so.[52] It is necessary for his death to coincide with this announcement, since it is inconceivable how the name K. is to fit in, how it is to find a home among the other simple names. Owing to his name, K. is only conceivable in transit, but not for a destination, not in a community.

But far be it from me to engage in exegesis of Kafka.

Nonetheless, we are still so accustomed to recognizing characters by their names and keeping track of happenings with the help of names that

---

50 Kafka, *The Castle*, 335.

51 Kafka, *The Castle*, 189–90.

52 See Brod's afterword to *The Castle*: "Kafka never wrote the concluding chapter. But he told me about it once when I asked him how the novel was to end. The ostensible Land Surveyor was to find partial satisfaction at least. He was not to relax in his struggle, but was to die worn out by it. Round his death-bed, the villagers were to assemble, and from the Castle itself the word was to come that though K.'s legal claim to live in the village was not valid, yet, taking certain auxiliary circumstances into account, he was to be permitted to live and work there." Kafka, *The Castle*, 181.

we believe we have understood the character once we have his name. We can still cling to the names even with Kafka; we are frequently pushed away, it is true, made to feel insecure, but we do cling to them. We are so accustomed to it and are also spoiled—spoiled not only by older literature but also by contemporaries of those writers who, for the first time, knock the names out of our hands. I am thinking principally of Thomas Mann. But the finesse with which he provides us most of his names is perhaps nothing more than an alarm signal. Names are given a great deal of importance in his works. Mann is the last great inventor of names, a conjurer of names.[53] But he drapes his names around his figures ironically, comical ones as well as tragic ones, with a very deliberate nuance. He wants to draw everything out of a name. Serenus Zeitblom,[54] Helene Oelhafen,[55] Madame Houpflé, the Marquise de Venosta, née Plettenberg[56]—the dignified-bourgeois, the common, the ordinary, the pale or exotic, the pseudo-exotic—indeed, all of that has been carefully taken into consideration, injected into the name, and even a serious name like Adrian Leverkühn[57] is specifically charged with the meaning that befits the person. Or the distinctly North German ones, the South German ones, the southern names, they help to herald the theme of the work; or, as in the case of *Tonio Kröger*,[58] to reveal the connections to two different worlds. The name already alludes to the conflict that the hero will be subjected to.

I am not sure if Thomas Mann is very expedient in this examination of names in recent literature, but his ironic, in the broadest sense ironic, aptitude for naming his characters may well arouse a suspicion that ingenuous naming has come to an end for now, not without bequeathing

53 Bachmann's term—literally "word magician"—is an allusion to Thomas Mann's nickname, "the Magician."

54 Zeitblom, literally "time blossom," is narrator of Mann's novel *Doctor Faustus* (1947).

55 Another figure from *Doctor Faustus*. The name "Helene" alludes to the famed beauty Helen of Troy, whose capture sparked the Trojan War in Greek legend. Her surname, however, translates as "oil harbor."

56 Houpflé and Venosta are characters in Mann's novel *Confessions of Felix Krull, Confidence Man* (*Bekenntnisse des Hochstaplers Felix Krull*, 1954; trans. 1955).

57 The main character of Mann's *Doctor Faustus*. His last name suggests a high degree of audacity and boldness, while his first may be a reference to the Emperor Hadrian, who had his young drowned lover Antinous deified, conferring immortality upon him.

58 Title character of Mann's 1903 novella.

us several exquisite, splendid names: Peeperkorn, Settembrini, Krull.[59] It would be a long list.

The names in James Joyce are also stable at first glance, almost as stable as in the novel of the nineteenth century. They promise sturdiness throughout, lulling us into a sense of security: there is the advertising agent Leopold Bloom,[60] Marion-Molly, his wife, and far more pointedly, Stephan Daedalus,[61] who carries a name around that is heavy with meaning. "The mockery of it," he is told, "your absurd name, an ancient Greek."[62] There would be nothing further to add if the names were not also affected by the linguistic upheaval, the aggressive dissolution of language in the work. Bloom's name is at first simply set before the reader, then shaken up, newly sampled; it is shouted from all sides and in all variations: Leo, Poldy, Siopold! Traveler Leopold, childe Leopold, Sir Leopold, the meekest man, meek sir Leopold, Master Bloom, Leop. Bloom, Stephen D. Leop. Bloom.[63]

In the night theater, in the brothel chapter, his name is summoned first by the gong: "Bang Bang Bla Bak Blud Bugg Bloo."[64] Then by a voice: "Poldy!"[65] Policemen appear, put their hands on his shoulders, saying: "Bloom. Of Bloom. For Bloom. Bloom."[66]

And a little later one of the watchmen snaps at him: "Come. Name and Address."

Bloom answers: "Dr. Bloom, Leopold, dental surgeon. You have heard of von Bloom Pasha. Umpteen millions. *Donnerwetter!* Owns half Austria. Egypt. Cousin."

The first watch asks: "Proof?"

Bloom hands him a card. Referencing this card, the watchman reads the name: "Henry Flower. No fixed abode."[67]

---

59 Peeperkorn and Settembrini are characters in Mann's novel *The Magic Mountain* (1924), and Krull the title character in his 1954 novel *Confessions of Felix Krull.*

60 Main character of Joyce's 1922 novel, *Ulysses.*

61 Character in Joyce's *Portrait of the Artist as a Young Man* (1916) and *Ulysses* (1922). Another example of the highly allusive nature of Joyce's names, this name calls to mind the Greek myth of Icarus and Daedalus.

62 James Joyce, *Ulysses* (New York: Random House, 1946), 5.

63 This selection of names for Leopold Bloom can be found in *Ulysses* on the following pages: "Poldy," 270; "Siopold!," 271; "Traveler Leopold," 380; "childe Leopold," 381; "Sir Leopold," 381; "the meekest man," 382; "meek sir Leopold" and "Master Bloom," 388; "Leop. Bloom," 391; "Stephen D.," 391.

64 Joyce, *Ulysses*, 428.

65 Joyce, *Ulysses*, 431.

66 Joyce, *Ulysses*, 445.

67 Joyce, *Ulysses*, 447.

(For Leopold allows his lover Martha to call him Henry Flower and has picked up in the course of the day, as we know, a general-delivery letter that was addressed to this name.)

Shortly after the police scene, Martha appears, calling:

"Henry! Leopold! Leopold! Lionel, thou lost one! Clear my name."[68]

Another woman testifies that she received a letter from him, signed with the name James Lovebirch.[69]

Kisses appear that twitter and warble: "Leo! . . . Leopopold! Leeolee! O, Leo!"[70]

Bloom slips into various roles as the scene progresses: as emperor and ruler he is called Leopold the First.

The archbishop who anoints him gives him the names: "Leopold, Patrick, Andrew, David, George, be thou anointed!"

Bloom (in his speech to his subjects) pronounces: "My beloved subjects, a new era is about to dawn. I, Bloom, tell you verily it is even now at hand. Yea, on the word of a Bloom, ye shall ere long enter into the golden city which is to be, the new Bloomusalem."

At that a man rises. "Don't you believe a word he says. That man is Leopold M'Intosh, the notorious arsonist. His real name is Higgins."[71]

As Professor Bloom he becomes an example of the first feminine man expecting to give birth. A voice asks him: "Bloom, are you the Messiah ben Joseph or ben David?"[72]

His daughter Milly: "My! It's Papli!"[73]

When the specters of the night theater have disappeared Bloom remains, but still with a name, Bloom, which suddenly triggers an association "Bloom blue blume"; and still Henry Flower remains, representing the name Bloom, which can appear in backstabbing translations.

For a house that is to be built or has been built for him the following are mentioned as possible names: Bloom Cottage, Saint Leopold's or Flowerville.[74]

Names are displaceable in meaning and sound in Joyce; they can be disjointed, misspelled, or distorted, yet in such a manner that the original name is alluded to, as in the acrostic that the young Bloom concocted.

Poets oft have sung in rhyme
Of music sweet their praise divine.

---

68 Joyce, *Ulysses*, 448.

69 The "other woman" is Mrs. Yelverton Barry, who makes the statement about James Lovebirch: Joyce, *Ulysses*, 457.

70 Joyce, *Ulysses*, 466.

71 Joyce, *Ulysses*, 475.

72 Joyce, *Ulysses*, 485.

73 Joyce, *Ulysses*, 530.

74 Joyce, *Ulysses*, 699.

Let them hymn it nine times nine.
Dearer far than song or wine,
You are mine . . .

(The first letters yield his name, Poldy.)

The way the name Bloom is taken on a merry-go-round until the name is as dizzy as we are can be shown by another passage (an anagram that Bloom made in his youth):

Leopold Bloom
Ellpodbomool
Molldopeloob
Bollopedoom
Old Ollebo, M.P.[75]

And with whom did Bloom travel, someone once asks.

With?

"Sinbad the Sailor and Tinbad the Tailor and Jinbad the Jailer and Whinbad the Whaler and Ninbad the Nailer and Finbad the Failer and Binbad the Bailer and Pinbad the Pailer and Minbad the Mailer and Hinbad the Hailer and Rinbad the Railer and Dinbad the Kailer and Vinbad the Quailer and Linbad the Yailer and Xinbad the Phthailer."[76]

And finally—how could we forget!—the book is titled *Ulysses*, and Leopold Bloom's journey through Dublin is undertaken in a single day under the shadow of the great name that is invoked—Odysseus. This name is enough and must be enough for us as a constant reference to the sufferer's journey and allows us to detect allegorical scenes everywhere.

Denial of names, ironic treatment of names, games with names, meaningful and meaningless, the unsettling of a name: those are the possibilities—but there is still a more radical one. As if it were too primitive to make a person distinguishable by a name, William Faulkner, in what is probably his most important work, *The Sound and the Fury*, drives his readers to desperation. I believe that almost no one could completely succeed in finding his way around in the web of the book, indeed not so much because the treatment of time by William Faulkner makes this difficult—in the book there is a continuous jumping back and forth among three different time frames; a few sentences can refer to the year 1928, the next ones again to the year 1910. The true difficulty of the work does not lie in this aspect, because we have long been familiar with texts that no longer employ chronological time as their model, but rather because we are totally left in the lurch as we grasp for names. One can only feel envious admiration for the author of the jacket text, who is able to describe

75 Joyce, *Ulysses*, 662.
76 Joyce, *Ulysses*, 722.

the text's content as though it were a family novel. Once entangled in the text, the reader feels as if he had been transformed into a bloodhound that loses the scent at every moment because his nose detects yet another smell. The name Caddy appears twice, once spelled with y, once with ie; Jason twice, Quentin twice, once as a male first name, once as a female one. But it also does not help us to understand this, of course, since we are not supposed to recognize the characters by their names at all. The names feel like traps. Instead, we are supposed to recognize them by something entirely different, by an aura surrounding each and every person, by a constellation they appear in that is drawn in very delicate hues. It is expressed in short quotes, which we are supposed to take note of, and in each reappearance of the person, be it Quentin-he or Quentin-she and in whichever time—as a child, as a student, as a young girl—this quote is sent along with the person by the author. More important than noting the name is paying attention to the context in which the name is mentioned. It can be in a flower, honeysuckle, a meadow sold, a wedding announcement. We suddenly discover that this is the only way to make progress, that the figures would otherwise remain hidden from us forever. And they want to hide since there is a reason, a mystery that makes the names diffident. Something happened in the past, incest, and the guilty do not want to be named—the child from the liaison is not to be named. The event is evoked repeatedly and immediately suppressed again, and the names are evoked and then muffled.

When we hear about it for the first time, the text reads: ". . . milkweed. I said I have committed incest, Father I said. Roses."[77]

The next time, this sentence occurs in connection with a name that we cannot make any sense of at first, but that name is evoked again and again until we grasp its importance. "I have committed incest I said Father it was I it was not Dalton Ames And when he put Dalton Ames. Dalton Ames." (A sentence is inserted here that belongs to a different time period, and then that name is mentioned again, three times.) "Dalton Ames. Dalton Ames. Dalton Ames."[78]

The roses appear repeatedly as a quote: a flower frequently mentioned in connection with the idiot Benjamin; but the scent of honeysuckle always appears in connection with the hushed-up incident.

He, Quentin, recounts: ". . . she held my head against her damp hard breast I could hear her heart going firm and slow now not hammering and the water gurgling among the willows in the dark and waves of honeysuckle coming up the air . . ."[79]

77 William Faulkner, *The Sound and the Fury* (New York: Vintage, 1990), 77.

78 Faulkner, *The Sound and the Fury*, 79–80.

79 Faulkner, *The Sound and the Fury*, 152.

Somewhat later: “damn that honeysuckle I wish it would stop”[80]

Somewhat later: “the honeysuckle drizzled and drizzled . . .”[81]

Objects that were connected to a situation or person remain so and encompass the respective persons better than a name. Objects testify to the presence of a person or the memory of objects.

Faulkner’s method is actually to divert us from the names in order to thrust us straight into reality without any explanation. It is not he, the author, who appropriates the names, who introduces them to us and averts confusion. Rather, it is only the characters among themselves who know each other, call themselves and one another by name, and we have to do our best to see—as in reality—how far we can progress and what relationships we can establish among people whom no one fashions for us in advance, preserves and labels for our greater understanding.

This would probably be the time to say that the thought of names came to me for the first time while reading Proust’s *Remembrance of Things Past.* There is no book that manages to draw one’s attention to the treatment of names better, their functioning, their density or transparency. Indeed, the reason for the radiance of names or for the stillbirth of names becomes obvious if one keeps track of every single name in Proust. For he has not only left behind a cemetery full of famous names, but has made names and the experiencing of names one of the themes in his novel. He said everything about names that can in any way be said, and he had an impact in two directions: he enthroned the names, dipped them in a magical light, then destroyed and blotted them out; he filled them with meaning, charged them with it, and at the same time revealed their emptiness; he threw them away like empty husks, branding them as property usurped.

80 Faulkner, *The Sound and the Fury*, 153.

81 Faulkner, *The Sound and the Fury*, 154.

The Fifth Frankfurt Lecture: Literature as Utopia[1]

Ladies and Gentlemen,

It was not too long ago that I myself sat in a lecture hall, not to hear about literature, to be sure—and what little I managed to pick up in passing from time to time only confirmed my distaste—at a time, in other words, when for someone young who writes and wants nothing but to write, writing had already been a central part of all thoughts and hopes for some time. My aversion to literature as it is treated in academia may have been one folly among others. You know that the study of literature is unnecessary and irrelevant for writers, that merchants and vagabonds, physicians and convicts, engineers, dandies, journalists, and yes, even professors, have managed to reap reputations of sorts as authors.

The ominous word "literature," that readily encompassing term for a seemingly unambiguous subject, has not only been turned over and put to use a hundred times by scholars. It is also a word for writers, one of the main words, even though now and then they use it in their own frivolous way. It is certain that not being counted among the literary fold or ceasing to be counted as part of it one day is a horrible thought to a writer, tantamount to a death sentence. Without admitting it, the writer constantly campaigns for admission to the fellowship of "literature," and even if he is never informed as to whether permanent membership has been granted to him, he hopes for it and never abandons that hope.

What that key word means, what it unlocks, to what realm it opens our eyes—that is a question, you would reckon, requiring little or no consensus. We know what German literature is, for one, and European literature and World literature. For now, let us cast aside the tendency in German lands to use the words "literature" and "literary" as pejorative, limiting terms or even as terms of abuse (and with the word "literati" the derogation has indeed almost succeeded!), and that we say things like "That's nothing but literature!" and "My, how literary!" Here in Germany we are more enamored of the "poetic" and the "creative," "poetry" and "creation," but because that terminology has taken on such ominous passions,[2] I should like to cast it aside and resort to the word "literature" as an objective term. But what exactly is that object? Is literature the sum of all literary works and beyond that the sum of all those who have left behind literary works?

Which works?—Only the outstanding ones? And outstanding by whose verdict? Which figures? Only those whose works have endured, and endured for whom? And those works and authors canonized in

1 The fifth lecture was held in Frankfurt on February 24, 1960. The title is taken from the heading of a diary entry by Robert Musil. See Musil, *Diaries*, 491.

2 Allusion to the misappropriation of these terms by the Nazis.

literature—do they occupy an unshakeable position? Is the treasure trove, that so-called reservoir of eternal poetry so zealously guarded and stewarded by literary historiography, worthy of such piety and continued invocation? Are all of those nuggets of the human spirit genuine? Do some not blacken, and do they not sometimes ring a little hollow? And is not what is made of gold also subject to the most incredible currency fluctuations?—Your teachers will be in a better position to tell you how often Goethe and Schiller were toppled, what market plunges the Romantics, the Naturalists, the Symbolists sustained. How often an author has been dismissed, then acclaimed again, forgotten, and resurrected once more—what works of the masters have been unduly praised or unduly ignored. And we ourselves, of course, are at the center of that process: we disdain, we reevaluate, we treat literature on the one hand as a fixture and on the other beat it into shape until it resembles an ideal.

A chain of circumstantial evidence in the form of literary works does in fact suggest that literature exists. Let us take German literature as an example—but at this point we are already stumped, even though every handbook tells us: From the Merseburg Spells to—well, to what exactly?[3] We are stumped, because we are also told that we have no literature, no continuous literature strictly speaking; it is described as lacking tradition and is suited least of all to the observation and perception of those elements by which we identify literature. Compared with French or English literature at any rate. There is more than a grain of truth in that assessment, as long as we stay within the boundaries of conventional wisdom. But if we place ourselves at a certain distance, then it is no longer self-evident why French literature, or any literature for that matter, would correspond to what we mean by literature. For what do we mean by literature?

It is an ideal that we have tailored to size by allowing certain facts to stand out, while eliminating others.

Let us take a good look around today at the opinions and views that prevail. When we do that, we can discover peculiarities in conversations with our friends day after day. In a conversation on painting, for instance, you can readily hear the names Giotto, Kandinsky, Pollock, but during the same conversation there is a reluctance to mention Raphael in the same tone of voice. When you are invited to someone's house and peruse the record collection, you can find Bach, a little Baroque music, Schoenberg, and Webern; Tchaikovsky will hardly be displayed among the assortment. In literary discussions in which participants pride themselves on their discernment, you can hear pronouncements on Joyce and

3 The "Merseburg Spells" ("Merserburger Zaubersprüche," c. tenth century), discovered in a German monastery in Merseburg in 1841, are two of the few written examples of Old High German literature.

Faulkner, Homer and Cicero, but the mention of Eichendorff or Stifter will possibly set off alarm bells. Those are not fabricated accounts; we witness them every day and play our own part in those tales. While there are functionaries engaged in an innocuous preservation of the monuments of literature and the other arts, an unofficial terrorism prevails that for stretches of time consigns entire parts of literature and art to oblivion. This kind of terror has always existed, and it helps little to be sensitive to it; we ourselves practice it out of necessity, our delight in one part of literature ultimately entails a rejection of the other. Necessarily, we also keep it alive in response to this injustice, measuring it against an ideal. And it is entirely conceivable that at a not-too-distant time our idols, the older ones as well as the newer ones, will be overthrown once again and have to abdicate for a while, that our tempo and our championing of the new, as we understand it, will incite another conflict. As long as we are here—and in this regard everyone is always in good faith here—there is no cause for concern.

Literature, although and even because it is always a conglomeration of things past and things inherited, always the hoped-for, the coveted, enriched by us from our inventory in keeping with our desire, is a realm of unknown boundaries, both open-ended and forward-looking. At the same time, our desire makes everything that has already been formed out of language share in what has not yet been articulated, and our enthusiasm for certain splendid texts is in fact an enthusiasm for the blank page, on which what is yet to be obtained also appears to be inscribed. In every great work, be it *Don Quixote* or the *Divina Commedia*, there is something that appears to us as withered, decayed. There is a flaw that we ourselves remove by giving the work a chance, by reading it today and wanting to read it tomorrow—a flaw that is so great that it impels us to treat literature as a utopia.[4]

What a quandary, then, for scholarship, since there is no objective judgment when it comes to literature, only a living one,[5] and that living judgment has such grave consequences. In the course of our life, we frequently change our judgment of an author more than once. At twenty, we write him off with a joke or call him a stuffed shirt who leaves us cold; at thirty, we discover his greatness, and after another ten years our interest has waned again or new doubts have been raised as well as a new intolerance. Or, inversely, we start by considering him a genius, later discover platitudes that disappoint us, and we write him off. We are merciless and

4 The concept of a "utopia," or ideal society, revolves around a pun in ancient Greek: it means both "good place" and "no thing."

5 Quote from Musil, *Diaries*, 426: "How often have I changed my judgment of Rilke, of Hofmannsthal! . . . there is no such thing as 'objective judgment,' only a 'living' one."

ruthless, but where we are not, we are not involved either. It always suits us to find examples of one thing or another in an era, in an author, and other elements pose obstacles and must be argued away. We quote triumphantly or damningly, as if it were the sole purpose of the works to prove something to us.

The alternating successes and failures of works, however, tell us less about themselves than about our own constitution and the constitution of our time; but the history of those constitutions has not yet been written, and what continues to be written is the history of literature, and it is arranged according to critical and aesthetic criteria, as if it were a finished undertaking, accessible to the unanimous verdict of those solemnly committed to the task—that is to say the readers, the critics, and the scholars.

But literature is not closed, neither the old literature nor the new. It is less closed than any other field, such as history, physics, and biology, in which every new discovery supersedes its predecessor. Literature is open-ended, given that its entire past presses into the present. With the force of all epochs, it presses against us, against the threshold of time on which we exist, and with powerful old insights and powerful new ones, its progress helps us to understand that none of its works wanted to be tied to a date and made innocuous. Rather, each of them contained all of the constitutive elements that elude final consensus and classification.

Those are the constitutive elements, lodged in the works themselves, which I would like to call, tentatively, "utopian."

If the works themselves did not contain those utopian premises, then literature, in spite of our sympathies, would be a graveyard. The only thing left for us would be to lay wreaths. In that case, each work would have been displaced and improved by another, each buried by a subsequent one.

But literature needs no pantheon; it knows nothing of dying, of heaven, of salvation; what it knows is the most ardent intention to produce an effect in any present, whether this one or the next.

But literature, always literature . . .[6]

That remains true even if in France, for instance, a book has recently surfaced that is entitled *L'Alitterature*[7] and attempts to prove that literature is shunned by writers, that writers reject literature or the state of being-in-literature. Those are nuances, alternatives to be taken somewhat differently, to be sure, from the sentimental German attempts to

6 Bachmann is quoting Georg Büchner's *Dantons Tod* (as cited by Paul Celan in his Büchner Prize acceptance speech) to underscore her point that literature always prevails. See Celan, "The Meridian," 40–41.

7 Claude Mauriac's 1958 work *L'alittérature contemporaine* was translated as *The New Literature* in 1959 by Samuel Stone.

distinguish between literature and poetry, for it is easy to understand what the author, Claude Mauriac, means, and yet it is irrelevant as to whether a work becomes a work of literature because it wanted to remain "outside" the literary or because it wanted to become a part of literature.

Indeed, the ideal of anti-literature is also a part of literature, and it tells us more about the current literary market, the social state of affairs, and the inevitable revolt of literary artists than about literature itself. An anti-literature is taking place within the realm of literature. But literature, which, unable to articulate what it is, is incessantly told what it is and what it ought to be—how could and should we pin it down and get to know it? An attempt might be made to do so in a roundabout way—one that immediately exposes a dozen false paths.

There is that wicked novel by Flaubert, *Bouvard and Pécuchet*, and the adventure of those two inquisitive scribblers with literature also exemplifies the grotesque nature of our own adventure with literature. Bouvard and Pécuchet, the two *bonhommes*, yearn for reassurance, and their discovery of the uncertainty of human perception not only makes the two of them ludicrous but also makes them our companions in misfortune. The tragicomedy in which Bouvard and Pécuchet play the leading roles also reflects the tragicomedy of scholarship. Since they cannot come to terms with the works by reading them on their own, they seek succor in scholarship, which is supposed to set them on the right path. Pécuchet entertained a good idea:

"If they were having such trouble, it was because they didn't know the rules.

"They studied the *Practice of Theatre* by d'Aubignac, plus a few works that weren't so outdated.

"The key questions were discussed: Can comedy be written in verse? Does tragedy cross the line when it takes its subject from modern history? May the hero be virtuous? What kinds of crimes are admissible? What degree of horror is still allowed? The details should all point toward a single end and thus increase the interest of the plot; the ending should correspond to the beginning—of course!

"'Show us a new wonder in each line,' says Boileau.

"How does one show a new wonder?

"In all you Write, observe with Care and Art to move the Passions, and incline the Heart.

"How do you go about inclining the heart?

"So rules were not enough: you needed genius as well.

"And even genius wasn't enough. Corneille, if you listened to the French Academy, had no understanding of theater. Geoffroy disparaged Voltaire. Racine was mocked by Subligny. La Harpe roared at the very mention of Shakespeare's name.

"[They were] disgusted by the classical critics . . ."[8]

"'Let's deal with prose first,' said Bouvard.[9]

"It is strictly recommended that a classical piece be chosen as a model. But each one has its drawbacks—and all of them have committed offenses not only against style, but also against language.

"Such an assertion perturbed Bouvard and Pécuchet, and they began studying grammar. . . .

"The grammarians themselves disagreed, some finding beauty where others saw errors. They admitted principles but ignored the consequences, proclaimed consequences but refused the principles, leaned on tradition but rejected the masters, and came up with bizarre refinements. . . .

"They concluded that syntax was a fantasy and grammar an illusion. . . .

"Perhaps the science designated as aesthetics could help them through their differences. A friend . . ., a philosophy professor, sent them a list of works on the subject. They worked separately, communicating their reflections to each other.

"First of all, what is beauty?

"For Schelling, it is the infinite expressed by the finite; for Reid, an occult quality; for Jouffroy, an integral fact; for de Maistre, something that pleases virtue; for Father André, what suits reason. And there are several types of beauty. . . .

"They broach the question of the sublime.

"Certain objects are sublime in and of themselves: the roar of a torrent, deep shadows, a tree felled by the tempest. A protagonist is beautiful when he triumphs, sublime when he struggles.

"'I understand,' said Bouvard. 'The beautiful is beautiful, and the sublime the very beautiful. How can we tell them apart?'

"'By means of tact,' answered Pécuchet.

"'And where does tact come from?'

"'From taste!'

"'What is taste?'

"It is defined as special discernment, rapid judgment, the mastery of recognizing certain relations.

"'So in the end, taste is taste—and none of that tells us how to have it.'"[10]

---

8 Gustave Flaubert, *Bouvard and Pécuchet*, trans. Mark Polizzotti (Normal, IL: Dalkey Archive Press, 2005), 125–26. Ellipses indicate omitted sections of Flaubert's text.

9 Bachmann adds "said Bouvard" to her version of the quote.

10 Flaubert, *Bouvard and Pécuchet*, 127–29.

But how has literature actually been discussed seriously, and how has it come down to us, affected by what methods and strokes of fate? That is not an idle question, for a trace of all that it has withstood still clings to it.

A literary history has only existed since the nineteenth century, since Romanticism. It was then that historical studies were undertaken as a patriotic duty. The result was a fastidious indexing of national literature, and often—though not always—national pride prohibited the chronicler from realizing that over entire stretches of time this literature runs dry. Those confident surveys of something that was not an integrated whole but rather a poorly supported, optimistic ideal, projected from national grandiosity, were to leave their mark on our school books for a long time to come, and we know of course that this increasingly degenerated historiography of literature bore unexpected and unimagined fruit in twentieth-century Germany. Likewise, at the beginning of the nineteenth century, Goethe had found a formulation that continued to have an effect, albeit a more providential one.

"I am more and more convinced . . . that poetry is the universal possession of mankind, revealing itself everywhere and at all times in hundreds and hundreds of men. One makes it a little better than the other and on the surface a little longer than another, that is all."[11]

And again, speaking to Eckermann:

"National literature is now rather an unmeaning term; the epoch of World literature is at hand, and everyone must strive to hasten its approach. But, while we thus value what is foreign, we must not bind ourselves to anything in particular, and regard it as a model. We must not give this value to the Chinese, or the Serbian, or Calderón, or the Nibelungen; but if we really want a pattern, we must always return to the ancient Greeks, in whose works the beauty of mankind is constantly represented. All the rest we must look at only historically, appropriating to ourselves what is good, so far as it goes."[12]

As exquisite as the beginning of that formulation still seems to us today—the spirited wish for something exemplary and the substantiation of the exemplary in the Greeks as well as the challenge to take a solely historical view of everything—those instructions for dealing with literature, like most admonitions that have come down to us, have, it seems safe to say, been sorely tested by time. But the wish to link exemplariness back to a beginning obscures another wish, the wish to project something

11 Johann Wolfgang von Goethe, Conversation from January 31, 1827, in *Words of Goethe: Being the Conversations of Johann Wolfgang von Goethe Recorded by His Friend Johann Peter Eckermann, Editor of Goethe's Collected Works* (New York: Tudor Publishing Company, 1949), 174–75.

12 Goethe, Conversation from January 31, 1827, 175.

forward, something unmeasured more than a measure, something that, however close we come, can never be attained.

Nonetheless, we are not disposed today to accept such and similar Olympian propositions slavishly. But when they appear to us in a new guise, then they move to a new place on the horizon. Goethe's Greeks may be read as a symbol.

In the twentieth century, a previously inconceivable, frenzied fever curve of criteria has superseded the succession of changing views and standards that ensued so slowly until the end of the nineteenth century that there was still time to view them individually. Each of them left its mark, whereas now the only constant, as if in mockery, seems to be commercial success. One of the reasons for this is what Jacob Burckhardt asserts about the situation in his *Reflections on History*: "The fate of modern poetry as a whole is the consciousness, born of the history of literature, of its relationship to the poetry of all times and peoples. . . ."[13] So that state of affairs, which was bound to appear and which comes to us from the nineteenth century, has made us richer, to be sure, than any generation before us, but also less stable and more endangered, more vulnerable to any association. For today we are familiar with not only the literature of all peoples, even including that of Africa; we are also aware of the existence of all grammars, treatises on poetics and rhetoric, aesthetics, and all of the prospects for law and form in literature. For every factual aspect of literature is accompanied by theory or is at the same time theoretical, and alongside a credit there also looms a debit that realigns or would like to realign it or has sprung from it, as a dream of realignment, and often transcends it to such a degree that it damages or no longer reaches it.

All of us want to test literature or test something about it. Moreover, philosophy, psychiatry, and every manner of disciplines jump on it, and it is forced into legalities or conditions or disclosures with which, and that is astonishing, it complies with them today, only to contradict them tomorrow. Literary historians—we have gradually become inured to this—break it up into time periods, shading it to match notions of ancient, medieval, and modern. Literary criticism and literary scholarship of a philosophical bent analyze it with respect to metaphysical and ethical problems—but literary scholarship has also resorted to other tools: sociology, psychoanalysis, and art history, not just philosophy—the span is that broad. Scholars examine literature with regard to stylistic periods, risking a substantive assessment or hoping for an existential gain. And because a writer lacks sufficient knowledge of too many details to negotiate that

13 Jacob Burckhardt, *Reflections on History*, trans. M. D. Hottinger (Indianapolis, IN: Liberty Classics, 1979), 110. The English translation italicizes "all." Bachmann adds the ellipsis at the end of the quote.

maze, let me seek assistance from someone, one of our great scholars, who should know. In the preface to his book *European Literature and the Latin Middle Ages*, Ernst Robert Curtius writes about modern literary scholarship and some of its schools:

"It wishes to be intellectual history. The trend which finds its support in art history operates on the extremely questionable principle of 'mutual illumination of the arts' and thus begets a dilettante beclouding of facts. It then proceeds to transfer to literature the art-historical system of periodization by successive styles. Thus we get literary Romanesque, Gothic, Renaissance, Baroque, etc., down to Im- and Expressionism. Then, by the process of 'essence-intuition,' each stylistic period is endowed with an 'essence' and peopled with a special 'man.' The 'Gothic man' (to whom Huizinga has added a 'pre-Gothic' comrade) has become the most popular, but 'Baroque man' cannot be far behind him. Concerning the 'essence' of Gothic, of Baroque, etc., there are profound views, which to be sure are partly contradictory. Is Shakespeare Renaissance or Baroque? Is Baudelaire Impressionist, George Expressionist? Much intellectual energy is expended upon such problems. In addition to stylistic periods, there are Wölfflin's art-historical 'basic concepts.' Here we find 'open' and 'closed' form. Is Goethe's *Faust* in the last analysis open, Valéry's closed? A vexing question! Is there, as Karl Joël attempted to show with much acumen and much historical knowledge, even a regular succession of 'binding' and 'loosing' centuries (each equipped with its own 'secular spirit')? In the Modern Period, the even centuries are 'loosing' (the 14th, 16th, 18th; and to all appearances the 20th too), the uneven 'binding' (the 13th, 15th, 17th, 19th), and so on *ad infinitum*."

And, Curtius continues: "Modern literary scholarship—i.e., that of the last fifty years—is largely a phantom."[14]

I do not know whether you, as students fifteen years after me, still find yourselves in the same situation; I hope not, but optimism in dealing with literature no longer seems to hold, because its historiography has not been exempted from pessimism. *Geschichte der poetischen Nationalliteratur der Deutschen* [History of the Poetic National Literature of the Germans] is the title of one of its primary tomes, and the last one that is known to me is *Tragische Literaturgeschichte* [Tragic History of Literature]. But why does literature so fatefully elude literary research? Why are we unable to understand it as we would like to? It cannot solely be the incompetence of the scholars and the critics that is to blame, can it? The contradictory pronouncements cannot be their fault alone. There must be a reason that is not only to be found in the shifting constitution of the age and ourselves.

14 Ernst Robert Curtius, *European Literature and the Latin Middle Ages*, trans. Willard R. Trask (New York: Pantheon Books, 1953), 11–12.

If only we were as gullible and credulous as the two poor fools Bouvard and Pécuchet—and sometimes we are—then we should have to drop the subject and every subject amidst a great, anonymous burst of laughter that would bury us and literature as well.

Literature, which is itself unable to say what it is and only reveals itself as a thousand-fold and multi-millennial infraction against flawed language—for life has only a flawed language[15]—and which therefore confronts flawed language with a utopia; this literature, then, however closely it might cling to the time period and its flawed language, must be praised for desperately and incessantly striving toward the utopia of language. Only for that reason is it a source of splendor and hope for humankind. Its most vulgar languages and its most pretentious ones still share in a dream of language; every word, every syntax, every period, punctuation, metaphor, and symbol redeem something of our dream of expression, a dream that is never entirely to be realized.

The dictionary tells us that "literature corresponds to the totality of written intellectual products." But that totality is accidental and unfinished, and the intellect reflected therein is imparted to us not only in written form. When we douse the searchlights and shut off every source of light, literature, in the dark and left to its own devices, gives off its own light, and its genuine products display emanations, palpable and exciting. They are products both gleaming and with blind spots, pieces of realized hope for the whole language, the entirety of expression for the changing human being as well as the changing world. What we call perfection in art only sets the imperfect in motion anew.

Because art is in motion, writers are not intimidated by the great works written before them—and yet these would have to intimidate them if they are indeed great, as something unattainable, unsurpassable. And it would also have to intimidate them if here, as elsewhere, there were achievements at stake that could be surpassed by greater ones, in which case they would be the victims tomorrow that they have been spared from becoming today. But there are no finish lines in literature, no achievements of that sort, no accelerating and no falling behind.

Nevertheless, it looks at present as if literature only existed as an overpowering past, pitted against a present condemned to fail from the beginning. Writers themselves suffer under the weight of the past and at the

15 Bachmann appears to referring to Robert Musil here: "The awe of those born later in the face of a man whose spirit they revere, more precisely, whose language they revere (in that it penetrates into the particulars of life) stems in part from the fact that life has a faulty language (and intends to have a faulty language)." Robert Musil, *Tagebücher I* [Diaries I], ed. Adolf Frisé (Reinbek bei Hamburg: Rowohlt, 1983), 884 (our translation).

same time under a present in which they secretly feel themselves and their contemporaries to be nugatory.

There is a passage of great candor in Robert Musil's diary, in which he confesses to have opened himself to only a few writers, Dostoyevsky, Flaubert, and others, but not a single contemporary among them, since the authors cited had written twenty to a hundred years previously.[16] If we subtract the small dose of vanity and resentment that resonates in Musil's words, what remains, to our astonishment, is the impossibility—genuine and pure in its motivation—of acknowledging his contemporaries. In another passage he notes: "Who is there then today? This pessimistic judgment on the value of contemporary literature, including mine." And further: "At the same time, the average standard is decidedly high. Reasons: Related to the longing for the 'Redeemer."[17] But that figure, too, the object of such longing, is nothing but an ideal figure, and as he thinks back, it occurs to him: "Virgil, Dante, Homer . . . aside. A certain degree of illusion and a certain love of their surroundings is an essential element in the love one feels for them. But what of Balzac, Stendhal, etc.? Just imagine they were alive and were 'colleagues.' What a weight of loathing for Stendhal, the scribbler, and Balzac, the gusher! Their imaginary worlds would be mutually incompatible if one did not think of them as being set in different places and epochs. Can they be added to each other or are they mutually exclusive? What is the nature of the problem that the sharpness of effect is toned down in the reception of an artist from a past age together with his epoch."[18]

And this note bears the heading: "On the Utopia of Literature." In Musil, the words "utopia" and "utopian" also crop up now and then in connection with literature, with the existence of the writer; he never elaborated on those thoughts, but only gave the cue for what I have tried to take up today.[19]

---

16 Musil, *Diaries*, 453: "I was receptive, in a specifically literary way, to Dostoevsky, Flaubert, Hamsun, d'Annunzio, and others—there was not one contemporary in the whole group! They wrote 20–100 years earlier!"

17 Musil, *Diaries*, 317. Musil's text reads: "Reasons: related to the longing for the 'Redeemer.' . . . At the same time, the average standard is decidedly high."

18 Musil, *Diaries*, 491.

19 Musil did, however, reflect further on the relationship of writing and utopian visions: "Writing is a reduplication of reality. Those who write lack the courage to acknowledge their utopian existence. They posit a country called Utopia, where they would hold their proper place; they call it culture, nation, and so forth. A utopia is not a goal, however, but rather a direction. But all narratives pretend that there is something that has been or is present, albeit in an unreal setting." See Musil's "Frühe Studien und 'Ideenblätter,'" [Early studies and "idea sheets"], in Musil, *Der Mann ohne Eigenschaften I*, 1636.

But if those who write had the courage to declare themselves utopian beings, then they would no longer need to appropriate that land, that dubious utopia—the entity that we are accustomed to call culture, nation, and so on and in which they have struggled to establish themselves until now. That was the old state of affairs, and I believe that even for Hofmannsthal and Thomas Mann, it had long ceased to be a natural one and could only be upheld by desperate measures.

But was it ever that natural? Did not, fortunately, that utopia of culture contain a much purer element of utopia, as a direction that we can still pursue after our culture has ceased to save face on major holidays and literature no longer poses as a "spiritual realm of the nation"[20]—in essence an impossibility today—but reverberates, from the exile of the here and now into the unspiritual realm of our sad countries? For this does remain: having to struggle with the flawed language that has been passed onto us, towards that one language that has never yet ruled but that governs our intuition and that we imitate, though it might also be said that it resembles the imitation of an ancient model, one that we are unable to escape because it is too deeply embedded in our consciousness. There is the feeble imitation, in the usual sense, and that is not what I mean; and there is the imitation about which Jacob Burckhardt spoke and that conservative critics today invoke with approval or reproach, imitation fated to remain mere echo, and that is not what I mean either. What I mean is the imitation of that very language that we divine without quite being able to make it our own. We own it as a fragment in literature, made palpable in a line or a scene, and sigh with relief as we grasp that, in them, we have come to language.

We must continue to write.

It is true that we must keep struggling with that word literature, and with literature, with what it is and with what we think it is, and often our chagrin at the unreliability of our critical tools will still be great, the chagrin at our nets, out of which it will continue to slip. But let us be glad that it escapes us in the end, for our own sake, so that it remains alive and our lives join with its life in moments when we trade our breaths. Literature as utopia—the writer as a utopian existence—the utopian essentials of the works—

If, one day, the questions that those dashes call forth could be formulated properly,[21] then perhaps we could rewrite and write anew the history of literature and our own history with it. But the person who writes,

20 An allusion to Hugo von Hofmannsthal's 1927 work *Das Schrifttum als geistiger Raum der Nation* (Literature as the Spiritual Realm of the Nation).

21 Another allusion to the Musil diary entry "On the Utopia of Literature," in Musil, *Diaries*, 491: "I am not even capable of formulating the question properly."

who has always dwelled in this history, seldom has the words for it and lives in the hope of an abiding, secret covenant. Let me nevertheless close with the words of a poet, words that sound to me as if they had been written expressly to articulate what it has been my attempt to express, just one single sentence, all long stories made short. Those words are by the French poet René Char:

"To each collapse of proofs the poet responds by a salvo of the future."[22]

22 René Char (1907–1988), "Formal Share" in *Furor and Mystery & Other Writings* (Boston: Black Widow Press, 2010), 125.

On Receiving the Anton Wildgans Prize[1]

Ladies and gentlemen, honored guests,
I have come to Vienna to receive a gift, the prize that you are bestowing upon me, and thus to thank you for it. Now, it is customary that the recipient express gratitude to the donor with the proper words. Only in the case of a writer is it expected, beyond this, that he also give a speech, if possible a weighty, significant one that says a good deal, which can mean that it says nothing. And since it is at his discretion to speak about whatever he wishes, he may even address all of the problems and questions of the time, even the gravest, because it is thought that for this species it must be rather easy to talk about the gloomy enigmas of the day as well as the enigmas of the world. Only, that is unfortunately not the case.

The mere fact that someone goes to the public and speaks up, as I am doing at the moment, must cause him to think himself totally out of place, that a falsification of his person is taking place here,[2] even if he is surrounded by so much friendly attentiveness, because an hour like this one has absolutely nothing to do with all my other hours. My existence is a different one. Only when I am writing do I exist. I am nothing when I am not writing. I am a complete stranger to myself, have fallen out of myself, when I am not writing. And when I am writing, you do not see me, no one sees me then. You can observe a conductor when he is conducting, a singer while singing, an actor as he acts, but no one can see what writing is. It is an unusual, a peculiar kind of existence, asocial, solitary, damned.[3] There is something damning about it, and only the publications, the books, become social, associable, find a path to you, through a reality desperately sought and sometimes achieved. Everything that does not seem to me unworthy of being expressed thoughtfully goes into the work. But people have tried for a long time to define what "writing" is, and what has been said by the greatest minds does not ring pure for . . ., but rather arbitrary, even hollow. It is not important to know what ludicrous or noble, unworldly or . . . ideas some poets entertained, who have nevertheless left behind great works. It is these that have truly remained. They could have spared their confessions.

I only know my desk, which is onerous to me, yet I would not leave it, were it not for the cunning arts of persuasion, such as yours at this time, which make us stand up, relieved for a moment, albeit we recognize

1 Bachmann delivered this speech in Vienna on May 2, 1972. The title is not Bachmann's original.

2 Bachmann also discusses the public speaker's shift in identity at the outset of the Third Frankfurt Lecture, "Concerning the I," in this volume.

3 Here, Bachmann echoes her essay "Admittedly," also in this volume: "when the door to the room in which I work falls shut, then there is no doubt: Thinking is a solitary pursuit, being alone is a good thing."

it was flight in the next moment, a seduction, and we wish ourselves back on the galley. Who is it that exerts such force? No one, of course. It is a compulsion, an obsession, a damnation, a punishment.

But you expect—unfortunately, I do not know what you expect—that, if higher matters are not referenced, at least an observation, so I understand, will be made about burning topical issues. I disregard the fact that there is really too much that is dreadful, shameful, because to deliberate on that, and at a formal occasion no less, would be to make it too easy for myself. Nor am I in a position to instruct you about it, to lecture, to shock you, because the horror is in you, and if it were not in you, then no one would be able to help you.

The burning issues, however, which people everywhere come up with for writers and which do not perturb me, look something like this. At least three times a week you receive letters: you ought to right away, you have to right away, by the fifteenth, by the twenty-third, and even if it is merely a few pages—just think, only a few pages!—express an opinion about something. You should tell us why you write, and what you think about the writer in this day and age, and the writer and society, and he and current conditions, and he and mass media, and whether you believe that, whether you think that, and whether you write only for yourself or in order to transform the world. Leave immediately for London, for Moscow, for New York, because apparently something weighty awaits your decision there—except that it has never struck me that I or others have been able to contribute anything to these big decisions, with signatures for, with signatures against, and although it appears as though I too might have done my part to the best of my knowledge and conscience, I realize that I have not accomplished anything in this way. I have not yet been able to end a war, because writers have neither power nor influence at their disposal.

A dreadful confusion keeps so many from finding the time to write, and the speeches they flee to simply fade away; after a few years no one remembers all of the things that were spoken in good faith, and new issues are once again ablaze, something has to be done again and resolved again, by people that no one heeds.

Early on, I established one or two commandments for my life that I have kept. And they have kept me to this day, my only refuge. If I remain silent about them, it is because in articulating them I would betray both them and myself, and for that very reason I would simply like to be read. Everyone has opinions; those of a writer are of no consequence, and what is not found in his books does not exist. So to be read, just as I have read books that have changed me and others, since books that transform the world are scarce; and their authors could not have known that they would change a world that ultimately ended up changing in a different way from what was expected. The demands made on writers, most recklessly, that they should at the very least change the world, are completely pointless. An I that takes in, puts out, and is transformed, one transformed through the writing process, is another matter. And as for the issues of the day, I only have to say that the writer must write them away, must subvert the issues of his time, may not allow himself to be corrupted by the empty phrases with which these issues are forced upon him. A writer must destroy the phrases, and if there are recent works that endure, then it will be the few that do without empty phrases. So there is a need not so much for talents, for there are many, but for writers for whom it is possible to keep their character at the height of their talent, and that is what is most difficult.[4] I am aware of the cryptocrystalline nature of these words. We do not know what talent and what character may be, but in speaking I am only able to point, given the impotence of speech, toward something that seems more important to me than the idiotic chatter about the role of the writer yesterday, today, and tomorrow. The crystalline words do not appear in speeches. They are the singular, the irreplaceable. Now and again they appear on a page of prose or in a poem. Since I can only answer for myself, they have become for me the most extreme words: language is punishment. And in spite of that, also a final line: No dying word, you words.[5]

---

4 Loosely quoted from Honoré de Balzac's *Scenes from a Courtesan's Life*,: "it is impossible to honor too highly men whose character stands as high as their talent." Honoré de Balzac, *Scenes from a Courtesan's Life*, in *The Works of Honoré de Balzac*, 32 vols. (New York: Kelmscott Society, 1900–1901), vol. 23, 9.

5 Final line of Bachmann, "You Words," 173.

Bibliography

THIS BIBLIOGRAPHY LISTS not only all works cited, but also other works that significantly contributed to the translators' understanding of the subject, as well as previous translations of writings by Bachmann. It includes German-language works; for the benefit of non-readers of German, English translations of their titles are provided in square brackets.

An asterisk at the end of an entry indicates that the cited work was in Bachmann's personal library in some form: whether in translation or in the original language. For authoritative notes in German on Bachmann's library holdings, including specific editions that she owned, see Monika Albrecht and Dirk Göttsche, "Sachkommentar," in *Kritische Schriften*, 633–785.

For an extensive listing of Bachmann's poems in English translation, see Achberger, *Understanding Ingeborg Bachmann*, 23–30.

* * *

Achberger, Karen R. *Understanding Ingeborg Bachmann*. Columbia: University of South Carolina Press, 1995.

Adorno, Theodor W. "Kulturkritik und Gesellschaft." In *Gesammelte Schriften*. Edited by Rolf Tiedemann. 20 vols. Vol. 10.1, *Kulturkritik und Gesellschaft I: Prismen; Ohne Leitbild*, 11–30. Frankfurt am Main: Suhrkamp, 1977.

Anders, Günther. *Franz Kafka*. Translated by A. Steer and A. K. Thorlby. London: Bowes and Bowes, 1960.

Andersen, Hans Christian. "The Nightingale." In *Eighty Fairy Tales*. Translated by R. P. Keigwin, 95–103. New York: Pantheon, 1982.

Arnim, Bettina von. *Die Günderode*. In *Werke und Briefe*, edited by Gustav Konrad. 5 vols. Vol. 1, 216–536. Darmstadt: Wissenschaftliche Buchgesellschaft, 1959–1963.

Auden, W. H. "Some Reflections on Music and Opera." *Partisan Review* 19 (January–February 1952): 10–19.

Bachmann, Ingeborg. "A Deal in Dreams." In *Three Radio Plays*. Translated by Lilian Friedberg with an afterword by Sarah Colvin, 1–54. Riverside, CA: Ariadne Press, 1999.

———. "Biographical Note." Translated by Mark Anderson. In *In the Storm of Roses*, 193–94.

———. "Diary of a Librettist." In *Encounter* 110 (November 1962): 75–76.

———. *Die kritische Aufnahme der Existentialphilosophie Martin Heideggers* [The critical reception of the existential philosophy of Martin Heidegger]. Edited by Robert Pichl. Munich: R. Piper, 1985.
———. "Early Noon." Translated by Mark Anderson. In *In the Storm of Roses*, 49–51.
———. *Ein Ort für Zufälle.* [A place for coincidences] With original drawings by Günter Grass. Berlin: Klaus Wagenbach, 1965.
———. "Enigma." Translated by Mark Anderson. In *In the Storm of Roses*, 185.
———. *Enigma: Selected Poems.* Translated by Mike Lyons and Patrick Drysdale. Preface by Heinz Bachmann. Afterword by Hans Höller. Riverside, CA: Ariadne Press, 2011.
———. "Every Day." Translated by Mark Anderson. In *In the Storm of Roses*, 53.
———. "In Apulia." Translated by Mark Anderson. In *In the Storm of Roses*, 127.
———. *In the Storm of Roses.* Edited, translated, and introduced by Mark Anderson. Princeton, NJ: Princeton University Press, 1986.
———. *Kritische Schriften* [Critical writings]. Edited by Monika Albrecht and Dirk Göttsche. Munich: R. Piper, 2005.
———. "Leaving Port." Translated by Mark Anderson. In *In the Storm of Roses*, 27–29.
———. *Male Oscuro: Aufzeichnungen aus der Zeit der Krankheit.* [Dark evil: Notes from the time of illness]. Edited by Isolde Schiffermüller and Gabriella Pelloni. Vol. 1 of *Ingeborg Bachmann Werke und Briefe*, Salzburger Bachmann Edition. 30 vols. Munich: R. Piper and Berlin: Suhrkamp, 2017.
———. *Malina: A Novel.* Translated by Philip Boehm. Afterword by Mark Anderson. New York: Holmes & Meier, 1990.
———. "Mortgaged Time." Translated by Mark Anderson. In *In the Storm of Roses*, 43.
———. "No Delicacies." Translated by Mark Anderson. In *In the Storm of Roses*, 187–89.
———. ["On the Origin of the Title 'In Apulia'"]. Translated by Mark Anderson. In *In the Storm of Roses*, 201–2.
———. *Requiem for Fanny Goldmann.* Translated by Peter Filkins. New York: Holmes & Meier, 2010.
———. *Songs in Flight: The Complete Poetry of Ingeborg Bachmann.* Translated and introduced by Peter Filkins. Foreword by Charles Simic. New York: Marsilio Publishers, 1994.
———. *The Book of Franza.* Translated by Peter Filkins. New York: Holmes & Meier, 2010.
———. *The Book of Franza and Requiem for Fanny Goldmann.* Translated by Peter Filkins. Evanston, IL: Northwestern University Press, 2010.
———. "The Poem for the Reader" [Sketch]. Translated by Mark Anderson. In *In the Storm of Roses*, 205.

———. *The Radio Family.* Translated by Mike Mitchell. Afterword by Joseph McVeigh. London: Seagull, 2014.

———. *The Thirtieth Year: Stories by Ingeborg Bachmann.* Translated by Michael Bullock. Introduction by Karen Achberger. New York: Holmes & Meier, 1987. First paperback 1995.

———. *Three Paths to the Lake.* Translated by Mary Fran Gilbert. New York: Holmes & Meier, 1989.

———. *Three Radio Plays.* Translated by Lilian Friedberg. Afterword by Sarah J. Colvin. Riverside, CA: Ariadne Press, 1999.

———. "Time on Loan." In *Enigma: Selected Poems*, 19.

———. *"Todesarten"-Projekt.* Edited by Monika Albrecht and Dirk Göttsche. 4 vols. Munich: R. Piper, 1995.

———. "Undine Goes." In *The Thirtieth Year*, 171–81.

———. "Undine's Valediction." Translated by Lilian Friedberg. *Trivia: A Journal of Ideas* 22 (1995): 103–11.

———. *Werke in vier Bänden* [Works in four volumes]. Edited by Christine Koschel, Inge von Weidenbaum, and Clemens Münster. 4 vols. New edition. Munich and Zurich: Piper, 1993.

———. "What I Saw and Heard in Rome." Translated by Mark Anderson. In *In the Storm of Roses*, 195–200.

———. *Wir müssen wahre Sätze finden: Gespräche und Interviews* [We must find true sentences: conversations and interviews]. Edited by Christine Koschel and Inge von Weidenbaum. Munich: R. Piper, 1983.

———. "Wozu Gedichte" [To what end poetry?]. *Westermanns Monatshefte* 96, no. 4 (April 1955): 77.

———. "You Words." Translated by Mark Anderson. In *In the Storm of Roses*, 171–73.

———. "You Words." Translated by Peter Filkins. In *Songs in Flight*, 303.

———. "You Words." Translated by Michael Hamburger. In *Anthology of Modern Austrian Literature*, edited by Adolf Opel, 16. London: Oswald Wolff, 1981.

Bachmann, Ingeborg, and Paul Celan. *Correspondence.* Translated by Wieland Hoban. London: Seagull, 2010.

———. *Herzzeit: Briefwechsel.* [Heart-time: Correspondence]. Frankfurt am Main: Suhrkamp, 2009.

Balzac, Honoré de. *Scenes from a Courtesan's Life.* In *The Works of Honoré de Balzac.* 32 vols. New York: Kelmscott Society, 1900–1901. Vol. 23, 1–412 and vol. 24, 1–146.

Baudelaire, Charles. "The Gulf." In *The Flowers of Evil.* Translated by James N. McGowan, 343–45. Oxford: Oxford University Press, 1998. *

Beckett, Samuel. *The Unnamable.* Translated by Samuel Beckett. New York: Grove Press Inc., 1958. *

Benjamin, Walter. "Doctrine of the Similar." Translated by Knut Tarnowski. *New German Critique* 17 (1979): 65–69.

———. "Little History of Photography." In *Selected Writings Volume 2, Part 2: 1927–1934.* Edited by Michael W. Jennings, Howard Eiland, and Gary

Smith. Translated by Rodney Livingstone et al, 507–31. Cambridge and London: The Belknap Press of Harvard University Press, 1999.

———. "The Work of Art in the Age of Mechanical Reproduction." Translated by Harry Zohn. In *Illuminations*, edited by Hannah Arendt, 219–54. New York: Harcourt, Brace, and World, Inc., 1968. *

Benn, Gottfried. *Essays, Reden, Vorträge*. Vol. 1 of *Gesammelte Werke in Vier Bänden*. Edited by Dieter Wellershoff, 4 vols. Wiesbaden: Limes, 1959.

———. "Probleme der Lyrik" [Problems of lyric poetry]. In *Essays, Reden, Vorträge*, 494–532. *

———. "Problems of Lyric Poetry." In *Selected Poems and Prose*, 451–54. [Contains extracts from the lecture.]

———. "Should Poetry Improve Life?" In *Selected Poems and Prose*, 459. [Contains an extract (one paragraph) from the essay.]

———. *Selected Poems and Prose*. Translated by David Paisey. Chicago: Carcanet Press Ltd., 2013.

———. "Soll die Dichtung das Leben bessern?" [Should poetry improve life?]. In *Essays, Reden, Vorträge*, 583–93. *

Bernhard, Thomas. *Playing Watten*. In *Three Novellas*. Translated by Kenneth J. Northcott, 61–110. Chicago: University of Chicago Press, 2003.

Brecht, Bertolt. *Bertolt Brecht: Poems 1913–1956*. Edited by John Willett and Ralph Manheim with the co-operation of Erich Fried. Second edition. New York: Methuen, 1979.

———. "Concerning a Drowned Girl." Translated by H. R. Hays. In *Selected Poems*, 49. *

———. "Concerning Poor B.B." Translated by H. R. Hays. In *Selected Poems*, 15–17. *

———. "Da das Instrument verstimmt ist" [Since the instrument is out of tune]. In *Werke: Große kommentierte Berliner und Frankfurter Ausgabe*, edited by Werner Hecht, Jan Knopf, Werner Mittenzwei, and Klaus-Detlef Müller. 30 vols. Vol. 14, *Gedichte 4*, 418. Berlin and Weimar/Frankfurt am Main: Aufbau/Suhrkamp, 1988–1998. *

———. "In the Second Year of my Flight." Translated by Michael Hamburger In *Bertolt Brecht: Poems 1913–1956*, 251. *

———. "Nimm Platz am Tisch" [Take a place at the table]. In *Werke: Große kommentierte Berliner und Frankfurter Ausgabe*, edited by Werner Hecht, Jan Knopf, Werner Mittenzwei, and Klaus-Detlef Müller. 30 vols. Vol. 15, *Gedichte 5*, 215–16. Berlin and Weimar/Frankfurt am Main: Aufbau/Suhrkamp, 1988–1998. *

———. "Now the instrument is out of tune." Translated by Tom Kuhn. In *The Collected Poems of Bertolt Brecht*, 643–44.

———. "Remembering Marie A." Translated by John Willett. In *Bertolt Brecht: Poems 1913–1956*, 35–36. *

———. *Selected Poems*. Translated by H. R. Hays. New York: Reynal and Hitchcock, 1947.

———. "Sit down to eat." Translated by David Constantine. In *The Collected Poems of Bertolt Brecht*, 961.

———. "Solomon Song." Translated by H. R. Hays. In *Selected Poems*, 73–75. *

———. "Tercets on Love—The Lovers." In *Love Poems*. Translated by Tom Kuhn and David Constantine. Foreword by Barbara Brecht-Schall. New York: Liveright Publishing, 2015. Readable PDF: http://poetrysociety.org.uk/poems/tercets-on-love-the-lovers/. *

———. *The Collected Poems of Bertolt Brecht*. Edited and translated by Tom Kuhn and David Constantine. London: Liveright, 2019.

———. "The Leavetaking." Translated by Naomi Replansky. In *Bertolt Brecht: Poems 1913–1956*, 275. *

———. "The Prince of Homburg." Translated by Eric Bentley. *Evergreen Review* 4, no.12 (March/April 1960): 53. *

———. *The Rise and Fall of the City of Mahagonny*. Translated by W. H. Auden and Chester Kallman. Boston: David R. Godine, 1976. *

———. "To Those Born Later." Translated by Naomi Replansky. In *Bertolt Brecht: Poems 1913–1956*, 318–20. *

———. "Washing (C.N.)." Translated by Michael Hamburger. In *Bertolt Brecht: Poems 1913–1956*, 290. *

Brecht, Bertolt, Kurt Weill, and Dorothy Lane. "What the Sailormen Say (The Sailors' Tango)." In the CD liner notes to *Ute Lemper Sings Kurt Weill*, translated by Chris Hazell, 2:11–14. RIAS Sinfonietta Berlin. John Mauceri. Decca Compact Disc 436 417-2. *

Breton, André. "Second Manifesto of Surrealism." In *Manifestoes of Surrealism*. Translated by Richard Seaver and Helen R. Lane, 117–94. Ann Arbor: University of Michigan Press, 1969.

Brinker-Gabler, Gisela, and Markus Zisselberger. *"If We Had the Word": Ingeborg Bachmann, Views and Reviews*. Riverside, CA: Ariadne Press, 2004.

Broch, Hermann. *The Sleepwalkers. A Trilogy*. Translated by Willa and Edwin Muir. New York: Vintage, 1996.

Brod, Max. "Afterword." In Franz Kafka. *Amerika*. Translated by Willa and Edwin Muir, 276–77. New York: New Directions, 1946.

———. "Afterword." In *The Penguin Complete Novels of Franz Kafka*. Translated by Willa and Edwin Muir, 177–81. Harmondsworth: Penguin Books, 1983.

Brokoph-Mauch, Gudrun. *Thunder Rumbling at My Heels: Tracing Ingeborg Bachmann*. Riverside, CA: Ariadne Press, 1998.

Burckhardt, Jacob. *Reflections on History*. Translated by M. D. Hottinger. Indianapolis, IN: Liberty Classics, 1979.

Carnap, Rudolf. "The Elimination of Metaphysics Through Logical Analysis of Language." In *Logical Empiricism at Its Peak: Schlick, Carnap, and Neurath*. Edited by Sahotra Sarkar, 10–31. New York: Garland, 1996.

Celan, Paul. "Count Up the Almonds." Translated by John Felstiner. In *Selected Poems and Prose of Paul Celan*, 49. *

———. "Death Fugue." Translated by Michael Hamburger. In *Poems of Paul Celan*, 61–63. *

———. "Matière de Bretagne." Translated by John Felstiner. In *Selected Poems and Prose of Paul Celan*, 109. *

———. *Poems of Paul Celan.* Translated by Michael Hamburger. New York: Persea Books, 1988

———. "Rubble Barge." Translated by Michael Hamburger. In *Poems of Paul Celan*, 127. *

———. *Selected Poems and Prose of Paul Celan.* Translated by John Felstiner. New York: W. W. Norton, 2001.

———. "Sketch of a Landscape." Translated by John Felstiner. In *Selected Poems and Prose of Paul Celan*, 115. *

———. "Speech on the Occasion of Receiving the Literature Prize of the Free Hanseatic City of Bremen.". In *Selected Prose.* Translated by Rosmarie Waldrop, 33–35. Riverdale-on-Hudson, NY: The Sheep Meadow Press, 1986. *

———. "Stretto." Translated by John Felstiner. In *Selected Poems and Prose*, 119–31. *

———. "The Meridian." In *Collected Prose.* Translated by Rosemarie Waldrop, 37–55. New York: Routledge, 2003. *

———. "Train-Tracks, Roadsides, Vacant Lots Rubble." Translated by Michael Hamburger. In *Poems of Paul Celan*, 194. *

Céline, Louis-Ferdinand. *Journey to the End of the Night.* Translated by Ralph Manheim. New York: New Directions, 1983. *

Char, René. "Formal Share." In *Furor and Mystery & Other Writings.* Edited and translated by Mary Ann Caws and Nancy Kline. Introduction by Sandra Bermann. Foreword by Marie Claude Char, 107–27. Boston: Black Widow Press, 2010. *

Curtius, Ernst Robert. *European Literature and the Latin Middle Ages.* Translated by Willard R. Trask. New York: Pantheon Books, 1953. *

———. *Französischer Geist im zwanzigsten Jahrhundert* [French spirit in the twentieth century]. Bern: Francke, 1952.

———. *Marcel Proust.* Frankfurt am Main: Suhrkamp, 1952. *

Dostoyevsky, Fyodor. *The House of the Dead.* Translated by Constance Garnett. London: W. Heinemann, 1967. *

Droste-Hülshoff, Annette von. "Die tote Lerche" [The dead lark]. In *Sämtliche Werke*, 432–33. Munich: Winkler Verlag, 1973. *

Eich, Günter. "Examine Your Fingertips." In *Günter Eich.* Translated and edited by Teo Savory, 14. Volume 3 of the Unicorn German Series. Santa Barbara, CA: Unicorn Press, 1971. *

———. "Moment in June." In *Contemporary German Poetry: An Anthology.* Translated and edited by Gertrude Clorius Schwebell, 53–55. New York: New Directions, 1964. *

Eliot, T. S. "Preface." In Simone Weil, *The Need for Roots: Prelude to a Declaration of Duties Toward Mankind.* Translated by Arthur Wills, v–xii. New York: G. P. Putnam's Sons, 1952. *

Empiricus, Sextus. "Pyrrhonic Sketches." Translated by Mary Mills Patrick. In *Sextus Empiricus and Greek Skepticism.* Cambridge and London: Deighton Bell and Company and George Bell and Company, 1899. Accessed via Project Gutenberg, February 18, 2021, https://www.gutenberg.org/files/17556/17556-h/17556-h.htm#PYRRHONIC_SKETCHES.

Enzensberger, Hans Magnus. "bildzeitung." In *verteidigung der wölfe*, 80–81. Frankfurt am Main: Suhrkamp, 1963.

———. "the wolves defended against the lambs." In *Poems of Hans Magnus Enzensberger*. Translated by Jerome Rothenberg, 23–24. Harmondsworth: Penguin Books, 1968. *

Faulkner, William. *The Sound and the Fury*. New York: Vintage, 1990. *

Flaubert, Gustave. *Bouvard and Pécuchet*. Translated by Mark Polizzotti. Normal, IL: Dalkey Archive Press, 2005. *

George, Stefan. *Blätter für die Kunst* [Leaves for art]. Berlin: Verlag Georg Bondi, 1899.

Gide, André. *The Journals of André Gide, 1889–1949*. Translated by Justin O'Brien. New York: Vintage Books, 1956. *

Goethe, Johann Wolfgang von. Conversation from June 20, 1831. In *Conversations of Goethe with Johann Peter Eckermann*. Edited by J. K. Moorhead. Translated by John Oxenford, 414–15. New York: Da Capo Press, 1998. *

———. Conversation from January 31, 1827. *Words of Goethe: Being the Conversations of Johann Wolfgang von Goethe Recorded by His Friend Johann Peter Eckermann, Editor of Goethe's Collected Works*, 174–75. New York: Tudor Publishing Company, reprinted 1949.

Gombrowicz, Witold. *Berliner Notizen*. [Berlin notes]. Pfullingen: Neske, 1965. *

Gray, Francine du Plessix. *Simone Weil*. New York: Penguin, 2001.

Hauff, Wilhelm. "The Young Englishman." In *Tales of the Caravan, Inn, and Palace*. Translated by Edward L. Stowell, 353–73. Chicago: Jansen, McClurg & Co., 1882.

Heidegger, Martin. *An Introduction to Metaphysics*. Translated by Ralph Manheim. New Haven, CT: Yale University Press, [1959] 1968. *

———. *Being and Time*. Translated by John Macquarrie and Edward Robinson. Oxford: Blackwell, 1962. *

———. *Existence and Being*. Translated by Ralph Manheim. New Haven, CT: Yale University Press, 1959. *

———. "Letter on Humanism." Translated by Frank Capuzzi and J. Glenn Gray. In *Basic Writings*. Edited by David Farrell Krell, 193–242. New York: Harper and Row, 1977.

———. "What is Metaphysics?" Translated by David Farrell Krell. In *Basic Writings*. Edited by David Farrell Krell, 93–110. New York: Harper and Row, 1977. *

Heine, Heinrich. Letter from March 16, 1822. In *Heine in Art and Letters*. Translated by Elizabeth A. Sharp, 134. London: W. Scott, 1895.

Hofmannsthal, Hugo von. *The Lord Chandos Letter*. Translated by Russell Stockman. Marlboro, VT: The Marlboro Press, 1986. *

Hölderlin, Friedrich. "Bread and Wine." In *Poems and Fragments.* Translated by Michael Hamburger, 243–53. Ann Arbor: University of Michigan Press, 1967. *

Höller, Hans. *Ingeborg Bachmann.* Reinbek bei Hamburg: Rowohlt, 1999.

Huml, Ariane. *Silben im Oleander, Wort im Akaziengrün: zum literarischen Italienbild Ingeborg Bachmanns* [Syllables in oleander, word in acacia foliage: on Ingeborg Bachmann's literary image of Italy]. Göttingen: Wallstein, 1999.

Jahnn, Hans Henny. *Die Niederschrift des Gustav Anias Horn II* [The record of Gustav Anias Horn II]. In *Romane III*, vol. 3 of *Werke und Tagebücher in sieben Bänden.* 7 vols. Hamburg: Hoffman & Campe, 1974.

——. *The Ship.* Translated by Catherine Hutter. New York: Scribner, 1961.

Joyce, James. Letter to Ettore Schmitz [Italo Svevo], January 30, 1924. In *Selected Letters of James Joyce*, edited by Richard Ellmann, 299–300. New York: Viking Press, 1975. *

———. *Ulysses.* New York: Random House, 1946. *

Kafka, Franz. *Amerika.* Translated by Willa and Edwin Muir. New York: New Directions, 1946.

———. "Before the Law." In *The Complete Stories.* Translated by Willa and Edwin Muir. Edited by Nahum N. Glatzer, 3–4. New York: Schocken, 1976. *

———. Letter to Oskar Pollack, January 27, 1904. In *Letters to Friends, Family, and Editors.* Translated by Richard and Clara Winston. Originally edited by Max Brod, 15–16. New York: Schocken Books, 1977.

———. *The Castle.* In *The Penguin Complete Novels of Franz Kafka.* Translated by Willa and Edwin Muir, 177–432. Harmondsworth: Penguin Books, 1983. *

Kant, Immanuel. "The Critique of Pure Reason." In *The Critique of Pure Reason, The Critique of Practical Reason and other Ethical Treatises, and The Critique of Judgment*, translated by J. M. D. Meiklejohn, 1–250. Chicago: Encyclopaedia Brittannica, 1952. *

Kaschnitz, Marie Luise. "The Frog Prince Bridegroom." In *Selected Later Poems of Marie Luise Kaschnitz.* Translated by Lisel Mueller, 17–19. Princeton, NJ: Princeton University Press, 1980. *

Kleist, Heinrich von. Brief an Christian Ernst Martini, 19 März 1799 [Letter to Christian Ernst Martini, March 19, 1799]. In *Sämtliche Werke und Briefe*, vol. 2, 478–86 Munich: Hanser, 1982. *

———. Brief an Ulrike von Kleist, 13.–14. März 1803 [Letter to Ulrike von Kleist, March 13–14, 1803]. In *Sämtliche Werke und Briefe*, vol. 2, 729–31. *

———. Brief an Wilhelmine von Zenge, 15. August 1801 [Letter to Wilhelmine von Zenge, August 15, 1801], in *Sämtliche Werke und Briefe,* vol. 4, 680–85. *

———. Letter to Wilhelmine von Zenge, October 10, 1801. In *An Abyss Deep Enough: Letters of Heinrich von Kleist.* Edited and translated by Philip B. Miller, 130–33. New York: E. P. Dutton, 1982. *

———. *The Prince of Homburg*. Translated by Hermann Hagedorn. In *The German Classics: Masterpieces of German Literature translated into English*. Edited by Kuno Francke. 20 vols. Vol. 4, 416–98. Albany, NY: J. B. Lyon, 1913. *

———. *Sämtliche Werke und Briefe*, edited by Helmut Sembdner. 2 vols. Munich: Deutscher Taschenbuch Verlag, 2001. *

Kraft, Victor. *Der Wiener Kreis: Der Ursprung des Neopositivismus; Ein Kapitel der jüngsten Philosophiegeschichte* [The Vienna Circle: The origin of Neopositivism; a chapter in the most recent history of philosophy]. Vienna: Springer, 1950. *

Kraus, Karl, *Die Fackel* [The torch]. 12 vols. Frankfurt am Main: Zweitausendeins, 1968–1976.

———. "Ich bin berühmt" [I am famous]. *Die Fackel* (March 1931) 847. In *Die Fackel*, vol. 11, 48–54.

———. "Sprachlehre" [Grammar]. *Die Fackel* (October 1925) 697–705. In *Die Fackel*, vol. 8, 92.

———. "Zur Sprachlehre" [On grammar]. *Die Fackel* (June 1921) 572–76. In *Die Fackel*. Vol. 8, 12.

Leibniz, Gottfried Wilhelm. *Dissertatio de arte combinatoria* [Dissertation on the art of combination]. Leipzig: John Simon, Fickium, and John Polycarp, Seuboldum, 1666.

Lennox, Sara. *Cemetery of the Murdered Daughters: Feminism, History, and Ingeborg Bachmann*. Amherst & Boston: University of Massachusetts Press, 2006.

———. "Gender, the Cold War, and Ingeborg Bachmann." *Studies in 20th & 21st Century Literature* 31, no. 1 (2007): 109–32.

———. "The Feminist Reception of Ingeborg Bachmann." *Women in German Yearbook* 8 (1992): 73–111.

Marinetti, Filippo Tomasso. "The Founding and Manifesto of Futurism." In *Marinetti: Selected Writings*. Edited by R. W. Flint. Translated by R. W. Flint and Arthur A. Coppotelli, 39–44. New York: Farrar, Straus, and Giroux, 1972.

Marino, Giambattista. *Adonis: Selections from L'Adone of Giambattista Marino*. Translated by Harold Martin Priest. Ithaca, NY: Cornell University Press, 1967.

Mates, Benson. *The Skeptic Way: Sextus Empiricus's "Outlines of Pyrrhonism"*. New York: Oxford University Press, 1996.

Maurois, André. *Proust: A Biography*. Translated by Gerard Hopkins. New York: Meridian Books, 1958. *

Mauriac, Claude. *The New Literature*. Translated by Samuel Stone. New York: G. Braziller, 1959.

Mayakovsky, Vladimir. *How Are Verses Made?* Translated by G. M. Hyde. London: Jonathan Cape, 1970. *

McVeigh, Joseph. "Afterword." In Bachmann, *The Radio Family*, 297–341.

———. "Ingeborg Bachmann as Radio Script Writer." *German Quarterly* 75, no. 1 (2002): 35–50.

———. "'My Father, . . . I would not have betrayed you . . .': Reshaping the Familial Past in Ingeborg Bachmann's *Radiofamilie*-Texts." *New German Critique* 93 (2004): 131–41.

Melchinger, Siegfried. "Wozu Gedichte? Anmerkungen zu einigen Lyrikbänden" [To what end poems? Notes on some volumes of lyric poetry]. *Wort und Wahrheit* 8 (August 1952): 618–21.

Musil, Robert. *Diaries: 1899–1941*. Translated and selected by Philip Payne. Edited by Mark Mirsky, 337–43. New York: Basic Books, 1999.

———. *Der Mann ohne Eigenschaften I*. Edited by Adolf Frisé, Sonderausgabe, 13th edition. Reinbek bei Hamburg: Rowohlt, 2006 (based on the 1978 edition).

———. "From the Posthumous Papers." In *The Man Without Qualities*. Translated by Sophie Wilkins, 1131–801. New York: Alfred A. Knopf, 1995. *

———. "Helpless Europe." In *Precision and Soul: Essays and Addresses*. Edited by Burton Pike and David S. Luft. Translated by Philip H. Beard, 116–33. Chicago and London: The University of Chicago Press, 1990.

———. *Tagebücher I* [Diaries I]. Edited by Adolf Frisé. Reinbek bei Hamburg: Rowohlt, 1983.

———. *The Confusions of Young Master Törless*. Translated by Christopher Moncrieff. London: Alma Classics, 2013.

———. *The Man Without Qualities*. 2 volumes. Translated by Sophie Wilkins. New York: Alfred A. Knopf, 1995. *

Nestroy, Johann. *Der Schützling* [The protégé]. In *Gesammelte Werke in sechs Bänden*. Edited by Otto Rommel. 6 vols. Vol. 4, 603–714. Vienna: Schroll, 1962. *

Nietzsche, Friedrich. *Beyond Good and Evil*. Translated by Judith Norman. Cambridge: Cambridge University Press, 2002. *

———. *Human, All-Too-Human*. Translated by Helen Zimmern. Edinburgh and London: Foulis, 1910.

———. *The Birth of Tragedy Out of the Spirit of Music*. Translated by Shaun Whiteside and edited by Michael Tanner. London: Penguin, 1993.

Pascal, Blaise. *Pensées*. In *The Provincial Letters, Pensées, and Scientific Treatises*. Translated by W. F. Trotter, 171–352. Chicago: Encyclopaedia Brittannica, 1952. *

Plath, Sylvia. *The Bell Jar*. Cutchogue, NY: Buccaneer Books, 1971. *

Proust, Marcel. "A propos de Baudelaire." *La Nouvelle Revue Française* 16, no. 93 (1921): 641–63.

———. *Auf der Suche nach der verlorenen Zeit*. Translated by Eva Rechel-Mertens. Frankfurt am Main: Suhrkamp, 1958.

———. *In Search of Lost Time*. Translated by Lydia Davis. New York: Penguin, 2002.

———. *Swann's Way*. In *Remembrance of Things Past*. Translated by C. K. Scott Moncrieff. 3 vols. Vol. 1, 1–325. New York: Random House, 1981. *

———. *The Captive*. In *In Search of Lost Time*, translated by C. K. Scott Moncrieff and Terence Kilmartin. Revised by D. J. Enright. New York: Random House, 2012. Kindle Version. *

———. *Time Regained*. In *In Search of Lost Time*. Translated by C. K. Scott Moncrieff and Terence Kilmartin. Revised by D. J. Enright. New York: Random House, 2012. Kindle Version. *

Sachs, Nelly. "To you that build the new house." In *O the Chimneys: Selected Poems, including the verse play, Eli*. Translated by Michael Hamburger, 5–6. New York: Farrar, Straus, and Giroux, 1967.

———. "Without Compass." In *The Seeker and Other Poems*. Translated by Ruth and Matthew Mead and Michael Hamburger, 301–3. New York: Farrar, Straus, and Giroux, 1970. *

Smith, Marjorie N. "An Annotated Translation of Gottfried Benn's 'Probleme der Lyrik.'" MA diss, Southwest Texas State University, 1970.

Solomon, Maynard. *Mozart: A Life*. New York: HarperCollins, 1995.

Spinoza, Benedict de. *Ethics*. Edited and translated by Edwin Curley. London: Penguin, 1996. *

Svevo, Italo [Ettore Schmitz]. *Confessions of Zeno*. Translated by Beryl De Zoete. New York: Vintage Books, 1958. *

———. *Zeno Cosini*. Translated by Piero Rismondo. Reinbek: Rowohlt, 1959. *

Thibon, Gustave. "Introduction." In Simone Weil. *Gravity and Grace*, 3–44. New York: G. P. Putnam's Sons, 1952.

Tolstoy, Leo. "My Confession." In *My Confession, Dogmatic Theology, My Religion, On Life*. Translated and edited by Leo Wiener, 3–92. Volume 7 of *Works*. 24 vols. Boston: C. Page, 1904.

———. *The Kreutzer Sonata*. Translated by Aylmer Maude. In *Short Novels*. 2 vols. Vol. 2, *Stories of God, Sex, and Death*, 114–212. New York: Modern Library, 1966. *

———. *Die Kreutzersonate*. Translated by Arthur Luther. Wiesbaden: Insel, 1957.

Ulfers, Fred. "The Utopia and Essayism of Robert Musil 1/4." European Graduate School video lectures. Filmed 2007. Accessed January 30, 2021, https://egs.edu/lecture/the-utopia-and-essayism-of-robert-musil-2007-1-4/.

Ungaretti, Giuseppe. "Freude der Schiffbrüche." Translated by Ingeborg Bachmann. In Bachmann, *Werke in vier Bänden*. Vol. 1, 556–57. *

———. "Morgen." Translated by Ingeborg Bachmann. In Bachmann, *Werke in vier Bänden*. Vol. 1, 514–15. *

Weil, Simone. "Evil." In *Gravity and Grace*, 119–130.

———. "Factory Journal." In *Formative Writings, 1929–1941*. Edited and translated by Dorothy Tuck McFarland and Wilhelmina Van Ness, 149–226. Amherst: University of Massachusetts Press, 1987. *

———. *Gravity and Grace*. Translated by Arthur Wills. With an introduction by Gustave Thibon. New York: G. P. Putnam's Sons, 1952. *

———. “He Whom We Must Love is Absent.” In *Gravity and Grace*, 162–66.

———. “Imagination Which Fills the Void.” In *Gravity and Grace*, 62–64.

———. *La condition ouvrière* [The labor condition]. Paris: Édition Gallimard, [1951] 1976. *

———. “Last Thoughts.” In *Waiting for God*, 88–104. *

———. “Prerequisite to Dignity of Labour.” In *Simone Weil: An Anthology*. Edited and introduced by Sian Miles, 244–56. New York: Weidenfeld & Nicholson, 1986. *

———. “Readings.” In *Gravity and Grace*, 188–90.

———. “Renunciation of Time.” In *Gravity and Grace*, 65–66.

———. “Spiritual Autobiography.” In *Waiting for God*, 61–83. *

———. “The Great Beast.” In *Gravity and Grace*, 216–22. *

———. “The Love of God and Affliction.” In *Waiting for God*, 117–36. *

———. “The Mysticism of Work.” In *Gravity and Grace*, 232–36. *

———. *The Need for Roots: Prelude to a Declaration of Duties toward Mankind*. Translated by Arthur Wills. With a Preface by T. S. Eliot. New York: G. P. Putnam’s Sons, 1952. *

———. “The Ring of Gyges.” In *Gravity and Grace*, 191–93.

———. “The Social Imprint.” In *Gravity and Grace*, 212–15.

———. “Training.” In *Gravity and Grace*, 177–81.

———. *Waiting for God*. Translated by Emma Craufurd. New York: Putnam, 1951. *

Witte, Bernd. “‘Ich liebe Dich und will Dich nicht lieben’—Ingeborg Bachmann und Paul Celan im Briefwechsel” [“I love you and don’t want to love you”—Ingeborg Bachmann and Paul Celan in correspondence]. In *Die Waffen nieder! Lay down your weapons!: Ingeborg Bachmanns Schreiben gegen den Krieg* [Lay down your weapons: Ingeborg Bachmann’s writing against war], edited by Karl Solibakke and Karina von Tippelskirch, 85–94. Würzburg: Könighausen und Neumann, 2012.

Wittgenstein, Ludwig. “A Lecture on Ethics.” *The Philosophical Review* 74, no.1 (1965): 3–12.

———. *Philosophical Investigations*. Bilingual edition. Translated by G. E. M. Anscombe, P. M. S. Hacker, and Joachim Schulte. Revised fourth edition, edited by P. M. S. Hacker and Joachim Schulte. Chichester: Wiley-Blackwell, 2009.*

———. *Tractatus Logico-Philosophicus*. Translated by D. F. Pears and B. F. McGuinness. New York: Routledge, [1961] 1974. *

Wolf, Christa. “The Truth You Can Expect.” In *The Author’s Dimension*. Translated by Jan Van Heurck, 99–109. Chicago: University of Chicago Press, 1995. Also published in *The German Library* 94, 101–12. New York: Continuum, 1998.

Zweig, Stefan. *Master Builders: A Typology of the Spirit*. Translated by Eden and Cedar Paul. New York: Viking Press, 1939.

Index